YEATS ANNUAL No. 13

Edith Wingate Rinder (1864–1962).

YEATS ANNUAL No. 13

Edited by
Warwick Gould

First published 1998 by
MACMILLAN PRESS LTD
Houndmills, Basingstoke, Hampshire RG21 6XS
and London
Companies and representatives
throughout the world

ISBN 0–333–71639–6
ISSN 0278–7688

A catalogue record for this book is available
from the British Library.

This book is printed on paper suitable for recycling and
made from fully managed and sustained forest sources.

10   9   8   7   6   5   4   3   2   1
07   06   05   04   03   02   01   00   99   98

Yeats Annual No. 13 was set in Garamond
and page-made using Nota Bene 4.2
by Warwick Gould. It was finished on
17 September 1997.

Printed and bound in Great Britain by
Antony Rowe Ltd, Chippenham, Wiltshire

Contents

'MASTERING WHAT IS MOST ABSTRACT': A FORUM ON *A VISION*

SHORTER NOTES

REVIEWS

List of Plates

Frontispiece: Edith Wingate Rinder (1864-1962) Photograph courtesy William F. Halloran and the family of Edith Rinder.

1. *Bagdad* (1927) oil painting by Wyndham Lewis. Reproduced by courtesy of the Wyndham Lewis Memorial Trust and the Tate Gallery.

2. *ATHANATON* (1933), pen, ink and gouache, by Wyndham Lewis, in the possession of Hugh Kenner. Photographed from Walter Michel, *Wyndham Lewis: Paintings and Drawings* (London: Thames and Hudson, 1971), plate 2.

3. Cover design for Yeats's *Selected Poems* (New York: Macmillan, 1921). Photograph by courtesy of the Robert W. Woodruff Library, Emory University.

4. Stage design by W. B. Yeats for the first production of *The King's Threshold*, reproduced by permission of the Houghton Library, Harvard University.

5. Liam Miller's transcription of p. 23 of W. B. Yeats's 'Scene Notebook', in his *The Noble Drama of W. B. Yeats* (Dublin; Atlantic Highlands, N. J., 1977), fig 42, p. 158, reproduced with the kind permission of Maire Miller.

6-8. John Butler Yeats's marginalia and drawings in a copy of *The Wanderings of Oisin and Other Poems* (1889), reproduced by courtesy of the Thomas Fisher Rare Book Library, University of Toronto.

9. Yeats with Members of the Oxford University English Club, *Oxford Mail*, 6 June 1933, 1.

10. Undated letter from John Masefield to Jack B. Yeats, partly in code, reproduced by permission of the Houghton Library, Harvard University.

Abbreviations

The standard works listed below are cited in *Yeats Annual* by standard abbreviations, including volume number (where appropriate), and page number. Volumes in *The Collected Edition of the Works of W. B. Yeats (CEW)*, edited by Richard J. Finneran and George Mills Harper, are cited by abbreviations of their individual titles. Manuscripts are cited using abbreviations for the main collections, listed below. Second or later citations of other works frequently referred to are usually by abbreviation or acronym as explained in the footnote accompanying the first citation in a particular essay.

Au	*Autobiographies* (London: Macmillan, 1955).
AVA	*A Vision: An Explanation of Life Founded upon the Writings of Giraldus and upon certain Doctrines attributed to Kusta Ben Luka* (London: privately printed for subscribers only by T. Werner Laurie, Ltd., 1925). See also *CVA*.
AVB	*A Vision* (London: Macmillan, 1962).
Berg	Books and Manuscripts, The Berg Collection, New York Public Library (Astor, Lenox and Tilden Foundations).
B.L. Add. MS	Additional Manuscript, The British Library, London (followed by number). Manuscripts as yet uncatalogued are cited as *B.L. Uncat.*
Bodley	Bodleian Library, Oxford.
Brotherton	Manuscript, The Brotherton Collection, Brotherton Library, University of Leeds.

CH   *W. B. Yeats: The Critical Heritage* ed. A.
               Norman Jeffares (London, Henley & Boston:
               Routledge & Kegan Paul, 1977).

CL1,2,3   *The Collected Letters of W. B. Yeats: Volume I,
               1865-1895*, ed. John Kelly and Eric Domville;
               Volume II, 1896-1900, ed. Warwick Gould, John
               Kelly, Deirdre Toomey, *Volume III, 1901-1904*,
               ed. John Kelly and Ronald Schuchard (Oxford:
               Clarendon Press, 1986, 1997, 1994).

CM   *W. B. Yeats: A Census of the Manuscripts* by Con-
               rad A. Balliet with the assistance of Christine
               Mawhinney (New York and London: Garland
               Publishing, Inc., 1990).

CV A   *A Critical Edition of Yeats's* A Vision *(1925)*, ed.
               George Mills Harper and Walter Kelly Hood
               (London: Macmillan, 1978).

CW1-8   *The Collected Works in Verse and Prose of Wil-
               liam Butler Yeats* (Stratford-on-Avon: The
               Shakespeare Head Press, 1908, 8 vols.).

DC   *Druid Craft: The Writing of* The Shadowy
               Waters, *Manuscripts of W. B. Yeats* transcribed,
               edited & with a commentary by Michael J. Sid-
               nell, George P. Mayhew, David R. Clark
               (Amherst: The University of Massachusetts
               Press, 1971).

Diaries   *Lady Gregory's Diaries 1892—1902*, ed. James
               Pethica, (Gerrards Cross: Colin Smythe, 1996).

E&I   *Essays and Introductions* (London and New
               York: Macmillan, 1961).

Emory   Books and Manuscripts in the Robert W.
               Woodruff Library, Emory University, Atlanta.

Ex	*Explorations*, sel. Mrs W. B. Yeats (London: Macmillan, 1962; New York: Macmillan, 1963).
G-YL	*The Gonne-Yeats Letters 1893-1938: Always Your Friend*, ed. Anna MacBride White and A. Norman Jeffares (London: Hutchinson, 1992).
Harvard	Manuscript, Houghton Library, Harvard University
HRHRC	Books and Manuscripts, Harry Ransom Humanities Research Center, University of Texas at Austin.
I&R	*W. B. Yeats Interviews and Recollections* ed. E. H. Mikhail, (London: Macmillan, 1977), 2 vols.
J	*W. B. Yeats: A Classified Bibliography of Criticism* second edition, revised and enlarged, by K. P. S. Jochum (Urbana and Chicago: University of Illinois Press, 1990). Item nos. or page no. preceded by 'p.'.
JS&D	*John Sherman AND Dhoya (CEW XII)*, edited by Richard J. Finneran (New York: Macmillan, 1991).
Kansas	Manuscripts in the Kenneth Spencer Research Library, University of Kansas, Lawrence.
L	*The Letters of W. B. Yeats*, ed. Allan Wade (London: Rupert Hart-Davis, 1954; New York: Macmillan, 1955).
LBP	*Letters from Bedford Park: A Selection from the Correspondence (1890—1901) of John Butler Yeats* edited with introduction and notes by William M. Murphy (Dublin: The Cuala Press, 1972).
LDW	*Letters on Poetry from W. B. Yeats to Dorothy Wellesley*, intro. Kathleen Raine (London and New York: Oxford University Press, 1964).

LJQ   *The Letters of John Quinn to W. B. Yeats* ed. Alan B. Himber, with the assistance of George Mills Harper (Ann Arbor: UMI Research Press, 1983).

LMR   *"Ah, Sweet Dancer": W. B. Yeats / Margot Ruddock, A Correspondence* ed. Roger McHugh (London and New York: Macmillan, 1970).

LNI   *Letters to the New Island: A New Edition (CEW VII)* edited by George Bornstein and Hugh Witemeyer (London: Macmillan, 1989).

LRB   *The Correspondence of Robert Bridges and W. B. Yeats* ed. Richard J. Finneran (London: Macmillan, 1977; Toronto: Macmillan of Canada, 1978).

LTWBY   *Letters to W. B. Yeats* ed. Richard J. Finneran, George Mills Harper and William M. Murphy with the assistance of Alan B. Himber (London: Macmillan; New York: Columbia University Press, 1977). 2 vols.

MBY   Manuscript in the Collection of Michael Butler Yeats.

Mem   *Memoirs: Autobiography - First Draft: Journal* transcribed and edited by Denis Donoghue (London: Macmillan, 1972; New York: Macmillan, 1973).

Myth   *Mythologies* (London and New York: Macmillan, 1959).

MYV1, 2   *The Making of Yeats's "A Vision": A Study of the Automatic Script* by George Mills Harper (London: Macmillan; Carbondale and Edwardsville, Ill.: Southern Illinois University Press, 1987). 2 vols.

NC   *A New Commentary on the Poems of W. B. Yeats* by A. Norman Jeffares (London: Macmillan; Stanford: Stanford University Press, 1984).

NLI   Manuscripts in the National Library of Ireland.

NLS   Manuscripts in the National Library of Scotland.

NYPL   Manuscripts in the New York Public Library.

Norwood Manuscripts, Norwood Historical Society, Day House, Norwood, Mass.

OBMV   *The Oxford Book of Modern Verse 1895-1935,* chosen by W. B. Yeats (Oxford: Clarendon Press, 1936).

P&I   *Prefaces and Introductions: Uncollected Prefaces and Introductions by Yeats to Works by other Authors and to Anthologies edited by Yeats (CEW VI),* edited by William H. O'Donnell (London: Macmillan, 1988).

PR   *The Poems: Revised* edited by Richard J. Finneran (New York: Macmillan Publishing Company, 1989; London: Macmillan, 1989). (*CEW 1* replacing *The Poems: A New Edition* ed. Richard J. Finneran [New York: Macmillan Publishing Company, 1983; London: Macmillan London Ltd., 1984], *PNE*).

SB   *The Speckled Bird, With Variant Versions* ed. William H. O'Donnell (Toronto: McLelland & Stewart, 1976).

SQ   *A Servant of the Queen: Reminiscences* by Maud Gonne MacBride, edited by A. Norman Jeffares and Anna MacBride White (Gerrards Cross: Colin Smythe, 1994).

SS   *The Senate Speeches of W. B. Yeats* ed. Donald R.
            Pearce (Bloomington: Indiana University Press,
            1960; London: Faber and Faber, 1961).

TB   *Theatre Business: The Correspondence of the First
            Abbey Theatre Directors: William Butler Yeats,
            Lady Gregory and J. M. Synge* ed. Ann
            Saddlemyer (Gerrards Cross: Colin Smythe;
            University Park, Penn.: Pennsylvania State
            University Press, 1982).

TSMC   *W. B. Yeats and T. Sturge Moore: Their Cor-
            respondence, 1901-1937* ed. Ursula Bridge
            (London: Routledge and Kegan Paul; New
            York: Oxford University Press, 1953).

UP1   *Uncollected Prose by W. B. Yeats*, Vol I, ed. John
            P. Frayne (London: Macmillan; New York:
            Columbia University Press, 1970).

UP2   *Uncollected Prose by W. B. Yeats*, Vol 2, ed. John
            P. Frayne and Colton Johnson (London: Mac-
            millan, 1975; New York: Columbia University
            Press, 1976).

VP   *The Variorum Edition of the Poems of W. B. Yeats*
            ed. Peter Allt and Russell K. Alspach (New
            York: The Macmillan Company, 1957). Cited
            from the corrected third printing of 1966.

VPl   *The Variorum Edition of the Plays of W. B. Yeats*
            ed. Russell K. Alspach assisted by Catherine C.
            Alspach (London and New York: Macmillan,
            1966). Cited from the corrected second printing
            of 1966.

VSR   *The Secret Rose, Stories by W. B. Yeats: A
            Variorum Edition*, ed. Warwick Gould, Phillip
            L. Marcus and Michael J. Sidnell (London: Mac-
            millan, 1992). Second edition, rev. and enl.

Wade	Allan Wade, *A Bibliography of the Writings of W. B. Yeats*, third ed., rev. Russell K. Alspach (London: Rupert Hart-Davis, 1968). Item nos. and/or page nos. preceded by 'p.'.
WWB1, 2, 3	*The Works of William Blake Poetic, Symbolic, and Critical*, edited with lithographs of the illustrated "Prophetic Books," and a memoir and interpretation by Edwin John Ellis and William Butler Yeats, 3 vols. (London: Bernard Quaritch, 1893).
YA	*Yeats Annual* (London: Macmillan, 1982-) cited by no.
YAACTS	*Yeats: An Annual of Critical and Textual Studies* (publishers vary, 1983-) cited by no.
YL	Edward O'Shea, *A Descriptive Catalog of W. B. Yeats's Library* (New York and London: Garland Publishing, 1985).
YO	*Yeats and the Occult*, ed. George Mills Harper (Toronto: Macmillan of Canada; Niagara Falls, New York: Maclean-Hunter Press, 1975).
YP	*Yeats's Poems* ed. & ann. A. Norman Jeffares, with an appendix by Warwick Gould (London: Macmillan, 1989). Cited from the third, revised edition of 1996.
YT	*Yeats and the Theatre*, ed. Robert O'Driscoll and Lorna Reynolds (Toronto: Macmillan of Canada; Niagara Falls, New York: Maclean-Hunter Press, 1975).
YVP1, 2, 3	*Yeats's* Vision *Papers* (London: Macmillan, 1992), George Mills Harper (General Editor) assisted by Mary Jane Harper, Volume 1: *The Automatic Script: 5 November 1917—18 June*

1918, eds. Steve L. Adams, Barbara J. Frieling and Sandra L. Sprayberry; Volume 2: *The Automatic Script: 25 June 1918—29 March 1920,* eds. Steve L. Adams, Barbara J. Frieling and Sandra L. Sprayberry; Volume 3: *Sleep and Dream Notebooks,* Vision *Notebooks 1 and 2, Card File,* eds. Robert Anthony Martinich and Margaret Mills Harper.

Editorial Board

Notes on the Contributors

Richard Allen Cave is Professor of Drama and Theatre Studies in the University of London (at Royal Holloway). He is the author of *New British Drama in Performance on the London Stage, 1970-1985* (1987), and he has edited George Moore's *Hail and Farewell: Ave, Salve, Vale* (Colin Smythe, 1976, 1985) and *The Lake* (1980), and is General Editor of the *Theatre in Focus Series*. His edition of Yeats's *Selected Plays* was published by Penguin in 1997 and his edition of *Selected Plays* of T. C. Murray will shortly be published by Colin Smythe Ltd.

Peter L. Caracciolo is Senior Lecturer in English at Royal Holloway, University of London. He has written widely on Wilkie Collins, Stevenson, Conrad, Lessing, and Aldis, and has major essays on Wyndham Lewis in Robert Fraser (ed.), *Sir James Frazer and the Literary Imagination* (1990), Andrew Gibson (ed.), *Pound in Multiple Perspective* (1993) and Ian Willison, Warwick Gould and Warren Chernaik (eds.) *Modernist Writers and the Marketplace* (1996). He edited *The Arabian Nights in English Literature* (1988), and is a member of the editorial board of the *Wyndham Lewis Annual*.

Maneck H. Daruwala is Associate Professor of English at Florida International University (the State University of Florida at Miami). She writes, and teaches a variety of courses, especially in Romanticism and late Romanticism. She has published on Keats, Pater and Wilde, and is currently writing on Yeats and children's stories.

Gregory N. Eaves is a Lecturer in English at Kingston University, Surrey, having previously taught as a Lecturer in English and Comparative Literature at the University of California, Davis. He has previously written on *The Wild Swans at Coole*.

Paul Edwards is a Lecturer at Bath College of Higher Education. He is editor of the *Wyndham Lewis Annual*, and author of *Wynd-*

ham Lewis: Arts and War (1992). He has edited several books by and about Wyndham Lewis for Black Sparrow Press, including *Time and Western Man* and *Creatures of Habit and Creatures of Change: Essays on Art, Literature and Society 1913-1956*, and *Volcanic Heaven: Essays on Wyndham Lewis's Painting and Writing* (1996). He is currently writing a study of Lewis for Yale University Press.

Philip W. Errington is currently researching John Masefield for his Doctorate at University College London after specialising on that for his MA. An active member of the recently formed John Masefield Society, he delivered the annual lecture in 1997 and takes up the editorship of the *John Masefield Society Journal* in 1998.

Adrian Frazier is Professor of English at Union College, Schenectady, New York, and the author of *Behind the Scenes: Yeats, Horniman, and the Struggle for the Abbey Theatre* (1990). He is currently working on an authorized life of George Moore.

Warwick Gould is Professor of English Literature in the University of London, where he teaches at Royal Holloway and is Programme Director of the Centre for English Studies in the School of Advanced Study. He is co-author (with Marjorie Reeves) of *Joachim of Fiore and the Myth of the Eternal Evangel in the Nineteenth Century* (1987), and co-editor of *The Secret Rose, Stories by W. B. Yeats: A Variorum Edition* (1992), and of *The Collected Letters of W. B. Yeats*, II, 1896-1900, (Clarendon, 1997), and is working on editions of Yeats's *Early Essays* and *Mythologies* for the new Macmillan *Collected Edition*, and of *Yeats's Occult Diaries (1898-1901)*. He is a Fellow of the Royal Society of Literature.

William F. Halloran is Professor of English Literature at the University of Wisconsin, Milwaukee, where he was Dean for many years. He is currently preparing for publication an edition of the letters of William Sharp and Fiona Macleod.

T. Jeremiah Healey III is an honours graduate in English Literature and Theology from Georgetown University. He spent a year at Royal Holloway, University of London, conducting the research upon which this article is based. He is now involved in mortgage finance at Credit Suisse First Boston, New York.

Elizabeth Heine is Editor of the *Abinger Edition* of E. M. Forster (Edward Arnold). She is currently completing a study of W. B. Yeats and Astrology.

Ron Heisler is a former trade union research worker; later an economics lecturer, and author of numerous articles on the early Rosicrucian movement. He is currently completing a history of Freemasonry down to 1700.

Virginia Hyde is Professor of English at Washington State University, Pullman and the author of *The Risen Adam: D. H. Lawrence's Revisionist Typology* (Penn. State University Press, 1992).

K. P. S. Jochum is Professor of English at Universität Bamberg, Germany. He is the heroic compiler of *W. B. Yeats: A Classified Bibliography of Criticism* (2nd ed., rev. & enl., 1990).

Declan Kiely is completing an MPhil in the University of London entitled 'Creating an Audience: Yeats's Lectures'. In 1997 he lectured to the Yeats Society of New York.

W. J. Mc Cormack is Professor of Literary History at Goldsmiths' College (University of London). His most recent books are *From Burke to Beckett* (1994) and *The Pamphlet Debate on the Union between Great Britain and Ireland* (Irish Academic Press, 1996). He is working on an edition of Yeats's political writings for Penguin.

Colin McDowell is a public servant in the Australian Bureau of Statistics. He is a regular contributor on Yeats and *A Vision*, and the author of many articles on Ezra Pound.

Colleen McKenna is completing a Doctorate in the University of London on W. B. Yeats and Seamus Heaney, and teaches at the University of Kingston.

James Pethica is Associate Professor of English at the University of Richmond, Richmond, Va. His edition of *Lady Gregory's Diaries 1892—1902* was published by Colin Smythe in 1996 and is reviewed in this volume. His edition of the manuscript materials of Yeats's *Last Poems* was published by Cornell University Press in 1997.

Masaru Sekine, a trained Noh actor, is Professor in the Department of Politics and Economics at Waseda University. He founded IASAIL-JAPAN, and is the author of *Ze-Ami and His Theories of Noh Drama* (1985) and (with Christopher Murray) of *Yeats and the Noh: A Comparative Study* (1990). He is editor of *Irish Writers and Society at Large* (1985), *Irish Writers and the Theatre* (1986), and, with Okifumi Komesu of *Irish Writers and Politics* (1990). He is currently experimenting with the blending of Japanese minimalism and the drama of Yeats and Beckett, in the Drama Centre, University College, Dublin.

Michael Sidnell is Emeritus Professor of English at Trinity College, University of Toronto. Co-editor of *Druid Craft: the writing of* "The Shadowy Waters" and of *The Secret Rose, Stories by W. B. Yeats: A Variorum Edition*, he is author of *Dances of Death: The Group Theatre of London in the Thirties* and co-editor of *Mythologies*, forthcoming in the Macmillan *Collected Edition*, and of *The Countess Cathleen* in the Cornell Yeats Manuscripts Series. His volume of essays, *Yeats's Poetry and Poetics* was published in 1996.

Colin Smythe is a publisher with a unique range of interests in Irish and Anglo-Irish culture. He is currently preparing a new edition of *A Bibliography of the Writings of W. B. Yeats* for the Clarendon Press. He is the General Editor of the Coole Edition of Lady Gregory's works, and co-editor of *Lady Gregory Fifty Years After* (1987).

Deirdre Toomey is editor of *Yeats and Women: Yeats Annual No 9* (1991), a revised and augmented edition of which appeared from Macmillan as *Yeats and Women* (1997). She is co-editor of *The Collected Letters of W. B. Yeats*, Vol II, (1896-1900) (Clarendon, 1997) and is working on editions of Yeats's *Early Essays* and *Mythologies* for the *Collected Edition of the Works of W. B. Yeats*, and on an authorised edition of *Yeats's Occult Diaries (1898-1901)*.

Preface and Acknowledgements

WE ARE ESPECIALLY DELIGHTED to include in this volume the first of a two part study of Yeats, William Sharp and his secondary personality, 'Fiona Macleod' by William F. Halloran. The second part of this study, which is based on letters long unavailable to scholars, will appear in *Yeats Annual No 14: Yeats and the Nineties* (1998), a special issue of which John Harwood will be co-editor, and which will contain essay reviews of Roy Foster's *W. B. Yeats: A Life, I: The Apprentice Mage* and *The Collected Letters*, II (1896-1900).

In July 1996, the National Gallery of Ireland instigated *The Yeats Network*, a quarterly newsletter. The Gallery's former Icon Gallery is being refurbished as a Yeats Gallery, and a new wing is currently being designed by Benson and Forsyth to house the Yeats Museum, looking out onto Lincoln Place. It will include a study room.

Anne Yeats has graciously donated Jack B. Yeats's complete archive to the Gallery. This generous gift includes her uncle's personal library, including a complete set of his own published work and first editions of works by W. B. Yeats, as well as 190 sketchbooks from the late 1890s to the 1950s. There are also seven volumes of *Lives*, original fantasy drawings, as well as his manuscripts of plays and other writings.

Tina Roche at the Development Office, National Gallery of Ireland, Merrion Square West, Dublin 2 (phone +353 1 6615 133; fax + 353 1 6761 620) is eager to hear from potential contributors to the Yeats Museum's Purchase Fund. Donors have also already made gifts in kind of letters, photographs and papers, including Jack B. Yeats's personal account book. A British Fund for the National Gallery of Ireland has been established as a Charity (no. 1055428), and offers tax relief on donations in the U.K. (c/o Bank of Ireland, 18 Lower Regent St., London SW1Y 4PU).

Professor Roy Foster, FBA, Carroll Professor of Irish History in Oxford (c/o Hertford College, Oxford) is working on the second volume of his authorised life of W. B. Yeats for the Clarendon Press,

Oxford. Professor Ann Saddlemyer, c/o Massey College, University of Toronto, continues to work on her authorised life of George Yeats. Professor John Kelly of St. John's College, Oxford, General Editor of *The Collected Letters of W. B. Yeats* (Clarendon Press) and his co-editor Professor Ronald Schuchard of Emory University, Atlanta, Ga., are currently finishing Vol IV, which covers the years 1905-1907. Colin Smythe (PO Box 6, Gerrards Cross, Bucks, SL9 8EF, UK) is completing his revision of the Wade-Alspach *Bibliography* for the Clarendon Press. An authorised edition of *Yeats's Occult Diaries, 1898-1901* is being prepared for the Macmillan Press by Deirdre Toomey and myself. All the above would be very grateful to hear of new letters, and to receive new information from readers.

Submissions for *Yeats Annual No. 14* should reach me by 31 October, 1997 (and those for *No. 15* by the same date in 1998), at the editorial address:

> The Centre for English Studies
> School of Advanced Study,
> University of London,
> Senate House, Malet Street,
> London WC1E 7HU.
>
> E-mail w.gould@sas.ac.uk.

Yeats Annual is now presented to the publisher in camera-ready form. Contributions should be supplied on 3.5" disks, and preferably in Nota Bene 4.5, the program used in the preparation of *Yeats Annual*. We can translate from other PC programs, and from texts prepared on Macintosh machines if they have been written to PC formatted disks. It is essential to send with the disk three copies on paper, and we advise that you send submissions in two separate parcels. Further information for contributors and a style sheet are also available upon request. We are grateful to receive offprints and review copies and other bibliographical information (which is acknowledged at the end of each volume). *Yeats Annual* can now be ordered from Macmillan Press's website. The URL is http://www.macmillan-press.co.uk/.

An error in *Yeats Annual 12* which was not corrected before the volume went to press is on p. 310 where '*Poems 1899-1905*' in line 21 should read '*Poems Second Series*'.

Our chief debt of gratitude is to Miss Anne Yeats and Mr. Michael B. Yeats for granting permission (through A. P. Watt Ltd.) to use published and unpublished materials by W. B. Yeats. Many of our contributors are further indebted to Michael Yeats and Anne Yeats for making unpublished materials available for study and for many other kindnesses, as is the Editor.

Other unpublished materials have been made available to us through the kindness of Colin Smythe Ltd. and the Houghton Library, Harvard University. Patricia Willis, Curator of American Literature at the Beinecke Rare Book and Manuscript Library, Yale University, Catherine Fahy of the National Library of Ireland, Dr Rodney Phillips and Dr Philip Milito of the Henry W. and Albert A. Berg Collection, New York Public Library (Astor, Lenox and Tilden Foundations), Dr Cathy Henderson and Professor Thomas F. Staley at the Harry Ransom Humanities Research Center, provided us with research assistance. The British Library, The University of London Library, and Mr David Ward of the library of Royal Holloway (University of London), have also been unfailingly helpful, and Professor Robin Alston of University College, London provided invaluable assistance with on-line databases and the preparation of digitised images supplied by the Thomas Fisher Library and Richard Landon, Director of the Rare Books and Special Collections at the University of Toronto. Many other helpful scholars and librarians have been thanked within the compass of individual contributions to this volume.

Grateful acknowledgement for access to and permission to print unpublished material is offered to the Wyndham Lewis Memorial Trust; James Dolman, C. J. Fox, Omar Pound and Michael Wood.

The following institutions are also acknowledged with thanks for access and for (in some cases) permission to include hitherto unpublished material from their various collections: The British Library; the BBC Sound Archives, the Carl A. Kroch Library, Cornell University, the Poetry and Rare Books Collection in SUNY at Buffalo, the Harry Ransom Humanities Research Center, University of Texas at Austin, the Rare Books and Manuscripts Division; the Yale Collection of American Literature, Beinecke Rare Book and Manuscript Library, Yale University.

At Macmillan Press, Charmian Hearne, Julian Honer and Tim Farmiloe were particularly helpful during the preparation of this volume, as were Lara Bell and Rebecca Dawson at the Centre for English Studies, University of London.

The late Riette Sturge Moore graciously allowed us to use on the front board of *Yeats Annuals* a symbol adapted from Thomas Sturge Moore's designs for the H. P. R. Finberg translation of *Axël* (1925). Linda Shaughnessy of A. P. Watt & Son, Professor Roy Foster, F.B.A. and Professor John Kelly on behalf of Oxford University Press were generous with permissions. Members of the Advisory Board continue to read a large number of submissions and we are grateful to them, and also to Dr Michael Baron, Professor Richard Allen Cave, Professor Elizabeth Butler Cullingford, Mr R. A. Gilbert, Mr Colin McDowell, Mr Roger Nyle Parisious, Professor Stephen Parrish and Professor John Stokes.

Deirdre Toomey as Research Editor took up in the research libraries those challenges which had defeated contributors and thus found innumerable ways to make this a better book. All associated with *Yeats Annual* (as well as its readers) will continue to be grateful to her for her learned and restless curiosity, and for her innate awareness of where, for the moment, research must have a stop.

WARWICK GOULD

ESSAYS

Yeats and Maud Gonne: Marriage and the Astrological Record, 1908-09

Elizabeth Heine

OF ALL THE EXTANT astrological manuscripts recording Yeats's relationship with Maud Gonne, the most important are those in the large, beautifully bound writing book which she gave to him in Paris in June 1908.[1] Her gift marked the revival of their earlier 'spiritual marriage'; in the course of the next year and a half Yeats used the book to record the dreams, visions, and planetary positions marking the development of their renewed partnership. This unusual journal provides not only basic biographical information but also extensive evidence of his techniques of meditation and prediction, both those stemming from his early training in the Hermetic Order of the Golden Dawn and those he was developing from his later practice of astrology. As he wrote to Florence Farr on 7 October 1907, 'I am hoping to find in the aspects a basis of evocation, which is really what interests me.' (L 500). The journal of 1908-09 preserves what is known of these evocations of the planets, while the surrounding astrological records testify to a mixture of vision and astrological inquiry surpassed only after Yeats's marriage to Georgie Hyde-Lees in 1917, in the creation of his final metaphysical work, *A Vision*.

3

In the same letter of 7 October to Florence Farr, Yeats shows both his enthusiasm for the art of astrology and the state of his technique in 1907: 'Astrology grows more and more wonderful every day. . . . I am trying to work at primary directions, but my head reels with all the queer mathematical terms.' These are not the remarks of a neophyte but of a practitioner whose earlier notebooks are full of horary charts, meant to judge the answer to a question from the positions of the planets at the time it was asked, and natal horoscopes progressed into the future by means of secondary directions, which take the movements of the planets during each day after birth as equivalent to the events in each year of the life. Few amateur astrologers master techniques beyond those of erecting a natal chart and following the transits of the planets as they move on in their normal orbits in what we now call 'real time', continuing to form 'aspects' to each other and to the positions they held at the time of birth, recorded in the natal chart. The earliest grades of the Golden Dawn, which Yeats joined in 1890, required training in several divinatory techniques, including horary astrology, and Yeats and his uncle, George Pollexfen, also a member of the Golden Dawn, furthered their astrological studies together in Sligo during the winter of 1894-95.[2] A few horoscopes cast by Yeats survive from the 1890's; many more are preserved in the notebooks he used in the Edwardian years. Those for Maud Gonne are recurrent, but others also recur, particularly those for his friends involved with the theatre, like Annie Horniman, Florence Farr, and Lady Gregory. The notebooks are particularly rich for 1907, as his letters to Florence Farr indicate.

Yeats's work in 1907 on the collected edition of his works, published from September to December 1908, may have prompted a review of his own past that increased his admiration for the predictive powers of astrology, which always seem most clear in retrospect. Certainly his advance from a mastery of secondary directions to a desire to learn the techniques of primary directions helps to account for much of the astrological record surrounding and supporting the journal begun in June 1908. Primary directions were the most mathematically difficult of the astrological methods of prediction available at the turn of the century; the terms sometimes differ among astrologers, but those Yeats was interested in are so-called because they are worked from the arcs formed at and after the moment of birth by the earth's rotation, not by the movements of the planets in their orbits (always, in astrological terms, including the sun and the moon as 'planets', wandering stars).

Interpretations of all astrological 'directions' and 'progressions' depend on symbolic uses of time. In primary directions each degree of arc is taken as equivalent to a year of life, and they are thus related to the most basic of all predictive techniques, in which one simply counts the number of degrees between any pair of planets in the natal horoscope, expecting some correspondence with the activities of the equivalent year of the life. Secondary directions, the major and most common form of 'progression', are solar, taking a day for a year, while tertiary directions are lunar, sometimes taking a day for a month, or equating the lunar months after birth to years of the life. Secondary directions resemble primaries in that the daily movement of the sun approximates one degree, but both secondaries and tertiaries require knowledge of the planetary movements in the days and years after birth for their calculation, while primaries depend for their accuracy purely on the natal horoscope and calculations related to spherical trigonometry. The moment of birth must therefore be known very exactly; since the earth rotates daily at the rate of four minutes to a degree, an error of five minutes can put predictions more than a year askew. Thus birth-times were often 'rectified' by matching dated events of the life to related arcs; the basic precept of all astrology, 'as above, so below', necessarily operates also in reverse, 'as below, so above'.[3]

Yeats may have been interested in primaries partly as a means of rectifying the birthtimes of himself and his friends. There are efforts to rectify and progress the horoscopes of Maud Gonne and Lady Gregory in his earlier astrological notebooks, but not in terms of these 'primaries'. Moreover, the calculations in those pre-computer days were both complex and time-consuming, so much so that by May 1908 he had hired J. R. Wallace ('Mercury') to do the calculations for his own horoscope. Wallace provided both a list of Yeats's primary directions and a set of forms, headed 'Progressed Horoscope "Directions"', giving Yeats's secondary directions and major transits from January 1907 to June 1917. Yeats had these forms interleaved with blank pages and bound into what it seems sensible to call the 'Wallace' notebook; into it Yeats copied Wallace's lists of his primary directions as well, and used the notebook for his personal predictions until 1917. It was very probably the workbook he refers to in 'The Return of the Stars', open upon his knee on 20 May 1908, when a transit of Mars to his natal Uranus, neatly noted and dated by Wallace, coincided, 'like the fulfilment of the oracle in a Greek play', with a journalistic 'attack' upon the 'management of the Abbey Theatre'.[4]

Yeats was so pleased with Wallace's work that he also ordered horoscopes for Lady Gregory, her son Robert and his wife Margaret, and Maud Gonne, all anonymously identified by 'Nata' or 'Natus' and the date and place of birth; Lady Gregory's horoscope, with Wallace's interpretation and five years of directions and progressions, survives among Yeats's papers. Wallace, who was penniless and desperate for work, corresponded with Yeats throughout the summer of 1908, his letters a mixture of sorrow and intense interest in rectifications. Maud Gonne's uncertain birthtime, in the late afternoon or early evening of 21 December 1866, meant that her rising sign, determined by the point of the zodiac ascending on the eastern horizon at the time and place of her birth (her 'ascendant'), could be either Cancer or Leo. Wallace's letter of 1 September 1908, his last before a silence not broken until 1910, shows that he and Yeats had been discussing Maud Gonne's life in some detail. Wallace wrote to ask Yeats's agreement with his proposed rectification to a birthtime of 6:40 p.m., giving about 4 degrees Leo as the ascendant, before he did the full calculations; the primary arcs he offered for consideration are those related to her marriage to Major John MacBride, on 21 February 1903, the 'trouble' with him in autumn 1904 and the resulting separation of January 1905, and a time of great 'trouble and excitement' in summer 1891. Only the last is understood wrongly, since Yeats seems to have told Wallace that it was caused by a 'false report' rather than by the death of her baby son, the child of Lucien Millevoye, on 31 August 1891.

By December 1908 Claude Dumas had taken Wallace's place. Dumas' calculations of primaries for Yeats were also entered in the Wallace noteboook, and his interpretation of Yeats's horoscope is clearly the one that evoked Maud Gonne's comments in her letter of 13 January 1909: 'The horoscope is very interesting, I think you ought to heed what it says about marriage, I always feel that marriage for you would be a mistake, I always have felt this . . . .' (G-YL 261). Yeats had accepted Wallace's birthtime for Maud Gonne, providing it to Dumas, but I think perhaps Yeats did not show her the comparison Dumas made of her horoscope and his own in terms of a possible marriage; Dumas advised very strongly against it, regarding some of the mutual aspects as very good, but other, less harmonious ones as destructive, not at all conducive to domestic tranquillity.

The calculations and comments of Wallace and Dumas provide the bulk of the astrological record for 1908-09 not created by Yeats himself. A horoscope for Maud Gonne done late in 1908 by 'Ely Star' of Paris also survives, but 'Star' seems to have guessed at the sun's position and decided those of the rest of the seven visible planets by lot rather than calculation—they are fraudulently wrong.[5] By contrast, Wallace and Dumas are clearly writing for Yeats as an astrologer, using the symbols and explaining their astrological reasoning. Wallace's calculations seem to have had the greatest effect on Yeats, stirring him to follow transiting Mars and its aspects through the summer of 1908, as he recorded the initial dreams and visions of the 'spiritual marriage' in his journal. There are also, scattered throughout Yeats's astrological manuscripts, a number of charts he erected on printed forms headed 'R. A. of M. C.' (Right Ascension of Medium Coeli), designed for horoscopes to be accompanied by a 'speculum', the listings of degrees and arcs necessary for the calculation of primary directions. These also belong to the record of 1908-09.

Yeats apparently obtained the 'speculum' forms as part of his investigation of primary directions, but then used many for more general astrological purposes. Several, like a natal horoscope he cast for Mabel Dickinson, with whom he began an affair in the spring of 1908, can be dated fairly precisely; hers has some notes for lunar positions of June and July 1908 written in future terms, so it must have been drawn up no later than May. Yeats used another of the forms for his own 'Lunation/43 years/(Nov 5 & 6) 1868'. Born on 13 June 1865, with the waning moon in Aquarius forming a 'trine' aspect of about 120 degrees to his sun in Gemini, he celebrated his 43rd birthday in 1908, and he is in this case experimenting with a tertiary direction dependent on the monthly synodic returns of moon and sun to his natal aspect of the waning trine; his notes show that in business he expected 'strife—with good result', and a 'not very good' 'Neptune-Uranus love affair' marked by 'unexpected events'.[6]

Another of the datable 'speculum' forms was cast near the time when he began the journal of 1908-09, but three other charts on the same forms, all concerned with Maud Gonne, need to be considered first, since they help to explain the astrological and biographical groundwork underpinning the journal of 1908-09. Two are obviously paired in their focus on her marriage; they are an event chart and a secondary progression of her natal planets for the time of her marriage. The third is a natal chart, necessary for basic comparisons with all future matters. Yeats's written judgements on the two marriage charts reflect both his knowledge of the aftermath and his opinion, which he may have expressed to Maud Gonne at the time of the marriage, that she was not only moving away from the promise of their 'spiritual marriage' of 1898, but also lowering herself (*CL3* 315-17). She seems to have told him that the marriage ceremony occurred between 10 a.m. and noon. He drew up the positions of the orbiting planets at Paris for about 11:30 a.m. on 21 February 1903, and wrote, among other notes: 'If Sun signifies the woman then she is in 10th house showing greater position, and conjunct Jupiter money etc., and trine Neptune mystic dreams. If Moon is the man then he is represented by the Moon terribly afflicted showing immorality and drunk etc.'. Usually the symbolism would take man as sun and woman as moon, which explains Yeats's 'If' and reflects his opinion of the match. On the progressed chart, a deletion shows that he was at first disappointed to find no 'evil' aspects to match those of the transiting planets, but he then noted that 'radical evil—violent emotion' would develop as her progressed moon reached the tense 'square' angle of ninety degrees to her natal Mars and Jupiter in the course of 1903.

Wallace's rectified birthtime for Maud Gonne is so close to the zero Leo ascendant which Yeats had been using for years that it is not possible to say whether these two charts were drawn up before or after Wallace proposed his rectification, but the natal chart on the 'R. A. of M. C.' form uses Yeats's earlier choice of ascendant. This chart is marked in pencil for Maud Gonne's progressions and transits for 1906-07, but it shows no evidence of natal calculations and appears to have been copied directly from an earlier natal horoscope. Written on a different, smaller form, creased and battered from much use, this earlier chart probably dates from 1896 or so, since an identical form preserves a 'Horary', so labelled, timed for 'Midnight', 25 May 1896, and headed 'concerning PIAL'; Yeats's use of the initials of Maud Gonne's Golden Dawn motto, 'Per Ignum Ad Lucem', identifies her now, though it preserved her anonymity then. It seems likely that the horary was precipitated by her letter of Saturday, 23 May 1896, written to ask Yeats, rather teasingly, whether he had indeed married a widow: 'At first I thought this could not be as having seen you in London I thought we were sufficiently friends for you to have told me, but on reflection this is absurd as marriage after all is only a little detail in life . . . .' (*G-YL*, 60) In casting the horary, Yeats must have been asking about the relationship. His judgement reads: 'Saturn and Sun receding from

opposition. Moon approaching opposition to Sun. This shows separation first caused by her action will continue because of his action.
Venus is approaching conjunction with Sun showing some affinity
which should be at its strongest 12 years from now. . . . Moon opposite to Venus makes for separation. . . . .' The twelve years' time lag
returns us to 1908, perhaps explaining the careful preservation of the
horary.

When the 1896 horary and the worn natal chart for Maud Gonne
are taken together, they remind us of the long, obsessive history of
Yeats's relationship with her. They also help to focus some of the
fundamental questions about astrology: Are aspects 'real'? What can
that mean? Does conviction that they are 'real' make any difference
to the way a life is lived? So far as Yeats is concerned, the answers to
the first and last questions are 'yes', and his answers to the second, in
1908-09, occupy us now. The only way I know of for others to answer the first two is to test the system, as Yeats did, though his
predisposition, given the hermetic belief that all realities are interre-
lated, would have been to see connections. The third answer, should
one reach that far in our modern and post-modern western culture,
is the individual's choice. Planetary positions are observational,
objective—but interpretations of their 'influences' vary among cultures and within cultures, from practitioner to practitioner. Yeats's
astrological links to Maud Gonne are powerful enough to make it
reasonable to ask whether his devotion was in part a conscious
choice supported by his knowledge of astrology, and also reasonable
to assume that the astrological links for the attraction he felt would
support his conviction that aspects are real in their effects. The
journal of 1908-09 shows him tracking the aspects of the planets,
particularly Mars, very closely. Necessarily, as he finds varying elements of support, questions of destiny and fate arise. On an individual basis most astrologers think and act as though there is no point
in looking ahead unless one is willing to take measures to avoid
'evil' and encourage 'good'. But in trying to manipulate the world to
shape itself to our desires, are we merely fulfilling the desires of the
universe? This last question, by no means limited to astrologers, is
perhaps more conscious in astrologers than in most people. And it
underlies much of the irony in Yeats's plays, particularly, perhaps,
in *The Player Queen*, which began its long gestation in the prose
drafts of the summer of 1908.

What Yeats saw when he first studied Maud Gonne's natal chart
in relation to his own were strong links of the most traditional sort.

She was born on 21 December 1866. He labelled both the early and the later horoscope 'Nata', with the date and a queried time of 5 p.m., probably provided by the nata herself. On the day of her birth the sun was in the last degree of Sagittarius, and by late afternoon the ascending moon, in Gemini, was almost full and approaching the planet Uranus, or Herschel, as it was often called then. Yeats was a year and a half older, born when the sun was in Gemini and approaching Uranus. Astrological aspects have 'orbs' of exactness, from the ten degrees allowed for oppositions and conjunctions of major planets down to the two or three degrees permitted to smaller aspects like quintiles (seventy-two degrees), sextiles (sixty degrees, half the trine) and semi-squares (forty-five degrees, half the square). Maud Gonne's moon, in Gemini, was 'conjunct' Yeats's sun and Uranus, about five degrees past his sun and within a degree of his Uranus. His Jupiter, in Sagittarius, was conjunct her sun by about five degrees, and her Jupiter, at four degrees of Aquarius, was conjunct his ascendant at zero Aquarius. The resulting polarity, with her sun opposite his and close to his Jupiter, and her moon and Uranus close to his sun and Uranus, is the sort of pairing of opposites that brings up terms like alter ego and the Jungian anima-animus, not altogether dissimilar from the roles of the daimons in the earlier version of *A Vision*.

But what Yeats did, faced with these polarities, was to rectify Maud Gonne's birthtime to an ascendant of zero Leo, directly opposite his own. Sun, moon, and ascendant are regarded as the three strongest elements in a horoscope; Yeats would also have seen that his own moon, in Aquarius, squared Maud Gonne's Saturn in Scorpio. Saturn represents restriction and delay, which he had certainly experienced in the course of their relationship, but he and she were firmly linked by an axis of opposition and conjunction for sun and moon, supported by Jupiter, traditionally the 'Great Benefic'. Why not oppose the ascendants as well? Maud Gonne was born at Aldershot, where the first degree of Leo would not ascend until about 6:30, but Yeats never marked either the earlier or later birthchart to indicate that he had revised the clocktime by his choice of ascendant. His own birthtime of 10:40 p.m. had been recorded in the family Bible and functioned well enough in astrological terms; he rectified hers by the experience of their relationship, and Wallace eventually praised Yeats's 'intuition' when he calculated her primaries for an ascendant of four degrees Leo.

Yeats, whose own motto in the Golden Dawn was 'Demon Est Deus Inversus', was always fascinated by opposites, whether represented by masks and by dramatic characters like those in *The Player Queen*, or by the orbital dance of sun and moon, traditionally symbolic of the polarity of male and female. By contrast, Claude Dumas begins his comparison of the two charts by finding the opposed suns 'fundamentally divergent' and the opposed ascendants 'anything but a desirable aspect'. Of 'male Uranus in conjunction with female moon' he writes: 'This is not good. The higher intuitions and aspirations of male would disturb and worry the calmer or more conventional imagination of female'. Dumas finds the mutual Jupiter positions beneficial and approves of the traditionally fortunate joining of male sun and female moon. But Maud Gonne's Saturn in Scorpio seems to him so troublesome that he quotes Sepharial, 'one of the best known astrologers of today', on its position: 'The native is prone to excess and folly in love affairs. The passions need to be bridled, many enemies arise against the native, and secret enmity from females may be expected. In marriage there will be trouble. The passions are quick and volatile and the nature is capable of great passional devotion which, however, is liable to bring disastrous results'.[7] Moreover, Yeats's Venus was opposite Maud Gonne's Saturn, to Dumas 'most decidedly unfavourable', and the square to his moon is for Dumas 'one of the worst afflictions in the two horoscopes': 'The female Saturn would certainly depress and worry the Aquarian moon in male natus. Not improbably there would be much jealousy on part of female, which might be aroused by misapprehending the male desire for platonic friendship'. Not only that, but Dumas takes the mundane positions of Maud Gonne's Saturn and Yeats's Sun, both in their respective fifth houses, at the same angles from the ascendant-descendant axis, to be equivalent to a zodiacal conjunction, and very evil: 'Gemini and the sun in male gives delight in the higher philosophy, in mental and ethical studies and interests, and manifests the higher phases of the "Reasonable Soul", while in the female we have Saturn in Scorpio. This gives a very opposite nature to the male. There would be brooding and dwelling upon morbid passional and sexual subjects, and perhaps, a love of mystery, intrigue, and desire for power over the male, the delight in wielding a secret and strange power'. These are the interpretations that I doubt Yeats showed to Maud Gonne. He wrote comments on Dumas' interpretations of his own horoscope, which she saw, but not on these.

There is no way of knowing how Yeats may have described the 'nata' in question, but Dumas' comments are well within astrological traditions. Dumas seems perhaps too conventionally patriarchal, expecting reason from the male and distressing passion from the female, but Saturn in Scorpio in the fifth house of children and creativity, love affairs and leisure, even theatre and gambling, is astrologically baleful, and Maud Gonne did have great sorrow from her love affairs, and a child who died. However, even if Dumas knew who she was and had heard the attacks on her reputation related to the dispute with MacBride, he also performs the useful role of the professional, pointing out negatives that are easy to deny in self-analysis. Yeats's actions seem to prove that he preferred his own interpretations, but he quotes from Dumas' analysis later in the 1908-09 journal, when he analyzes the evocations of the planets he undertook with Olivia Shakespear and Florence Farr, two of his 'seers', as he dealt with his feelings in June 1909, after Maud Gonne had told him that she must renounce their physical relationship. He is reconsidering her sun opposite her moon and Uranus, which are conjunct his sun and Uranus: 'This would mean that her active being [sun] would be repelled by my intellectual side [his sun and Uranus], while her imaginative side [moon] is attracted by dreams—think this Uranus aspect evil also and that my Uranus would "worry and disturb" her "calmer and more conventional imagination"' [see above]. Maud Gonne's imagination, especially if figured by her moon, can easily be regarded as extremely unconventional, shaped by Uranus to the same degree as Yeats's sun, but in his depression Yeats is finding negatives where he might otherwise see positives, focusing on her sun, her conscious 'active being', in opposition to his own.

Earlier, in December 1908 or January 1909, Yeats did take issue with the comparison provided by Dumas, whose answering comments survive to show him defending his interpretations and discussing Yeats's view of the possible spiritual role of Neptune. Neptune and Uranus were then relatively new planets in terms of discovery, and Pluto was unknown. These outer planets orbit so slowly, often appearing to go backwards for long periods, in 'retrograde' motion from our geocentric viewpoint, that their positions are to some extent generational, and their astrological interpretations still in process of development. At the turn of the century Saturn, outermost of the visible planets, was the traditional ruler of Aquarius, and Yeats, with his ascendant and moon in Aquarius, usually referred to himself as an Aquarian, ruled by Saturn, rather than use his sun-sign of Gemini, ruled by Mercury. Astrologers now regard Uranus as the ruler of Aquarius, electric and eccentric, a kind of 'higher' Mercury, as Dumas' and Yeats's own comments suggest, always surprising but not necessarily 'evil'. Neptune, now having displaced Jupiter as ruler of Pisces, is still seen as spiritual and vision-ary but is also associated with illusion, with narcotics, with Hol-lywood. Moreover, despite Yeats and Maud Gonne's difference in age, the to-ing and fro-ing of the planets had brought Neptune to the same degree (10 Aries) when they were born, placing it in her birthchart near or at the powerful midheaven zodiacal point. What Yeats knew of her visionary powers and her ability to enthrall crowds must have contributed to his knowledge of Neptune; his own was in his second house, less powerfully placed but trine his Mars in Leo. Also, though neither knew it, Pluto was at the same degree at their births (13 Taurus), and exactly conjunct Yeats's Venus, planet of love and beauty. Discovered only in 1930, Pluto is still in process of astrological definition, but seems to be an intensifier, with the explosive power of the atom and the profundity and finality of the god of the underworld. If the difficult Gonne-Yeats relationship seems both inescapable and apparently eternal, preserved and celebrated in Yeats's poems and plays, then the unusually exact planetary conjunctions and oppositions can be inter-preted as astrological correlatives.

As Yeats's judgement of the horary for 25 May 1896 indicates, he had been willing to put up with Saturnian restrictions for a long time. When he drew up a chart after the Paris revival of their old 'spiritual marriage' in June 1908, he labelled it first as a 'Horary' for 20 June at 11 p.m., then changed it to 21 June at 10:30 p.m., a time which brought the moon to conjunction with Saturn in Aries, approaching their joint natal Neptune. He marked the chart doubly and triply to diminish the semi-fatalistic character of the horary moment, which is traditionally seized as a question arises, shaping itself out of our usual random chaos in a moment expected to be 'radical'—relevant and significant in astrological terms. Instead Yeats chose the 'radical' moment. The three notes read: 'Did not think this moment radical at the time.' 'Was not quite sure of moment—no precise significant moment.' 'Incline for 10.30 which gives radical figure.' A fourth note looks back: 'Night before at same hour however also significant—moon at about 25 Pisces.' For the moment Yeats chose, Aquarius ascended and thus Saturn ruled, con-junct the moon and square both Uranus in Capricorn and the collec-tion of planets in Cancer, including the sun, Neptune, Mercury, Mars and Venus. Only Jupiter was fortunate, trine moon and Saturn and conjunct Yeats's natal Mars in Leo. Thus he reaches his judge-ment: 'a tragic passionate relation—present depression leading to painful or troubled time—passionate feeling or bond mixed up with mystic life but accompanied by a noble or religious influence'.

Just when Yeats cast the figure for 21 June 1908 and began the journal is uncertain, but the first entry and the horoscope are closely related. Of the dates in the entry, quoted below, '(20th)' was added later, inserted above the first line; the final '8' of 1898 replaced a '9'; and the inch-long blank space after the initial 'June' looks very much as though it was left open for a date or dates; 'the night' was inserted before 'June 24'. Clearly Yeats checked the dates after writing the entry, and may have cast the horoscope in the process. On the verso of the 21 June chart he wrote the caption and the aspects for a figure he did not finish drawing: 'On night of 24 when mystic marriage again showed itself'. Parts of the first entry in the journal have been published before, but the whole is relevant here, particularly in relation to the non-physical character of the 'mystic marriage'.[8] The complete first entry, with Yeats's ellipsis, reads:

> June   at Paris with PIAL. On Saturday evening (20th)
> she said something that blotted away the recent past and brought all
> back to the spiritual marriage of 1898. On Sunday we talked more
> plainly. She believed that this bond is to be recreated and to be the
> means of spiritual illumination between us. It is to be a bond of the
> spirit only and she lives—[from] now on she said—for that and for
> her children. I was ill a little and slept heavily and so got nothing
> for two or three days. Then on the night [of] June 24 I had a long
> poetical dream—not perfect vision for there was not bright light. I
> was sailing a gay and painted boat on some narrow sea. People ran
> upon the shores and pointed to a shrouded figure lying in the boat.
> I sang in answer words I have forgotten except these words
>
> > We call it . . . .
> > It has such dignity of limb
> > By the sweet name of Death.
>
> The next day she said she had been with me. I said 'There is something I want you to give me, a book to write such visions in.' She
> said triumphantly, 'I have already planned to give you that. I came
> back from you with that thought.' She then gave me this book.

This entry, like all Yeats's earlier visionary experiences of 'marriage' with Maud Gonne, reflects the sublimation of sexual passion that was so fundamental to their relationship. The revival of the dreaming astral meetings of the mystic marriage of 1898 carries through the summer and autumn of 1908, at last becoming physical when Yeats again visited Paris in December 1908, to judge from the change in tone in Maud Gonne's letters and Yeats's insistence on the possibilities of ordinary marriage in his exchanges with Dumas. In astrological terms, the initial revival could have been physically sexual, but then Yeats's reading of the horoscope for 20 and 21 June 1908 might more reasonably have focused on the transit of fortunate Jupiter over his natal Mars, in his seventh house of marriage and partnerships, and the conjunction of transiting Venus and Mars in Cancer, trine Maud Gonne's Saturn in Scorpio. Wallace had noted the Jupiter transit, which might have moved Yeats to choose this time to visit Paris. But even if the 20th saw a more intimate meeting, the spiritual focus of the 21st caused Yeats to choose the restriction of moon by Saturn, trine Jupiter and nearing Neptune, to signify a mystic, noble, religious quality for the reunion—and then he sang of the body lying still as death.

The poem thus inspired was published in *The Nation* on 11 July 1908 as 'A Dream', with a note describing the vision almost exactly in the words of the journal. Yeats reprinted it later as 'His Dream', the first in the series he grouped under the title 'Raymond Lully and his wife Pernella' in the first edition of *The Green Helmet and Other Poems* (1910), inadvertently naming Lully, as an erratum slip explained, instead of the alchemist Nicholas Flamel (*VP* 253). It was apparently Maud Gonne, in a letter of September 1910, who pointed out the error, after having thanked Yeats for the series, 'these beautiful things created for me' (*G-YL*, 294).

Mystical and alchemical elements appear throughout the dreams and visions of the renewed 'spiritual marriage', described most fully by Virginia Moore.[9] Alchemy and astrology share the symbols of the planets, so that some of Yeats's uses of the symbols have more to do with the archetypal symbolism of alchemy than the specifics of astrology. For instance, the intersecting circles of silver and gold that Yeats used to evoke the spiritual union represent moon and sun, or night and day, and then Venus and Mars when he shifts the colours to green and red, but the female-male pairing in the symbolism is mythical and mystical, not tied to real planets or aspects. In the summer of 1908 the astrology runs concurrently with the visions, appearing in Yeats's habit of drawing up horoscopes for moments of receiving and writing letters, and in his continuing exploration and testing of Wallace's primary and secondary directions. He also customarily used the verso pages of the journal for additions, not only contemporary horoscopes or the pasted-in envelopes that hold Maud Gonne's letters of 26 June and 26 July 1908, but also later comments which are sometimes difficult to date. By the summer of 1909, however, Yeats's descriptions of his astrological evocations of the planets dominate the entries, and the alchemy is represented by an account of his reading of Basilius Valentinus.

Yeats's second and third entries in the journal are for 3 July and 11 July 1908. That for 3 July is a brief account of his use of the 'old symbol' of the 'gold sun' and 'silver moon' on going to sleep, and then a dream of a 'talking machine that argued out egoism (Sun) and altruism (Moon), a confused expression of the symbol of no importance'. That for 11 July links a recent evocation of 'a red and green globe mingling' to an indistinct dream of making verse, and the advice that weaker poetry is the 'price for an inner intensity'. Yeats also notes that a letter from PIAL arrived on 10 July at about 2:30 p.m., probably the letter of 26 June preserved in the envelope facing the entry, though it is missing its last page or pages and does not now match Yeats's report that PIAL wrote she had 'not yet tried to come' and that her dreams were 'also confused'.

At the end of the entry for 11 July Yeats drew up a horoscope for the letter's arrival, beginning his commentary with a note on the fortunate Jupiter in the 'figure for Paris meeting'; at his reception of the letter the moon was again trine Jupiter, and Yeats now sees 'a long course of friendship which brings us to gentleness, under the influence of high feeling (Jupiter) and steadfast purpose and time (Saturn) . . . . emotional nature of affection—soft and gentle (Cancer) and yet commingled with intellect. Then suffers under Saturn influence—absence a hindrance or the like—and trine of Jupiter to Saturn softens this as well as lunar trine'. Then, on the facing verso page, he drew up another horoscope for the reception of another letter at 9 a.m. on 10 July. The zodiacal positions of the planets are the same, except that the moon is three degrees earlier, just entering Sagittarius and approaching the trine to Mars in early Leo, rather than separating from it, but the ascendant degree is quite different, changing the houses into which the planets fall and their rulers. As Yeats notes, 'Chief difference is Mercury and Jupiter are now significators. I doubt that is to say if any resolve or emotion was born or greatly strengthened at this moment . . . . events coming first under Mars (parallel Neptune) and then under that of Time or prudence which is hostile to sender, though much softened by Saturn trine Jupiter and Moon trine Saturn. Passionate Mars involvement and then waning'. Because of Yeats's judgement, it is probable that this letter was from Mabel Dickinson, who obviously stood no chance with Yeats against Maud Gonne. Yeats appears to be looking for astrological support for his different feelings toward the two women, and finding it.

A letter of 13 July 1908 from Lady Gregory to Synge places Yeats with her and her son and daughter-in-law in the Burren, on the west coast of Ireland, from 11 July to the end of the month. He was dictating both the scenario for *The Player Queen* and also some of the essays which accompany 'The Return of the Stars', and he was making no secret of his interest in tracking Wallace's directions and progressions: 'Yeats' stars mean a row on the 14th! but he is not sure where it will fall' (*TB* 286). His next journal entry, of 21 July, records the event: 'On July 14th Mars conjunct progressed Sun by transit—letter full of emotion from PIAL which affected me deeply'. This letter, like others from this period, seems to have been lost; in the same entry Yeats also mentions that in her 'last' letter PIAL wrote that she had succeeded in coming to him only once since he left Paris, on the night of the seventh, which he thinks may have been the night 'when I found myself making verse'.

The next two entries are dated 23 and 29 July. Yeats notes a more vivid dream or vision of 'cascades on cascades of white roses' on 23 July,[10] but the most spectacular of the dream unions is that of the night of Saturday, 25 July 1908. Maud Gonne described her astral union with Yeats, who figured in it as a great serpent, in her letter of 26 July, which Yeats pasted, in its envelope, to the page facing the second installment of his journal entry of 29 July. He added, 'Letter from PIAL' at the bottom of the first installment; the implication is that the letter arrived shortly after he finished the first part of the entry, his record of the night of 25 July:

29 July. On night of 25th made evocation of [*interlocking circles*]. Saw it for the first time bright and shining. Sought union with PIAL. Slept without dream. Next day was extraordinarily well. . . . Noticed also that for the first time in weeks physical desire was awakened. Made evocation again on Sunday night and had confused dream, an amorous dream of the ordinary kind. . . .

Curiously, Yeats does not dream at all, and the results are physical. Maud Gonne's letter also moves from the 'wonderful spiritual vision' to more worldly cares, reporting that in her vision Yeats had said it would 'increase physical desire', which troubled her, 'for there was nothing physical in that union—Material union is but a pale shadow compared to it . . . .' (*G-YL*, 257)

The rest of Yeats's journal entry for 29 July, headed 'Later same day', describes the evocations he made between 3:30 and 4:30 in the afternoon, alone in the woods. There he successfully achieved union in the figure of a serpent 'as in letter', and then again in 'a great

mouse-grey veil or shroud', which is now a more vital shroud, in
that it leads to a 'dazzling, dark "green and red"' and 'an intense
inner life'. The entry ends with his attempt to 'become PIAL':

> Once when I tried to become PIAL to see what I was to be to her I
> saw a rippling wavy yellow flame. Is she to be Venus (green) and I
> Mars (red) and am I day and Sun and is she night and Moon. Years
> ago she used to put on Moon she said to come to me.

But although Yeats uses the astrological symbols here, and Maud
Gonne's method of travel might have something to do with her
moon conjunct Yeats's sun, the meanings are essentially archetypal,
as much alchemical as astrological. Yeats's astrological comment is
buried at the very back of the writing book, where he was reviewing the effects of his primaries and the transits of Mars for May,
June, July, and August 1908. For July he wrote:

> Mars conjunct progressed Sun (14th) letter from PIAL which deeply
> affected me. Nothing for Mars conjunct natal Mars except that if I
> had not refused invitation to Dublin would have spent 26th with
> Neptune-Mars [Mabel Dickinson] and so on day she was somewhat
> in my mind. On 25th matter referred to in PIAL letter happened (?
> may have been caused by Mars conjunct natal Mars in deep sleep
> self).

The question mark in the last supposition is Yeats's, and his acceptance of some causality that could link his moods even unconsciously
to the cycles of the planets is fully astrological, but for him not only
astrological. In 'The Return of the Stars' he argues that the Renaissance began a process still being completed, the task of 're-uniting
the mind and soul and body of man to the living world outside us', a
work undertaken by painters, poets, spiritists and also astrologers,
who are returning to us, he concludes, the knowledge of 'lucky
hours that double time's mystery, and hours that measure the tides
of being, setting stars to keep the bounds of pleasure and excitement'
('Return' 83).

Yeats was using the back of the writing book because he was
working out Lady Gregory's aspects from Wallace's calculations for
her, and finding causative correlations between the opposition of
her progressed moon and progressed Mars and 'a family quarrel
which though a slight thing has affected her very much as it is the
first she has had.' She had had to go to her family home in Roxborough on 10 August, experiencing 'a very bad day'. Yeats was

writing on 11 August, and wondering whether the moon's transit of her progressed stellium (group) of planets on 17 August would be eventful. His later comment is: 'Yes, a bother about geese on lake—tenant's geese driven off by herd without order.' Lunar aspects are often minor, and whatever environment is available has to provide the 'effects', but Yeats was obviously enjoying the quest for precise effects brought about even by transits of the moon, effectuating the background trends provided by primaries and secondaries and the natal chart itself.

Another list of Yeats's primaries with his notations of events from February 1908 to March 1909 faces the journal entries of 21-29 July 1908. The list and the comments for August and earlier seem to have been written in August, for Yeats notes that his primary direction of M.C. (midheaven) trine his moon was probably exact in June or July: 'In which case this may refer to PIAL matter. It brought her into my life again and a great change in all life.' To this he adds that his progressed moon square his natal sun, which he recalculated and moved from July to June in the Wallace chart, 'is working in PIAL affair'; such a square operating in June and during the summer would help to account for the sexual tensions and separation. Sometime later he bracketed the primaries for October-December 1908. They involved Saturn and Uranus and his moon: 'Performance of my play [*Deirdre*]. Is Mrs Campbell a Saturn woman or Saturn Moon—and led to my visit to Paris (Uranus sextile Moon).'

From August through November 1908 there is relatively little astrology in the entries of the journal. Yeats drew up a horoscope on the facing verso page for the time of his writing a letter to PIAL on 6 August, when he was feeling ill. He noted that Venus passed through the seventh house of partners and marriage as he wrote, from 3 to 4:30 p.m., and that Jupiter was important in the chart and lord of the ascendant, which led him to 'notice that Jupiter seems lord of the union. It has been strong in all figures.' In this figure, he takes Saturn opposite the midheaven to 'explain depression perhaps'. But the major entries describe his visionary dreams. One for the night of 8 August was based on the Rosicrucian patterns of the Golden Dawn; he did not rise through the Rose or raise his own cross, but successsfully imagined the union 'as a mingling of gold and silver flame'. Another, on the night of 18 September, was less directly concerned with the union itself, and suggests again that some of the PIAL dreams brought him poetry, like 'His Dream', and ideas for poems.

In the September dream, 'the first clear and logical since that in June in Paris', Yeats conquered a stone man by dismantling him, naming the parts of his body and sending them back to the elements until 'only his heart was left and that lay on my hand as a spider' which he told 'to go to the centre of the earth', whereupon it vanished into a hole in the ground. He writes that he felt that 'the vision was from PIAL and that the evil, which I thought to be my own destruction, had to be dealt with in detail. Was the stone man an image of a fixed idea? Spider a false critic of some kind.' The dream prefigures his later images of limited, stony hearts created by fanaticism, and may also be related to his comments on alchemical processes later in the journal, in June 1909, when he was concerned about the deadening effects of his studies of philosophy, 'a daily rooter out of instinct and guiding joy'.[11] 'The Fascination of What's Difficult', which follows the marriage poems in *The Green Helmet and Other Poems*, deals with a similar conflict between his 'Theatre business', drying his veins and his heart, and a freer poetic voice. In 1908 the dream of the stone man is followed by Maud Gonne's own entry of 20 October, in which she wrote of a visionary union with Yeats, who was in Liverpool at the time.[12] She calls him 'Aleel', after the adoring poet in *The Countess Cathleen*; Yeats edited the name to DEDI, his Golden Dawn identity.

Yeats also notes his sexual difficulties. On 24 August he wrote: 'Nerves upset—erotic dream last night. Never till this have I had one of this kind about PIAL. Wretched all day wanting to be with her.' On November 7, directly after Maud Gonne's entry, he wrote his last of 1908: 'This morning about 7 or 7:30 went through ceremony of spiritual union. Have been for two days much troubled with desire. (Note—the union always takes place in a world where desire is unthinkable—desire in the ordinary sense—that is before and after.)' It is no wonder that these two visionaries came down to earth for a while at least during Yeats's visit to Paris in December 1908.

Yeats's next entries after 7 November 1908 are dated for 5 January, 26 February, and 26 May 1909. Maud Gonne, not following Yeats's practice of leaving the versos blank for additional comments, had written her entry on the verso page of his for late September, and his cramped note of 7 November was fitted in beneath her account. He then continued his entries for 1909 on the recto pages, returning on 21 June 1909 to the verso facing the entries of 26 February and 26 May in order to add his well-known account of his response to her renunciation of their physical relations. His opening sentence begins, 'On May [*space*] PIAL told me that we must be apart', but his 'June 21' could easily be read 'Jan 21', and has been, especially since the June entry lies between those of 5 January and 26 February.[13] The date for the space is most probably 27 May. Maud Gonne stopped in London before sailing for Dublin on the night of Thursday, 27 May; she wrote her letter of further explanation to Yeats 'On the boat going to Ireland', and refers to 'things I said yesterday evening' (*G-YL*, 271-2). Certainly Maud Gonne convinced Yeats of her rejection of the physical after he wrote his journal entry of 26 May, which records an astrological session with a seer—his friend Olivia Shakespear—on 25 May; she foretold a coming loss, uncertain in its nature.

In January 1909 there was no renunciation of the physical, and it seems that from December 1908 until June 1909 Yeats considered himself essentially as well as spiritually married, though Maud Gonne was separated rather than divorced from her husband. In December 1908 he also began a second, less private journal, opening it with 'No Second Troy', another of the marriage poems printed in *The Green Helmet and Other Poems*. This later journal has been published in *Memoirs*[14] and Yeats's extensive work through the spring on the brief essays in the new journal, some of which deal with astrology, helps to explain the relatively few entries in the earlier one. But in the earlier journal there is also a change in the depth, or perhaps height, of Yeats's astrological practices, now directed not only to tracing the effects of transits and directions, but also toward evoking the planets themselves, apparently as both psychological and spiritual presences.

Yeats's entry for 5 January 1909 in the earlier journal begins with his descriptions of invocations of sword and cauldron, spear and stone, elements used in his and Maud Gonne's earlier efforts to found a Celtic Mystical Order. Then it moves on to an evocation of sword and cauldron followed by Yeats's setting of 'her own horoscope about her' as he 'invoked vision of the planets and aspects'. Maud Gonne had been haunted by a 'grey woman' in her earlier years; now she was told that the woman 'was the spirit of Moon opposite Sun but that the effect of this aspect had been conquered', and also, more ominously, that 'Uranus opposite Sun would destroy her in the end—that this was unalterable'. She and Yeats moved on to 'questioning Mars', which had led her into her battles and 'externality', and when Yeats asked how the influence might be checked, 'she was told that as she had not feared she might evoke Saturn'. After they did so 'certain fears troubled her much', and

Yeats writes that he had 'since noticed that during those days Mars by transit was passing [her natal] Saturn', which dates these events to 26-27 December 1908.

Yeats records that their 'evocations of Saturn' were failures because Maud Gonne had such difficulty 'seeing', which was 'unusual with her'. The entry ends with his account of their accompanying quarrels about the worth of an unnamed 'Dublin girl' who annoyed him, echoed also in the second journal entry in *Memoirs*, where he attributes his anger, as usual, to his own Mars opposite Moon. In the PIAL journal, instead of simply attributing the difficulties to his own aspect or to Mars transiting Maud Gonne's Saturn, he wonders about more occult causes, suspecting that the disputes were the result of 'one of those curious attacks which so often drive one from the threshold of wisdom. Her fears and my irritations were in each case of all things the most likely to separate us.' But there was no major separation.

Chronologically, Yeats's next relevant astrological commentary, dated 9 February 1909, appears as the sixtieth journal entry in *Memoirs*. He states his lesser thesis immediately, using 'radical' as equivalent to 'natal': 'There is an astrological sense in which a man's wife or sweetheart is always an Eve made from a rib of his body. She is drawn to him because she represents a group of stellar influences in the radical horoscope.' The paragraph was composed with an eye to public rather than private reading, so Yeats goes through a logical balancing of possible good or bad interconnections of man and wife before advancing to his greater thesis:

> All external events of life are of course an externalization of charac-
> ter in the same way, but not to the same degree as the wife, who
> may represent the gathering up of an entire web of influences. A
> friend if represented by a powerful star in the eleventh house may
> be the same, especially if the Sun apply to that star. We are mirrors
> of stellar light and we cast this light outward as incidents, magnetic
> attractions, characterizations, desires. This casting outward of the
> light is that fall into the circumference the mystics talk of. (*Mem*
> 167)

Maud Gonne, of course, is the 'friend' represented by Yeats's Jupiter in Sagittarius in his eleventh house of friendship, conjunct her sun. So disguised, she seems nonetheless necessary to him here, but his surrounding statements, moving as they do from psychology to metaphysics, reach far beyond the ordinary astrology of aspects and houses. They resemble his much later 'Seven Propositions', in which he declares that 'The horoscope is a set of geometrical relations between the Spirit's reflection and the principal masses of the universe and defines that character.'[15]

In the PIAL journal, only the entry of 26 February stands before the extensive entries of 26 May and the days after Maud Gonne's renunciation of the physical. It records a dream on 'night of Feb 23 or 24 (wrote it to PIAL)', in which Yeats in the company of Lady Gregory turns away in terror from a longing to throw himself into an abyss and then discovers an ancient house full of beautiful things which he 'should have gone into before'. Knowing that he can find wisdom in it he asks for the 'wisdom of love' and opens a book in which he knew he 'would learn of PIAL', but the writing is too small. He looks at the pictures instead and sees genealogical charts: 'I longed for time to understand but woke. Old John brought in letter from PIAL.' There is a matching entry in the later journal, where Yeats noted his activities for 26 February, when 'Venus just passed conjunction [his natal] Moon'; his timetable shows that he devoted the time from noon to 1:30 to 'Letters and writing mystical notes, etc.' (*Mem* 172). Venus here is loving and positive, as the dream seems to be, and the entry following the timetable is Yeats's revision of 'Reconciliation', another of the 'marriage' poems. He writes that it was initially composed six months earlier, but then begins revising, and it is clear that the final lines were added here, at the end of February 1909. He had turned to the theatre and plays about warring kings when Maud Gonne shocked him by marrying MacBride, but now the case is different:

> And while we're in our laughing, weeping fit,
> Hurl helmets, crowns and swords into the pit.
> But, dear, cling close to me; since you were gone,
> My barren thoughts have chilled me to the bone.

Renunciation was yet to come, but perhaps there was already some foreboding.

The entry of 26 May in the more private journal is fascinating both for its messages and for Yeats's astrological means of evoking them. Olivia Shakespear was his first lover, in an affair which became physical in 1896, shortly before Maud Gonne's letter querying a Yeats marriage. His affiliation with 'PIAL' eventually broke up the affair with Mrs. Shakespear in early 1897, but they renewed their friendship later. All Yeats's close women friends, with the possible exception of Mabel Dickinson, shared to some extent in his occult interests and would 'see' for him if they could. The entry

begins, 'Yesterday awoke vision of horoscope—my own—with S.'
She knew no astrology and apparently he did not name the planets,
but she described what she 'saw' as he 'questioned Jupiter in Sagittarius in eleventh house':

> It took various forms as I connected it by line and light with the
> aspecting planets, at first a white-haired, though seemingly young,
> figure robed in blue, holding a vessel of red liquid (? blood) in left
> hand and in right an ivory spoon, or what seemed so, but darkened
> as I evoked Saturn, grew more lovely when I evoked Moon, and
> wore crown of wheat when I evoked Sun.

Yeats had forgotten how the figure of Jupiter changed when he
evoked Uranus, lying in opposition to it, but it 'disliked' Uranus,
calling it the 'witchery of intellect' which 'had much to do with'
Yeats's plays. Jupiter wanted Yeats to give up *The Player Queen* for
four years. It then reached its final form in the figure of an armor-
clad young knight, with 'a large ruby on breast', and provided a
three-part message.

The first part of Jupiter's message was frightening, but Yeats's
record of it shows no thought of trouble with PIAL: 'Owing to the
influence of Saturn I shall very soon receive a violent shock. I shall
lose something and until this has taken place I shall not have found
myself. This loss did not seem to be illness.' The second part was
more encouraging. A 'strange new influence' was coming from the
Sun 'through the vehicle of a loving person who involuntarily on
both our parts would give to my personality something like "a
transfusion of blood". I might think myself going mad when this
strange thing began to happen, but I was not to fear.' Jupiter then
provided advice on means of meditation and for the third prediction
foretold a letter enabling Yeats to give up *The Player Queen*, which
would be 'an abortion' if written then, and here Yeats added a
facing note dated June 1912: 'no letter came'. For the second part of
the message, it seems possible that Yeats may have adapted it, in
time, to his acceptance of Maud Gonne's decision, although, looking
back now, it seems more applicable to his marriage with Georgie
Hyde-Lees and the coming of *A Vision*.

Yeats's next journal entry, of 3 June, shows that he had returned
to Olivia Shakespear the day before, giving her Maud Gonne's letter
to 'see' from, 'not saying what it was but after a moment or two she
recognized whose it was but first said writing had to do with my
stars.' Here the 'stars' turn out not to be the planets, but certain of
the fixed stars, many of which do have traditional astrological mean-

ings. They become elements in six 'obstacles' seen for Maud Gonne, not Yeats, to cross. The six are a double set in the order human, spiritual, and material, the second set much less clear than the first, and in a facing note Yeats added, 'The vision about PIAL suggests alchemical symbolism by the order human, spiritual, material, the black, white, and red of the operation.' In the vision, Maud Gonne's first obstacle was 'Human love to do with a child and two women', the second something related to the star Aldebaran, and the third related to a star called Egidion and, he quotes, 'the transvaluation of all bodily values'.

Yeats then records a full evocation of Olivia Shakespear's horoscope, in which the fixed stars again appear, driving him to consult his 'planisphere', a form of horoscope in which the planets' places at the moment of one's birth are drawn on a sky map with the arcs related to the earth's daily rotation. His facing note reads: 'Must get Right Ascension of line of Orion. The line may be mundane.' In his following notes, having found from his planisphere that the line probably ran from 17 or 18 degrees of Gemini to the end of Gemini, he both wonders whether 'S' speaks 'from some state of heaven before precession of equinox had carried sign round to present position', and takes the result as 'good news as my stars must have crossed PIAL's probable ascendant'. Proficient astrologers, unlike their critics, know that the precession of the equinoxes gradually carries the constellations associated with the names of the signs of the zodiac around the whole circle, in the 'Great Year' so essential to Yeats's later ideas of the history of civilization. Astrologers may choose a 'sidereal' zodiac centered on the fixed stars, but the usual 'tropical' beginning of 'Zero Aries', by Ptolemaic convention and no doubt before, is set each year at the point of the vernal equinox, whatever fixed stars may have 'precessed' to provide the sky map behind the sun.

Yeats's pursuit of visionary astrology also led him to consult Florence Farr on the evening of 3 June. His journal entry of Friday, 4 June, begins with a note that a week earlier he had had 'a curious confused dream of a ghost' so that he wondered whether Maud Gonne had tried to come then, and on the Monday night as well. Clearly the 'spiritual marriage' was expected to continue despite the absence of a physical relationship, and in evoking his horoscope with Florence Farr, first 'setting all stars in place', Yeats called up the troublesome Uranus. Reflecting Florence Farr's interest in Egypt, the planetary spirit appeared in the guise of an Egyptian woman in a nun-like habit. When connected with Saturn the vision shifted to a mummy case, and when with Jupiter, in opposition, 'the case opened and swathings loosened and fell from mummy which came to life—a tall woman in brown dress—with Moon smaller white woman'. Uranus then proceeded to 'denounce' Jupiter for leading Yeats into quarrels, and caring, he writes, only for 'sensuous things, whereas Uranus tried to drive me to make me progress'. Uranus and Sun also said he need not take Jupiter's advice about the play. Yeats's facing notes appear to be contemporary, asking first why the seers make Jupiter so war-like, and then considering that Lady Gregory, his 'most Jupiter friend', 'by giving me a sense of order and dignity in life has made me quarrel with the reverse in Ireland—hence most of my quarrels.' His further notes have to do with Uranus and PIAL. They begin with a question reflecting the change in Uranus from the earlier 'seeing'—'Does the comparative friendliness of Uranus and Sun come in this case from my not having asked about the vehicle of the Sun—PIAL—who has Sun opposite Uranus?'—and end with the words of Claude Dumas quoted above.

Yeats's methods of evoking the stars blend astrology with his Golden Dawn training as a magician, and so far as I can tell these methods are both age-old and new age, as obvious as the solar elements in an Easter morning ritual of high mass and as psychologically intriguing as Fritz Perls' methods of having his patients embody and enact the different elements of their dreams. Yeats's evoking of planets probably involved ritual movements around a circle in the pattern of the zodiac, somehow marking out the different angles of the aspects, for at the end of his description of Florence Farr's vision he adds a separate paragraph referring to R. W. Felkin's experiences in Arabia:

> Felkin told me that he had seen a Dervish dance a horoscope. He went round and round on the sand and then circle to centre. He whirled round at the planets making round whorls in the sand by doing so. He then danced the connecting lines between planets and fell in trance. This is what I saw in dream or vision years ago.

Yeats and Felkin had worked together first in the Golden Dawn and then in the Stella Matutina branch, which broke away partly in order to preserve and develop the rituals and magical practices from which A. E. Waite's Independent and Rectified Rite was moving away. In the early journal entry of 11 July 1908 Yeats also noted, before drawing up the horoscope for his reading of Maud Gonne's letter, 'Began to work out meditation for Order of the SM', which probably refers to the Stella Matutina and his continued involvement in the creation of rituals.

In 1909, immediately following the description of the Dervish, Yeats writes on 'Monday, 21 June', that he had dreamed an alchemical dream on the Saturday before, after reading Basil Valentine. In the dream he met a floating wizard who disappeared into 'a furnace or stove of some kind', but remained alive, and told Yeats that he listened 'too much to supernatural and philosophic voices', ignoring what was under his feet, which Yeats thought in the dream meant the 'poetical voice'. Yeats then asked whether he and his 'friend for twenty years' would 'ever be nearer', and was told there would be death. Yeats then goes on to ask himself whether the wizard was 'a voice of fermenting—instinctive life—a voice out of the athanor', and goes on to recall that 'Years ago I was told by S.[16] that my pursuit of the perfect love lacked the "liquefaction of the gold" and I found this on page [*space*] of Basil Valentine as a prelude to the marriage of Sol and Luna; but my dream was not concerned with liquefaction—which is surely an enhancement purely—but rather with its opposite—fermentation, Nature. The liquefaction is surely one of those "supernatural and philosophical" things the voice blamed me for.'

Whatever stage Yeats was rejecting in the 'liquefaction', he seems still to be searching for a physically creative force, 'fermentation, Nature'. His love—and perhaps the anniversary date of the revival of the mystic marriage a year earlier—seem to have moved him to go back through the journal. He marked the envelope containing Maud Gonne's letter of 26 July 1908, of the serpent vision, with a querying question mark and 'marriage of Sol and Luna', dating the words 'June 21 1909', the '9' replacing a confusing '8'. The comment he wrote over her earlier letter of 26 June, pasted opposite the entry of 11 July 1908, is linked by a line drawn to the space between his report that PIAL 'had not yet tried to come' and the thinking out of a 'meditation' for SM. The comment reads: 'Think meditation should be representative of initiation in the coffin of Father Rosy Cross. Must work out relation between this and mystic marriage.' The comment was most probably written near the time of the entry, and may relate both to the 'SM' meditation and to Yeats's early efforts to perfect his own methods of meditation to reach the visionary dreams of the mystic marriage. In these he usually entered the cave with the Rosicrucian coffin, or 'pastos', and then seems to have endeavored to ascend the jointly Kabalistic and Rosicrucian 'tree' of the Sephiroth, with its central rose and serpentine paths of ascension linked to the Tarot Trumps; his entry of 21 July 1908 notes 'Twin [? *two*] trumps but it seems as if the Gemini Trump is the one when two souls ascend.' The Gemini Trump in the Golden Dawn Tarot is The Lovers, and it is probably worth remembering, in the range of Yeats's symbols, that the sisters of the Gemini twins, Castor and Pollux, are Clytemnestra and Helen of Troy, who in his poetry so often represents Maud Gonne.

The last entry of 21 June 1909 is the well-known one, attributing Maud Gonne's renunciation of their physical relationship both to her religious objections to divorce and her reawakened 'dread of physical love', which Yeats, referring indirectly to the alchemical dream, equates in its effect to his attraction to philosophy: 'a daily rooter out of instinct and guiding joy—and all the while her beauty grows nobler under the touch of sorrow and denial.' Still, he 'was never more deeply in love', and 'She too seems to love more than of old.' His desires must lead him elsewhere—there are horoscopes late in his older astrological notebook of 1907 for 5 June and 13 June 1909, the earlier for 'MD's first visit to 18 Woburn Buildings', his flat, and the later for 'letter to MD reopening negociation'—but he was on 21 June, writing of Maud Gonne, 'in continual terror of some entanglement parting us, and all the while I know that she made me and I her.' The second paragraph is the least quoted:

> Of old she was a phoenix and I feared her, but now she is my child more than my sweetheart. Who was it said of the old Irish, 'They love their horses even unto witchcraft'? Always since I was a boy I have questioned dreams for her sake—and she herself always a dream of deceiving hope, has all unknown to herself made other loves but as in the phoenix nest, where she is reborn in all her power to torture and delight, to waste and to enoble. She would be cruel if she were not a child, who can always say, 'You will not suffer because I will pray.'

This is a sadder and a wiser love, and for all its protestation Maud Gonne appears less frequently in the few remaining entries of the 1908-09 journal. On 3 July Yeats reported a consultation with Olivia Shakespear in which he tried to evoke answers to his questions about some threatening primary directions for October 1909, Sun parallel Mars and Mars square Moon, but he learned nothing intelligible. On 8 July he recorded a discussion in Dublin with AE's young friend, the visionary Evans, who had been 'seeing' an ancient sacrifice at New Grange. They discussed the willingness of the sacrificial victim. Yeats writes that he remembered his own dream experience 'years ago' of a 'curious initiation ceremony': 'How I lay on a stone trough while men who stood round seemed to pour certain forces into me—piercing my eyes and I think heart. Was not I the entranced victim.'[17] Then he and Evans discussed 'the soul receiving divine life through a mediation of the soul of a woman', and Yeats 'spoke of the love hymn in Wolfram's Parsival'; the entry concludes as he 'thought of the mediation of PIAL and saw her as the mystic victim.' As in his interpretation of the mystic marriage a year earlier, he sees both noble and spiritual qualities in Maud Gonne's 'sorrow and denial'.

Nonetheless, in his next entry, for 1 August at Coole, Yeats records an attack by 'merely physical desires', so strong and distressing that he used an evocation of the sun to cure them. In the long following entry, of 10 August, 'a damnable day', he struggled to calculate the position of his progressed moon exactly enough to know whether transiting Mars was in precise opposition. He calculated that it was, and then went on to a series of his own astrological predictions, again based on Wallace's list of his primaries. Yeats foresaw worsening conditions for a theatre row; for the 'Quinn affair' caused by his indiscreet talk about John Quinn's friend, Dorothy Coates; for 'strife and excitement' in October, probably having to do either with 'MG' or the theatre; and for a Venus event with influence from a Sun-Mars person in December. He was 'very much afraid of the violent Sun and Mars aspects of October disturbing things more and more as that date gets near', and he added a further note on October: 'If the October aspects refer to the theatre they will transform it or end it—the one certain thing about all these aspects is that my life will be utterly changed in some way before next Xmas (Sun parallel Moon).' For astrologers, it must be noted that these 'parallels' of sun to Mars and moon are primary directions, noted in the Wallace list as 'rapt parallels', calculated as equal distances from the meridian axis of the birth chart, or from the ascendant-descendant axis. Ordinary transiting parallels form when planets are at equal distances north or south of the equator.

Journal entries for 11 August and 17 August in *Memoirs* match and explain Yeats's concerns for the theatre and Quinn, and he there attributes the problems to transiting Mars, nearly stationary at its retrograde turn, and thus opposite his progressed moon all month; the October primaries seemed still to come, though Yeats decided later that they had deployed ahead of time. On 25 August he and Lady Gregory succeeded in producing G.B. Shaw's *The Showing up of Blanco Posnet*, banned in England, despite the Lord Lieutenant's opposition. In the PIAL journal, the first part of the entry following that for 10 August, dated 29 August, adjusts the astrology to the events: 'contest with and victory over Viceroy can only have come from Sun parallel Mars acting two months before event for it has been too triumphant for Moon sesquiquadrate Mars to account for it.' (The sesquiquadrate, a kind of distant semi-square, is a relatively weak aspect of 135 degrees.)

The following entry of 16 September, a note on Lady Gregory's loss of her diamond brooch (later found), shares its date with one of Yeats's additional comments on the verso facing his predictions of 10 August. He had predicted worsening troubles in the theatre as a result of the sesquiquadrate; the September comment reads: 'Yes—Lord Lieutenant affair swirled up two or three days later and lasted to end of month, but how did the evil Moon sesquiquadrate Mars give us so much triumph in the end? Is it effect of Sun parallel Mars which is described as giving "preferment in a military horoscope".' A later addition, in the bottom left-hand corner of the same verso, sums up the 'October aspects' which had seemed so fearful in August: 'Sun parallel Mars seems to have worked in change in theatre—raising money to purchase—etc. No event of moment in October or November—Mars entirely discharged himself in August.'

Sun parallel Mars may account for too much, but it is clear that Yeats was pleased with his growing skills in prediction. One further additional comment on the predictions of 10 August, 'Yes. D', dated 'July 1910', suggests that Mabel Dickinson was the predicted Venus influence for December 1909. Here the date of July 1910 matches that of a later set of astrological predictions on what appears to be the final page of the 1908-09 journal of the mystic marriage, but it is not. Uncharacteristically, Yeats wrote the last entries, dated from 29 August to 8 November 1909, on the verso of the predictions of 10 August. His predictions of July 1910, later marked 'Came true', foretell eventual victory in the purchase of the Abbey Theatre on the basis of his 'Moon going to rapt parallel Jupiter', and make no mention at all of Maud Gonne, though there are several for 'D'. These later predictions face the last of the 1908-09 entries, which are written in a cramped and tiny hand and are increasingly perfunctory. The parenthetical addition to the first, undated but in somewhat clearer penmanship, gives details not in Maud Gonne's September letter (G-YL, 281), a lack that suggests some later communication; 24 October was a Sunday, so Yeats probably wrote the penultimate entry on 25 October:

Sept 17

PIAL wrote to say she had vivid dream of me on night of 10th and that my letter shows I dreamed of her the same night. My dream was I remember vivid but not very important—hers of me good but refers to some past incarnation in India of which she 'had never remembered anything before.' She wrote about dream, was entangled and then got my letter. (She dreamed that we were together among sunlight and great fruit like melons which we sold. We were dark, we were lovers.)[18]

Oct 5

End of last month ill same cause as on August 1.

Oct 24 (Monday)

Last week—Wednesday night I think—went through the ritual of union.

Nov 8

Last Friday night dreamed of PIAL.

Here in the last of the entries in the journal of the mystic marriage, Yeats is still dreaming of Maud Gonne, but loose among the final pages of the writing book is a draft of 'King and No King', the poem that in the marriage series in *The Green Helmet and Other Poems* follows 'Reconciliation'. The draft, written on a sheet of two-holed looseleaf paper, is dated 7 December 1909, and in it Yeats contrasts the success of the theatrical king in the old romance, whose love was satisfied when words were proven false, with his own lost dream of a real marriage with Maud Gonne. The draft is nearly identical to the printed version and the similar draft written in the newer journal (*Mem* 236); the major difference is that it is the only version to show 'I'll find' rather than 'We'll find' in the concluding lines, so very far from mystical:

> And I that have not your faith how shall I know
> That in the blinding light beyond the grave
> I'll find as good a thing as that we have lost?
> The hourly kindness, the day's common speech
> The habitual content of each with each
> When neither soul nor body has been crossed.

NOTES

1. The astrological manuscripts are among those available for study in the William Butler Yeats Microfilmed Manuscripts Collection, Special Collections Department, Library, State University of New York at Stony Brook. The originals of all those mentioned here are in the possession of Michael Yeats unless otherwise noted. I am most grateful to Senator Yeats for the opportunity to compare photocopies with originals, and to A. P. Watt Ltd on behalf of Anne and Michael Yeats for permission to quote unpublished passages. I have not been able to trace heirs of the two professional astrologers whose analyses are also part of the Yeats Collection, James Richard Wallace (1852-1910?) and Claude Dumas. The writing book itself is large, about 32.4 cms x 24.1 cms., and bound in white leather, with now worn or lost thongs for tying. Yeats left the first leaf blank and began his entries for 1908-09 on the second leaf, ending on the verso of the seventeenth. He later used the book for records of seances, and occasional horoscopes, from 1912 until 1917. The last few leaves, also part of the 1908-09 record, were not microfilmed. In transcribing I have used words for all astrological symbols; capitalized 'Sun' and 'Moon' in quotations are the only indication.

2. The grades of the society are described by Israel Regardie, *The Golden Dawn* (St Paul, Minn.: Llewellyn Publications, 1971). On 29 September 1910, Yeats wrote to Lady Gregory about Pollexfen's funeral: 'I found it hard to see George's house again, every detail as it was when I stayed with him and worked at Astrology'. (*L* 553).

3. Attributing this 'hermetic axiom' to the *Smaragdine Tablet* of Hermes Trismegistus, Madame Blavatsky uses it pervasively in the first volume of *Isis Unveiled* (1877). See, for example, pp. 22, 35, 294, 330, 507. Yeats uses it himself much later, in 'Ribh Denounces Patrick': 'For things below are copies, the Great Smaragdine Tablet said' (*VP* 556).

4. 'The Return of the Stars', in 'Discoveries: Second Series', ed. Curtis Bradford, in *Irish Renaissance: A Gathering of Essays, Memoirs, and Letters from* The Massachusetts Review, ed. Robin Skelton and David R. Clark (Dublin: Dolmen Press, 1965), p. 82. Further references are noted parenthetically as 'Return'. For the 'attack' and Yeats's rejoinder, see 'Mr. W. Fay and the Abbey Theatre' (*UP2* 363-4).

5. Ellic Howe identifies Ely Star as Eugene Jacob (1847-1942), who used 'a curious kind of Cabalistic astrology that was unknown outside France', in *Astrology and the Third Reich* (Wellingborough: Aquarian Press, 1984), p. 74. Howe's book is a revised edition of his *Urania's Children: The Strange World of the Astrologers* (1967).

6. By my count, taking the first month of Yeats's life as equivalent to his first year, he ought to be using the waning trine of 4 December 1868 to predict the year beginning at his forty-third birthday. Mistakes in calculation are not uncommon even in these days of computers, but astrologers usually detect inapplicable charts. In other cases, it sometimes seems that the act of concentration in interpreting can override errors in reading tables or entering data.

7. Sepharial was Walter Gorn Old (1864-1929), whose many books are no longer easily available: see Ellic Howe, p. 64.

8. In particular, Virginia Moore, *The Unicorn: William Butler Yeats' Search for Reality* (New York: Macmillan, 1954), p. 197; George Mills Harper, *Yeats's Golden Dawn* (London: Macmillan, 1974), p. 168; Nancy Cardozo, *Lucky Eyes and a High Heart: The Life of Maud Gonne* (New York: Bobbs-Merrill, 1978), p. 258.

9. Moore, *The Unicorn*, pp. 197-204. Cardozo also describes and quotes from the journal (*Lucky Eyes and a High Heart*, pp. 258-63). I differ from both in readings of dates and words. For instance, both Moore and Cardozo read 'arrested' rather than 'awakened' in Yeats's entry of 29 July, in which he notes 'that for the first time in weeks physical desire was awakened'.

10. This Yeats would have interpreted as a dream of marriage (see *Aut* 260).

11. The 'stone man' might also be development of the crucial experience of December 1898, when he shared a double vision with Maud Gonne: 'She thought herself a great stone statue. . .and I felt myself becoming flame and mounting up through and looking out of the eyes of a great stone Minerva' (*Mem* 134).

12. Largely quoted by Cardozo, *Lucky Eyes and a High Heart*, pp. 262-3.

13. Moore, *The Unicorn*, p. 202; Cardozo, *Lucky Eyes and a High Heart*, p. 263.

14. The 'Autobiography—First Draft' is particularly informative about the early years of the Gonne-Yeats relationship.

15. Moore, *The Unicorn*, p. 379. On Mrs Yeats's authority, Moore dated the typescript to 1937, but Yeats wrote the 'Propositions' as 'Astrology and the Nature of Reality' in his Rapallo Notebook of 1928-29, now in the National Library of Ireland (NLI 13,581).

16. The incident is recalled from a diary marked 'VISIONS—Begun—July 11. 1898' (private collection). Edited by Warwick Gould and Deirdre Toomey, it will be published by Macmillan in 1998. 'S.' in this case is William Sharp.

17. See *Mem* 127-8 for a fuller account of this experience which is of 1898-99.

18. Maud Gonne's dream of a past incarnation in fact does recall a dream of July 1891, which Yeats used as the basis of 'Cycles Ago', his unpublished poem of October 1891. See *YA11* 124-137 cf., *YA7* 184-93.

The Anti-Theatre and its Double

Gregory N. Eaves

I

AT A TIME OF RENEWED INTEREST in his plays, Yeats's *The Only Jealousy of Emer* deserves re-examination not only for the most familiar of reasons, its immense beauty and difficulty, but also in response to the recent publication of much of the textual material preliminary to the writing of *A Vision* (1925).[1] George and W.B. Yeats's sittings with spiritual Instructors, recorded in what is known as the 'Automatic Script,' have been known for a long time to have provided the immediate inspiration for the writing of *A Vision* and to have generated much of the raw material for Yeats's (W.B.'s) poems, plays, and prose of the 1920's and 1930's. One of the major surprises for those of us acquainted for the first time with the automatic materials (courtesy of George Mills Harper and his team of editors) has been the sheer prominence of *The Only Jealousy of Emer*—the most frequently indexed of all Yeats texts. The writing of this play coincided largely with the first six months of the Automatic Script and prompted numerous exchanges recorded in its sessions.[2] Yet the play is mentioned only once in the 1925 edition of *A Vision*; by this time the preoccupations shared between play and Script—frequently autobiographical and with marital and sexual implications—had presumably been worked out by the Yeatses.[3]

34

The Only Jealousy of Emer is, then, a text situated at the very inception of *A Vision*, and is that much more intriguing for it. Equally, the automatic materials provide the reader with invaluable, however baffling, insights into this most difficult of plays. In taking this opportunity to re-examine *The Only Jealousy of Emer*, I do not propose to cover comprehensively the references to it in the Script. Rather, I prefer to be selective and to use the Script to unfold a set of related issues: the critically neglected role of Bricriu in the play and, in particular, his relation as outsider to the remaining characters (and the fourfold structure they comprise). This approach generates an unfamiliar reading of the play and its characters; it opens up the anti-realist aesthetics structuring the mythological surface of this, theatrically the richest of Yeats's plays. For *The Only Jealousy of Emer* is, I will argue, the key anti-theatrical exhibit among his *Four Plays for Dancers* and an enactment of his newly formulated poetics of the Mask.[4]

II

Most commentators on *The Only Jealousy of Emer* have neglected Bricriu. Unprepossessing he may be, a pagan god of discord with a cold disdain for the emotions of others; worse still, he is ugly and deformed. Excluded from the extended discussion devoted to Emer or Fand, this character has been dismissed as 'malignant' or 'wicked' and treated as a mere plot function (as Fand's opponent and the occasion of a series of thematic conflicts).[5]

Perhaps most constructive have been the attempts, albeit inconclusive, to locate Bricriu within the symbolic structure laid out in *A Vision*—in other words, to specify his appropriate lunar phase. No easy task, this; and part of the difficulty may be that discussions have tended to concentrate on Bricriu's relation to a single one of his fellow characters. The god of discord has been identified as Fand's opponent and, therefore, as belonging to the opposite phase on the lunar wheel of 28 phases.[6] To her fifteenth phase, that of the full moon and of the perfection of individual form, corresponds Bricriu's initial phase (phase 1), that of the dark moon and of the dissolution of all form. He has been identified by another critic as the Daimon and lunar opposite of Cuchulain, the play's ostensible hero—in other words, phase 26 (the phase of the Hunchback) as opposed to phase 12 (that of the hero).[7] Still another analysis has made Bricriu the Daimon of Emer, Cuchulain's queen and arguably the heroine of the piece; here, however, the lunar phases do not work out.[8] More recently, another critic has suggested that Bricriu acts as Daimon to both Cuchulain and Emer and has argued against undue reliance on classification by phase.[9] She is right; one has to remember that the dramatic action of this play was being formed at a time when the lunar System of *A Vision* was still evolving. Besides, as well as being a cosmic designer, Yeats was a dramatist with stage sense.

The trouble is, each of these competing antithetical pairings of Bricriu with another character appears plausible. I suggest rather that Bricriu be considered in his relationship to all the other characters simultaneously, including Cuchulain's mistress, Eithne Inguba, who is missing from the above equations. My plea on behalf of the handicapped and neglected Bricriu focusses, then, on his complex relations with the remaining four characters and, since he is the outsider in relation to this foursome, on his eccentric status. In keeping with the deformity of the spirit presiding over my analysis, I offer a reading biassed to his point of view.

Eccentric Bricriu is, and in a manner critical for the play's symbolic structure. The Automatic Script makes this clear. Those sessions relevant to *The Only Jealousy of Emer* place consistent emphasis on the play's fourfold or tetradic structure. As always, Bricriu is the character left out—and for important reasons, which I will attend to shortly. For now, it is worth considering that the foursome in question comprises those characters with obvious autobiographical equivalents: Cuchulain (W.B. Yeats), Emer (George Yeats), Fand (Maud Gonne), and Eithne Inguba (Iseult Gonne).[10] Since the Script consistently and strategically converts personal facts and events into universal principles or types and, besides, adds little fresh autobiographical information about these four, I shall follow its lead and leave the historical personages behind. A structural analysis of texts seems to me to promise more. Suffice it to say that the play, like the Script, testifies to Yeats's need to make aesthetic sense of immediate and troublesome personal experience.

Later in a series of classifications and tabulations the Automatic Script develops the four characters into a series of tetrads, some traditional (the Four Elements), some familiar only to dedicated readers of Yeats. Pre-eminent among the more esoteric sets are the Four Principles of supernatural experience which, along with the Four Faculties, their equivalents in human experience, will become the key structuring devices for the Symbolic System published as *A Vision*. Such systematisations lie mostly further ahead in the Script and are homologous with rather than predicated upon the tetradic formation of *The Only Jealousy of Emer* (the writing of which developed in parallel with, yet independently of, the early Script).[11] As regards the play, what is new to anyone hitherto unacquainted with the Script is the suggestion that the three female characters of *The Only Jealousy of Emer* are in an ideal or eternal sense one, and that the tetrad they form with Cuchulain corresponds to a Blakean or archetypal conception of the human self, to be viewed perhaps, in the words of the Script's editor-in-chief, as 'divine man united with ideal woman.'[12]

An unsettlingly schematic perspective threatens to impose itself on the play. Are the four not, then, to be viewed as independent characters? To which the answer must be both 'yes' and 'no,' depending on the perspective adopted. From a traditional perspective they may be taken as four individual characters interacting on stage (though one has to allow for the awkward fact that one of the four, Fand, is non-human and another, Cuchulain, is in limbo). But the Script views the same four from a more esoteric or, in Yeatsian terms, a daimonic perspective;[13] according to this, the foursome is interdependent and its interactions describe a quasi-geometrical pattern. Their drama is that of a divided and conflict-ridden self; any alteration in its interrelations, as there must be if there is to be drama at all, testifies to a disunity or imbalance in the (potentially) unified self of which they are aspects. Thus, while this play has been said to take its inception from Yeats the man's sexual relations with three women, its textual intricacies may be said to gesture towards his visionary self-portrait—the artistic construction of a unitary, more inclusive sense of self. Yet the play is tragic; there is no promise of harmony or transcendence. Rather, its discursive momentum is circular and conflictual; the universalizing, androgynous vision of being developed in the Automatic Script remains a distant point of reference.

The Automatic Script, together with the Four Principles and their attendant schematisms, will play a limited part in the rest of my argument. I have dwelt on them mainly to draw attention to the combined personal and esoteric structural design in the writing of *The Only Jealousy of Emer* and, its correlative, the division of its characters into a foursome and an outsider, Bricriu. In so doing, I believe I have unearthed an unlikely but promising parallel between

Yeats the dramatist and Bricriu, the god of discord: each interacts with an amorous foursome that both excludes and includes him, in which he has both a place and no place. I suggest that, upon closer examination, this structural analogy will extend critical understanding of Bricriu's commonly underestimated role. For now, it is worth pointing out that an analogy between Yeats the writer and Bricriu, a character, promises to reveal a strand of artistic reflexivity woven into the play.[14]

III

The earlier of the two published versions of *The Only Jealousy of Emer*, that written synchronously with the first six months of the Script, makes it quite clear that, far from being a mere plot function, Bricriu as outsider makes the plot function.[15] Fand (the Woman of the Sidhe), frustrated at her loss of Cuchulain, blames the god of discord (Bricriu, or the Figure of Cuchulain, who has taken over the hero's corpse) for the whole scenario. The play as we have it is a plot—*his* plot—and this identifies him as the playmaker within the play:

Woman of the Sidhe [*to figure of Cuchulain*]. To you that have no
    living light, but dropped
From a last leprous crescent of the moon,
I owe it all.

Figure of Cuchulain. Because you have failed
I must forego your thanks, I that took pity
Upon your love and carried out your plan
To tangle all his life and make it nothing
That he might turn to you.

Woman of the Sidhe. Was it from pity
You taught the woman to prevail against me?

Figure of Cuchulain. You know my nature—by what name I am
    called.

Woman of the Sidhe. Was it from pity that you hid the truth
That men are bound to women by the wrongs
They do or suffer?

Figure of Cuchulain. You know what being I am.

Woman of the Sidhe. I have been mocked and disobeyed—your power
Was more to you than my good-will, . . . (*VPl* 559, 561vv.)

In this dialogue Fand lists all the significant actions of the play so far
and holds Bricriu responsible for them. The 'power' she refers to is
of the dramaturgic kind; this shaping power has consigned her to a
subordinate and tragic role within an action of Bricriu's making.
According to Fand, he has engineered the crisis of choice facing
Cuchulain; the audience knows he has similarly engineered that
facing Emer. In respect of each of the other four, his superior
knowledge has enabled him to exploit a weakness: Fand's ignorance
of the abiding nature of human attachments, Emer's ignorance of
relations between human and divine, Eithne Inguba's ignorance of
her own powers, and Cuchulain's unconsciousness. Certainly, if
little of interest may be said of Bricriu's motivation as a character (a
lack largely responsible for his critical neglect), his omniscience
seems little short of authorial.

To take the deformed Bricriu as in any sense a Yeatsian surrogate
may seem preposterous. Cuchulain, the hero, has always been taken
as the poet's exclusive surrogate in this and in all the other plays in
the heroic cycle. Yet in this play Cuchulain is a passive figure; and
Bricriu enjoys a special relationship with the fallen hero, one which
enables the trickster god to take his place. Bricriu it is who, as
changeling, usurps the lifeless body of Cuchulain in order to appear
in a play of his own making. And all this by virtue of his being the
hero's daimon and, therefore, of an opposite lunar phase.

Critics reading *The Only Jealousy of Emer* have quite regularly
identified Bricriu as the daimonic figure. But Yeats himself proposes
a dramatic art of the daimon, as follows; and, I believe, it is a mere
extension of his argument for me to attribute to Bricriu the role of
surrogate dramatist. A well known passage from *A Vision* (prominent in both versions and in the Automatic Script) uses the *Commedia del Arte* to explain Yeats's model for the human personality,
the Wheel of the Four Faculties. Here I sidestep theoretical considerations (Faculties, Wheel, etc.) in order to focus on Yeats's
idiosyncratic analysis of the *Commedia*; it might be taken equally
for a commentary upon Bricriu's daimonic relationship to the other
four characters in *The Only Jealousy of Emer*. The striking structural
resemblance between the two dramatic forms has not, to my knowledge, been remarked on hitherto by critics; but then it is only in the

Script that the reference to the *Commedia* appears in the context of a discussion of *The Only Jealousy of Emer*.[16] For the purposes of my argument all three versions of Yeats's analogy fit snugly together. Here is the one from *A Vision* (1925):

> One can describe *antithetical* man by comparing him to the *Commedia del Arte* or improvised drama of Italy. The stage manager having chosen his actor, the *Will*, chooses for this actor, that he may display him better, a scenario, *Body of Fate*, which offers to his *Creative Mind* the greatest possible difficulty that it can face without despair, and in which he must play a role and wear a *Mask* as unlike as possible to his natural character (or *Will*) and leaves him to improvise, through *Creative Mind*, the dialogue and details of the plot (*CVA* 17-18).[17]

Like Bricriu, the 'stage manager' sets in motion a theatrical representation of a conflict in which there are four participants. The 1937 version of *A Vision* further identifies Bricriu's equivalent as 'the stage manager, or *Daimon*' (*CVA* 84)—stage manager, in each case, presumably because the dialogue of the *Commedia* was traditionally improvised.

The context for the above quotation is Yeats's account of what he calls, again in the 1925 version, the '*Drama* of the Faculties . . . etc.' (my italics). His purpose is to describe structurally the mental predispositions of such as himself and, for that matter, Cuchulain, both of whom occupy antithetical positions within the Wheel of the lunar phases.[18] His rhetorical strategy is to describe those lives in terms of a fourfold drama. Dramatic self-portraiture, in other words, on the universal level and according to the self-same pattern that I have already identified in my discussion of the foursomes in *The Only Jealousy of Emer* and the Script.

If drama is to occur, the set of relationships common to the four characters of *The Only Jealousy of Emer* and of the *Commedia* has to vary, to be unstable to the point of crisis. And dramatic crisis, as all the texts agree, is the business of the daimon or stage manager. This tendency of the four characters (Faculties) to follow a pattern of changing relationships corresponds, in the schematic accounts offered in the Script and *A Vision*, to the technical term 'Discord,' which brings to mind the official attribute of Bricriu in the play under consideration: 'Maker of discord among gods and men' (*VPl* 543).

IV

I hope my argument so far has introduced an unfamiliar and more essential Bricriu: to sum up, not only the god of discord, but Yeats's surrogate as the dramaturge of the discordant drama of the Four Faculties, the Four Principles, and of the four key persons in the writer's now fully universalized love life. These fourfold structures with their attendant daimons will reappear in my argument in due course. But first I need to introduce a further dimension of the protean Bricriu—one that will enable me to explicate rhetorically the symbolic discourse peculiar to *The Only Jealousy of Emer* (and its immediate textual kindred). There are at work here a predominant rhetorical figure and an allied philosophy, of which Bricriu is the presiding genius; together, their workings articulate the thematization of the theatrical in this most reflexive of plays.

Bricriu embodies the very spirit of Heraclitus. In the words of *A Vision* (1937): 'Discord or War . . . Heraclitus called "God of all and Father of all, some it has made gods and some men, some bond [sic] and some free."'[19] Another 'thought of Heraclitus' came so to epitomize Yeats's ontology and aesthetics of antithesis that he repeated it constantly: 'the immortals are mortal, the mortals immortal, each living in the other's death and dying in the other's life'.[20] Like Heraclitus's god, Bricriu delights in conflict between opposites; a shape-changer and essentially formless himself, he lords it over change for change's sake, at least in the world of finite beings, mortal or immortal. And in the text in which Bricriu is enscribed, as in certain of the surviving fragments of Heraclitus, a chiastic logic obtains: opposites do not merely oppose each other conflictually; they reciprocate each other in inverse, like mirror images; in the course of conflict they even change into one another, reciprocally. These are what Yeats calls, in another passage of exposition quoting Heraclitus, 'true opposites' (*CVA* 214).[21] Frequently, this pattern of inversion will reduplicate itself in language, in the ab/ba figure of chiasmus, as Yeats explains elsewhere in an adaptation of Heraclitus: 'opposites are everywhere face to face, dying each other's life, living each other's death'.[22]

The introduction of the figure of chiasmus enables me to refine my earlier treatment of a group of key terms: the relationship between 'daimon' and everyday 'self' (or 'Will'), like all 'antithetical' relationships, follows a chiastic pattern. Further, the encounter of these opposites requires the activity of a 'mask.' In Yeats's words,

> the Daimon comes not as like to like but seeking its own opposite, for man and Daimon feed the hunger in one another's hearts. Because the ghost is simple, the man heterogeneous and confused, they are but knit together when the man has found a mask whose lineaments permit the expression of all the man most lacks, and it may be dreads, and that only (*Myth* 335).

Self and daimon are not only 'true' Yeatsian opposites in that they are each other's inverse; they are also attracted toward each other and are joined, as it were, by the mask. Acting almost as a hinge or fold joining the two mirror images, the mask is the self's imagining of all that he/she is not (gender opposition often being part of the design) and, therefore, finds most threatening. The congruency of this set of relationships with the figure of chiasmus (abba) and, to move further back, its similarity to the structure of the *Commedia del Arte* as Yeats sees it will, I hope, be evident (though I will return to the *Commedia* shortly).

The contribution of the theatrical metaphor at work here deserves attention. The mask is material; it is actualized. It is a piece of artwork, of theatrical magic—a painted mask, a text, an image in the text, an actor acting. It is also a fictive representation, the product of the self's imagining of its own very antithesis. As such, it allows that self, by playing a role, to become one momentarily with his or her buried archetypal or permanent self and antagonist, the daimon.

A few details will, perhaps, silhouette a marked similarity between the self-daimon-mask relationship (as described above) and Yeats's model of the *Commedia del Arte*. 'Will' in the *Commedia* is the equivalent of self (or 'man') while the 'stage manager' or daimon

> chooses for this actor . . . a scenario, *Body of Fate*, which offers to his *Creative Mind* the greatest possible difficulty that it can face without despair, and in which he must . . . wear a *Mask* as unlike as possible to his natural character (*CVA* 17-18).

Given, then, that the *Commedia* works as a Yeatsian staging of the chiastic relations between self and daimon, the same will be true of the plot of *The Only Jealousy of Emer* itself, which, as I have earlier pointed out, is structurally congruent with the *Commedia*. Thus, *The Only Jealousy of Emer* may be said to be a play that allegorizes the theatrical metaphor of the mask so central to Yeats's poetics. Of course, there is the obvious structural discrepancy between a drama setting in motion a foursome of characters with a presiding daimon and a pair of inverse terms (self and daimon) linked by an interface (the Mask). That the four + one pattern of *The Only Jealousy of Emer* nevertheless follows a similarly chiastic logic I hope next to demonstrate.

V

In two cases pairs of characters in *The Only Jealousy of Emer* sustain geometrically strict chiastic relationships. To the extent that one can plot a pair of mutually antithetical characters accurately on the Great Wheel of 28 lunar phases, their relationship will inevitably be chiastic. Self (or Will) and Mask, which represents the self's antithesis or anti-self, will occupy exactly opposite phases, as do, for instance, Cuchulain (phase 12, that of the hero) and Bricriu (phase 26, that of the Hunchback).[23] In this case Cuchulain and Bricriu are fourteen phases apart, which places them geometrically opposite on the circumference of the Wheel and thus makes them each other's exact inverses. But what *links* them chiastically (since chiastic opposites also meet)? The two characters are linked theatrically by the elaborate masks worn by their respective actors; these masks are distinct, for Bricriu's is 'distorted,' but are similar enough to be recognizable versions of the same Mask. The mask as stage property, then, is what allows a substitution (behind a partially closed curtain) to take place between the two characters—a visual sleight-of-hand true to the spirit of Bricriu the shape-changer. At the same time the switch stages the chiastic relationship between Cuchulain and his Daimon: man and god, dying each other's life, living each other's death.

A second tidy pair of opposed lunar phases is that matching Fand ('one hour' short of phase 15, the phase of perfectly individualized form, we are told) against Bricriu (now in his own phase, phase 1, that of formlessness and discord).[24] Bricriu, it will be noted, now occupies a different phase from the one he occupied when opposed to Cuchulain. In his feud with Fand Bricriu plays himself, a god acting on a supernatural plane, rather than the role of a visiting

Daimon acting out the borrowed Mask of Cuchulain. More important than the numerology is the impact of his chiastic relationship with Fand on the dramatic action. The exchanges that result are pivotal and deserve close attention.

At two critical points in the play the fate of the unconscious Cuchulain, the issue around which the whole plot revolves, is decided by a kiss, or the lack thereof. And these kisses compose an antithetical pair. The first kiss, delivered by Eithne Inguba in the attempt to lure Cuchulain's Ghost back into his body, instead lures the changeling Bricriu. This is the 'Kiss of Life.' In the Symbolic System of *A Vision* such kisses link mortals and immortals sexually and are delivered by 'Spirits at One' (P1), who 'give help' (*AVA* 240). Appropriately enough, Bricriu has arrived to tell Emer how to rescue Cuchulain from Fand and return him to the natural world. The second kiss is the 'Kiss of Death,' dreaded in Irish folklore and denounced by Emer, representing sexual 'contact' between mortals and 'Spirits at Fifteen' (P15), who 'need help' from a mortal.[25] Fand's kiss promises eternal oblivion to Cuchulain; for her it means the completion of her being and her escape from the cycle of reincarnations:

> When your mouth and my mouth meet
> All my round shall be complete
> Imagining all its circles run. (*VPl* 555)

Bricriu's intent in exchanging the first kiss with Eithne Inguba is to prevent Cuchulain kissing Fand; by showing Emer how to break Fand's hold on Cuchulain, he plays his role perfectly as god of discord. As Fand's supernatural opponent, he has to oppose her plan as a matter of policy; and in doing so, he maintains discord between human and divine.[26]

The two Kisses, of Life and of Death, are thus perfectly and dramatically opposed in both their purpose and their provenance. The one may even be said to cancel out the other since the conclusion of the play's action amounts to something like a return to status quo. Meanwhile, on a thematic level, exchanges between the elemental oppositions of life and death, mortal and immortal, male and female have been played out with the formal precision of dance.

Even Bricriu's relation to Eithne Inguba, the one pairing which has attracted no attention, partakes of the pattern of formal inversion. Initiated by a kiss and linking mortal female to immortal male, their relationship entails a further antithetical twist: Bricriu's presence entails Eithne Inguba's absence—a parallel to Fand's kiss of oblivion, perhaps.[27] Upon Bricriu's emergence, wearing the 'distorted' version of the heroic mask, Eithne Inguba immediately leaves the stage. Is the kiss of the consuming type, that of an incubus? Or does his ugliness drive away her beauty? Whichever account one favors, the situation is reversed when Bricriu leaves Cuchulain's body vacant for the hero's return; Eithne Inguba returns simultaneously to claim that her kiss has brought Cuchulain back. It is as if all that has intervened has occurred on some plane insensible to her and as if, to borrow Fand's account of her own kiss, time has 'seem[ed] to stay his course' (*VPl* 555).

Chiastic structures abound, for Yeats was clearly conscious of reciprocal patterning in his organization of the text in each version of *The Only Jealousy of Emer*. The relationship between Bricriu and Emer deserves particular attention since the transformation she undergoes following his bullying receives much more focus in the 1934 version of the play. As a result, a reader comparing the two versions observes the dramatist's (presumed) recognition of a further opportunity for antithetical patterning. As critics have pointed out, Fand's closing squabble with Bricriu is all but eliminated in the rewritten play in order to heighten the plot's tragic appeal. Emer's choice now constitutes the dramatic crisis and prompts the denouement of the entire plot. And her renunciation of Cuchulain's love not only frees him from Fand's hold, but places herself under the daimonic power of Bricriu. The supernatural combat between the diametrically opposed Fand and Bricriu is thus fought out to the latter's satisfaction, with the estranged human couple as counters.

This account ignores the human dimension of Emer's drama of choice, which, especially in the later play, can command considerable empathy from audience or reader; but to claim, as some critics do, that it is her play is to ignore Yeats's attention to design.[28] The struggle between Emer and Fand over Cuchulain is conducted in a highly formalized manner. Emer, equipped by Bricriu with a second sight that enables her to witness but not participate in Cuchulain's dialogue with Fand, can only state her hostility before Bricriu; it is his *mise en scène* and, as always, he controls the action. Cuchulain, visited by Fand in a dream, is perceptually restricted to her image; like Emer he can communicate only with his supernatural interlocutor. Yet the separate dialogues are so organized as to allow Emer and Fand to engage in an indirect rhetorical duel.

From Emer's perspective gods or spirits such as Bricriu and Fand represent untruth, for they distort the evidence of the senses. Bricriu has just arrived to take over Cuchulain's lifeless body when Emer dismisses his supernatural powers: 'You people of the wind | Are full of lying speech and mockery' (*VPl* 543). Yet she is dependent upon powers of vision lent her by the same shape-changer in order to witness Fand's attempted seduction of Cuchulain. Her comment upon seeing Fand's performance in the guise of a beautiful woman reasserts her empiricist self-righteousness: 'And so that woman | Has hid herself in this disguise and made | Herself into a lie' (*VPl* 549). A point of view unashamedly earthly; Emer is a creature of the hearth, symbol of domestic integrity, to which she has once already turned for protection against supernatural changelings such as Bricriu and Fand. For Emer truth is a question of sense perception and of human loyalties, and it precludes supernatural interference with either.

But in the world of Irish folktale, especially as modified to fit Yeats's symbolic requirements, the supernatural also has its claims to make. Fand presents the epistemological issue clearly, for all her rhetorical bias. Her Kiss, promising a Death out of worldly experience, is at odds with all prior human experience:

> Then kiss my mouth. Though memory
> Be beauty's bitterest enemy
> I have no dread, for at my kiss
> Memory on the moment vanishes:
> Nothing but beauty can remain. (*VPl* 555)

Finding Cuchulain 'impure with memory,' Fand points out that he has sacrificed experience on a superhuman level, one where

> . . . all have washed out of their eyes
> Wind-blown dirt of their memories
> To improve their sight?[29]

The supernatural perspective values vision over memory, beauty past all change. If, in reference to Cuchulain's particular past, Fand offers him escape from the 'intricacies of blind remorse,' on a more symbolic level her offer represents the purification of all lived experience, the individuation and permanence of the image in art; hence, the claim she makes for 'beauty.' Stripped of its mythological trappings, Fand's perspective is an aesthetic one, and one any Yeatsian artificer would share.[30]

The contest for Cuchulain thus may be said to pit Fand's aesthetics against Emer's ethics. For Emer, beauty is a trick, a lie, and vision a temporary borrowing, forced on her by Bricriu.[31] Yet Bricriu and the daimonic perspective triumph even in her case. Emer's borrowed vision leads her to 'renounce Cuchulain's love for ever' (*VPl* 561). In so doing, she inversely matches Cuchulain's own gesture of renunciation; just as Cuchulain rejects supernatural vision (in the form of Fand) for memories (those of Emer), so Emer renounces the Cuchulain she remembers for . . . what? Should I insert 'vision'? Not exactly, but a supernatural transformation does overtake her. In being brought (by Bricriu) to this moment of heart-rending choice—the moment when she becomes dearest to the audience, Emer enters into a reluctant relationship with Bricriu. When she enters into his 'bargain,' he becomes her Daimon. In an ironic inversion of her values Emer, by thus resolving the play's action as its tragic heroine, accedes to tragic beauty and, no longer mistress of the hearth, accepts the marmorean permanence and the isolation of art.

All but one of the chiastic interactions between characters that I have examined involves Bricriu as one of the interested parties. This is no accident. His relationships to all four of the other characters reveal how centrally Bricriu belongs in Yeats's theoretical program for *The Only Jealousy of Emer*. Simply put, wherever Bricriu's impact is felt, discord opens up and assumes chiastic form. As I have suggested, even the inverse movements of Cuchulain and Emer, respectively back to and away from worldly attachment, follow Bricriu's orchestration.

VI

A previously unpublished Yeatsian dialogue entitled 'The Poet and the Actress' was published in *Yeats Annual 8* (123-43). Dated 1916, the text agrees with many of the proposals for 'a mysterious art . . . that would ally acting to decoration and to the dance' appearing in essays such as 'The Tragic Theatre' (1910) and 'A People's Theatre' (1919).[32] It seems to anticipate the call in the latter essay for 'an unpopular theatre' or 'the theatre's anti-self' and, in the words of the dialogue's editor, to 'herald Yeats's "plays for dancers," the first of which, *At the Hawk's Well*, was produced on 2 and 4 April of that year'.[33] Peculiar to 'The Poet and the Actress' is an explicit advocacy of the Mask, with which it begins and ends. Even though the Mask's *modus operandi* is deliberately left mysterious and the poetics associated with it is as yet relatively undeveloped, this dialogue offers insights crucial to an understanding of *The Only Jealousy of Emer*; while the dialogue introduces the Mask as a theatrical strategem, the play dramatizes and simultaneously theorizes mask at its supernatural (and theatrical) work.[34]

As in the subsequent visionary prose, from *Per Amica Silentia Lunae* to the Automatic Script and *A Vision*, the mask in 'The Poet and the Actress' is a representation of everything the artist most lacks; and with its help 'we,' Poet and Actress alike, 'transcend circumstance and ourselves' and are elevated to tragic stature (Emer's fate). The work of the mask is described only indirectly, in terms of a 'phantasmagoria' or mythological scenario explicitly antithetical: 'there must be fables, mythology that the dream and the reality may face one another in visible array' (*YA 8* 135). More specifically, in this phantasmagoria 'dream' and 'reality' correspond to the mutually antagonistic worlds of the supernatural (as in the Irish world of faery) and the natural (that of the poet's and actress's everyday selves). The theatre that the Poet describes to his Actress is antithetical in the technical Yeatsian sense; it has built into it the relation of antithesis that permeates *The Only Jealousy of Emer* and the whole Symbolic System:

> the art I long for is also a battle but it takes place in the depths of the soul, and one [of] the antagonists does not wear a shape known to the world or speak a mortal tongue. It is that struggle of a dream with the world (*YA8* 132-33).

To this art corresponds an artist who stages a scenario in which the self, it might be said, 'must . . . wear a mask as unlike as possible to [its] natural character' (*AVA* 18). This repeat of an earlier quotation identifies familiar ground. The Poet of the dialogue is a Yeats surrogate in the mould of the 'stage manager' of the *Commedia* and Bricriu in *The Only Jealousy of Emer*.[35] Like both, he presides theatrically over a 'discord' which, as in Bricriu's version, sets at odds human and divine. The phantasmagoria is designed specifically to bring their worlds into confrontation; and the techniques of this theatre of the mask—'music,' 'dance,' 'rhythmical speech'—have as their aim the heightening of that confrontation until it is a 'violent antithesis,' for 'the greater the contest, the greater the art' (*YA8* 136, 133).

This emphasis on the degree of antithesis may seem puzzling without an insight into its basis in Yeats's sense of the Irish folktale. He is characteristically fascinated by those tales in which the invisible boundary separating the human world from the super-natural one of faery is located, only to be violated. In *The Celtic Twilight* (1901) he expresses his theme thus:

> There is a war between the living and the dead, and the Irish stories keep harping on it. They will have it that when the potatoes or the wheat or any other of the fruits of the earth decay, they ripen in Faery, . . . and that one hears the bleating of the lambs of Faery in November (*Myth* 116).

These two worlds are not just in conflict; they are inversions of one another. Now an art, such as the Poet's, devoted to heightening the conflict between such Yeatsian true opposites will be one that brings into focus the very point of encounter, the interface, as it were. A liminal art, an art of the threshold between worlds, it will be poised at the point of crossing, where inversion finds its hinge or common ground and opposing perspectives are chiastically aligned. It will not have escaped the reader that I am describing the art of *The Only Jeal-ousy of Emer*. Its vicissitudes of plot are assembled in accordance with the antithetical 'war' referred to above; and over the threshold, focal point of the same war, presides its tutelary god of discord, Bricriu, mastermind of each instance of liminal transgression.

This 'struggle of a dream with the world' is for Yeats the essential task of mythic discourse (what he calls a 'whole phantasmagoria') and that which *par excellence* distinguishes it from mimetic dis-course, as the Poet argues in the dialogue. But the relationship between phantasmagoria and mask he leaves unspecified. At the dialogue's end the Poet mystifies the Actress with a parting dismissal of the very theatrical mask he has been urging on her: 'there is no mask. I have never been to Fez.' This mask is no mere stage prop-erty; rather, it is a gesture countering the same realist theatre—'its power of mimicry, or of stating facts'—with which the Actress is familiar and comfortable (*YA 8* 133, 139 and 131). The mask mounts a critique of theatrical materialism; and it represents everything its intended wearer is not. Like all Yeatsian masks to come, it makes the self, or rather the theatre this self identifies with, conjoint with its opposite or anti-self. Thus, the mask, a gesture that is also an artifice, initiates and mediates a confrontation between opposing sides, even as it does in this dialogue. The antithetical theatre implicit here is not just the theatre's opposite, but rather an enactment of that very opposition, 'the two halves of the [self] separate and face to face,' as Yeats puts it in 'A People's Theatre' (*Ex* 259). For, as he formulates this dynamic in *Per Amica Silentia Lunae* (1917),

> they are but *knit together* when the [self] has found a mask whose lineaments permit the expression of all the [self] most lacks, and it may be dreads, and that only (*Myth* 335, emphasis added).

Perhaps into this adapted quotation one may also read the resistance of the Actress.

Yet the mask suggests more than an anti-realist manifesto. Repellant to the humanist assumptions of the bourgeois theatre of Yeats's time, it also opens up a theatrical space of intersection between this world and its supernatural other. And just as the Poet's mask is not merely some device to be worn, so this space answers to no topographical designation. The mask has as its purpose to heighten the point of confrontation between earthly and spiritual forces, to bring their opposition to the point of dramatic crisis. And the phantasmagoria—plot, character, *mise en scène* assembled out of folk materials and obeying their chiastic logic—is its rendering in theatrical and textual space.

Figuratively speaking, and the mask in the dialogue is as yet only figurative, the wearing of the mask opens up a theatrical space in between opposing worlds, at their hinge. It is liminal, this space: the place of passage and the moment of transformation. As such, it is ritual, a space where culture (traditional Irish lore) and a sense of the sacred meet. It was the spiritual allure offered by this liminality that drew Yeats in his life to seance rooms and to the rituals of more than one occult order. For him, a true 'last romantic,' spiritual ambition and aesthetics, 'sanctity and loveliness' join forces in traditional form.[36] An art form rooted in 'myth and fable,' such as the theatre proposed by Yeats's Poet, will be designed so as to evoke this threshold joining and separating contrary worlds and to embody theatrically their encounter. In fact, for Yeats such encounters are quintessentially theatrical. They presuppose the mask, both figurative, as in the dialogue, and visible as well as figurative, as in *The Only Jealousy of Emer*.

VII

If, as I have suggested, *The Only Jealousy of Emer* puts into practice the poetics of the mask, particularly as described in 'The Poet and the Actress'—if it was designed as the flagship of that poetics, so to speak, then one might expect to find the mask prominently exhibited. One might further expect to find a more or less explicit refutation of realist principles. Both, I propose, are the case. The refutation, to take that first, is enacted most subtly in the play's lyric framework. Here, especially in the opening lyric, the encounter of antithetical natural and supernatural worlds receives thematic treatment; and the same liminal space that eluded Yeats's literal-minded Actress is chosen for the play's dramatic location.

In its opening lyric Yeats's play stakes out its ground at the place of passage between opposing worlds, 'lingering,' as it is phrased elsewhere in Yeats, 'on the storm-beaten threshold of sanctity' (*Au* 522). More specifically, the lyric renders womanly beauty in terms of the stormy passage and safe landing of 'a frail sea bird'; the metaphor of passage is then repeated for an analogous arrival, that of 'A fragile, exquisite, pale shell' (*VPl* 531). A reading of the rest of this lyric reveals an interpretation of physical beauty, not as the attribute of a individual female, but as the culmination of a process of refinement ('measurement,' 'discipline') in a succession of reincarnations of the same soul. Even its sexuality alternates.[37] Hardly the stuff of realist discourse! And, browsing in the automatic Script, one is able to piece together more of Yeats's allegory: the frail bird corresponds to Eithne Inguba, whose physical beauty makes her an 'image of desire' appropriate to the hero Cuchulain;[38] such images, one learns, have their origin in *Anima Mundi*, a version of what Jung called the collective unconscious. Thus, the bird's passage, like that of the shell, is a psychical as much as a sea passage. An image crosses from the unconscious to the conscious mind; a soul undergoes reincarnation in a form corresponding to that image and crosses from the world of faery ('the Country under Wave') to the human shore. Yet for all the complication of the underlying allegory, Yeats's lyric images do not lack theatrical impact. Even without the benefit of prior reading and research, a listener receives the distinct impression of passage, of 'daybreak after stormy night' (liminal rather than chronological time) and of the singer's location on the sea's margin.

Not only does the opening lyric expound a reincarnationist aesthetics and unfold a liminal space for the ensuing action; it mounts a refutation of mimesis. I find it almost too obvious to point out that the framing of a dramatic plot within elaborate lyrics, to be both sung and mimed, constitutes an immediate affront to realist theatrical protocol.[39] But Yeats's polemic goes further. The song's performance accompanies a theatrical ritual peculiar to his Plays for Dancers. A cloth held by three Musicians, one at each end and one at the pivotal point in the middle, is first unfolded, then folded again, while the Musician holding the still pivot or fold of the cloth sings the lyric of passage. The implication for a dramatic text poised at a threshold between mirrored worlds is obvious; the implication for an anti-mimetic theatre is, I find, startling. For the conventions of mimesis are in this ritual both parodied and turned inside out. I suggest that this cloth replaces the curtain of the realist theatre, by convention a removable fourth wall virtually separating the audience from the mimetic representation of a reality in which it shares. Instead of including the audience in an illusion of reality, the Yeatsian theatre here presents the encounter of that reality with its antithetical dream. The human world, in its folktale or phantas-magoric version, confronts its antithesis, a spiritual world that a human may experience only in an induced vision (as does Emer) or in a dream state (as does Cuchulain). The traditional theatrical curtain, prohibited in Yeats's unpopular theatre, thus shifts to centre-stage; from being a fourth wall that is raised to invisibility during scenes, it becomes a threshold that is only realized in performance. Unfolded and then refolded, it symbolizes the chiastic relations between 'the dream and the reality.' Threshold in performance, the cloth ritual announces a theatre of the threshold; further, it frames a drama whose action follows threshold logic, whose vicissitudes of plot unfold quasi-geometrically about a virtual axis, as mimed by the Musicians during the lyric song.

Secondly, as suggested at the beginning of this section, the prominence of the mask in *The Only Jealousy of Emer* is such as to need little elaboration. The passive Cuchulain's passage out of and back into human form, reciprocated by the corresponding arrival and departure of the instrumental Bricriu, sets in motion and concludes the action of the play. And this alternating exchange is performed onstage by two actors, one of whom switches from a 'heroic' to a 'distorted' mask to indicate Bricriu's manifestation in Cuchulain's empty form. Although the mask-switching is managed behind a pulled curtain, that curtain hangs onstage and the change of mask is made immediately evident; upon arrival in response to Eithne Inguba's kiss, Bricriu publicly distinguishes himself from 'the man' Cuchulain.

Not only does this conspicuous sleight-of-mask stage the poetics of mask outlined in my previous section; the switch appears to have been one of the founding ideas in Yeats's conception of this play. To a letter (10 April 1916) addressed to Lady Gregory, Yeats adds a postscript:

> I want to follow *The Hawk's Well* with a play on *The Only Jealousy of Emer* but I cannot think who should be the changeling put in Cuchulain's place when he is taken to the other world. There would be two masks, changed upon the stage. Who should it be—Cuchulain's grandfather, or some god or devil or woman? (*L* 612).

Nearly two years before the play's completion the staging of the mask is already in place, regardless of the identity of the changeling. And later in the 'Preface' to *Four Plays for Dancers* (1919) Yeats comments that

> *The Only Jealousy of Emer* was written to find what dramatic effect one could get out of a mask, changed while the player remains upon the stage to suggest a change of personality (*VPl* 1305).

However overstated this fascination with the technical possibilities of mask may appear to be, one should bear in mind the continuing appeal this episode of the Cuchulain legend seems to have exercized over Yeats.[40] In a 'Note' appended to Lady Gregory's *Visions and Beliefs in the West of Ireland* and commenting on the story of Cuchulain's enchantment, Yeats seems almost disappointed that, although Cuchulain is 'away' (that is, carried off by the 'touch' of the people of faery), the usual substitution goes unmentioned:

> We have here certainly a story of trance and of the soul leaving the body, but probably after it has passed through the minds of story-tellers who have forgotten its original meaning. There is no mention of any one taking Cuchulain's place . . . .[41]

If I add that Bricriu is a character imported by Yeats into the Cuchulain legend for the express purpose of substituting for

Cuchulain, the central and structural importance of mask and mask exchange in the construction of this play becomes inescapable. The tradition of faery (daimonic) intervention, with its folk metaphysics of shape-changing, facilitates the self-conscious staging of mask, with all its implications for an anti-realist theatre.[42]

VIII

In Yeats's antithetical theatre the centrality of mask, of threshold, and of a poetics of transformation points once again to the structural and thematic importance of Bricriu—daimon or gatekeeper, changeling, and motivator in this drama of inversions. It justifies, I feel, the writing of an essay following his distorted perspective. Distorted it may be, if viewed from a humanist standpoint; but supernatural interference is instrumental in Yeats's dramatizing accounts of artistic creation:

> There are, indeed, personifying spirits that we had best call but Gates and Gate-keepers, because through their dramatic power they bring our souls to crisis, to Mask and Image[43]

Here the apparently obscure epithet 'personifying' may be taken as proleptic, alluding to 'persona' or mask.

Still, this daimonic perspective so far leaves one structural feature unaccounted for. The framing of the dramatic action within lyrics of such conspicuous beauty and mystery has exercised the inventiveness of all critics of *The Only Jealousy of Emer* thus far; the relationship of lyric frame to chiastically designed plot therefore demands my comment.

The thematic relevance of both opening and closing lyrics to the play's action is easily established: both focus in their imagery on the crossing of a threshold between reality and dream, natural and supernatural. The closing lyric, for all its ambiguity of reference, certainly alludes to Fand's masquerade as a woman of statuesque beauty:

> I have met in a man's house
> A statue of solitude,
> Moving there and walking;
> Its strange heart beating fast. (*VPl* 563)

In fact, the threshold encounters of all three female characters may be read into the mysterious closing stanzas. But while the lyric serves as an epilogue, its opening counterpart leads directly into the play's first scene. The elision of lyric into opening scene is smoothly managed: sea storm imagery melts into dramatic setting and the 'frail bird' of 'woman's beauty' into the hesitant Eithne Inguba. Meanwhile, the arrival of the frail bird, an image of desire 'dragged into being' from *Anima Mundi* (the collective unconscious), coincides with and presupposes the passage of Cuchulain beyond the threshold of consciousness.[44] Counterparts, each other's inverse, in psychic passage, the landing of the feminine image and Cuchulain's being 'away' are the essential antecedents and the keys to the ensuing dramatic action. Dream image and dreaming hero introduce the Yeatsian slant on this story within the Cuchulain legend. They announce a pattern of liminal crossing and recrossing; they establish the zone of influence of the shapechanger and presiding genius of the threshold, Bricriu.

By their encirclement of the plot, the twin poles of its lyric framework insist on the formalism of its organization. The action of *The Only Jealousy of Emer* is both circular and oppositional in that nothing happens that is not reciprocal. Cuchulain, having left, returns to his abandoned earthly body; Bricriu enters and leaves that same body; meanwhile Eithne Inguba remains Cuchulain's mistress, and Emer, his estranged wife. The only sustained change takes place across the intangible threshold that separates the permanence of art (Choice, in the Yeatsian jargon of *A Vision*) from the accidence of lived experience (Chance). Emer and Cuchulain traverse this polarity of Choice and Chance in opposite directions: while Cuchulain traverses the threshold in an earthly direction, allowing the particulars of memory to defeat the eternity of Fand's art, Emer crosses in the direction of archetype, abandoning her dearest earthly tie in a gesture of tragic self-isolation. In her self-less response to the crisis of choice that Bricriu has engineered, she is transfigured from keeper of the hearth, her domestic self, to a human version of the 'statue of solitude' evoked in the closing lyric.[45] Thus, the dramatic action, in tune with the circularity of its frame, dances out its own pattern of inversion.

Yeats's lyric frame, then, draws attention to a circular quality in the action, one that has aesthetic implications. To suggest a homology between between his *mise en scène* of the traditional tale and the evolving dynamics of the Great Wheel is not, I think, to exceed the evidence. As the Automatic Script demonstrates, the writing of *The Only Jealousy of Emer* coincides with the very earliest systematic elaboration of the Symbolic System later published as *A Vision* (1925). And, like the System, the play derives its tetradic structure from a dilemma of sexual choice—that is, as Yeats himself perceived it. The Script suggests that, in a series of universalizing or sublimating steps, Yeats and his three choices (Maud Gonne, Iseult Gonne, and George Yeats) become Cuchulain and the three women competing for him, become the Four Principles, the Four Faculties, the intersecting gyres, and the other tetradic figures described on the Wheel of the twenty-eight lunar phases.

If one regards the play's characters as enacting a fourfold alternation under the supervision of a fifth, Bricriu, who is able at will to replace one of the four and merge into the formal pattern, then one may perhaps perceive a dramatist who is learning the art of distancing himself aesthetically from a disturbing fourfold sexual drama. As I have suggested, Yeats had to supplement his four autobiographically based characters with Bricriu, or the 'dramatic power' of the Daimon. Further, since the Mask, whereby one becomes conjoint with one's daimonic opposite, is Yeats's central figure for the moment of artistic creation, Bricriu's interchangeability with Cuchulain may represent the aesthetic or, in this case, dramaturgic solution to the personal dilemma. Dramaturgic because daimonic, that is. If the entanglements of his sexual life are to become drama, pattern, the poet has to become conjoint with his daimonic other, to assume the dramatizing powers of the daimon, of his own genius; Cuchulain has to turn into Bricriu.

And this transformation, too, describes a reciprocal or chiastic pattern, one that *The Only Jealousy of Emer* may be said to perform. On the one hand, the autobiographical poetic material underlying the play may be said to reduplicate Emer's progression from the accidence of worldly attachments to the permanence of tragic art; on the other hand, the poet, like Cuchulain, will always return after the moment of visionary contact with the daimonic to resume his affiliations with the sublunary world. In accordance with the wisdom of *Per Amica Silentia Lunae*,

> the poet, because he may not stand within the sacred house but lives amid the whirlwinds that beset its threshold, . . . [must] be content to pass at moments to that hollow image and after become [his] heterogeneous sel[f].[46]

NOTES

1. The entire Cuchulain cycle, including *The Only Jealousy of Emer* (*OJE*), was performed during the Yeats International Theatre Festival at the Abbey Theatre, Dublin, in 1989. See the cumulative review compiled by James W. Flannery and A. James Wohlpart in *YAACTS 10* 183-256. References to the Automatic Script will be to *MYV1&2*, and *YVP1-3*. See also George Mills Harper's 'Editorial Introduction' to *CVA* xi-l.

2. According to a letter written by Yeats to Lady Gregory, the play was finished on 14 Jan 1918, while the first Automatic Script has been dated 27 Oct 1917 by Harper. Harper suggests that the writing of the play, which had begun in 1916, was postponed this long because Yeats 'could not comprehend its symbolic meaning' without the Script. See *L* 645 and *MYV1* 25.

3. See *MYV1* 2-4, 6, 42, 83 and *passim* for references to the direct relationship of *OJE* to the 'personal dilemma' in which the Script and *A Vision* also had their roots. Yeats's editor comments that by the completion of *OJE* in January, 1918 the dramatist had 'eliminated his personal problems through the therapy of art' (*MYV1* 153).

4. What I refer to here as 'anti-theatre' is a concept Yeats introduces in the essay 'A People's Theatre' (*Ex* 244-59). Frustrated by the popular appeal of the realist play, particularly bourgeois comedy, Yeats announced that he would 'create for [him]self an unpopular theatre' and that he sought 'not a theatre but the theatre's anti-self' (*ibid.* 254, 257). The reference is to his own concept of a hidden, antithetical self, the opposite of all that comprises the familiar, daily self—spiritual where the self is material, archetypal where the self is individual. See *Myth* 317-69, for Yeats's exposition of these ideas.

5. Knowland and Martin are notable exceptions. See A. S. Knowland, *W. B. Yeats: Dramatist of Vision* (Gerrards Cross: Colin Smythe, 1983), p. 127, and Heather C. Martin, *W. B. Yeats: Metaphysician as Dramatist* (Waterloo, Ontario: Wilfred Laurier U.P., 1986), pp. 61-2. Even so, I suspect that their analyses of Bricriu would have been considerably expanded had the Script been as available to them. The epithets quoted are from F. A. C. Wilson, *Yeats's Iconography* (New York: Macmillan, 1960), p. 76, and Leonard E. Nathan, *The Tragic Drama of W.B. Yeats: Figures in a Dance* (New York: Columbia University Press, 1965), p. 228.

6. Wilson, in *Yeats's Iconography* pp. 112-13, established this phasal correspondence. See also Helen Vendler, in *Yeats's 'Vision' and His Later Plays* (Cambridge, Mass.: Harvard University Press, 1963), pp. 221; Knowland, *Dramatist of Vision* p. 125; and Nathan, *The Tragic Drama* p. 233. These later critics agree about the exactitude of the Bricriu-Fand opposition but seem hesitant to ascribe Bricriu a phase other than phase 26.

7. Reg Skene, *The Cuchulain Plays of W.B. Yeats: A Study* (London: Macmillan, 1974), p. 210.

8. Nathan, *The Tragic Drama* p. 239. His discussion does not consider their relative lunar phases. It is difficult to imagine how Bricriu could be allocated a phase opposite to phases 18 or 24, the two phases given to Emer in the Automatic

Script. For all that, his argument, based on the dramatic action of the later edition of *OJE*, is convincing.

9.   Martin, *Metaphysician as Dramatist* p. 53.

10.   Nowhere in the Automatic Script does the dialogue explicitly identify the three female characters of *OJE* with Iseult Gonne, Maud Gonne and George Yeats. Still, George Mills Harper insists *passim* upon the correspondence, and it makes eminent sense to me since the two female threesomes are attributed equivalent characteristics in the Script. In any case, the autobiographical analogy, if that is what it is, plays little part in the structural argument of this essay, which concerns itself with a tetradic structure adumbrated in *OJE* and expanded and diversified later in the Script and in *AV*.

11.   As I have mentioned above, the writing of the first published version of *OJE* was more or less simultaneous with the first six months of the Script. However, neither text appears to derive directly from the other; the allusions to *OJE* recorded in the Script mostly represent attempts to gain guidance about or explication of characters or incidents already included in the text, or at least the overall design, of the play. See, for instance, *MYV1* 25-6 and *YVP1* 72 on the significance of Bricriu's 'withered hand'.

12.   *MYV1* 152. Harper is collating complex textual material at this stage and is pointing out that the Four Principles in the Yeatses' classifications correspond to another fourfold account of whole or prelapsarian being: Blake's Four Zoas. The idea of completed or whole human being as androgynous is standard in much alchemical and hermetic writing; Aristophanes's myth of the androgyne in Plato's *Symposium* was basic to Yeats's treatment of sexual love.

13.   That is, the perspective of the anti-self mentioned in Footnote 4. The daimon is the anti-self; and the 'eternal self' referred to in Footnote 9 corresponds to self and anti-self united (since the anti-self is, in *AVA*, the self's opposite in gender too).

14.   The familiar analogy is, of course, that between Yeats and Cuchulain; Harper's discussion of the Automatic Script even uses the term 'surrogate' to describe this relationship (*MYV1* 81). But I promised an 'unfamiliar' reading of this play, and I invite my reader to consider that Bricriu and Cuchulain are only a Mask's change apart.

15.   *OJE* was first published in several editions, the earliest of which was William Butler Yeats, *Two Plays for Dancers* (Churchtown, Dundrum: Cuala Press, 1919). Most critics of the play have focussed on the later version, which first appeared in *The Collected Plays* (London: Macmillan, 1934), 279-96. I shall refer mostly to the earlier version for reason of its contemporaneity with the Script, but will identify any occasion when a discrepancy between the two versions is pertinent to my discussion. In general, Bricriu is more conspicuous as surrogate dramatist in the 1919 version. But even in the 1934 version he runs the show, and he maintains the same daimonic relationships with the others; his presence is now more shadowy, though, for he is given fewer lines and is no longer singled out by Fand for attack.

16.   See *MYV1* 158-59; *YVP1* 270.

17.   See *AV B* 83-4 for the very similar later version.

18.   The AS compare this pattern of the Four Faculties as it appears in *OJE* to both the *Commedia* and the Japanese Noh drama and indeed 'all great art'; they des-

cribe it as 'partially a dramatisation of the soul' (*MYV1* 158; *YVP1* 270).

19. *AVB* 67. Yeats is quoting Heraclitus, Fragment 25 from (probably) John Burnet, *Early Greek Philosophy*, (London: Adam & Charles Black, 1892, *YL* 308), 136. Hereafter, Burnet.

20. Heraclitus, Fragment 66 (Burnet 138), first quoted by Yeats in *Mem* 216. See also *AVB* 68.

21. The context makes a theoretical distinction between the chiastic or 'true' opposites of the Heraclitean formula and any 'mere alternation between nothing and something.'

22. *Ex* 430. I have found most helpful a discussion of the philosophical implications of the rhetorical figure of chiasmus in Rodophe Gasché's 'Introduction' to Andrzej Warminski, *Readings in Interpretation: Hölderlin, Hegel, Heidegger, Theory and History of Literature*, Vol.26 (Minneapolis: University of Minnesota Press, 1987), xvi-xix. Using Heraclitus, Gasché develops this definition of chiasmus: 'opposites are linked into pairs of parallel and inverted oppositions on the ground of an underlying unity, a *tauto*, which manifests itself through what is separated' (xvii).

23. A reference to Bricriu's deformity when in human form. Although as a spirit or god Bricriu has a being completely other than that of Cuchulain, when he chooses to enter the human world courtesy of Cuchulain's lifeless body, as Cuchulain's adoptive Daimon, he assumes Cuchulain's physical appearance (and his heroic mask), though in deformed versions, for his phase is now Cuchulain's opposite, that of the Hunchback. As god of Discord and formlessness, Bricriu seems perhaps an appropriate candidate to assume a Mask of deformity.

24. Martin makes the point that Fand is only approaching phase 15 (of harmonious artistic form) and has designs on Cuchulain for that reason (*Metaphysician as Dramatist*, p. 54). I would add only that, if this is the case, the Phase she is attempting to leave would be phase 16 (that also of Maud Gonne); the reason might be that, whereas a human would approach phase 15 from phase 14, that of Eithne Inguba, the Wheel of the immortals rotates *in inverse motion*. George Mills Harper's interpretation of the Script supports the assignment of phase 16 to Fand (see *MYV* 126, 149-53); however, as Colin McDowell has pointed out to me, the Script itself explains that Fand is 'not yet midway in 15' (*YVP1* 218). Whatever the true plight of Fand, the Bricriu of phase 1 (her opposite—see Note 6) must be regarded as the god in his own right, not as 'The Figure of Cuchulain' (and belonging in phase 26), as he is called in the 1919 version of *OJE*.

25. The Script material on the two Kisses is assembled rather inadequately in *AVA*, 241-44; even Yeats apologizes for the confusion. Still, this section of the text is fascinating if read with *OJE* in mind. See Wilson, *Yeats's Iconography* p. 76, on the ritual aspect of Eithne Inguba's kiss.

26. There is also the question whether Bricriu might also want to block Fand's union with Cuchulain in order to prevent her breaching her antithetical relationship with himself (i.e., her phase 15 to his phase 1) when she leaves the cycles of phases.

27. Bricriu's explanation of her absence is, however, in terms of his own daimonic relationship with Cuchulain: 'I show my face and everything he loves/Must fly away' (*VPl* 543). As his Daimon, Bricriu stands for everything opposed to

Cuchulain's ordinary self, everything the hero lacks.

28.   Nathan, for instance, gives the earlier version of *OJE* to Fand, the later version to Emer (see *The Tragic Drama* p. 236).

29.   *VPl* 557. This epistemological contest between memory and vision is equally conspicuous in both versions of the play.

30.   This is an over-simplification. Sometimes one has to reserve a complex analysis for a later occasion. In terms of Yeats's mature aesthetics, Bricriu, as well as Fand, is essential for the work of art, as, I think, 'The Double Vision of Michael Robartes' demonstrates. Still, even in that programmatic poem it is the dancer's image of P15 that lingers in the speaker's mind. See Peter Allt and Russell K. Alspach, eds., *The Variorum Edition of the Poems of W.B.Yeats* (London: Macmillan, 1956), 382-84.

31.   This attitude applies not only to Fand's beauty but to Eithne Inguba's, too, for Emer reduplicates Fand's tactic of 'fish[ing]' for men with dreams on the hook' when she gets Eithne Inguba to kiss the corpse; both the embodied Fand and Eithne Inguba are dreams of feminine beauty. Another chiastic pair.

32.   See in particular 'A People's Theatre', *Ex* 255 and 258.

33.   *Ex* 254 and 257; 'The Poet and the Actress,' in *Yeats Annual No.8* (Basingstoke: Macmillan, 1991), 124. Yeats's theatrical and aesthetic interests during the later 1910's coincide with and anticipate to a remarkable degree those expressed by Antonin Artaud in his essays (1931-36) collected under the heading of *The Theatre and Its Double*. (See *Antonin Artaud: Selected Writings*, Susan Sontag, ed. [Berkeley: University of California Press, 1988], 213-76). Like Yeats, Artaud was frustrated with the dominant bourgeois realist theatre and its obsessive psychologism and turned to Asia, Bali in his case, for a theatrical model that would restore mystery, ritual and spiritual encounter to the stage. For his 'pure theatre' or 'theatre of cruelty' Artaud proposes incantation, music, dance and hieratic images to induce a state of trance; spectacle—ritual costume, mask, gesture, puppetry, hieroglyph—is to surround the spectator, who is to be deprived of the private comforts of the fourth wall. Located instead in a liminal space, the spectator witnesses a human encounter with its own emotional 'double,' 'a specter who is fluid and never finished, . . . on whom [the actor] imposes the forms and image of his sensibility' (*Artaud* 261). Here is Artaud's treatment of the stage itself, reminiscent surely of Yeats's turning to 'the theatre's anti-self' and of the 'great dining-room or drawing room' (*Ex* 257 and 255) envisaged for performance of the Plays for Dancers: 'we are eliminating the stage and the auditorium and replacing them with a kind of single site, without partition or barrier of any kind, which will itself become the theatre of the action. A direct communication will be reestablished between the spectator and the spectacle, between the actor and the spectator, because the spectator, by being placed in the middle of the action, is enveloped by it and caught in its cross fire. . . . The room will be enclosed by four walls, without any kind of ornament' (*Artaud* 248).

34.   I believe *OJE* to be closer in spirit to the dialogue than the other plays for dancers in that its treatment of folk material is explicitly reflexive and, thus, theoretical in its implications.

35.   The poet especially resembles the Bricriu who, Yeats-like, explains the rules of the life after death to an unknowing Emer; also Michael Robartes in his poetic

dialogue with a 'Dancer' who appears similarly ignorant of spiritual lore. See 'Michael Robartes and the Dancer' in *VP* 385-87.

36. I allude, of course, to Yeats's elegiac statement of allegiance in 'Coole Park and Ballylee, 1931' in *VP* 491.

37. According to the 'Note' to *OJE* in *Four Plays for Dancers*, a 'saint or sage' has 'one reincarnation as a woman of supreme beauty' (*VPl* 566).

38. See *MYV1* 123-24, *YVP1* 217-18 (on Eithne Inguba as bird and shell); *MYV1* 233, cf *YVP1* 385-6 (on the connection between the Passionate Body—Eithne's Principle—and *Anima Mundi*) and *MYV1* 254-55, *YVP1* 412-14 (on Passionate Body/Eithne, art, and sex). See also *AVA* 63, for the susceptibility of the hero of P12 to such 'sexual images.'

39. The same may be said of the lyric framework to *At the Hawk's Well* and, to a lesser extent, of the later plays for dancers (See the 'Preface' to *Four Plays for Dancers* in *VPl* 1304). The difference is that in *OJE* the work of the threshold—the passage between worlds—is explicitly thematized both in the lyrics and in the framed action.

40. Wilson (*Iconography* 75) comments on Yeats's 'characteristic exaggeration' here. I insist on taking Yeats's exaggerations seriously; the alternative is to risk his domestication as thinker and as artist.

41. *VBWI* 364. Yeats's note follows quite closely his earlier account of the same Cuchulain story in 'Away,' the last of a set of six essays on Irish folklore: see *UP2* 279-82. 'Away' was first published in April 1902 and, like the other five essays, was the result of research undertaken in collaboration with Lady Gregory. At any rate, this earlier source reveals a Yeatsian interest in shape-changing and substitution that predates the writing of *OJE* by many years.

42. Certainly, *OJE* exemplifies perfectly Yeats's account of the origin of his theory of the mask offered in *Au* 252. All the features listed here—changeling tale, ventriloquism, 'an image of him who sleeps'—are conspicuous in the play.

43. *Au* 272. Note how 'Gate' and 'Gate-keeper,' for which I substitute 'threshold' and 'daimon,' are virtually identified here.

44. Taken further, the bridging between lyric and plot follows a mazy logic of alternating absence and presence that is at best associative, never conclusive: the absent Cuchulain and the present 'frail bird' serve somehow as a double prerequisite to the materialization of Bricriu; this *substitute* Cuchulain exploits the duplicity of mask to trick the frail bird's *equivalent*, Eithne Inguba, into luring him onto stage by the vehicle of her kiss; whereupon she absents herself while he proceeds to stage manage the ensuing plot.

45. Nathan is the critic who most accurately identifies Emer's change in stature (*The Tragic Drama* pp. 229, 235). Unless Emer undergoes such a change, the closing lyric will appear to have little relevance to her and to distract attention away from the culmination of the dramatic action, in which her act of renunciation is paramount. Many analyses of the play create this problem for themselves.

46. *Myth* 333. This quotation suffers from a major join in my modified version of it, being taken from two adjoining sections of Yeats's text; but I believe my version remains true to the logic of Yeats's context.

W. B. Yeats, William Sharp, and Fiona Macleod
A Celtic Drama: 1887 to 1897

William F. Halloran

IN 'THE DISCOVERY OF THE CELT', Holbrook Jackson recognized Yeats as 'the chief figure of the Celtic Renaissance . . . the fullest expression of the intellectual Celt—poet, mystic, and patriot—expressing himself in an imaginative propaganda which has affected the thoughts and won the appreciation of the English-speaking world.'[1] To convey the dominant mood of nineties Celticism, however, Jackson placed at the head of his chapter a quotation from Fiona Macleod which reads in part:

> Through ages of slow westering, till now we face the sundown seas, we have learned in continual vicissitude that there are secret ways whereon armies cannot march. And this has been given to us, a more ardent longing, a more rapt passion in the things of outward beauty and in the things of spiritual beauty. Nor it seems to me is there any sadness, or only the serene sadness of a great day's end, that, to others, we reveal in our best the genius of a race whose farewell is in a tragic lighting of torches of beauty around its grave.[2]

Pushed to the fringes of Europe, the Celtic race has, nonetheless, produced artists, like Yeats and Fiona herself, whose torches of beauty light the ritual burial scene and preserve the Celtic flame. By featuring this passage, Jackson implied that Fiona Macleod's romantic Celticism, with its glow of fading twilight, typified the movement that grasped the popular imagination of the *fin de siecle*.

Who was Fiona Macleod? What was the nature of her relationship with Yeats? The simple answer to the first question is that she was the Scottish writer William Sharp who was born in 1855 and died in 1905 and who, for the last decade of his life, carried on two separate literary careers, writing and publishing under his own name and that of Fiona Macleod. Fiona was also an imaginary woman Sharp created by talking about her to his friends and in print and by writing letters from her which were sent in their own distinctive handwriting to editors and admirers. All but a few close friends believed until they read Sharp's posthumous confession, which was widely reported in December 1905, that the writings of Fiona Macleod were produced by a real woman of that name. In her 1910 *Memoir*,[3] Elizabeth Sharp affirmed that her husband was the author of the writings and said he sometimes experienced Fiona as a second personality. When writing some of the pseudonymous stories, poems, and essays, she said, he had the sensation of being Fiona. To complicate the matter further, Fiona was entwined inextricably in Sharp's mind and heart with a beautiful young woman he had come to love.

The answer to the first question is multi-layered and the second—her relationship with Yeats—raises a third: whom did Yeats think he was dealing with as he interacted with Fiona? That question is answered only by trying to determine how much Yeats learned of the truth as the years went by. Like many of his contemporaries, Yeats came under the spell of Fiona in the mid-nineties. In reading her first book—*Pharais, A Romance of the Isles*—in 1894 and the stories and poems that followed in 1895 and 1896, he accepted Fiona for what she claimed to be, a woman who embodied the spirit of the surviving Celtic peoples on the shores and off-shore islands of western Scotland. He praised her work in print and in letters to its author, and he applied to it criticisms that were partly self-directed. That Fiona was Scottish rather than Irish was so much the better, for Yeats in the nineties wanted the Celtic Revival to be inclusive.[4]

I believe that, sometime in late April or early May 1897, Sharp, pledging Yeats to secrecy, told him that Fiona Macleod was a pseudonym and that the writings resulted from his collaboration with a woman of great beauty with whom he was in love. To protect her identity, that woman was to be thought of and addressed as Fiona woman was to be thought of and addressed as Fiona Macleod. Sharp came close to telling him the truth, for there was such a woman in Sharp's life, and her inspiration and physical presence were necessary for him to continue writing the pseudonymous prose and poetry. Yeats continued to use the name Fiona Macleod when writing to her and about her, to others, and in print. Only in writing to Sharp did he, for a time, place the name in quotation marks.

Sharp's confidence must have raised other questions in Yeats's mind. What was the extent of the real woman's involvement in prose and poetry so different and so much better than any Sharp acknowledged as his own? Was her role similar to that of Maud Gonne in his own creative life? Was she an inspiration only, or did she participate actively in the writing? Were Sharp's contributions to the writings emerging from a female consciousness, or *anima*, that was activated by the presence of the woman? Were supernatural forces involved? Anxious to know more and to incorporate the person Sharp called Fiona into his Celtic fold, Yeats continued to press Sharp for information and for a meeting with her. In response to that pressure, and similar questions from others, Sharp built up in conversations and correspondence a persona and a fictional life for Fiona that was designed to enhance her attractiveness and to keep her out of reach. He did not fulfill his promise to introduce her to Richard Le Gallienne and Yeats, but he did take a beautiful woman, probably the woman he loved, to meet George Meredith in June 1897 and introduced her as Fiona Macleod.[5] As the months and years went by, it became more difficult for Sharp, whose health continued declining, to sustain the double life and for his friends to understand just what was going on.

That difficulty has persisted since Sharp's death in 1905. In writing the *Memoir*, Elizabeth Sharp was not fully informed about what had taken place, and she withheld some of what she did know for her sake and that of others. Before she died in 1932, she ordered the destruction of most of her husband's papers. Some letters from Yeats to Sharp and to Fiona have surfaced recently which increase our knowledge of the complex relationship that developed among the three in the latter half of the 1890s. Yeats and Fiona, through the agency of Sharp, were promoting each other's writings, working on plays for a Celtic Theatre, and exploring Celtic mythology for its associations with the occult and its potential for facilitating communion with the realm of spirits. By piecing together what we now have of the Yeats-Sharp-Macleod correspondence and setting it

against what the three said about each other in print and what their
friends wrote about them, it becomes possible to lift partially the
veil Sharp cast over Fiona and sketch with reasonable certainty the
outline of their interactions with Yeats. The tripartite relationship
sheds light on Yeats's principal concerns in the late nineties and on
Sharp's accomplishments as a writer and literary entrepreneur.

First Meetings

In January 1906, shortly after Sharp died, Yeats wrote to his widow,

> your husband was a man of genius, who brought something wholly
> new into letters & thousands will feel his loss with a curious per-
> sonal regret. To me he was that, & a strange mystery too & also a
> dear friend. . . . He was certainly the most imaginative man—I use
> the word in its old & literal sense of image making—I have ever
> known, not like a man of this age at all' (ALS, private).

Nineteen years earlier, when Yeats first met Sharp, he had recently
left his friends in Dublin and moved with his family to London
where he felt unappreciated and unhappy. In June 1887, he wrote to
Katharine Tynan, 'I was introduced to Sharpe of the 'sonnets of this
century' and hated his red British face of flaccid contentment'.[6]
    Ten years older than Yeats, Sharp was an established man of let-
ters. He had left his native Glasgow in 1878 and settled in London to
pursue a literary career. In 1879 he called on Dante Gabriel Rossetti
who accepted him into his circle and introduced him to many prominent writers and artists. After Rossetti's death in April 1882, Sharp
wrote and published within the year a biographical study of Rossetti
and a volume of his own poetry.[7] In 1884, Sharp married his first
cousin, Elizabeth Sharp, following a nine-year betrothal. Having
grown up in London, she moved in a set of intelligent, well-educated
young women who aspired to become writers and influence public
opinion. Ernest Rhys described Sharp coming to see him one morning in 1885: He 'towered up, a rosy giant, in the low-raftered room.
His fine figure and exuberant contours, set forth in unusually
resplendent clothes, suggested a stage Norseman. He talked fast and
excitedly, his bright yellow hair brushed up from an open brow,

under which blue eyes, rosy cheeks, full red lips, and a pointed yellow beard suggested a staring picture by some impressionist
painter.'[8] Rhys had produced a volume of George Herbert's poems
for the Canterbury Poets of which Sharp was General Editor.
Having heard Rhys would be General Editor of the complementary
Camelot prose series, Sharp produced a list of volumes he wanted to
do. Rhys gave him De Quincey's *Opium-Eater*. When Sharp came
down with scarlet fever and then rheumatic fever in the winter of
1886, Rhys generously wrote the introduction from Sharp's notes
and published it over Sharp's name.[9] In 1887 Sharp succeeded his
friend Eric Robertson as Literary Editor of the *The Young Folks
Paper*, a post that provided a reasonable and steady income.

By the early summer of 1887, when Yeats met him, Sharp was a
well published,[10] successful literary man who had influential friends
and access to literary assignments that provided modest incomes for
aspiring writers. According to Rhys, Sharp 'appeared to know
everybody, to have been everywhere.'[11] Mrs. Sharp recalled an
extensive list of people 'with whom we were in sympathy' who
came to their 'Sunday informal evening gatherings' at Wescam, their
house in South Hampstead. Among them was Yeats who, she said,
'came in the intervals of wandering over Ireland in search of Folk
tales' (*Memoir* 140-1). During his three years at Wescam, Sharp produced a steady stream of articles, reviews, and editions.

Despite his exuberant manner and apparently robust body, Sharp
had from childhood suffered frequent bouts of illness, and rheumatic
fever in 1886 permanently damaged his heart. Just as his handsome
appearance and enthusiastic manner masked physical weakness, so
he concealed from all but his most intimate associates a dreaming,
contemplative nature. Responding to Rhys's description of her husband, Elizabeth Sharp wrote

> From time to time the emotional, the more intimate self would
> sweep aside all conscious control; a dream, a sudden inner vision, an
> idea that had lain dormant in what he called 'the mind behind the
> mind' would suddenly visualize itself and blot out everything else
> from his consciousness, and under such impulse he would write at
> great speed, hardly aware of what or how he wrote, so absorbed was
> he in the vision with which for the moment he was identified. In
> those days he was unwilling to retouch such writing; for he thought
> that revision should be made only under a similar phase of emotion.
> Consequently he preferred for the most part to destroy such efforts
> if the result seemed quite inadequate, rather than alter them.[12]

In the late eighties and early nineties, Yeats knew nothing of this side of William Sharp. The extraordinary shift in Yeats's opinion of Sharp dates from the mid-nineties when Sharp, in his own name and that of Fiona Macleod, joined the Celtic Revival.

Though Yeats was dismissive of Sharp in the late eighties to Tynan,[13] he was anxious to produce books for Walter Scott. Rhys set him to collecting and editing material for *Fairy and Folk Tales of the Irish Peasantry*, published in September 1888. Yeats wanted his first English book to enhance his reputation and produce more commissions and in mid-June 1888 he wrote to Katherine Tynan that the 'book of selected fairy tales . . . for the Camelot Classics . . . must be done by the end of July. The time is too short to make a really good book I fear. I hope to get Davis to edit in Canterbury Poets. I have not yet asked but will if this fairy book looks well when done'.[14] Yeats then edited *Stories from Carleton* and T. W. Rolleston edited *Prose Writings of Thomas Davis*, both in the Camelot Series (1889).

In preparing *Fairy and Folk Tales*, Yeats familiarized himself with the major collections of folklore produced in the nineteenth century and recalled the stories he heard as a boy in County Sligo. The project strengthened his belief that Irish folklore, with its roots in ancient myths and legends, was a valuable heritage and a rich resource for his poetry.[15] Yeats, Sharp, and others prepared their Canterbury and Camelot books at the British Museum. Sharp's knowledge of Yeats's project surely caused him to recall stories he heard as a boy in the West of Scotland. In addition to its effect on the course of Yeats's development, *Fairy and Folk Tales* may well have sowed the seeds of Fiona Macleod.

The Birth of Fiona Macleod

In the Spring of 1890, the Sharps gave up their house in South Hampstead and their comfortable literary and social life so that Sharp could concentrate on serious literary work, giving voice to what he called his 'other self'. On 17 June 1890, Sharp explained his decision in a long letter to his American friend, E. C. Stedman:

> Most of my acquaintances think I am very foolish thus to withdraw from the 'thick of the fight' just when things are going so well with me, and when I am making a good and rapidly increasing income . . . . . But truly enough wisdom does not lie in money-making—not for

the artist who cares for his work at any rate. I am tired of so much
pot-boiling, such unceasing bartering of literary merchandise: and
wish to devote myself entirely—or as closely as the fates will
permit—to work in which my heart is. I am bouyant with the
belief that it is in me to do something both in prose and verse far
beyond any hitherto accomplishment of mine: but to stay here
longer, and let the net close more and more round me, would be
fatal.[16]

Sharp's break from editing was less complete than he had hoped it
would be, but his embarking on what he told Stedman would be a
'bohemian' life did produce a body of prose and verse that was far
superior to anything he had written earlier.

After moving from place to place during the summer, the Sharps
went to Germany in early October 1890 and then on to Rome in
December.[17] 'Winter in Rome,' according to Elizabeth, 'was one
long delight to the emancipated writer. . . . He revelled in the
sunshine and the beauty; he was in perfect health; his imagination
was quickened and [he] worked with great activity' (Memoir, 173).
Among British friends who were visiting Rome, Elizabeth mentioned Mrs. Wingate Rinder who 'joined us for three weeks, and
with her my husband greatly enjoyed long walks over the
Campagna and expeditions to the little neighbouring hill towns'. A
beautiful woman of 26, Edith Wingate Rinder (see frontispiece) had
come by herself from London to spend three weeks with her husband's cousin, Mona Caird,[18] a close friend of Elizabeth Sharp's.
Sharp, at 35, fell in love with Edith Rinder, and she with him, during their walks in the Italian countryside.

We know from Sharp's diary, which Elizabeth quoted selectively
for these months, that on 3 Jan. 1891, he and Mrs. Rinder went by
train to Albano (Memoir, 173-82). From there they walked to 'the
high ground, with its olive orchards, looking down upon the Lake
of Nemi. It looked lovely in its grey-blue stillness, with all the sunlit
but yet sombre winterliness around' (Memoir, 173-82). Ernest Rhys
recalled Sharp's telling him that his first meeting with Fiona
Macleod

> was on the banks of Lake Nemi, when she was enjoying a sun-bath
> in what she deemed was a virgin solitude, after swimming the lake.
> 'That moment began,' he declared, 'my spiritual regeneration. I was
> a New Man, a mystic, where before I had been only a mechanic-in-
> art. Carried away by my passion, my pen wrote as if dipped in fire,
> and when I sat down to write prose, a spirit-hand would seize my

pen and guide it into inspired verse. We found we had many common friends: we travelled on thro' Italy, and went to Rome, and there I wrote my haunting *Sospiri di Roma*' (*Everyman Remembers* 79-80).

The poems Sharp wrote that January and February in Rome and published privately as *Sospiri di Roma* before leaving Italy in the Spring exhibit a new energy and control of imagery that had not been evident in his earlier work.[19]

One of those poems is based on that magical day with Edith Rinder at Nemi. 'The Swimmer of Nemi' describes a handsome man with yellow hair, an idealized self-portrait, swimming in Nemi and trailing a branch of the red-berried ash:

> White as a moonbeam
> Drifting athwart
> The purple twilight,
> The swimmer goeth—
> Joyously laughing,
> With o'er his shoulders,
> Agleam in the sunshine
> The trailing branch
> With the scarlet berries.
> Green are the leaves, and scarlet the berries,
> White are the limbs of the swimmer beyond them,
> Blue the deep heart of the still, brooding lakelet,
> Pale-blue the hills in the haze of September,
> The high Alban hills in their silence and beauty,
> Purple the depths of the windless heaven
> Curv'd like a flower o'er the waters of Nemi.

Much could be said about this poem, with its impressionist strokes and indebtedness to the myths described in James Frazer's *The Golden Bough*. What is of interest here is the vital male figure who has captured in the ash branch the very essence of dynamic life. When Sharp told the story to Rhys some years later, he had been transformed into Fiona Macleod.

Sharp came to believe that Fiona Macleod had been born on that day he shared with Edith Rinder at Nemi. Edith Rinder was responsible, so Sharp came to believe, for the birth of Fiona in his mind and heart. In time, he came to identify Fiona with Edith. Reconstructing Sharp's voice, Rhys continued his account:

You, *amico mio*, who have a Celtic strain, and a touch of the 'sight,'
can understand how it was that Fiona, when we reached England,
was seen by very few. I took her to see George Meredith, at his own
earnest request; and he was enchanted by her dark Highland beauty.
. . . I had her portrait taken afterwards, and here it is [showing me
the photograph of a lovely young woman, dark, tall, with coils of
black hair, and mysterious eyes]. Ah, hers was the divine gift,
beauty, and everything she wore impressed her; but her first emanation, clad only in the golden light of Nemi, was the loveliest (*ibid.*).

In the poem, Sharp casts the event as his own rebirth; he is Apollo,
the god of poetry and beauty, arising from the water. Later he
reconstructed it as the birth of Fiona Macleod arising from Lake
Nemi as Aphrodite, the goddess of love and beauty. The transference of gender that occured between the poem and the conversation with Rhys eventually came to haunt Sharp. When the Fiona
Macleod persona began to assume a life of her own, a serious split
developed between his masculine nature which was attracted to
Edith Rinder and a feminine *anima*, or anti-self, that identified with
women, indeed became a woman, and released his creative powers.
In the winter and spring of 1891, however, Sharp's response to his
relationship with Edith Rinder was one of pure joy. She revitalized
him and released the creative impulse that produced *Sospiri di Roma*.

A Romance of the Isles

After another year of travel and temporary residences, the Sharps
leased a house in the summer of 1892 in the country south of
London. There, in relative isolation, Sharp began writing (in 1893)
Pharais, A Romance of the Isles, the first Fiona Macleod book, which
was published in 1894 and dedicated to E. W. R., or Edith Wingate
Rinder.[20] Writing with finesse and delicacy as Fiona in the
dedicatory preface, Sharp addressed the woman who had inspired
the story and changed his life:

While you gratify me by your pleasure in this inscription, you
modestly deprecate the dedication to you of this story of alien
life—of that unfamiliar island-life so alien in all ways from the life
of cities, and, let me add, from that of the great mass of the nation
to which, in the communal sense, we both belong. But in the
Domhan-Toir of friendship there are resting-places where all bar-

riers of race, training, and circumstance fall away in dust. At one of these places of peace [the reference must be to the Roman countryside and to Lake Nemi] we met, a long while ago, and found that we loved the same things, and in the same way.

Fiona shares with E. W. R., she says, a love for the West of Scotland not only 'in the magic of sunshine and cloud,' but also 'when the mists drive across the hillsides, and the brown torrents are in spate, and the rain and the black wind make a gloom upon every loch.' She draws a parallel between E. W. R. and Deirdre, the 'Celtic Helen,' identifies herself and E. W. R as children of Keithor, the Celtic 'god of the earth; dark-eyed, shadowy brother of Pan', and tells E. W. R. that a sense of kinship has led her 'to grace my book with your name'. In Fiona's description of the qualities she shared with E. W. R., Sharp was establishing her persona. He was also expressing his gratitude to and feelings of affinity with Edith Rinder. The persona, the imagined Fiona with Edith behind her obscured from view, soon came to exercise an enormous appeal on the minds and hearts of readers throughout the English-speaking world.

Fiona's dedication to *Pharais* also contains Sharp's first articulation of his concept of Celticism. Keats, she says, transmuted into his poetry 'something of the beautiful mythology of Greece,' but while he

spun from the inexhaustible loom of genius, and I am but an obscure chronicler of obscure things, is it too presumptuous of me to hope that here, and mayhap elsewhere, I, the latest comer among older and worthier celebrants and co-enthusiasts, likewise may do something, howsoever little, to win a further measure of heed for, and more intimate sympathy with, that old charm and stellar beauty of Celtic thought and imagination, now, alas, like so many other lovely things, growing more and more remote, discoverable seldom in books, and elusive amid the sayings and oral legends and fragmentary songs of a passing race?

The Celts are a passing race, Fiona continued, 'and yet, mayhap not so':

It may well be that the Celtic Dream is not doomed to become a memory merely. Were it so, there would be less joy in all Springs to come, less hope in all brown Autumns; and the cold of a deathlier chill in all Winters still dreaming by the Pole. For the Celtic joy in the life of Nature—the Celtic vision—is a thing apart: it is a passion; a visionary rapture. There is none like it among the peoples of our race.

In 'a few remote spots, as yet inviolate . . . Anima Celtica still lives and breathes and hath her being'. One purpose Fiona and E. W. R. share is that of crossing and diminishing the frontiers that separate Celtic peoples from others. The dedication also bows briefly to Yeats: 'The sweetest-voiced of the younger Irish singers of to-day has spoken of the Celtic Twilight. A twilight it is; but, if night follow gloaming, so also does dawn succeed night. Meanwhile, twilight voices are sweet, if faint and far, and linger lovingly in the ear'.[21] Acknowledging her debt to Yeats, Fiona Macleod strengthened the chance of his accepting her as the 'latest comer' on the Celtic stage.

The novel itself is the best piece of prose fiction Sharp had written. It tells the story of a young married couple on one of the remote Outer Hebrides. The husband, robust, fair-haired, and fairskinned like William Sharp, learns that he has an incurable mental illness that is sure to become worse. He and his wife, who resembles Edith Rinder in appearance, decide to lie down in a cave, bind themselves together with seaweed, eat berries that will put them to sleep, and drown when the tide fills the cave. They want to leave this world for the next before he lapses into insanity and his wife gives birth to a child who will surely inherit his illness. Before the cave fills with water, they are rescued, but separated. The wife remains on the island and bears a child who is blind. The husband drifts off to another island from which he eventually returns in a dream-like state, swims ashore, sheds his clothes, makes a crown of myrtles for his head, and meets his wife and baby.[22] They live happily for a time, but, as his mental and physical condition declines, they sail to a remoter island in the West from which they can more easily enter the gates of paradise. There, as snow begins to fall, the landscape comes to life as a protective and welcoming female. Snowflakes 'glisten like burnished gold' in the sunrise as the natural world merges with the eternal to ease the ascension of husband, wife, and child to paradise. Fusing classical myth and gaelicized Christianity, the novel encourages its readers to look past the pains of this world to the next. The hope it holds forth and the ease of the final passage accounted, no doubt, for the popularity of *Pharais* as the century was drawing to its close. Rich in local detail, the novel paints its natural settings in vivid strokes and draws its principal characters fully and convincingly. Readers who can see past its sentimentality will feel its appeal to those who yearned for a simpler life and assurance of a blissful paradise after death.

Pharais also carries in disguise the story of its author and the woman he loved. Strong, passionate love cannot long survive in this world, but lovers who are deeply committed will find fulfillment and peace in the afterlife. Sharp's identification with its doomed hero surely accounts for the depth of feelings that draws the reader into the novel. The mention of Yeats in the dedicatory note makes us wonder if Sharp's control of language and improvement of execution may be partly attributable to the example of *The Celtic Twilight*. The improvement is so dramatic, however, that we must also wonder if Edith Rinder was more than an inspiration. Did she provide advice during the work's composition? Did she play a more active role in structuring and executing it? Those questions may never be answered with certainty.

Lyra Celtica

In the autumn of 1894, after leaving Phenice Croft near Rudgwick, Sussex, to make their home again in London, the Sharps met Patrick Geddes who was forming a community at the top of the High Street in Edinburgh to promote the revival of Celtic culture in Scotland. He established a publishing firm to issue Celtic books and named Sharp manager. The firm issued a collection of Fiona Macleod stories in October 1895, *The Sin-Eater and Other Tales* which, according to Elizabeth Sharp, 'attracted immediate attention.'[23] In February 1896 (*Memoir*, 262), the firm published *Lyra Celtica: An Anthology of Representative Celtic Poetry*, edited by Elizabeth Sharp with an introduction and notes by her husband.[24] Linking his name with this volume, Sharp hoped to establish his credentials as a Celticist and reenforce the separate identity of Fiona Macleod whose poems appeared in the anthology. This book renewed Sharp's relationship with Yeats which had been in abeyance since he left some of his editing posts and London in 1890.

In late June or early July 1895, Elizabeth Sharp asked Yeats's permission to include five of his poems in the anthology. Her letter has not surfaced, but we have Yeats's reply.

> Your letter has found me after wandering in Ireland. Mr. Unwin has a share in my copyright, so far as I understand this matter which is but dimly, & I have written to ask him whether he objects

to your quoting the poems you name; so far as I am concerned you are welcome to them. I will let you know what he says as soon as I have heard. I shall look forward very much to "Lyra Celtica"' (*CL1* 469).

In a postscript Yeats asked, 'Do you know Miss Hopper's verse? She is very celtic'. On the same day, 12 July, Yeats wrote to Unwin seeking his permission for Mrs. Sharp 'to include "The Lake Isle of Innisfree" "The White Birds" and three other poems from my forth coming book [*Poems*, 1895] in an anthology of Celtic poetry' (*CL1* 468). On 17 July, Yeats told Mrs. Sharp that his publisher wanted him to 'limit the number of quotations' because he 'seems to have some objections to anthologies'. So he asked Mrs. Sharp to include only the three she had named. To demonstrate his commitment to the project, however, he said he had urged the case upon Unwin because 'celtic things were so completely "my business" & your anthology so desirable that we could not refuse' (*CL2* 654). *Lyra Celtica* included, besides the two poems named above, 'They went forth to the Battle, but they always fell' (later 'The Rose of Battle'). Sharp, however, quoted liberally from others in his introduction and lavished great praise on Yeats:

> If it be advisable to select one poet, still 'with a future,' as pre-eminently representative of the Celtic genius of to-day, I think there can be little doubt that W. B. Yeats' name is that which would occur first to most lovers of contemporary poetry. He has grace of touch and distinction of form beyond any of the younger poets of Great Britain, and there is throughout his work a haunting beauty, and a haunting sense of beauty everywhere perceived with joy and longing, that makes its appeal irresistible for those who feel it at all. He is equally happy whether he deals with antique or with contemporary themes, and in almost every poem he has written there is that exquisite remoteness, that dream-like music, and that transporting charm which Matthew Arnold held to be one of the primary tests of poetry, and, in particular, of Celtic poetry (*LC*, xliv).

To support his points, Sharp included, a long quotation from 'The Wandering of Oisin', the concluding stanza of 'The Madness of King Goll', a stanza from 'The Stolen Child', and the first two stanzas of 'The Rose of the World', all from Yeats's *Poems* published in early autumn 1895, after Mrs. Sharp had received her letter of permission and before Sharp wrote his introduction.

Yeats was not, in 1896, the melancholy young man Sharp had known in the late eighties. He had published three volumes of poems, two volumes of stories, and six editions of poems and stories by others. He had also completed with Edwin Ellis the three-volume edition of *The Works of William Blake*. By 1896 his reputation was established, but such was not the case for Sharp. The Fiona Macleod stories had attracted a surprising amount of favourable attention, but Sharp's own reputation had waned. Such patterns underlie the dynamic of their future interaction.

Sharp's concluding note on Yeats's poems in *Lyra Celtica* makes a further point. Irish and Celtic, his work nevertheless 'belongs to English literature'.

> Mr. Yeats himself would be the last man to nail his flag to the mast of parochialism in literature. He is one of the two or three absolutely poetic personalities in literature at the present moment; and in outlook, and, above all, in atmosphere, stands foremost in the younger generation. It is noteworthy that the two most convincingly poetic of all our younger poets . . . are predominantly Celtic; W. B. Yeats and John Davidson—and noteworthy, also, that both are too wise, too clear-sighted, too poetic, in fact, to aim at being Irish or Scoto-Celtic at the expense of being English in the high and best sense of the word. This, fortunately, is consistent with being paramountly national in all else. In the world of literature there is no geography save that of the mind (*LC*, 399).

Sharp assumes Yeats's concurrence in the view that he is both Celtic and English, both local and universal. Celtic poetry in English, Sharp believed, is English poetry. It must be seen as part of that tradition and judged accordingly. In the years ahead he would make this point repeatedly in reviews and essays signed Fiona Macleod. As the Irish literary movement gained force and became associated more closely with Irish nationalism, this position lost favour in Ireland.[25]

Sharp assessed Yeats's position in the mid-nineties correctly. He wanted the Celtic spirit to flourish in Scotland and Wales as well as in Ireland, and he did all he could to foster solidarity between the Irish and their Celtic brethren. His main concern was to unleash the possibilities he recognized in Celtic myth and legend to effect a spiritual renewal of western civilization. Such a renewal, he thought, would come about by infusing into the dominant culture the easy concourse with spirits he found among Irish peasants. In this visionary hope, Yeats was influenced not only by his contact with the people of his native Sligo, but by his reading of Irish myth and folklore and by his immersion in the works of Blake. He looked to Celticism, just as he was exploring Hermeticism, in his search for contacts with the supernatural, for a substitute for conventional religion that would give meaning and purpose to human life.

After August 1901, Yeats's interest in Pan-Celticism diminished (*CL3* 109-11). In writings over his own name and the pseudonym, Sharp remained committed to Pan-Celticism and to judging Celtic literature in English, regardless of its country or region of origin, as a distinctive—and inspired—subspecies of English literature. In his introduction to *Lyra Celtica,* Sharp credited Renan and Arnold with shaping his idea of Celticism and paraphrased with approval Renan's glorification of the Celtic race:

> One does not enough reflect on how strange it is that an ancient race should continue down to our day, and almost under our eyes, in some islands and peninsulas of the West, its own life, more and more diverted from it, it is true, by the noise from without, but still faithful to its language, its memories, its ideals, and its genius. We are especially apt to forget that this small race, contracted now to the extreme confines of Europe, in the midst of those rocks and mountains where its enemies have driven it, is in possession of a literature, which in the Middle Ages exerted an immense influence, changed the current of European imagination, and imposed upon almost the whole of Christianity its poetical motifs.[26]

It would be a shame, Sharp says, to lose 'this fading glory of the West,' but he concludes 'we are still far from believing that the Celtic race has said its last word'. For Sharp there was no contradiction between accepting a racial theory as a basis for the origin of a particular kind of literature in English and insisting that it be judged by the qualitative standards set for the whole of English literature. He had addressed this point two years earlier in the dedicatory note to *Pharais,* where Fiona identified herself as a British or Anglo-Saxon writer who aspired to capture and preserve the 'joy in the life of Nature' and the 'visionary rapture' of the Celtic people in the West of Scotland and bring those qualities into English literature. All influences that come into that literature, be they from the classical world or that of the Celts, Fiona Macleod said, are valuable both in themselves and for their enrichment of the whole.

Two years later Sharp closed his introduction to *Lyra Celtica* as follows:

No, it is no 'disastrous end': whether the Celtic peoples be slowly perishing or are spreading innumerable fibres of life towards a richer and fuller, if a less national and distinctive existence. From Renan, the high priest of the Breton faith, to the latest of his kindred of the gael, there is a strange new uprising of hope. . . . Let me conclude, then, in the words of the most recent of those many eager young Celtic writers whose songs and romances are charming the now intent mind of the Anglo-Saxon. 'A doomed and passing race. Yes, but not wholly so. The Celt has at last reached his horizon. There is no shore beyond. He knows it. This has been the burden of his song since Malvina led the blind Oisin to his grave by the sea. 'Even the Children of Light must go down into darkness.' But this apparition of a passing race is no more than the fulfilment of a glorious resurrection before our very eyes. For the genius of the Celtic race stands out now with averted torch, and the light of it is a glory before the eyes, and the flame of it is blown into the hearts of the mightier conquering people.[27] The Celt falls, but his spirit rises in the heart and the brain of the Anglo-Celtic peoples, with whom are the destinies of the generations to come' (*LC*, li).

The 'most recent' of the 'many eager young Celtic writers whose songs and romances are charming the now intent mind of the Anglo-Saxon' was, though unnamed, none other than Sharp himself. The passage he quotes is from the 'Prologue' to Fiona Macleod's *The Sin-Eater* which had been published by Geddes the previous year. There he turned Fiona from the non-Celt she was in the dedication to *Pharais* into an Anglo-Celt. The vacillation about her ancestry is to be explained, I believe, by the split in Sharp's own ancestry between his Scottish father and Swedish mother and by the fact that neither his parents nor his grandparents qualified as authentic Celts.[28] What mattered to Sharp was a writer's ability to identify with and portray accurately the life-style, values, and beliefs of the authentic Celts who survived in the remoter regions of the West. His objective was to break down what he called the 'frontiers,' to breath the Celtic spirit, following Renan and Arnold, into the mainstream of British, indeed, European culture.

In the nineties, Yeats shared that objective, and it is not surprising, given Sharp's high praise for his work, that he responded appreciatively to *Lyra Celtica*. In early June 1896, he wrote

I have now read . . . 'Lyra Celtica' & with the greatest delight. I do not think any book for a long time has given me so much pleasure. The book is certain to be very influential & to help forward a matter I have myself much at heart—the mutual understanding & sympathy of the Scotch Welsh & Irish Celts. The Welsh part was very new to me & very delightful & in the Scotch part Fiona Mac-Cleod's 'prayer of women' filled me with a new wonder it is more like anciant than any other modern poem & should be immortal.

Formal in tone, the letter projects sincere gratitude and moves on to the personal: 'You were so kind as to ask me to dine with you one day soon. Any day this week (except tomorrow) or next would suit me admirably & I have some celtic matters to talk over with you' (*CL2* 37-9).

Besides advancing Sharp as a knowledgeable Celticist, *Lyra Celtica* subtly promoted the poetry of Fiona Macleod. Seven of her poems were included in the 'Modern and Contemporary Scoto-Celtic' section of the volume, a larger representation than that of the other poets in the section. Sharp's note on Fiona Macleod advances her as

one of the younger writers most intimately associated with the Celtic Renaissance in Scotland. . . . Such of the poems scattered through her several volumes, and others, as she wishes to preserve in connected form, will be published by Miss Macleod early in 1896 (Patrick Geddes and Colleagues), under the title of *Lyric Runes and Fonnsheen*.[29]

Fiona Macleod is not mentioned by name in the introduction, but those who knew *The Sin-Eater* might have recognized that Sharp praised and quoted her. It is not known if Yeats made that connection, but his choice of Fiona Macleod for special praise among all the poets in the volume suggests that he knew that Sharp and Fiona Macleod were friends. A letter from Fiona Macleod to Yeats in September 1896 confirms that Sharp had told Yeats so in June or July 1896, as he slowly enticed Yeats into a drama that he was constructing around the imaginary Fiona. Motivated by a sense of common purpose and simple curiosity, Yeats became an ever more willing participant. *Lyra Celtica* meanwhile established Sharp's credentials as a Celticist, affirmed the pre-eminence of Fiona Macleod among young Celtic poets, and reinforced the independent identities of Sharp and Macleod.

The Archer Vision

On or about August 25, 1896, Yeats wrote a letter to Sharp from Edward Martyn's Tillyra Castle in County Galway in which he thanked him for a recent letter, reported on his visit to the Aran Islands where he was 'studying' for the opening chapters of the story that became 'The Speckled Bird,' and said he had met a man who 'hears the fairies . . . every night.[30] On his way to Galway to stay with Martyn, Yeats said, he found the Dublin mystics, referring to George Russell and his friends, 'afire, as I never knew them to be, with their new-old celtic mysticism'. He then described a recent vision:

> I have had some singular experiences myself. I invoked one night the spirits of the moon & saw between sleep & waking a beautiful woman firing an arrow among the stars. That night she appeared to Symons who is staying here, & so impressed him that he wrote a poem to her, the only one he ever wrote to a dream, calling her the fountain of all song or some such phrase. She was the symbolic Diana.'[31]

Concluding by asking Sharp to 'give my greetings to Miss Macleod' Yeats foresaw that he would return to London in 'the first week of October'. Between his letter of early June and this one, Yeats had come to think of Sharp as a friend with whom he could discuss his work and share his interest in the occult, and Sharp had told him that he and Fiona Macleod were friends. He may also have told him they were related, for he claimed to others they were distant cousins, and he may have implied they were involved romantically. If so, Yeats might have recognized the similarities between the Sharp-Macleod relationship and his own relationship with Maud Gonne. As Sharp portrayed her to others,[32] Fiona was supremely beautiful and highly accomplished. That she was not involved in politics and directed her energies to the production of prose and poetry would have made her appealing to Yeats who wanted Maud Gonne to be less involved in public life. Clouding his romantic relationship with Fiona, as Sharp said to others (and perhaps to Yeats), was the fact that both were married: Sharp to Elizabeth and Fiona to an older, well-off Scottish laird who allowed her great freedom to move about in the world.[33] Strong, passionate love that cannot be fulfilled in this world is a constant theme of the stories Sharp was writing under the feminine pseudonym, just as unrequited love that is too great to be realized in this world is a constant theme of the poems Yeats was writing in the nineties.

In addition to telling Yeats about his relationship with Fiona Macleod, Sharp must also have told him that he and Fiona had the capacity to see visions. Only to a fellow visionary would Yeats have described so casually in his August letter to Sharp the vision he had seen at Tillyra. Yeats mentions in this letter that he had written a letter to Fiona Macleod, and we know from her response, that it also contained a description of his archer vision.

Having received two letters from Yeats describing his vision of the beautiful woman shooting arrows, Sharp appropriated it for the conclusion of a Fiona Macleod story on which he was working in Scotland. Originally entitled 'The Last Fantasy of James Achanna' , the reworked story became 'The Archer'.[34] It begins with the authorial voice of Fiona saying she will tell a story she heard from Coll McColl, a fisherman in the Southern Hebrides, who told it to her in Gaelic while mending his nets. It is a story about 'two men who loved one woman'. Ian Macleod, a poet and dreamer, has fallen in love with Silis, the wife of his friend and fishing partner, Seumas Maclean. After a night on the water in which the two men speak in guarded terms about their problem, Seumas returns to his cottage and kneels beside his sleeping wife. As she wakes in a dreamlike state, she thinks the kneeling figure is Ian and breathes his name. In despair, Seumas goes to Ian's cottage where they draw to see who will go to Silis and ask her to name the one she loves best. Seumas wins the draw, goes back to his cottage, and returns to bring Ian back to hear what Silis has said. In a tearful scene, Silis remains faithful to her husband. Although passionately in love with Ian, she knows that her choosing him would kill Seumas. So she says, 'Yes, it is a true thing, Ian. I abide by Seumas'. Ian whispers 'dear love of my heart', but Silis is frozen, and 'the deadly frost of her lie slew that in him without which life is nothing'.[35] Ian leaves, and his body is found three days later 'face upward, among the green flags by the water-edge'.

The night they found Ian's body, Coll McColl, while walking in the moonlight, saw a fawn. 'While he watched, amazed, he saw a tall shadowy woman pass by. She stopped, drew a great bow, and shot an arrow which 'went through the air with a sharp whistling sound—just like *Silis—Silis—Silis*'. The arrow passed through the fawn, and the fawn went leaping away into the night while its heart remained 'suspended, arrow-pierced, from the white stem of a silver birch'. To this day, Coll says, he does not know 'who that archer was, or who that fawn,'

> But I have this thought of my thinking: that it was only a vision I saw, and that the fawn was the poor suffering heart of Love, and that the Archer was the great Shadowy Archer that hunts among

the stars. For in the dark of the morrow after that night I was in Cnoc-na-Hurich, and I saw a woman there shooting arrow after arrow against the stars. At dawn she rose and passed away, like smoke, beyond those pale wandering fires.

Coll's second vision of a woman shooting arrows against the stars is derived from 'a beautiful woman firing an arrow among the stars', which is how Yeats described his Tillyra vision to Sharp in his August letter. Neither the fawn nor the arrow-pierced heart on the birch in Coll's first vision had appeared to Yeats, and they aroused his curiosity.

Arthur Symons had asked Fiona Macleod, upon Yeats's encouragement, for a story for *The Savoy*.[36] After returning to London from Sligo sometime after 20 September, Symons received 'The Archer' and two other Fiona stories to consider for publication. When Yeats returned to London in late September or early October and saw 'The Archer', he assumed Fiona had written it before she received his letter from Tillyra. Having been seen by three people (Yeats, Symons, and Fiona), the archer vision, Yeats thought, must have been a real event containing a message from beyond. 'It seemed impossible that Sharp could have heard of my vision in time, and part of it was new'. Determined to learn more about it, Yeats consulted Dr. Wynn Wescott, a founder of the Order of the Golden Dawn, who

opened a drawer and showed me two drawings, one of a woman shooting at a star and one of a centaur. They were the symbolism of a kabalistic grade I had not yet attained to, a secret imagery. Then he showed me that what seemed a star was a little burning heart, and he said this heart was Tiphereth, the centre of the kabalistic tree, the heart of Christ, also. The archer woman and the centaur were the higher and lower genii respectively of the path Samek, which leads from Yesod to Tiphereth, from sun to moon. I remembered that Christ was sometimes the mystic fawn (*Mem* 103).

In *The Trembling of the Veil*, in 1922, Yeats described the vision again and recalled the questions it brought to mind:

Had some great event taken place in some world where myth is reality and had we seen some portion of it? . . . or had we but seen in the memory of the race something believed thousands of years ago, or had somebody—I myself perhaps—but dreamed a fantastic dream which had come to those others by transference of thought? I came to no conclusion, but I was sure there was some symbolic meaning could I but find it (*Au* 373-4).

Yeats puzzled over his Archer Vision for many years and used its imagery in his poetry.[37] Its immediate effect was to establish in his mind Fiona Macleod's credentials as a visionary.

Where Sharp found the fawn and the heart, for he was not a member of the Golden Dawn, remains a mystery. In Coll's first vision, the faun whose heart is removed by the arrow and pinned to the tree represents Ian who dies when he is rejected by Silis. Sharp may have intended an association with Oisin whose name means 'little fawn.' Oisin's mother (Blai, of the *sidhe*) had been changed into a fawn and was in that form when Oisin was born.[38] Sharp surely intended the vision to reaffirm symbolically the point of the story which is that Silis, knowing her husband will die if she chooses Ian (whom she truly loves), remains loyal to Seumas, and continues in a loveless marriage. The body of the story, which dates from 1893, grimly recasts the hopeless situation in which Sharp and Edith Rinder found themselves in 1893 and to which they accommodated themselves in the years ahead.[39]

The Shadows are Here

Sometime in May 1896 Yeats received a copy of the latest book of Fiona Macleod tales, *The Washer of the Ford and other Legendary Moralities*, and the following note from its author[40]

9. Upper Coltbridge Terrace | Murrayfield | Midlothian

Dear Sir,
Please accept from me, in return for so much pleasure, the new book of mine I have directed to be sent to you.
    I hope you will find something both in the prose and verse of this volume to appeal to you.

Yours very sincerely
Fiona Macleod

The next Fiona Macleod letter to Yeats, which was written in late September 1896, is a response to a 'long and deeply interesting as well as generous letter' she received from him regarding *The Washer of the Ford*. This Yeats letter, which was written at Tillyra in mid-August and contains, besides comments on *The Washer of the Ford*, a description of Yeats's archer vision, has not surfaced.

Elizabeth Sharp said her husband 'during the most active years of the Fiona Macleod writings . . . was usually in a highly wrought condition of mental and emotional tension, which produced great restlessness, so that he could not long remain contentedly anywhere' (*Memoir* 266). They spent the summer of 1896 'moving about from one place to another [in Northern England and Scotland] that had special interest for him'. At the end of the summer they 'moved to one of William's favourite haunts, Loch Tarbert, off Loch Fyne, where our friends Mr. and Mrs. Frank Rinder had taken a house for the summer. There I left him with his secretary-sister, Mary [who provided the Fiona Macleod handwriting], and returned to London to recommence my work on *The Glasgow Herald*'.[41] On 23 September, Sharp reported to his wife that he was 'now well in writing trim' and that he had finished, among other stories and poems, 'the Savoy story "The Archer"'. At Tarbert, Sharp wrote the following Fiona Macleod letter to Yeats. The letter survives in two manuscripts: a pencil draft in Sharp's hand which is among the Sharp papers in the National Library of Scotland and a final version, now in the Yale Library, which Mary transcribed into the Fiona Macleod hand and sent to Yeats.[42] The final version reads as follows:

Strath-Ma-Mara | Tarbert of Loch Fyne | Argyll

Dear Mr. Yeats

Unforeseen circumstances have prevented my writing to you before this, and even now I must perforce be more brief than I would fain be in response to your long and deeply interesting as well as generous letter. Alas, a long pencilled note (partly apropos of your vision of the woman shooting arrows, and of the strange coincidence of something of the same kind on my own part) has long since been devoured by a too voracious or too trustful gull—for a sudden gust of wind blew the quarto-sheet from off the deck of the small yacht wherein I and my dear friend and confrere of whom you know were sailing, off Skye.

Private matters have combined to distract me very much just now—and this, and much sailing about and faring in remote places—and the work we are doing, and putting together the volume of verse[43]—have together frayed the edges of my small fragment of actual leisure for writing.

How good of you to write to me as you did. Believe me, I am grateful. There is no other writer whose good opinion could please me more—for I love your work, and take an endless delight in your poetry, and look to you as not only one of the rare few on whose lips is the honey of Magh Mell but as one the dark zone of whose mind is lit with the strange stars and constellations of the spiritual life.

Most cordially I thank you for your critical remarks. Even where I do not unreservedly agree, or where I venture to differ (as for example, in the matter of the repetition of the titular words in 'The Washer of the Ford' poem) I have carefully pondered all you say.

I am particularly glad you feel about the 'Annir Choille' as you do.[44] Some people whom I would like to please do not care for it: yet I am sure you are right in considering it one of the most vital things I have been able to do.

With what delight I have read your lovely poem 'O'Sullivan Rua to the Secret Rose.'[45] I have read it over and over with ever deepening delight. It is one of your finest poems, I think: though perhaps it can only be truly appreciated by those who are familiar with legendary Celtic history. We read it to each other, my friend and I, on a wonderful sundown 'when evening fed the wave with quiet light,' off one of the Inner Hebrides (Colonsay, to the south of Oban). The only thing we both note is the use of 'heavy' in the 7th as well as in the sixth line. Is not the effect of that in the 7th consequently lost? And would not 'slumbrous' or some other apt epithet be better? It is but a suggestion—and it is only because you love so truly what is beautiful and so are heedful to any suggestion, right or wrong, that I venture to make it. I cannot quite make up my mind, as you ask, about your two styles.[46] Personally, I incline not exactly to a return to the earlier but to a marriage of the two: that is, a little less [of the] remoteness, or subtlety, with a little more of [the earlier] rippling clarity.[47]

After reading your Blake paper[48] (and with vivid interest and delight) I turned to an early work of yours which I value highly, *Dhoya*: and I admit that my heart moved to *it*.[49] Between them lies, I *think*, your surest and finest line of work—with the light deft craft of *The Celtic Twilight*.

I hope you are soon going to issue the promised volume of poems.[50] When my <our> own book of verse is ready—it is to be called *From the Hills of Dream*—it will give me such sincere pleasure to send you a copy. By the by, I must not forget to thank you for introducing my work to Arthur Symons. He wrote to me a pleasant letter, and asked me to contribute to the *Savoy*, which I have done.

I daresay my friend (who sends you comradely greetings, and says he will write in a day or two) will tell you more from me when he and you meet. I had a strange vision the other day, wherein I saw the figure of a gigantic woman sleeping on the green hills of Ireland. As I watched, the sun waned and the dark came and the stars began to fall. They fell one by one, and each fell into the woman—and lo, of a sudden, all was wan[51] running water, and the drowned stars and the transmuted woman passed from my seeing. This was a waking dream, an open vision: but I do not know what it means, though it was so wonderfully vivid. In a vague way I realise that something of tremendous moment is being matured just now. We are on the verge of vitally important developments. And all the heart, all the brain, of the Celtic races shall be stirred. There is a shadow of mighty changes. Myself, I believe that new spirits have been embodied among us. And some of the old have come back. We shall perish, you and I and all who fight under the 'Lifting of the Sunbeam'—but we shall pioneer a wonderful marvellous new life for humanity. The other day I asked an old isles woman where her son was buried: he was not buried,' she said, 'for all they buried his body. For, a week ago, I saw him lying on the heather, and talking swift an' wild with a Shadow.' *The Shadows are here.*

I must not write more just now.

My cordial greetings to you—
Sincerely
Fiona Macleod

This letter is carefully constructed to fix in Yeats's mind the persona Sharp was fashioning for Fiona. He begins by having her mention her note about Yeats's archer vision and 'something of the same kind' on her part. Since that something was a 'strange coincidence', Yeats was to assume that she had also seen an archer. By invoking the 'too voracious or too trustful gull' to devour the note, he avoids having Fiona Macleod describe what she saw or comment directly on Yeats's vision. Yeats must wait until he returns to London to learn about Fiona's archer from Symons. The strategy of indirection and delay lessened the possibility of Yeats concluding that Fiona had not seen an archer, but simply used his. The gull that made off with Fiona's note thus became an agent in moving the drama forward.

The 'dear friend and confrere of whom you know' is, of course, Sharp whose arrival and the ensuing activity explain her delay in responding. The 'private matters' might also refer to Sharp, who could have told Yeats in London in early summer not only that he and Fiona were close, but also that he was involved in Fiona's writing. Her casual mention of 'the work we are doing' could refer simply to collecting material among the people for her stories since she distinguishes that work from 'putting together the volume of verse'. The second reference to *From the Hills of Dream* shows, however, that Sharp wanted to claim a collaborative role for himself in its production. In drafting the letter, he had Fiona share the credit with him: it is 'our' volume. Then he demurred, crossed out 'our,' and wrote 'my', thus removing himself and having Fiona claim full authorship. Mary copied 'my'. In reading Mary's final copy, however, Sharp wrote '(our)' above the line between 'my' and 'own.' The 'our' is wrapped in parentheses, and then lightly crossed out. The final impression is that Fiona is the author of the poems, but that she wants to give Sharp some recognition for the important role he is playing in their composition and arrangement.

Though Sharp had praised Yeats in his introduction to *Lyra Celtica* as the leader of the Celtic movement, he also wanted recognition, which is why he had given up his editorial positions and left London in 1890. Now, having finally produced work that was widely read and admired, he could receive no credit: worse, since that work depended on the mystique of its authorial persona, its popularity would plummet if he admitted authorship, and he would be unable to continue writing as Fiona, or so he believed. (There was the additional problem of gender identification in the wake of the Oscar Wilde scandal.) Writing privately to Yeats as Fiona, however, Sharp equivocated. Within a few months, he would tell Yeats that he was the author of the Fiona Macleod writings and that a woman was a necessary accomplice in their production, thus reversing the genders of the authorial relationship implied in this letter.

There was a further problem of credit. At Tarbert Sharp was with Edith Rinder, the woman who enabled him to attain the state of mind in which he could write as Fiona Macleod, and he was writing at great speed. Fiona Macleod was a fictional character, indeed Sharp's most vital creation, but significant aspects of her being had their origin in Edith Rinder, who might have been assisting Sharp in assembling and arranging the poems. If so, the true 'we' and 'our' were William Sharp and Edith Rinder. The volume's final section,

'The Silence of Amor,' a series of impressionistic prose sketches, is dedicated to Esclarmoundo, a name Sharp used for Edith which casts her as the brightest star in the sky and also implies the impossibility of his possessing her.[52] Since both were married, Sharp could recognize her essential role in the Fiona Macleod drama only by initials and secret names.

In the letter's last paragraph, a high point in Sharp's construction of the persona, he establishes Fiona's credentials as a visionary. And what a vision she describes! A gigantic woman is sleeping on the hills of Ireland. It becomes dark, the stars fall one by one into the woman, and the entire scene turns to water. This 'waking dream' is intended to appeal to Yeats's hopes for the regeneration of Ireland through the work of her artists. The falling stars represent visionary or imaginative insights; and they fall into Mother Ireland who, transmuted by their agency, is flooded by regenerative waters. The symbolic landscape is not difficult to read, but Sharp has Fiona Macleod say, 'I do not know what it means', suggesting that as a seer she is less interested in unravelling the meaning of her visions than with their immediacy and beauty.

Fiona then moves from her 'waking dream' to prophecy. Something 'vitally important' is about to happen. From the Celts will come a new age, 'a wonderful marvelous new life for humanity'. She and Yeats will be the pioneers of that new life, though they may not live to experience it. The agency of rebirth will be the faculty of vision such as that possessed by 'the old isles woman, who sees her dead son lying on the heather talking with a shadow'. It is those shadows, those disembodied spirits, who are 'here'. The principal agents of rebirth will be those who can commune with the shadows and transform the results of that communion into works of art. Yeats and Fiona Macleod, having the gift of sight, are two such people: he had described his archer vision for Fiona, and she now shares hers with him. Both involve a woman and stars. Indeed, Fiona's, with its stars falling into Mother Ireland, offers Yeats a way of reading his vision.

In his August letter to Sharp, Yeats had mentioned the Dublin mystics. Two months earlier, in June, he had received a letter from George Russell about 'the Ireland behind the veil'. 'The gods have returned to Erin', Russell wrote, 'and have centred themselves in the sacred mountains and blow the fires through the country. They have been seen by several in vision, they will awaken the magical instinct everywhere, and the universal heart of the people will turn to old druidic beliefs'.[53] Russell had seen a vision of an Avatar, a ruler and a sage, who was about to appear. Few shared that secret, but, he said, there will soon be many, and a 'branch of the school for the revival of the ancient mysteries to teach real things' will 'be formed here soon'. It was in this heightened atmosphere of apocalyptic expectation that Yeats was planning his order of Celtic Mysteries. In time, Yeats thought, and with sufficient visionary insight and energy, that Order would bring about the transformation of Ireland that Russell was expecting any minute. Early in 1897 Yeats would invite Sharp and Fiona to assist him with Celtic Mysteries. The visionary enthusiasm Sharp has Fiona evoke in her September letter to Yeats is too close to Russell's not to have been influenced by it. Yeats might have shared Russell's letter with Sharp or described its content when they met in early summer. Or he might have said more about what was occurring in Dublin in his missing letter to Fiona. Either or both would explain Sharp's effort in this letter to impress upon Yeats not only Fiona's visionary capabilities but also her recognition that the apocalypse would begin in Ireland.

The Fiona letter of September 1896 was brilliantly contrived to convince Yeats that he had found in her a fitting compatriot in the Celtic cause. Sharp presents her as a wise woman steeped in the Celtic heritage and an authentic seer, a true visionary. She is also slightly frail and depends on the steadying presence of her male friend. Was Yeats convinced of the authenticity of Sharp's construction? His review of Fiona's *From the Hills of Dream* in December and his answer, in January 1897, to Fiona's September letter show beyond doubt that Sharp's artifice had succeeded.

From the Hills of Dream

In reviewing the volume of Fiona Macleod's poetry, Yeats mixed lavish praise with comments designed to discourage her impressionistic mood poems which he found too vague.[54] Writing to Sharp the previous June, he had singled out Fiona's 'The Prayer of Women,' a rune that appeared first in *Pharais* and then in *Lyra Celtica*, for praise (see above p. 78). Six months later, in the review, he focused again on that poem. French literary circles believe, he said, that 'a return to the subjective' is 'the great change in our time'. Poets no longer wish to describe nature or society, but 'to make our work a mirror, where the passions and desires and ideals of our own minds can cast terrible or beautiful images'. Without that change, he says, some of the poems in *From the Hills of Dream* 'would have been almost impossible'. 'We should probably have lost' he continues, 'one of the most inspired, one of the most startling, one of the most intense poems of our time, her incomparable "Prayer of Women"'. He then quotes twenty lines from that forty-three-line poem choosing the best and wisely omitting, for example, these:

> Save us from the springing of the cruel seed
> In that narrow house which is as the grave
> For darkness and loneliness . . .
> That women carry with them with shame, and weariness, and long
>   pain,
> Only for the laughter of man's heart,
> And for the joy that triumphs therein,
> And the sport that is in his heart.
> Wherewith he mocketh us,
> Wherewith he playeth with us,
> Wherewith he trampleth upon us . . .
> Us, who conceive and bear him;
> Us, who bring him forth;
> Who feed him in the womb, and at the breast, and at the knee:
> Whom he calleth mother and wife,
> And mother again of his children and his children's children.[55]

Reading that poem a century later, we wonder what moved Yeats to praise it so lavishly while ignoring or bestowing fainter praise on others in the volume that are much better. For one thing, he assumed it had been 'first written in Gaelic' and he thought 'Miss Macleod is always best when she writes under a Gaelic and legendary and mythological influence'. 'Emotions which seem vague or extravagant when expressed under the influence of modern literature,' he continued, 'cease to be vague and extravagant when associated with ancient legend and mythology, for legend and mythology were born out of man's longing for the mysterious and the infinite'. If not a translation of an ancient prayer, the rune was, Yeats thought, a close approximation of something Fiona heard from a country woman in the West of Scotland. It had been spoken by such a woman in *Pharais*. Yeats's critical faculties, not unlike those of other Celtic enthusiasts, were tempered by his belief that things old are necessarily good, and he wanted to encourage Fiona to pursue that vein.

Other considerations were at play. The hard life of women is a constant in the folk tales Yeats heard in the West of Ireland and Sharp in the West of Scotland. Women mistreated by men and women punished for trying to escape the yoke of demanding and uncaring husbands appear in the stories both Fiona and Yeats were writing during these years. One thinks, also, of Yeats's short play *The Land of Hearts's Desire*. Assuming, of course, that Fiona Macleod *had* written the poem, Yeats read it as the lament of a woman as retold by a woman who was close to Celtic sources in the West of Scotland. He heard in it real feelings expressed by a real woman.

The poem deals not simply with the general travail of women, but with their special misfortune, the pain and indignity of pregnancy and childbirth. Having used women for their pleasure, men cast them off and laugh at their suffering. Sharp considered himself at the forefront among men of the nineties in supporting improved conditions for women. This poem, which champions that cause and which Yeats called 'one of the most intense poems of our time', now appears, apart from the false archaism of its diction, intensely regressive in its depiction of relations between the sexes. Women see themselves only as victims of male aggression and take no pleasure in bearing children. Given the pain they suffer throughout their lives, so the poem argues, they should be pitied for what men do to them. Sharp in writing the poem and Yeats in praising it seem only to be assuaging male guilt, their own and others.

Sharp's fascination with childbirth traces back to his first book of poetry in 1882 and a poem therein called 'Motherhood' which casts an idealistic glow over the experiences of three females giving birth—a tigress, a primitive woman, and a proper Victorian girl. Childbirth reappeared occasionally in Sharp's writing during the eighties, but it became a persistent concern of Fiona Macleod.[56] In a letter to his wife from Tarbert on 26 September 1896, Sharp described his composition of another poem that appeared in the 'Lyric Runes' section of *From the Hills of Dream*, 'Rune of the Sorrow of Women.'

> I went alone for an hour or so to revise what had stirred me so unspeakably, namely the third and concluding 'Rune of the Sorrow of Women.' This last Rune tired me in preliminary excitement and in the strange semi-conscious fever of composition more than anything of the kind since I wrote the first of the three ['The Prayer of Women'] in *Pharais* one night of storm when I was alone in Phenice

Croft. I have given it to Mary to copy, so that I can send it to you at once. Tell me what you think and feel about it. In a vague way not only you, Mona, Edith and others swam into my brain, but I have never so absolutely felt the woman-soul within me: it was as though in some subtle way the soul of Woman breathed into my brain—and I feel vaguely as if I had given partial expression at least to the inarticulate voice of a myriad women who suffer in one or other of the triple ways of sorrow (*Memoir*, 267).

The poem that resulted from this feverish creative act is prefaced by the following three lines:

> *This is the rune of the women who bear in sorrow:*
> *Who, having anguish of body, die in the pangs of bearing,*
> *Who, with the ebb at the heart, pass ere the wane of the babe-month*

The poem proper opens with an eight-line 'rune' in which a mother who has just given birth laments that she is going to die and says farewell to her newborn baby. There follows a description of a dream the new mother has before she dies. She sees therein the Virgin Mary who is about to give birth to Jesus. In her suffering Mary is visited by God who tells her she will bear the Prince of Peace and, consequently, be blessed. Mary remains courteous, but has no use for God. She lapses into a dream state wherein the poet reproduces a rune which God sees in her heart. This rune of Mary's heart reverses the true gender traits with heavy handed irony. Men are portrayed as long suffering and ever constant, while women expect to be cared for, lack constancy, expect everything, give back nothing. Addressed to God, the rune characterizes him as an overbearing authoritarian and chastises him for creating men in his likeness. Following the retelling of Mary's dream, the poet says, 'And high in his Heaven God the All-Seeing troubled'. The ungrateful message upsets God who cannot understand why such a dream would occur in any woman's 'heart,' least of all that of the chosen Mother of Christ. Sharp expected his readers to see that Mary has struck a blow to God's manly core. Responsible for all the suffering of women, he is too myopic or, as we would say, gender-bound, to see the truth. The poem concludes with a repetition of the rune of the dying mother who has returned briefly from her dream. Its last line is 'Bitter the sorrow of bearing only to end with the parting'.

In writing this poem and 'The Prayer of Women,' Sharp placed himself imaginatively in what he thought to be the minds of three women he knew well. He was trying to think and speak as they would. In the second edition of *From the Hills of Dream,* he moved the two runes to a section called 'From the Heart of a Woman.' He thought the sentiments he expressed in these poems were close to the real feelings of Elizabeth Sharp, Mona Caird, and Edith Rinder, three intelligent and well-read women. Was their view of childbirth and women's role in the reproductive process so grim? They certainly encouraged Sharp in the Fiona Macleod writings, and they may have encouraged him to believe he was expressing their thoughts in these and similar poems. In any case, the poems struck a positive chord for many readers, Yeats among them.[57]

Referring to these poems, Yeats said in his review, 'We are at the beginning of a franker trust in passion and in beauty than was possible to the poets who put their trust in the external world and its laws'. He had in mind the serious strain of Victorian poetry that was meant to be, in Arnold's phrase, a 'criticism of life'. Fiona Macleod's runes from and about women purport to be frank statements of how people feel about deeply personal matters. All that separates them, however, from hundreds of Victorian poems about the burdens of women and the pains of childbirth is greater frankness in alluding to physical processes. But that frankness simply moves them toward bathos because their idiom remains that of Victorian platitude. For the frankness of subject matter, moreover, Sharp was less indebted to the French than to a strain of what he called Paganism that emanated more directly from Whitman than Baudelaire.

'The Prayer of Women' and similar runes are not a fair representation of the quality of *From the Hills of Dream.* Yeats divided the volume's poems arbitrarily into two kinds and said Fiona had mastered those with a 'Gaelic influence', but not those with an 'influence from modern literature'. An example of the latter is 'The White Peace':

> It lies not on the sunlit hill
> Nor on the sunlit plain:
> Nor ever on any running stream
> Nor on the unclouded main—
> But sometimes, through the Soul of Man,
> Slow moving o'er his pain,
> The moonlight of a perfect peace
> Floods heart and brain.

In this brief mood piece, Yeats found the thought 'too vague greatly to move or impress' him. In contrast, he was 'altogether moved and impressed' by 'The Rune of the Four Winds', which ends as follows:

> By the three dark winds of the world;
> The chill dull breath of the Grave,
> The breath from the depths of the Sea,
> The breath of To-morrow:
> By the white and dark winds of the world,
> The four and the three that are seven,
> That Man knoweth,
> That One dreadeth,
> That God blesseth—
>
>> Be all well
>> On mountain and moorland and lea,
>> On loch-face and lochan and river,
>> On shore and shallow and sea.

It would be hard to distinguish between these two poems with respect to 'vagueness' of thought or image. Neither is flawless, but the first certainly outshines the second in economy and control of language. 'The White Peace' is an effective mood poem which, largely due to the initial metre-breaking 'Floods' of its last line, surprises, delights, and sticks in the mind.

Anxious to promote the Gaelic influences in Fiona Macleod, Yeats preferred the runes because he thought they were authentic translations or representations of originals. At the close of the review, however, his critical sense returned. He singled out for praise too fine Fiona Macleod poems which are in 'rhyme and in regular measures' and which 'seem to be latest in date.' They are, he said, 'a great advance upon their fellows, and have occasional passages of a charming phantasy.' The first of these is 'The Moon-Child':

> A little lonely child am I
> That have not any soul:
> God made me but a homeless wave,
> Without a goal.
>
> A seal my father was, a seal
> That once was man:
> My mother loved him tho' he was
> 'Neath mortal ban.

He took a wave and drowned her,
She took a wave and lifted him:
And I was born where shadows are
I' the sea-depths dim.

All through the sunny blue-sweet hours
I swim and glide in waters green:
Never by day the mournful shores
By me are seen.

But when the gloom is on the wave
A shell unto the shore I bring:
And then upon the rocks I sit
And plaintive sing.

O what is this wild song I sing,
With meanings strange and dim?
No soul am I, a wave am I,
And sing the Moon-Child's hymn.[58]

Yeats's high opinion of this poem may have been influenced by its affinities with 'The Stolen Child,' his own lyric in which the fairies entice a human child to join them in a seacoast fairy land of play and pleasure.[59]

Yeats was also attracted to the poem because he had first-hand knowledge of its 'authenticity'. When he visited the Aran Islands in August 1896, he had been reading a Fiona Macleod story from *The Sin-Eater and Other Tales* (1895) called 'The Dan-nan-Ron' (The Song of the Seal) which depicts a man of the western islands who is rumoured to be descended from a seal and who is torn apart by the seals when he tries at the end of the story to join them in the sea. In reprinting that story in the spring of 1897, Sharp prefaced it with a note that begins: 'This story is founded upon a superstition familiar throughout the Hebrides. The legend exists in Ireland, too; for Mr. Yeats tells me that last summer he met an old Connaught fisherman, who claimed to be of the Sliochd-nan-Ron—an ancestry, indeed, indicated in the man's name: Rooney'.[60] In his review, Yeats described his conversation with the fisherman to demonstrate that 'The Dan-nan-Ron' is based in authentic legends and beliefs and that Fiona Macleod 'felt about the world, and the creatures of its winds and waters, emotions that were of one kind with emotions of these grave peasants, the most purely Celtic peasants in Ireland, and that she had become their voice, not from any mere observation of their ways, but out of an absolute identity of nature'.[61]

The second of the poems Yeats singled out for praise is 'In the Shadow', and again there is a special association. Before encountering it in the volume of collected poems, Yeats had seen it in the manuscript of Fiona Macleod's 'The Archer'. Near the beginning of that story, a fisherman sings 'In the Shadow' while his boat drifts near that of Ian Macleod and Seumas Maclean. The poem foreshadows the plot of the story:

Oh, she will have the deep dark heart, for all her face is fair;
As deep and dark as though beneath the shadow of her hair:
For in her hair a spirit dwells that no white spirit is,
And hell is in the hopeless heaven of that lost spirit's kiss.

She has two men within the palm, the hollow of her hand:
She takes their souls and blows them forth as idle drifted sand:
And one falls back upon her breast that is his quiet home,
And one goes out into the night and is as wind-blown foam.

And when she sees the sleep of one, ofttimes she rises there
And looks into the outer dark and calleth soft and fair:
And then the lost soul that afar within the dark doth roam
Comes laughing, laughing, laughing, and crying, Home! Home!

And is there any home for him whose portion is the night?
And is there any peace for him whose doom is endless flight?
O wild sad bird, O wind-spent bird, O bird upon the wave
There is no home for thee, wild bird, but in the cold sea-grave![62]

For Yeats, the poem contains a passage 'which expresses something almost beyond the range of expression'. It surely stands on its own as an evocation of the tragic feelings engendered in a man and woman who cannot consummate their love, yet it gains added poignancy by its placement in a realistic story about simple people who make their living from the sea. In his review, Yeats surely remembered that the story ended with a 'tall, shadowy woman' shooting an arrow at a fawn who leaps away sobbing into the night, its heart suspended, arrow-pierced, from a silver birch.

This poem and the story in which it occurs represent one of Sharp's most compelling attempts to dramatize his relationship with Edith and Frank Rinder.[63] Yeats did not know about that triangle when he reviewed *From the Hills of Dream*, and he thought the poem and the story were written by Fiona Macleod. It being likely, as I have said, that Sharp told Yeats in the spring of 1896 that he was in love with Fiona and that she was married, Yeats might have seen in poem and story a statement by Fiona Macleod about her personal circumstances, and might have identified her with the woman who must make a tragic choice. He would not have identified their author with the man who is rejected, as was the case, but in that rejected lover, he may have seen a reflection of his own situation.

There are many fine poems in the first edition of Fiona Macleod's *From the Hills of Dream*. Yeats recognized the quality of some of the best and overpraised others, demonstrating what he valued most in his own and others' work at the time. Throughout the review one senses his effort to bring Fiona Macleod in line with his own agenda and to dissuade her—and perhaps himself—from indulging in impressionism at the expense of expressing the real thoughts and feelings of real people. For poems such as 'The Moon Child' and 'In the Shadow', which combine the experiences and superstitions of Celtic people with symbolist methods, Yeats's praise was deserved.

A Cafe in Paris

Yeats's wrote his response to Fiona's September 1896 letter in early January 1897 in a cafe in Paris. Relaxed and friendly in tone, it demonstrates his full acceptance of the Fiona Macleod whom Sharp had created for him. Yeats had gone to Paris in early December where he was trying to start his novel, taking advice from Mac-Gregor Mathers about his projected Celtic Mystical Order, and meeting J. M. Synge, who was staying at the same hotel in the Latin Quarter (*CL2* 62-63, 69). It was there Yeats told Synge he should go to the Aran Islands. He planned, with Maud Gonne, her l'Association Irlandaise (founded 1 Jan. 1897) and, partly under her influence, moved into a period of intense public activity in the cause of Irish nationalism.

203 Boulevard Raspail, | Paris. | Tuesday

My dear Miss Macleod: I owe you a letter for a very long time & can only promise to amend & be more prompt with my replies in future. I have had a breathless autumn, always trying to make myself do more work than my disposition will permit; & at such times I am the worst of correspondents. I have just finished a certain speech in 'The Shadowy Waters', my new poem, & have gone to 'The Cafe de Musse du Cluny' to smoke & read the Irish news in the *Times*. I should say much about your book of poems but you will have seen my review in the *Bookman*. (I hope it was not misprinted my proof sheet was sent in rather late) & I have not the book here; I will return to it when I write from London. I have just now <at the moment> a plan I want to ask you about. Have you ever thought of writing a short play? Our Irish literary & politico-literary organizations are pretty complete now (I am trying to start a *Young Ireland Society*, among the Irish here in Paris, at this moment) and I think it would be very possible to get up celtic plays through these societies. They would be far more effective than lectures & might do more than anything else, we can do, to make the Irish, Scotch, & Other, celts recognize their solidarity. My own plays are too elaborate, I think, for a start & have also the disadvantage that I cannot urge my own work on committees. If we had two or three short & direct prose plays, of (say) a mythological and folk lore kind, by you & by some Irish writer (I may be able to move O'Grady. I have already spoken to him about it but vaguely) I feel sure we could get *The Irish Literary Society* to make a start. They have indeed for some time talked of doing my *Land of Heart's Desire*. My own theory of poetical or legendary drama, is that it should have no realistic or elaborate, but only a symbolic & decorative setting. A forest for instance should be represented by a forest pattern not by a forest painting. One should design a scene which would be an accompaniment but not a ref[l]ection of the text. This method would have the further advantage of being fairly cheap, & altogether novel. It would give one's work the remoteness of a legend. The acting should have an equivalent distance from common reality. The plays might be almost, in some cases, modern mystery plays. Your *Last Supper*[64] for instance would make such a play, while your story in *The Savoy*[65] would arrange as the strongest of plays of merely human tragedy. I shall try my own hand, possibly, at some short prose play also but not yet. I merely suggest these things because they are a good deal on my mind & not that I wish to burden your already full hands.

You know I am an occult student. Well I am trying to found some celtic invocations on certain medieval invocations. I have traced the four talismans of the Tuatha De Danaan, the sword, the lance, the cauldron, & the stone, further than Nutt has done, & found them in Medieval magic. I am working on this foundation &

trying to go back, from the medieval magic, with which they became connected, to the old celtic gods. I have seen a very learned & indeed powerful kabalist here on the subject & hope for the beginning of what might become a celtic magic. I have made some practical use of them but not enough yet to know their value. My 'Shadowy Waters' is magical & mystical beyond anything I have done. It goes but slowly however, & I have had to rewrite all I did in Ireland some years ago. Mr Sharpe heard some of it in London in its first very monotinous form. I wish to make it a kind of grave exstasy. I am also at the start of [a] novel which moves between the Islands of Arran & Paris, & shall have to go to Arran again about it. After these books I start a long cherished project—a poetical version of the great celtic epic tales Deirdre, Cuchullin at the ford & Cuchullins death & Dermot & Grania. I have some hope that Mr Sharpe will come to Paris on his way back to England.[66] I have much to talk over with him. I am fealing more & more every day that our celtic movement is aproaching a new phase. Our instruments are sufficiently perfect, so far as Ireland is concerned, but the proper use of them still remains & this can only be done by the <energy> imagination of a very few acting upon all.

My book 'The Secret Rose' was to have been out in December but it has been postponed to February.[67] If I have any earlier copies you shall have one. I am especially curious to know what you will think of a story called 'The Adoration of the Magi' which is a half prophecy of a very veiled kind.

                              Yrs ever, | W B Yeats[68]

In this letter Yeats raised with Fiona three topics that were of great concern to him. Inviting her to write short plays to promote the Celtic cause (and so identifying himself with 'Pan-Celticism'), he demonstrates that by early 1897 he had given considerable thought to the kind of plays he wanted for the movement. Based in Celtic myths and legends and in the lives of peasant people, they would portray—by their absence of realism, use of rituals, and evocation of spirits—interactions between the material world and the realm of spirits. In response to the request in this letter, Sharp planned many and finished—in 1900—two Fiona Macleod plays of the kind Yeats requested. But they came too late. The Celtic Literary Theatre, so postulated (according to Lady Gregory) as to accommodate plays by Fiona Macleod,[69] had by then, under the influence of Irish Nationalism, become the Irish Literary Theatre, and Fiona's plays were not welcome. But in January 1897, Yeats could even see which of Fiona Macleod's stories might become successful plays.

Second, Yeats introduced Fiona to his plan for the Order of Celtic Mysteries, a project that remained one of his principal preoccupations for many years. What he said about the project here casts some light on its background. One of three founding Chiefs of the Order of the Golden Dawn in London, MacGregor Mathers and his wife Moine, Henri Bergson's sister, had moved to Paris in 1892 where Mathers opened a new Ahathoor Temple of the Order and began to function as the leading personality of the Golden Dawn's Second Order which Yeats had joined in 1893. The Celtic Mystical Order had been on his mind since 1895. He received permission from Mathers to start it either during or shortly after this visit to Paris.

The new order would be modelled in form on the Golden Dawn but take its talismans and symbols from ancient Celtic myth. Its headquarters were to be on Castle Rock in Lough Key in Roscommon, but its membership would not be limited to Irish men and women. Yeats hoped to attract to his Irish Eleusis or Samothrace (*Au* 253-4) intellectuals and artists who could claim, by heritage or study, knowledge of or affinity with the ancient Celts. Mathers was already predisposed to the Celtic element of the proposed order. Having taken a new given name, 'MacGregor', and invented a Scottish ancestry for himself, and moving about Paris in a kilt and plaid in the MacGregor tartan.[70]

In this letter Yeats describes his current concerns regarding the order. He had equated the four traditional talismans of Irish myth and legend—sword, lance (or spear), cauldron, and stone—with the four suits of the tarot (*Mem* 125; *CL2* 74n.). Now he was trying to trace them back further to provide a concrete foundation for what 'might become a Celtic magic' and provide legitimacy for the order among hermeticists and other occultists. Under the influence of Mathers, Yeats believed the only way to develop a new authentically Celtic order was to combine knowledge of Celtic myth and legend with the power of vision. Thus he needed help from people who knew Celtic myth, who were committed to a revival of Celtic culture, and who could see through or beyond the material world. Since Yeats did not rate his own visionary capacity highly, he was on the lookout for new seers.

Far-fetched as such efforts appear in reconstructing them, they were inextricably bound up for Yeats with his determination to produce poems and stories and plays that would transform the lives of his contemporaries and live forever. 'The Shadowy Waters' at this stage still contained the eagle-headed beings called the *seabar*, and the 'grave exstasy' he envisaged for it approached the ritual he had in mind for the Celtic order. *The Speckled Bird* was also related to the Celtic Mysteries (which, in the last draft version, becomes a Grail Order).

Finally, Yeats shared in his letter to Fiona his concern about his own work. Writing to her in August, he had asked which of his two styles she preferred. Here he said he was 'curious' to know what she would think of 'The Adoration of the Magi' when it appeared in *The Secret Rose*.[71] There are strong affinities and significant differences between that story, which is informed by his plans for the Celtic Mystical Order, and Fiona Macleod's 'The Last Supper,' which Yeats had read the previous summer in *The Washer of the Ford* and which, he now says, would make 'a modern mystery play'. In 'The Last Supper' the authorial Fiona retells a story she heard from Art Macarthur, who as a child was visited by Iosa mac Dhe, or Jesus, an event that transformed his life. Art's story is simple and beautifully controlled. Feeling lonely and rejected, he was taken by Iosa to a huntsman's cottage at the far end of a Shadowy Glen where Iosa kissed his eyes so he would 'never be quite blind again' and so he could see the last supper: 'For I die daily', said Iosa, 'and ever ere I die the Twelve break bread with me.' Hereupon local legend enters for the twelve apostles are Weavers. Eleven in sequence take up three shuttles (identified as *Beauty*, *Wonder*, and *Mystery)* and weave their immortal forms, each associated with a positive human experience, before leaving to become part of the Web of Life that is Iosa. When the twelfth, Judas, weaves his immortal form with three different shuttles (*Mystery, Despair,* and the *Grave)*, that form is identified as Fear. He too enters the Web of Life where he will forever betray Iosa, the Prince of Peace. After this experience, we are told by Fiona Macleod that Art Macarthur, whose given name was not idly chosen by Sharp, possessed the gift of sight: 'His mind was a shell that held the haunting echo of the deep seas: and to know him was to catch a breath of the infinite ocean of wonder and mystery and beauty of which he was the quiet oracle'. Art now 'lies under the heather upon a hillside far away: but the Fisher of Men will send him hitherward again, to put a light upon the wave and a gleam upon the brown earth'. Simple, concrete, and fit for a child, Sharp's story also contains the hint of a coming apocalypse. Though Sharp was not a practicing Christian, Fiona Macleod retells a story about a saviour who is ever present in his spiritual form in the West of Scotland. He may make himself known at any time to poets and singers who, in turn, will bring their knowledge to others.

In contrast to this story, where Christianity is mediated only slightly by its Celtic context, Yeats's 'The Adoration of the Magi' is informed by his rejection of Christianity, his belief in magic, and his study and practice of hermeticism. It is a post-Christian story in which the Immortals, who may or may not number Jesus and the Christian God among them, control the world of spirit and flesh. Three wise men of the West of Ireland, learned in classical literature and philosophy, are drawn to a brothel in Paris where a prostitute lies dying. In the 1897 version of the story, she divulges the 'secret names' of the Immortals, in the 1925 version she gives birth to a unicorn (*VSR* 168 &v.). Either way, the event might constitute a turn of the cycle that will then begin working its way to its opposite, towards a rejection of the animalism and materialism represented by the house of prostitution and a regeneration of the spiritual dimensions of human life. That movement of regeneration will be centred in the West of Ireland where the new Magi live, a reflection of Yeats's interest in establishing there the headquarters of his Order. As Yeats told Fiona Macleod in this letter, the story is a 'half prophecy of a very veiled kind.' Central to the prostitute's message are the names of the 'immortals of Ireland and of their love for the cauldron, and the whetstone, and the sword, and the spear' (*VSR* 170v.). Yeats's story contains the seeds of apocalypse, but the differences of tone and underlying belief systems mark an important distinction between Yeats and Sharp that persisted, despite their efforts to bridge it, until Sharp died in 1905.

Yeats had found the shadows in the stories of Fiona Macleod and knew she saw visions, but he was not sure she was predisposed to using symbols, or talismans, to evoke them. Not everyone, after all, was a fitting recruit for the new Order whose forms and rituals would follow it closely. Yeats stopped short in his January letter of asking Fiona to join him in his great project. In describing his occult interests, however, he hoped William Sharp would stop in Paris on his way back to England; he had 'much to talk over with him'. One of those things, we can be sure, was the extent to which Fiona might be a suitable recruit for the work of the Celtic Mysteries. Yeats knew Sharp was not predisposed to join the Golden Dawn, but he saw visions, and was attracted to Celtic myth and lore because it moved so easily between the material world and the realm of spirits. For him, as well as for Yeats, the mystical vein of Celticism was an alternative religion.

Yeats might have thought Fiona the better recruit, because she was a more authentic Celt than Sharp. Fiona was retelling the stories she had heard from the people of western Scotland, and she was the more accomplished artist. She had a vital imagination and the ability to shape her raw materials into works of power and beauty. Finally, Yeats preferred the elusive Fiona as a co-worker on the new order's rituals because, unlike Sharp, she did not carry the baggage of London literary life wherein, as Yeats knew, Sharp was regarded by some as a comic figure. Fiona Macleod, as Sharp set her forth in print and in letters, was immune from all such impressions. She could never offend, and she was eminently proper and highly intelligent.

Yeats's letter demonstrates that he had become a willing participant in the drama of Fiona Macleod and that he wished to interact with her at a deep and personal level. Sharp, whose health had become more problematic as he struggled to carry on this drama and the literary double life its success demanded, was experiencing additional strain. Having created Fiona, he could not take credit for what he was writing. Committed as he was to maintaining that fiction, he was coming to the bittersweet recognition that he would not taste the rewards of her fame. That recognition had caused him to tell Yeats he was essential to Fiona Macleod's ability to write her stories and poems. Yeats accepted this, and his opinion of Sharp was greatly enhanced. Sharp did stop in Paris and, after testing Sharp's visionary powers with a tarot symbol and finding them acceptable, Yeats invited him and, through him, Fiona to participate with Maud Gonne and a few others in the effort to obtain by dream and vision materials for his Celtic Order. Flattered by the invitation, Sharp accepted for himself and for Fiona and set off to enlist the participation of Edith Rinder as a surrogate for Fiona Macleod. But those remarkable events take place in another act.

Meantime, the first act of the Yeats-Macleod-Sharp drama ends on a positive note. Yeats has become an enthusiastic participant. His self-interest is served by accepting Fiona Macleod as a colleague in retelling tales in prose, poetry and plays. He hopes that she will be able and willing to help him in the construction of the Celtic Mystical Order, and he values her opinion of his writing. After a shaky start a decade earlier, Yeats relationship with Sharp has progressed in 1896 to one of easy friendship. We know, but Yeats did not as yet, that the person who was responsible for bringing them together, Fiona Macleod, was a character of Sharp's invention, but a character who was based substantially on a real woman, Edith Rinder, with whom Sharp was deeply in love.

NOTES

1. *The Eighteen Nineties, A Review of Art and Ideas at the Close of the Nineteenth Century* (New York: Mitchell Kennerley, 1914), pp. 178-89.

2. This passage is from an essay called 'Prelude' which preceded 'Celtic: an Essay' when the latter was published in Fiona Macleod's *The Winged Destiny: Studies in the Spiritual History of the Gael* (London: Chapman and Hall, 1904). It may be found in vol. 5 of the Uniform Edition of *The Works of 'Fiona Macleod'* (London: William Heinemann, 1910), 167-79 (Hereafter cited *UE* in the text). 'Celtic: an Essay' was first published in the *Contemporary Review* in May 1900 and again, a few weeks later, in Fiona Macleod's *The Divine Adventure: Iona: By Sundown Shores* (London: Chapman and Hall, 1900), 291-308. When it appeared in the *Contemporary Review*, the essay was strongly criticized by some Irish nationalists because of its Pan-Celtic position. When it appeared as a separate publication (*Celtic: A Study in Spiritual History*, Portland, Maine: Thomas B. Mosher, 1901), it had been revised, and a Foreword was added which became the 'Prelude' from which Jackson took this passage.

3. *William Sharp (Fiona Macleod), A Memoir*, compiled by his wife Elizabeth A. Sharp (New York: Duffield & Company, 1910). Subsequent references to this single volume edition are noted in the text as *Memoir*.

4. Yeats was one of the founders of the Pan-Celtic Association in November 1898.

5. In *The Romantic '90s* (London and New York: G. P. Putnam's Sons, 114), Le Gallienne says Sharp further mystified him 'by saying that "Fiona Macleod" was shortly coming to London, and that he intended to introduce her to three people only—George Meredith, Mr. W. B. Yeats, and myself. The introduction to me was never made, and I believe it was all just part of Sharp's masterly game of hide-and-seek.' Ernest Rhys recalled Sharp's saying to him, 'I took her to see George Meredith, at his own earnest request; and he was enchanted by her dark-Highland Beauty' (*Everyman Remembers* [London and Toronto: J. M. Dent and Sons Limited, 1931], p. 79). The date of that visit can be pinned down precisely. In the *Memoir* (287), Elizabeth Sharp says, describing her husband's activities in 1897, 'On the 10th of June the author went for a night to Burford Bridge, in order to have some talks with George Meredith.' Meredith wrote as follows to Alice Meynell in a letter dated June 13, 1897: 'Miss Fiona Macleod was here on a day of last week: a handsome person, who would not give me her eyes for a time. One fears she was not playing at abashment. Even after I had brought her to laugh, the eyelids drooped. She spoke of your beautiful long letters. I repressed my start and moderated my stare'. See C. L. Cline (ed.) *The Letters of George Meredith* (Oxford: The Clarendon Press, 1970), III, p. 1268.

6. *CL1* 21-5. *The Sonnets of This Century* was published by Walter Scott in 1886 in the Canterbury Poets. Sharp's extensive preface is 'The Sonnet: Its History and Characteristics'. The anthology went through many editions (its name was changed after 1900 to *Sonnets of the Nineteenth Century*). When he wrote again to Katharine Tynan from Rosses Point in mid-August 1887, Yeats said he had been reading Phillip Bourke Marston's stories: 'Some of them are good—very good, but the most i[n]different and all a little feverish'(*CL1* 33-5). Sharp had produced an edition of Marston's stories, *For a Song's Sake, and Other Stories*, for Walter Scott soon after his friend died prematurely in February 1887. Yeats probably

received his copy from Sharp, but the volume evidently did nothing to alter Yeats's opinion of Sharp.

7. *Dante Gabriel Rossetti: A Record and a Study* (London: Macmillan and Co.) and *The Human Inheritance; Motherhood; Transcripts from Nature* (London: Elliot Stock).

8. *Everyman Remembers*, 76. Rhys's account of Sharp in 1931 drew on a perceptive and sympathetic article he published about his friend in the *Century Magazine* in May 1907: 'William Sharp and "Fiona Macleod."' Of Sharp's death in 1905, Rhys said in the article: 'The gate shut on one of the most vital spirits and one of the most imaginative men of our time.' Mrs. Sharp quoted extensively from Rhys's article in the *Memoir* (106-9). Rhys was also a close friend of Yeats and a member of the Rhymer's Club.

9. Thomas De Quincey, *Confessions of an English Opium Eater* (London: Walter Scott, 1886).

10. His second volume of poems was *Earth's Voices, Transcripts from Nature, Sospitra, and Other Poems* (London: Elliot Stock, 1884).

11. *Century Magazine* (May, 1907), 111.

12. *Memoir* 109 (in response to Rhys's comments in the *Century Magazine* article).

13. On 27 Feb. 1890 Yeats asked 'Have you heard Oscar's last good thing. He says that Sharps motto should be *Acutis decensus averni* (Sharp is the decent into Hell). The phrase as you know begins in the orthodox way *Facilis* (easy)' (*CL1* 212). Yeats assumed Katherine Tynan, who had met Sharp during her visit to London in summer, 1889, would share Wilde's derision.

14. *CL1*, 70-1. If Yeats did ask Sharp about a Canterbury edition of Thomas Davis, none appeared, possibly because his poems were so frequently reprinted by others for their Irish audience.

15. See Mary Helen Thuente's *W. B. Yeats and Irish Folklore* (Dublin: Gill and Macmillan, 1980) for a thorough and insightful discussion of the value and importance of Yeats's work on Irish folklore.

16. ALS, Huntington Library. See also *Memoir*, 166-8.

17. The Sharps spent six weeks in Heidelberg. He had received from Stedman an introduction to Blanche Willis Howard, the American novelist who had married the Court Physician of the King of Wurtenberg and become Frau Hof-Arzt von Teuffel. When Sharp visited her in Stuttgard in the autumn of 1890, they began planning an epistolary novel that became *A Fellowe and His Wife* (London: James R. Osgood and New York: Harpers, 1892). For this curious work, which consists of an exchange of letters between a German nobleman who stays home to attend to his business and his wife who goes off to enjoy the pleasures of Rome, Howard wrote the letters of the husband and Sharp, drawing on his experience in Italy, those of the wife. The letters he wrote for that novel during another visit to Germany in the autumn of 1891 are the first instance of his creating a female persona and speaking through her in a sustained fashion.

18. Edith Mary Wingate and Joseph Francis (Frank) Rinder grew up in Lincolnshire. The families were close friends, the Rinders having moved from Scotland to Skendleby Manor, Lincs. when Frank (b. 1863 at Barrogill Cottage, John O'Groats, Caithness) was a boy. Edith and Frank shared artistic aspirations felt to be 'advanced' in Lincs., where she was born in 1864. They were married in a registry office in London on 27 February, 1890. Frank's Scottish cousin, Henry Caird, and his wife Mona were their source of support in London. The Sharps

were also friends of the Cairds, and surely met the Rinders at least a year before the fateful trip to Rome. Mona Caird later wrote *The Morality of Marriage and Other Essays on the Status and Destiny of Women* (London: George Redway, 1897) and many other works championing the rights of women.

19. See my 'William Sharp as Bard and Craftsman', *Victorian Poetry*, X, 1, 1972.

20. Pharais, Macleod says in a footnote of the dedicatory introduction, is the genitive and dative case of Paras, the Gaelic for Paradise or Heaven. Elizabeth Sharp reported that '*Pharais* was not the first written expression of the new work. It was preceded by a short story entitled "The Last Phantasy of James Achanna" that in the autumn of 1893 was sent to *The Scots Observer*' where Henley declined it with 'a word of genuine encouragement'. According to Elizabeth Sharp, that story was rewritten several times and finally became "The Archer"' (discussed below). During 'the writing of *Pharais* the author began to realise how much the feminine element dominated in the book, that it grew out of the subjective, or feminine, side of his nature. He, therefore, decided to issue the book under the name of *Fiona Macleod,* that "flashed ready made" into his mind' (*Memoir*, 227). To avert speculation among critics that he was the author of *Pharais,* Sharp also arranged for Murray to publish simultaneously a collection of dramas and stories by William Sharp called *Vistas*. The frontispiece of *Vistas* reproduces Blake's engraving of Adam and Eve before the fall in *Paradise Lost*. Both books were published in Derby in Frank Murray's Regent Library series, and they were sold at his bookshops in Derby, Leicester, and Nottingham.

21. *The Celtic Twilight, Men and Women, Dhouls and Faeries* (London: Lawrence and Bullen) had been published in December, 1893.

22. This recalls Sharp's imagined rebirth in 'The Swimmer of Nemi'.

23. Elizabeth Sharp says, 'Owing to the publication of *The Sin-Eater* by a firm identified with the Scoto-Celtic movement the book attracted immediate attention. . . . No conspicuous modern Celtic work had hitherto been written in the English tongue [in Scotland] until the appearance of the writings of Fiona Macleod, and later of Mr. Neil Munro. *The Sin-Eater* was therefore warmly welcomed on both sides of the Irish Channel, and Fiona Macleod acclaimed as the leading representative of the Highland Gael, "our one and only Highland novelist"' (*Memoir*, 256-7). This volume (and the next two Geddes volumes appeared in blue boards with striking Celtic designs and lettering in gold, somewhat in anticipation of Althea Gyles's symbolical book covers for Yeats.

24. *Lyra Celtica: An Anthology of Representative Celtic Poetry*, Edited by Elizabeth A. Sharp, With an Introduction by William Sharp. Ancient Irish, Alban, Gaelic, Breton, Cymric, and Modern Scottish and Irish Poetry (The Lawnmarket, Edinburgh: Patrick Geddes and Colleagues, 1896). Hereafter noted in the text as *LC*.

25. Fiona Macleod's 'Celtic: an Essay' which appeared in the *Contemporary Review* in 1900 became a flashpoint for public arguments between Irish nationalists and Pan-Celticists. See fn 2.

26. *LC*, xlix. Walter Scott published in the autumn of 1896 in The Scott Library *The Poetry of the Celtic Races, and Other Studies by Ernest Renan*, trans., with introduction and notes, William G. Hutchison. Sharp's direct quotations from Renan show he was using an earlier translation. His paraphrase of Renan is very close to being a quotation as can be seen from comparing it to Hutchison (p. 2).

27. The torch and flame metaphor for the influence of Celtic writers reappeared frequently in the Fiona Macleod writings. Indeed, it became one of the metaphors

by which Sharp would try to explain to Yeats how a real woman generated within him the fictional Fiona Macleod and enabled him to produce the writings he signed with that name.

28. Edith Rinder, though married to an ardent Scot, was English.

29. Published by Geddes in Edinburgh in late November or early December 1896 as *From the Hills of Dream: Mountain Songs and Island Runes*.

30. *CL2* 47-9; partly in *Memoir* 269-70.

31. *CL2* 48n annotates these references.

32. Ernest Rhys and Richard La Gallienne, among others.

33. Sharp modeled Fiona's marriage on that of Mona Caird, Elizabeth's girlhood friend.

34. See above n. 20.. The story is included in the *Re-issue of the Shorter Tales of Fiona Macleod, Rearranged, with Additional Tales* (Edinburgh: Patrick Geddes & Colleagues, 1897), III, pp. 233-54. This three-volume, paper-covered edition (I. Spiritual Tales; II. Barbaric Tales; and III, Tragic Romances) was nicely designed, printed on heavy paper, and sold for a modest price. The volumes were issued in the early Spring. See also *UE*, III, 104-22, from which I have quoted passages. In the 1897 printing, Ian Macleod, one of the principal characters, is called Isla Macleod.

35. In the 1896 version, Isla whispers, 'My fawn,' and Silis's response is described as follows: 'the deadly frost in her eyes slew the dream that the brain of the poet dreamed. Then it slew the poet.'

36. See my 'W. B. Yeats and William Sharp: The Archer Vision' (*ELN*, VI, 4, 274-80). That article places the archer vision in early August. We now know it occurred on the night of 14 August. The later date does not affect the point of the article. Sharp would have received Yeats's letter to Fiona in late August. Yeats's Tillyra letter to Sharp was mailed from Rosses Point on 4 September, and Sharp would have received it a few days later, well before he completed 'The Archer' on 22 or 23 September and mailed it to Symons (*Memoir*, 227). Symons published in the November issue of *The Savoy* not 'The Archer', but another story Sharp sent him for consideration, 'Morag of the Glen'. In a letter to Fiona, he said he chose 'Morag' partly because ' you have had a difficulty in placing it elsewhere. It seems to me lunatic to object to it on the ground of morality; and it is certainly one of the most powerful things you have done' (ALS, National Library of Scotland).

37. See *CL2* 658-63.

38. See Kuno Meyer and David Nutt (eds.) *The Voyage of Bran*, I (London: David Nutt, 1895), pp. 151-2.

39. Coll's first vision, added three years later, injects immolation into Sharp's portrayal of the continuing frustration of his love for Edith and raises it to the level of myth. He has fallen victim to Diana, the shadowy huntress, who, in shooting out his heart and pinning it to a tree, has destroyed his capacity for love. Coll's second vision, that of the Great Shadowy archer shooting 'arrow after arrow against the stars' (directly mirroring Yeats's vision), casts the mythic love of Silias and Ian—Edith and Sharp—in cosmic dimensions as reflected in a vision sent by Sharp to Yeats from Fiona shortly after he had finished 'The Archer'.

40. The ALS, which remains in private hands, has no date. This return address was not used for the Fiona Macleod correspondence after June 1898. The formality

and brevity of the letter suggest it was written before the Fiona Macleod letter to Yeats of late September 1896. The most likely candidate for the book's identity is *The Washer of the Ford* which was published in May 1896 by Patrick Geddes and Colleagues. Many of the prose tales in that book contain poems.

41. Elizabeth Sharp had, by this time, taken over from her husband the post of art critic for the *Glasgow Herald* and wrote other occasional pieces for the paper. This work produced badly needed income.

42. Elizabeth Sharp printed most of this letter in her *Memoir*, but left out two important passages: (i) para. 2 in which Fiona Macleod implies she has been sailing about a good deal with William Sharp and says she and William Sharp are doing work together, and (ii) four sentences in para. 6 in which Fiona Macleod suggests an improvement in the Yeats poem.

43. i.e., *From the Hills of Dream.*

44. 'Annir Choille' is one of the stories in *The Washer of the Ford.*

45. This poem was first published in *The Savoy* 5 (Sept. 1896) 52. In *The Secret Rose* (London: Lawrence and Bullen, 1897), it became 'To the Secret Rose' and contained one revision in response to Fiona's suggestion: 'heavy' in line 7 became 'great', not 'slumbrous'.

46. In the missing letter, Yeats must have asked Fiona Macleod which of his two styles she preferred.

47. The bracketed words in this sentence do not appear in Sharp's pencilled draft. They are inserted above the lines in Mary's final copy in a hand that is probably Sharp's.

48. In his pencilled draft, Sharp first wrote 'Dante' and then crossed that out in favour of ' Blake'. Yeats's Blake paper, 'William Blake and his Illustrations to *The Divine Comedy*', was published in three parts in the July, August, and September issues of *The Savoy*. See also *CL2* 40 and Holbrook Jackson, *The Eighteen Nineties*, p. 50.

49. *John Sherman AND Dhoya* (London: T. Fisher Unwin, 1891).

50. *The Wind Among the Reeds*, not published until 1899.

51. Mrs. Sharp misread this word in Sharp's draft as 'bare'. In Mary's final copy it is clearly 'wan'.

52. When the next edition of *From the Hills of Dream* was published (Bangor, Maine: Thomas Mosher, 1901), another of its sections, 'Foam of the Past,' was dedicated to Yeats.

53. See Alan Denson (ed.) *Letters from AE* (London: Abelard-Schuman, 1961), pp. 17-8.

54. 'Miss Fiona Macleod as a Poet,' *Bookman* (December, 1896) (*UP1* 421-4).

55. Passages in the text are from the 1896 edition of *From the Hills of Dream*. When this poem first appeared in *Pharais*, the last two lines put a mother-in-law somewhat awkwardly into the picture: 'Whom he calleth Mother, | And Mother again of his wife and children'. Perhaps Sharp intended the man's mother to be the surrogate mother of his wife. In the final version, these lines have, at least, the advantage of maintaining mother and wife as separate persons.

56. Flavia Alaya, in a fine biographical and analytical study of Sharp, *William Sharp 'Fiona Macleod,' 1855-1905* (Boston: Harvard University Press, 1970), has written perceptively about Sharp's feminism and his preoccupation with the suffering of women. See especially pp. 123-33. She correctly points out that Sharp begins to focus on the pain and suffering accompanying childbirth in the mid-nineties, and

she raises the 'possibility that Sharp's anguished preoccupation with suffering in childbirth may have had its direct and immediate source in some miscarried attempts of his wife to have children.' Although entirely possible, there is no evidence that Elizabeth suffered a miscarriage. In any case, Sharp's concern with the suffering of women in childbirth pre-dates his marriage.

57.   'The Prayer of Women' translated into French by T. Rudmose-Brown appeared in *Vers et prose* (Dec. 1905-Feb. 1906), 84-5.

58.   In the second, 1901 edition of *From the Hills of Dream*, the last stanza reads:
>   I have no playmate but the tide
>   The seaweed loves with dark brown eyes:
>   The night-waves have the stars for play,
>   For me but sighs.

59.   This poem was first published in the *Irish Monthly* in December 1886 and then in *Poems and Ballads of Young Ireland* (1888), *Fairy and Folk Tales of the Irish Peasantry (1888), The Wanderings of Oisin and Other Poems* (1889), and *Poems* (1895). A favourite among Yeats's poems, it was probably known to Sharp at least as early as 1888 when it appeared in *Fairy and Folk Tales*, published by Walter Scott.

60.   *Re-issue of the Shorter Stories of Fiona Macleod,* III, 61.

61.   *UP2*, 42-5. Yeats may have described that conversation in the missing letter he wrote to Fiona in September 1896, or he may have 'told' it to William Sharp in person either in October in London or when they met in Paris in January 1897. Since Yeats knew that Sharp was close to Fiona Macleod, he would not have been surprised by her note.

62.   In the 1901 and subsequent editions of *From the Hills of Dream*, the last stanza reads:
>   There is no home in faithless love, O fool that deems her fair:
>   Bitter and drear that home you seek, the name of it Despair:
>   Drown, drown beneath the sterile kiss of the engulfing wave,
>   A heaven of peace it is beside this mockery of a grave.

63.   Sharp wrote a version of this story before beginning *Pharais*, and revised it several times. See n. 22.

64.   'The Last Supper' was one of the 'Legendary Moralities' in Fiona Macleod's *The Washer of the Ford* (Edinburgh: Patrick Geddes and Colleagues, 1896).

65.   i.e., 'Morag of the Glen', *The Savoy*, 7 (Nov. 1896).

66.   From mid-December 1896 until early January 1897, Sharp was in the south of France where he visited Catherine Ann and Thomas Janvier who were living in St. Remy (*Memoir*, 282-3). He met the Janviers during his first visit to the United States in September 1889 and described them in letter to his wife dated October 1 from New York: 'Among the new friends I care most for are a married couple called Janvier. They are true Bohemians and most delightful. He is a writer and she an artist . . . and both have traveled much in Mexico' (*Memoir*, 154). The Sharps and the Janviers became and remained close friends. William Sharp was particularly close to Catherine, and they corresponded frequently. She learned very early that Sharp was producing the Fiona Macleod writings. *The Washer of the Ford* was dedicated to C. A. J. and contained a long 'Prologue (To Kathia)' which began 'To you, in your far-away home in Provence, I send these tales out of the remote North you love so well, and so well understand. The same blood is in our veins, a deep current somewhere

beneath the tide that sustains us. We have meeting-places that none knows of; we understand what few can understand; and we share in common a strange and inexplicable heritage'. Sharp did stop in Paris on his return from Provence. In a letter to E. C. Stedman dated 25 January 1897, he said he had been in Scotland for about a week and that he had come there 'abruptly' from Paris where he spent a 'week or so' on his return from visiting the Janviers (ALS, Columbia University Library).

67. It was published on 5 April 1897.

68. *CL2* 72-5. Elizabeth Sharp printed this letter in the *Memoir* (280-2), but she omitted some portions and misread Yeats's handwriting in others.

69. *Our Irish Theatre, A Chapter of Autobiography, By Lady Gregory*, with a forward by Roger McHugh (Gerrards Cross: Colin Smythe, 1972), p. 20. Originally published in 1913, *Our Irish Theatre* contains the following sentences on this topic: 'I think the word 'Celtic' was put in for the sake of Fiona Macleod whose plays however we never acted, though we used to amuse ourselves by thinking of the call for 'author' that might follow one, and the possible appearance of William Sharp in place of the beautiful woman he had given her out to be, for even then we had little doubt they were one and the same person'. If Lady Gregory's recollection thirteen years after the fact is correct, others in the Irish Literary Theatre circle beyond her, Russell and Yeats knew by 1900 that Sharp was the author of the work of Fiona Macleod, that could well have been another reason not to produce the FM plays, especially in Dublin.

70. For a discussion of the early development of the Celtic Order, see Warwick Gould's ''The Music of Heaven': Dorothea Hunter,' *YA9*, 1992, esp. pp. 151-8.

71. This story and 'The Tables of the Law,' originally intended for *The Secret Rose,* were excluded from that volume by Bullen, the publisher, who printed them privately in a separate volume some months after he published *The Secret Rose* on 5 February 1897. See *VSR* 269-70.

In Fundamental Agreement:
Yeats and Wyndham Lewis

Peter L. Caracciolo and Paul Edwards

TWO MEN COULD HARDLY BE MORE DIFFERENT in style and ethos than Wyndham Lewis and W. B. Yeats. Yeats's feudalistic Irish Nationalism, mysticism and eccentric historicism are the antithesis of the younger painter-writer's cosmopolitan internationalism, anti-historicism and mechano-morphic vision of humanity. On closer inspection, Yeats and Lewis prove to have a surprising amount in common. The cultural vision of both extended way beyond Europe and they shared the view that a willed struggle with a contradictory version of the self was the basis of achievement in the arts. Each valued his apparent opposite at crucial moments. When Yeats was studying philosophy in the years following publication of the first version of *A Vision*, he suggested that the editor of *The Enemy* should read Plato's *Theaetetus*—advice that Lewis apparently took.[1] Yeats, in his turn, learnt from Lewis. *Time and Western Man* was one of the volumes the poet 'defied the doctors' by reading: 'Tell Wyndham Lewis . . . that I am in all essentials his most humble and admiring disciple', Yeats wrote to Olivia Shakespear in December 1927 (*L* 733-4). One of the longest chapters of Lewis's book is given over to a scathing attack on Oswald Spengler's *Decline of the West* ('this kind of sham does take in a great

110

many people, and it does have a far-reaching and extremely poisonous effect').[2] Yeats had acclaimed Spengler's book for its essential agreement with his own cyclical theory of history, but Yeats admired Lewis's intellectual passion, irrespective of whether he agreed with him. There was more to his admiration than this: he concluded that, beneath their disagreements, he and Lewis were 'in *fundamental* agreement' (*L* 733). An indication of what he meant is given by *A Packet for Ezra Pound* (1929), revised for the opening of *A Vision* (1937).

For Yeats it must have been particularly heartening that another artistic ally of Ezra Pound, and one even more closely associated with Pound than Yeats was himself, should share his own doubts about the *Cantos* and their author.[3] Lewis's criticisms, first published in *The Enemy* (Feb. 1927), and later incorporated into *Time and Western Man*, were directed as much against Pound's personality as his writing, and Yeats evidently agreed with Lewis that Pound was a 'Revolutionary Simpleton' and 'a kind of intellectual eunuch' (Yeats's 'sexless American professor') (*LDW* 23). Yeats used the philosophical analysis of the nature of reality that Lewis had provided in *Time and Western Man* as the basis of a critique of Pound's aesthetic in 'A Packet for Ezra Pound'. Lewis himself had formulated a critique of Joyce's *Ulysses* on this basis, but had not shown its (potentially greater) relevance to the *Cantos*. Lewis took his ideas from a loose interpretation of Hume and Kant. Perceived reality is the result of the shaping power of the mind (partly its habits) operating on raw sensation. This dualism can then be extrapolated to other orders of reality, as in the case of Yeats's criticism of the *Cantos* as 'without edges, without contours—conventions of the intellect—from a splash of tints and shades' (*AVB* 4), where the 'splash' can be thought of as 'raw sensation' (though of course raw sensation cannot literally be transmitted through language). The *Cantos* give this 'sensation', but lack the 'shape' given by the mind. Yeats has other things in mind besides Lewis's philosophy—Balzac's 'Chef d'oeuvre inconnu' above all[4]— but also Pound's own description of the composition of his famous Imagist poem, 'In a Station of the Metro': 'I do not mean that I found words, but there came an equation, not in speech, but in little splotches of colour'.[5] Pound equates his ambition with that of Wassily Kandinsky, who wanted his art to communicate directly, by-passing or dissolving the mental habits and conventions that enable us to navigate in (but apparently confine us within) a world of material objects. Significantly, in 1915,

Wyndham Lewis had criticised Kandinsky's painting (some aspects of which he nevertheless admired) as 'etherial', 'cloud-like' and generally lacking form: 'he is so careful to be passive and medium-like, and is committed, by his theory, to avoid almost all powerful and definite forms, that he is, at best, wandering and slack'.[6]

Lewis correctly attributed these characteristics of Kandinsky's work to his 'Blavatskyish' interests in theosophy, and his 'medium-like' attempts to convey the reality of the spirit-world in as unmediated a form as possible. Whether or not Yeats was familiar with Lewis's essay,[7] Lewis's apparent hostility to spiritualism would seem to embarrass an argument for their 'fundamental agreement'. For the raw material of *A Vision* is the product of precisely the kind of mediumistic enterprise that Lewis scorned in Kandinsky's splotches of colour and wandering lines. Since for both Lewis and Yeats the afterworld was actually a major preoccupation, and to some extent a region into which both could project their visions of a realm out of nature and time, this point needs some clarification. Yeats is often caricatured as a superstitious dupe of Romantic irrationalism and Lewis, because of his declared anti-Romanticism and predilection for satire (associated with a supposed Eighteenth Century 'Age of Reason') is often thought to be a rationalist, though of a peculiarly hysterical sort.[8] In fact Lewis was quite prepared to acknowledge the existence of a 'spiritual world', as he explained to a newspaper reporter who interviewed him about his decorative scheme for Lady Drogheda's drawing room in 1914. She was a believer in occult forces in general, and in her own psychic powers in particular, but there is evidence to suggest that Lewis was not merely supplying the reporter with a reply that would please his patroness.

> 'I believe the super-sensible will play a greater part in life and art as time goes on. The spiritual world is the Polar regions of our psychic existence, and useful ghosts will meet us on its borders, even if we do not adventure more. . . . The art of the future will reach out into these regions'.[9]

In *Time and Western Man* itself Lewis would affirm that 'If you say that creative art is a spell, a talisman, an incantation—that it is *magic* in short . . . I believe you would be correctly describing it. That the artist uses and manipulates a supernatural power seems very likely'.[10] Crucially, though, for Lewis these are powers to be used, not to be surrendered to in the fashion of a medium who would transmit them raw. Lewis would meet his ghosts on the 'borders' of the spirit world and negotiate, as he made clear in a 1919 article, 'The Credentials of the Painter'. He outlines two parameters within which human evolution could take place in the future. One is a virtually complete identification with matter, the other an equivalent dissociation from material existence in favour of religion or a 'superstitious fancy'. But between these defining limits some degree of dualism will always persist, and the function of art will remain to negotiate between the two realms of matter and spirit, whatever their relative importance in the future: Art can belong to neither realm exclusively, for it 'is a coin that is used on a frontier, but in neither of the adjoining countries, perhaps'.[11]

Yeats also, though far more committed to the practices of spiritualism than Lewis ever was, drew back from becoming merely a vehicle for the spirit world's messages. Like Lewis, he believed that that world was to be used—even though his enthusiasm for it was such that he had to be instructed by the spirits not to surrender to them: '"No," was the answer, "we have come to give you metaphors for poetry"' (AVB 8). Harper and Hood remind us that A Vision was an 'attempt to use the methods of empirical science' to order the revelations of the spirit world (CVA. xi). A Vision, as much as the poems that accompany it, is the result of the kind of negotiation that Lewis describes.

The empirical method, however, cannot be totally surrendered to, either, for, when taken to its logical extreme by Hume, it is a destroyer of all belief. It was Hume who drove the wedge between 'is' and 'ought', between our raw sensations logically broken down to their original components and the reality we actually experience, and he was notoriously unable to join them again. Hume himself was distressed by this, for it drove a wedge also between two parts of his life. One half was dissolved into a succession of raw sensation, or 'impressions', the other was reduced to a life of habit and imagination with nothing to underpin it. At the conclusion of the first book of A Treatise of Human Nature, having completed one of the most destructive analyses of phenomenal reality ever written, Hume is overwhelmed by the wreckage he has made (for he is himself the Humpty Dumpty his reasoning cannot put together again). But habit and imagination soon recover:

> Most fortunately it happens, that since reason is incapable of dispelling these clouds, nature herself suffices to that purpose, and cures me of this philosophical melancholy and delirium . . . I dine, I play

> a game of backgammon, I converse, and am merry with my friends;
> and when after three or four hour's amusement, I wou'd return to
> these speculations, they appear so cold, and strain'd, and ridiculous,
> that I cannot find it in my heart to enter them any farther.[12]

Perhaps Hume was easily satisfied (more probably he was aware that
the contrast between the enormity of the destruction and the trivi-
ality of the effective remedies actually added another turn of the
screw); but others have placed their faith in more imposing principles as a means of restoring coherence. Hence, it could be argued,
the Romantic Movement. But as faith in the efficacy of
Romanticism declined (as it was bound to, while science and reason
continued their processes of atomisation), those for whom backgam-
mon, chat and alcohol were not sufficient had to resort to constructs
that were frankly the products of artifice, conventions of the
intellect. Others, such as Ezra Pound (in Yeats's estimation), still
hoped that coherence would emerge from their impressions and
'splashes of colour' as an order of nature itself, a hierarchy showing
'That it is of thrones, and above them: Justice'.[13]

The Romantic and post-Romantic enterprises still work within
that bifurcated scepticism of Hume's, as Yeats appears to acknowledge in his own version of Hume's dilemma, the famous, magnificent conclusion to the 'Introduction' to *A Vision*. Here he
arrives at the same crux as Hume did, only he arrives from the
opposite direction:

> Some will ask whether I believe in the actual existence of my cir-
> cuits of sun and moon. . . . To such a question I can but answer that
> if sometimes, overwhelmed by miracle as all must be when in the
> midst of it, I have taken such periods literally, my reason has soon
> recovered; and now that the system stands out clearly in my
> imagination I regard them as stylistic arrangements of experience
> comparable to the cubes in the drawing of Wyndham Lewis and to
> the ovoids in the sculpture of Brancusi. They have helped me to
> hold together in a single thought reality and justice.[14]

It is part of Yeats's cunning that he chooses these two visual artists,
both championed by Ezra Pound, as a contrast with the 'Kandins-
kian' practice of Pound himself, alluded to earlier in the essay.[15]

The Kantian solution to Hume's dilemma provides a guarantee
for the reliability of our perceptual reality. Reality simply doesn't
show up for us in its 'raw' form, before the mind does its work on

it. But both Yeats and Wyndham Lewis were profoundly influenced by Nietzsche, who scorned the Kantian guarantee, and thought of consciousness in evolutionary terms as a factor of social (and by implication cultural) development:

> our becoming conscious of our sense impressions, our power of being able to fix them, and as it were to locate them them outside of ourselves, has increased in proportion as the necessity has increased for communicating them to *others* by means of signs.[16]

In this way, reality becomes relativised, and the philosophical idealism that both Yeats and Lewis espoused is consequently haunted by an anxiety about the solidity of the world, which now depends upon the continuance of a tradition of its actually being thought of as solid, rather than on immutable Kantian categories. Yeats's Berkeley is 'God-appointed', yet the world (that Berkeley, at least, was confident of having demonstrated to be 'solid'), in Yeats's post-Nietzschean formulation, 'Must vanish on the instant if the mind but change its theme'.[17] Elsewhere Yeats envisages a less abrupt disappearance of the solid world, prescribing a Nietzschean valuation of values—different ones for different cultural traditions—to prevent its atomisation:

> A table of values, heroic joy always, intellectual curiosity and so on—and a public theme: in Japan the mountain scenery of China; in Greece its cyclic tales; in Europe the Christian mythology; this or that national theme (*E&I* viii-ix).

Breaking from his inherited tradition—part of which, he says, comes to him 'in super-normal experience'—would be for Yeats 'breaking from some part of my own nature'. But though he has not abandoned this tradition, he is conscious that others have. Civilization has reached a point that all civilizations reach, at which 'Caesar is killed, Alexander catches some complaint and dies; personality is exhausted . . .' And, says Yeats, using an image of a bundle of firewood that cannot but remind us of Hume's atomisation of the personality into a collection of unrelated perceptions, when tradition is abandoned, 'we are broken and separate, some sort of dry faggot, and the time has come to read criticism and talk of our point of view'. (Yeats implicates himself in this fragmentation here, for he is introducing the reader to a collection including criticism.) In this situation, Yeats concedes (with a reluctance not noticeable in his

Introduction to *A Vision*) that 'cubes, triangles [and] ovoids, that are all stiff under the touch' may be an appropriate substitute for the description of 'desirable people, places [and] states of mind' that remains his own preference (*E&I* viii-ix).

Yeats's nostalgia can, somewhat surprisingly, be parallelled in an unpublished typescript of Lewis's, 'The Critical Realists'. Yeats cannot have seen it (though we cannot know what the two men discussed face to face).

> Art, and civilization generally, is in a sense a refinement of the old age of the race: the objects of a great civilization like the Chinese are (in the sense of Hume's psychology) its *images*. (Our western youth and newness without being dignified by the blasts of 'sensation' hardly attains to art in the chinese sense. Our barbary seems rather to be 'dying young'.[18]

Like Yeats, Lewis here sees the process of civilization as, if not continuous with, at the very least analogous to, the process by which raw sensation is solidified in ordinary perception. In both cases, the past and the dead have a crucial role: 'What life is busy doing, fundamentally and all the time, in its material evolution, is getting individuality; separating itself, fencing itself off, intensifying its particularity. But that can only be done by a progressive *hardening* and stabilizing—by a compromise between itself and death'.[19]

Desolate Places and the Great Wheel

Besides this 'fundamental agreement', Lewis and Yeats impinged on each other's work in a variety of ways. For Yeats, Lewis's example afforded a kind of moral encouragement by its implicit support of his own positions, and he was happy to repay in the form of endorsements of Lewis's writing.[20] It is possible that Yeats was alerted to the interest of Lewis's recent writings by their common friend, Thomas Sturge Moore, who had originally introduced them to each other around 1909, when Lewis, newly returned from several years' wandering in Europe as an art student, would attend lunches with Moore at the Vienna Café.[21] Around 1926, with the publication of Lewis's *The Art of Being Ruled*, Sturge Moore and Lewis renewed their connection. This did not lead immediately to a meeting between Yeats and Lewis; indeed, Lewis might well have felt that Yeats was unlikely to admire his work. He had written (somewhat cryptically) to Sturge Moore in 1916 when trying to place his recently-completed novel, *Tarr*, with a publisher. Sturge Moore had informed him that Yeats had refused to back an application to the Royal Literary Fund:

> As to Yeats: = Pound suggested that he should take a section of my book down to the country with him, and read it to Yeats, with a view to subsequent action in the direction of the *Fund*. = I did not fall in with this suggestion, as I knew Yeats would not like the book, and also that he can hardly approve of me? You see of course what I mean.[22]

Certainly Yeats admired the revised *Tarr* that Lewis issued in 1928 (*L* 762-63). He had however been fascinated earlier by Lewis enough to regard him as important in the scheme of *A Vision*. On 30 Nov. 1917, only a week into the mediumistic activities upon which the book is based, he asked the Control, 'Can you tell me where Wyndham Lewis comes?' (*YVP1* 131). The replies to this and later questions were perceptive about Lewis's character: 'Short passion—stiff vanity destroying emotion—long curiosity—supple kindness', and 'obscurity & passion (?) about self caused by the very desire to go to the root of the self'.[23] These perceptions go beyond mere approval or disapproval.

Whatever Lewis thought about Yeats's attitude, his own work had begun to take him into territory he would have known interested Yeats—the next world. Lewis regarded the world of art as 'out of nature' in Yeats's sense, and the condition of death as at least an effective analogy or symbol of this condition—'[a]nything living, quick and changing, is bad art, always', says his surrogate artist, Tarr. The living is bad art, paradoxically, because it can die, whereas art cannot.[24] In the twenties, Lewis began a complex fictional project ('Joint') that eventually developed into *The Childermass* (1928), *The Apes of God* (1930) and the unfinished *The Human Age*, (1955, a continuation of *The Childermass*). The exact development of this project has not yet been fully traced, but some tentative suggestions are possible.[25] First, it was based on the preoccupation identified in Yeats's scripts as a 'desire to go to the root of the self', and on the paradox that the stable self is a fictional projection, or emanation, from something more real yet less palpable and determined. 'Joint' was to be about a hierarchy of reality, and about the Calvinistic fatality inherent in the behaviour of fictional characters.[26] Among modern writers, the chief influences on this project were Joyce and

Pirandello.[27] The creations of the writer can be thought of as ghosts, dependent on a higher order of personality for their being; they are 'apes' of their creator (who is himself ultimately an ape of God).[28] This was a metaphysical critique of life (in the sense that the world of the dead, and the world of art, always constitute a critique of life), but Lewis sought to overlay this metaphysical level with another that could be read as an ideological critique of contemporary society. In the event, the offshoots of the 'Joint' project both present an ideological appearance that obscures their metaphysics (even though that metaphysics can be recovered).[29]

The Childermass presents an afterlife (the scene is laid 'Outside Heaven') in which the dead are insecure about their identity. In a corrupt process of 'judgement' that is a contemporary equivalent of Calvinistic determinism, the ruling authority, using all the techniques and tricks of modern cultural and political indoctrination, persuades the dead to settle for stereotypical roles as the identities in which they will be perpetuated in 'Heaven' (the walled city beyond the Styx). The presiding judge, a bombastic Mr Punch-like hunchback called the Bailiff, appears to have usurped St Peter's role as Heavenly Gate-keeper, and to be more a Zeitgeist than an eternal authority. He is opposed by some of the dead, organised into a band of militant enthusiasts for 'classical' and 'Aryan' values by a figure known as Hyperides. Although the *Childermass* project was set aside uncompleted after publication of the first part,[30] Lewis indicated in a letter to Sturge Moore that he planned the work to culminate in a version of Armageddon ('after the Hyperideans are disposed of'): 'the whole affair ends in chaos'.[31] *The Childermass* is evidently intended as a Dantesque myth through which contemporary history can be presented in several perspectives—some metaphysical, 'eternal', or religious, some secular and historical.[32] It was this use of the myth of the afterworld, particularly in placing the present in a vast cycle of history, that was one of the features of the work that must have excited Yeats, and prompted his enthusiastic letters about it to Olivia Shakespear and Lewis himself.

Not surprisingly, Yeats seized on the figure of the Bailiff: 'The Baily is of course my Hunchback—phase 28', he wrote to Olivia Shakespear (12 August 1928, *L* 745). The hunchback is actually discussed in Phase 26, and the coincidence with Lewis's Bailiff is indeed remarkable:

he is full of malice because, finding no impulse but in his own ambition, he is made jealous by the impulse of others.[33] He is all empha-

sis, and the greater that emphasis . . . the more does he display his
sterility. If he live amid a theologically minded people, his greatest
temptation may be to defy God, to become a Judas, who betrays,
not for thirty pieces of silver, but that he may call himself creator
(*CVA* 111).

Yeats wrote to Lewis, c/o Mrs Shakespear, mentioning the connection with *A Vision*, which he, apparently rightly, assumed Lewis had
not read. With *The Childermass* still only half-completed, Lewis
seems to have been more than simply politely desirous of seeing
Yeats's work. In a draft letter dated Sep. 18, 1928, Lewis writes, 'I
am very anxious to get your book 'Vision.' [I believe it contains
some things that might enlighten me (*deleted*)] I am now going to a
bookseller to see if it is still available in its first form. . . . I am very
curious to see what it contains'.[34] This might seem to rule out the
possibility of Yeats's psychical researches having influenced the
composition of the first section of *The Childermass*. Yeats assumed
that a letter sent to Olivia Shakespear would easily reach him. Her
acquaintanceship with Lewis was close; he had probably received
from her an account of the Yeatses' occult activities, and hints of the
system to which they led. In 1926 (when he was working on the
Childermass drafts) Lewis's relationship with Mrs Shakespear was
close enough for him to produce some of his most esoteric
paintings—a set of three elaborate watercolours of totemic
forms—particularly intended as a decorative scheme for her drawing
room. Lewis knew what would appeal to his patron, and no doubt
provided her with a key to these intriguing images.[35]

As well as having heard details from Mrs Shakespear, Lewis is
likely to have read the essay on the afterlife that Yeats composed in
1914, 'Swedenborg, Mediums, and the Desolate Places'.[36] The portion of *The Childermass* that Yeats (along with most readers) found
most fascinating was the first 120 pages, before the arrival of the
Bailiff at his theatrical court. 'These first 100 [*sic*] pages are the first
region of the dead as the ghosts everywhere describe it', Yeats's letter to Shakespear continues. His recognition is not altogether surprising.[37] Much of this section of the book was written in the later
stages of composition, after the publication of *Time and Western
Man*, and it may have been Yeats's reported enthusiasm for the book
that prompted Lewis to expand this portrayal of the desolate 'time-
flats' surrounding the encampment of souls awaiting judgement.

A closer consideration of *The Childermass*'s treatment of history
virtually reverses the supposition that Lewis's polemical attack on

Oswald Spengler could be taken as a sign of fundamental disagreement with Yeats over history. Whether Lewis's presentation of Western history in 1928 quite matches Yeats's *Vision* schema or not, he shares with Yeats a vision of the present moment in the perspective of a longer cycle. E. W. F. Tomlin drew attention to this cyclical underpinning of *The Childermass* in his 1955 pamphlet on Lewis, when he remarked on the significance of the *Maha-Yuga* symbol adorning the Bailiff's Punch-and-Judy booth: 'the *Maha-Yuga* is the name in Vedanta doctrine for a complete cycle of history.' Other symbols suggest to Tomlin that the 'successive decline in human righteousness' taking place across this cycle has reached a nadir.[38] The sense of eternal recurrence is increased by the narrator's description of the arrival of the dead at the encampment outside Heaven: 'With the gait of Cartophilus some homing solitary shadow is continually arriving in the restless dust of the turnpike'.[39] Separate souls here become one arriving repeatedly, the 'turnpike' evokes a sense of not just a toll-paying road but also of rotation (the *OED* records suggestions of a turnstile, indeed, of a spiral or winding stair[40]—another Yeatsian parallel), and 'restless dust' evokes a perpetual redistribution of particles. More important is 'Cartophilus', however; Lewis means Cartaphilus, or Ahasuerus, the 'Wandering Jew', condemned to live through the whole cycle of human history. This allusion also links *The Childermass*, through a passage deleted from his attack on Spengler's fatalism, to *Time and Western Man*. Lewis must have deleted the passage because it revealed more imaginative sympathy on his part with cyclical ideas of history (brought into consonance with Einsteinian physics) than his official polemical stance ought to have allowed:

> Slightly changed, changed into very slightly different people, we are, for the 'historic' mind, always passing again, in our periodic and cyclic course, the same objects, and historic features, and experiencing, with slight modifications, the same passions. 'I have been here before: How long ago I may not know: But when your head turned so' etc.—And these things are as *true*, and obvious, to us today at all events, as the rising of the sun or the disintegrating property of fire. These other selves, at other places in what we call Time, advancing on such and such 'world lines', in their eternal courses, like generations of a new Cartophilus, are the strictest realities.[41]

In his imaginative work, then, Lewis was prepared to entertain ideas he would not endorse in polemics. He had a particular polemical reason for repudiating cyclical versions of history. He wanted the European mind to break free from this habit of thinking: 'The Great War and the wars that are now threatened are the result of the historic mind. It is the time-mind at work: indeed it is peculiarly useful to the promoters of wars, hence its popularity. It says "*It's time for* another war."'[42] Lewis's fear is that subservience to ideas of recurrence will make the vision embodied in Yeats's 'The Second Coming' more likely.[43] It may have been a similar fear that became one of the obstacles preventing him from completing his own imaginative account of Armageddon in the thirties; what began as a warning increasingly came to look like a prophecy.[44] It reappears in a recognizably Yeatsian context in Lewis's other major imaginative work of the period, *The Apes of God.*

Likewise, just as Lewis was imaginatively compelled by Spengler's ideas, so eventually Yeats felt the necessity to break free from their determinism. In 'The Phases of the Moon' Aherne hints at an 'escape' from the Wheel; the revised version refines on the first edition, envisaging the mysterious possibility of transcendence onto the spiritual plane: this concept of the *Thirteenth Cycle* or *Cone* or *Sphere* 'may deliver us from the twelve cycles of time and space' (*AVB* 210). Neil Mann observes this 'anti-universe, akin to the angelic world of Swedenborg' (and standing 'in for an absconded god') is related to the world of 'the Return' in Yeats's spiritualism, that educative process successfully undergone by certain souls in the After-life; Yeats 'appears unconcerned by the almost Calvinistic separation of an elect of "God's athletes" . . . from the rest of humanity'.[45] Significantly, much the same spiritual conditions, philosophical attitudes and narrative patterns are discernible in Lewis's own Dialogue of the Dead, *The Childermass* and its various sequels. Mann emphasises, however, Yeats's fundamental indifference to this realm of absolute transcendence (where 'all the gyres converge in one . . . all the planets drop in the sun'), and stresses his 'anti-Religious conception of the divine', originating in 'a form of Romantic anthropocentrism'. Yeats's God has 'absconded' at such a distance that His attributes 'are so absolute as to become almost irrelevant to man.' (*YA8* pp. 161, 166). Lewis shares Yeats's Romantic anthropocentrism, and Yeats might have at times agreed with Lewis's pragmatic conclusion about his 'abdicated' God that 'it is most true and better to *say* there is *no* God'.[46]

Baghdad and Byzantium

Lewis and Yeats met again: 'in later years, the late twenties, I would meet him at Dulac's in Holland Park. I remember more than one tea, it seems to me, at Mrs Shakespears when Yeats was there. I seem to remember a meeting with him about the date you [Wade] mention in 1929'.[47] By Yeats's account of the 1929 meeting to Olivia Shakespear, both men were 'too cautious, with too much sympathy for one another not to to fear we might discover some fundamental difference' (4 May 1929, *L* 763). They met again at Lewis's Ossington Street flat, where Lewis showed Yeats some recent paintings of a tower. Mrs Lewis reported in a letter, 'I know Yeats was very intrigued by them, found some mystical interest in them, W[yndham] said', and to Lewis's biographer she reported more specifically that Yeats had remarked that the towers expressed 'just what I felt about life'.[48] If they did so, it may well have been at least partly because Lewis's new connection with Yeats had stirred his interest in Yeats's latest work, and the poems of *The Tower* had influenced his visual imagination. 'The Gift of Harun Al-Rashid' would certainly have interested Lewis, if not for its particular story, at least for its aura of *The Arabian Nights* and the Caliphate of Baghdad.[49] The only important large oil that Lewis produced in the late twenties is called *Bagdad* (Plate 1), and it is likely that Yeats or Sturge Moore would have seen it, either in Lewis's studio, or when it was exhibited by Curtis Moffat at the Redfern Gallery in the summer of 1929.[50] It represents a dream-vision of a white staircase-like form, half totem, half tower, standing in a blue vacancy and contemplated by floating sculpted heads and other forms.

In Lewis's personal mythology, Baghdad had a significance similar to that held by Byzantium in Yeats's. His 1919 pamphlet, *The Caliph's Design*, which is one of the great unknown manifestos for Modernism and contains some of the profoundest thinking about art produced by the movement, begins with a short parable set in Baghdad. The Caliph orders his engineers, on pain of death, to produce plans for a new street, based on some Vorticist sketches he has produced;

> and by ten o'clock next morning a series of the most beautiful plans that had yet been made in Baghdad (retaining with an exact fidelity the masses and directions of the potentate's design) were ready for

their master. And within a month a strange street transfigured the heart of that cultivated city.[51]

The parable presents in archaizing and orientalizing form Lewis's ambition for a Modernism that would transform the face of modern London. *Bagdad* has long been recognised as a visual translation of this fantasy: the 'staircase' form culminates in a stylised vista of a modern urban environment with sunny spots of greenery. But the image also brings nearer to the surface the perhaps unconscious historicism implicit in the original vision; that the modern utopia is conceived as a return to an ideal past. This aspect of the painting has recently been commented upon by Andrew Causey, who also notes the contrast between its air of dark mysticism and the sunlit assertiveness of *The Caliph's Design* itself. Causey draws attention to Lewis's anti-historicism and his hostility to Spengler but adds that Lewis was by no means unaffected by Spengler's cyclical morphology: 'Spengler's belief that history was cyclical not linear led him to envisage as contemporary, events occurring in the same chronological phase of different historical cycles. Lewis quotes Spengler saying that Baghdad and Washington are contemporary because they are similarly positioned in late phases of their respective civilisations'.[52]

There seems to be an overlay of secular and metaphysical (or eternal) levels in this painting (as in *The Childermass*), though without the novel's contemporary satirical dimension. The 'staircase' form, rising from chaotic elements at the base to an ideal order at the top can be interpreted temporally as a complete 'cycle' of civilisation, its forms equally those of Babylon, Baghdad and a Lewisian modernist architecture.[53] The cycle is contemplated by the dreaming, fictive heads of philosopher-rulers, floating like djinn in mid-air, outside time. At the top left of the image is a bird-like contemplative form. This can be identified with the Ancient Egyptian *ka*. W. J. Perry, an anthropologist and historian of the 'diffusionist' school (whose work Lewis knew well), offers an explanation that illuminates more than just Lewis's painting; for in Perry's account the admirer of Yeats recognises an avatar or type of the 'falcon' which gyres away from Christ 'the falconer' at the start of 'The Second Coming':

In Egypt . . . the king . . . was looked upon as a manifestaton of the sun-god. . . . This identification was accomplished at the coronation, when the ka, the double of the hawk . . . descended from the sky and incarnated itself in the king. When the king died, the hawk-double returned to Horus, to be incarnated in the next occupant of the throne.[54]

The *ka* is thus an eternal ruling spirit; its identification with the sun symbolises its role as source of all civilization. In Lewis's painting the sun can be seen as a small yellow disc in the centre, towards the top. As well as looking back to Lewis's earlier preoccupations, and summarising his earlier ambitions, this painting looks forward to the series of paintings on historical themes that he was to paint in the thirties. In these, too, architecture features prominently, as relics of a primeval civilization from which we have declined, and signs of a possible future renewal. These paintings also offer a critique of the particular cyclical repetitions of European history—migration, struggle, conquest and assimilation or destruction—that Lewis felt were leading a sleepwalking modern Europe once again to war on a terrible scale.[55]

It will readily be seen how the spirit of such a painting as *Bagdad* would evoke a sense of kinship between Lewis and Yeats. Although the particular terms of Lewis's mythology here are not quite Yeats's, it is certainly possible that Lewis's 'winding stair' may have influenced the cover design produced by Sturge Moore for Yeats's next volume of poems, produced in 1933 (making allowance for Moore's curious fusion of art-deco and fin-de-siècle styles). And there may be a more direct connection in *Bagdad* with Yeats's *A Vision*. In the first version of that book, the vision is revealed to the Caliph of Baghdad by Kusta ben Luka, and Book I, 'What the Caliph Partly Learned' commences with the poem 'The Wheel and the Phases of the Moon', in which Michael Robartes sings the phases of the moon (the phases of Yeats's cyclical version of history). While *Bagdad* encodes Perry's version of the sun-myth, far more prominent than the small solar disc in the painting is a large blue and white disk at the top of the picture, clearly representing the crescent moon. By comparing this image of partial occlusion with the diagram of the phases of the moon on p. 13 of *A Vision* (1925), it can be seen to be 'the crumbling moon' of the 28th phase (though in reversed, mirrored form). This, it will be remembered, is precisely the phase that Yeats had identified as being represented in Lewis's *The Childermass*.

In the 1930s, Wyndham Lewis returned to painting. *Bagdad* had been his only major painting since 1923, but over 50 oils are recorded as having been painted in the thirties, as well as many drawings and watercolours. The period was one of serious ill-health for Lewis, and he underwent several major operations. Although considerably younger than Yeats, he became imaginatively preoccupied with the perilous crossing the soul must make when the dying animal to which it is tied is finally consumed. Clinics and images from the sick-room feature among the series of oils that Lewis exhibited in his major 1937 exhibition at the Leicester Galleries.[56] Another set of images have a more direct reference to Yeats's imaginative world, taking the soul's journey as their subject: *One of the Stations of the Dead* (M P50), *Queue of the Dead* (M P56), *Departure of a Princess from Chaos* (M P64) and, most sublime and terrifying of all, *Inferno* (M P72)—a depiction of the damned painted in emulation of Signorelli's Orvieto fresco—in which, according to the artist, 'a world of shapes locked in eternal conflict is superimposed upon a world of shapes, prone in the relaxations of an uneasy sensuality which is also eternal'.[57]

In the works of the thirties where a direct influence from Yeats is most easily discerned, the connection is made through Sturge Moore. In his essay, 'The Visual World of Wyndham Lewis', which opens Walter Michel's *Wyndham Lewis: Paintings and Drawings*, Hugh Kenner discusses Lewis's *ATHANATON* (M 787, 1933 Plate 2) as a visual transposition of Yeats's 'Sailing to Byzantium'.[58] Certainly the nautical shapes in the picture recall the elements of a voyage-quest in the poem, and there is a strange wafer-thin profile on the right that suggest 'such a thing as Grecian goldsmiths make of hammered gold.'[59] A subtle amalgam of mysterious shapes, evocative of the epiphanies, elongations and not least the eyes of Byzantine mosaic, ivory and icon, the labyrinthine geometries and shape-changing zoomorphs of Celtic ornament, as well as the similarly expressive distortions of more exotic 'primitive' cultures the world over, out of such a potent mixture in *ATHANATON* Lewis conjures up this spell-binding abstract of a Yeatsian phantasmagoria. But in what Kenner perceptively views as a Modernist approach to an 'emblematic picture', Lewis's use of collage is more akin to a later poem of Yeats, 'Byzantium', where narrative is replaced by a haunting montage of spiritual manifestations. Indeed, over on the left of the composition beneath the Greek inscription signifying 'immortal', is depicted in wittily sartorial fashion 'an agony of flame that cannot singe a sleeve'.[60] There are other influences on the painting, some of them no less distinctly Yeatsian. Above 'the flames that no faggot feeds and no steel has lit', on the top of the tower 'floats an image, man or shade. | Shade more than man, more image than a shade'. Although only the eyes[61] and the grotesque hands and black wings of this ghostly presence are visible, gradually we discern that 'the superhuman' cradles what looks like a crying baby. Paradoxically this supernatural nursing 'humanises' a scene twice used by Sturge Moore as a telling detail in cover designs for books by Yeats, *Reveries* (1916) and *Selected Poems* (New York: Macmillan, 1921; see Plate 3). In both designs, emerging from the sky, a supernatural hand touches a baby perched on a pillar rising from the sea. At the bottom of this pillar, a door opens and a woman descends the last steps of the winding inner staircase. The same structure is depicted in cross-section on the cover design of *The Winding Stair*. We argue that Sturge Moore has been influenced by Wyndham Lewis, but *ATHANATON* suggests that the influence was mutual.[62] Employing the same X-ray technique[63] as Sturge Moore would use later the same year, in this gouache, made (it would seem) early in 1933,[64] Lewis shows two women below the crying baby—much as in the designs of the spine and front cover for *Reveries*, if these images are taken together.[65] Sturge Moore's design for *Selected Poems* is more complex than that for *Reveries* but the most significant new details are the waves that break at the foot of the now fluted column of the tower. Below this is a sort of frieze, perhaps a shore-line, crowded by faces; some of these hold antique masks. This strange beach scene of 1921 looks forward to significant details on the 1933 cover. Sturge Moore took pains to give *The Winding Stair* a cover that would practically function as the visual equivalent of the contents page. In this complex design there is an image at the foot of the tower which shows a man riding a dolphin and beating a drum. Although the figures evidently represent 'that dolphin torn and gong-tormented sea' of 'Byzantium', again they seem also to allude another poem dealing with that 'Other Shore' reached by the newly deceased soul of the greatest of Neo-Platonist philosophers on his passage to the Isles of the Blessed, 'The Delphic Oracle upon Plotinus' which Lewis gently mocks in *Count Your Dead* (1937) his affectionate burlesque of the origins and nature of *A Vision*.[66]

Awesome yet at the same time witty allusions to a 'rough beast slouching towards Bethlehem to be born' in a visionary 'sonnet'-like chapter, pivotally located, in *America and Cosmic Man* (1948) indicate that during his years as war refugee in the States and Canada, Lewis continued to be powerfully attracted by Yeats.[67] In these circumstances, it is tempting to speculate whether the strange series of beach scenes, idyllic yet unearthly, (on which Lewis worked in

Toronto during the Forties)[68] are contiguous with Yeats's 'Trans-
lunar Paradise':

> Straddling each a dolphin's back,
> And steadied by a fin,
> These Innocents relive their death
> . . . .
> Until, in some cliff-sheltered bay
> Where wades the choir of love
> . . . .
> They pitch their burdens off. (*VP* 612)

If so, both poet and painter were conscious of darker aspects in the
after-world. Certainly, the final stanza of Yeats's poem will remind
the Lewis scholar of that terrifying episode in *Malign Fiesta*
(1955)—the long-delayed continuation of *The Childermass*, and
Lewis's vision of a Twentieth Century Hell—where through the car
window the appalled Pullman glimpses what happens when Sammael throws the woman sinner to 'the ravening beasts'.[69] The resulting horror recalls the disturbing lines that conclude Yeats's otherwise transcendental message for the notoriously ambiguous Oracle
at Delphi:

> Foul goat-head, brutal arm appear,
> Belly, shoulder, bum,
> Flash fish-like; nymphs and satyrs
> Copulate in the foam. (*VP* 612)

Natural Magic: A Daniel Come to Judgement

Both Yeats and Lewis felt the need to quarrel with themselves in
order to create, but Lewis in particular also needed to quarrel with
others. He developed a devastating rhetoric in which to do so, but
confessed that private struggles lay behind the certainties he presented with such force. This is how Lewis describes the process of
reaching a point of view in *Time and Western Man*:

> . . . I have allowed these contradictory things to struggle together,
> and the group that has proved the most powerful I have fixed upon
> as my most essential ME. This decision has not, naturally, sup-
> pressed or banished the contrary faction, almost equal in strength,

indeed, and even sometimes in the ascendant. And I am by no means above spending some of my time with this domestic Adversary (*TWM* 132).

Among other things, *Time and Western Man* is an argument in favour of the stable personality, which in modern thought and ideology has been broken down—into a bundle of faggots, in Yeats's formulation; or, according to Lewis, has become a mere characterless site where realler things meet and struggle. So Lewis's statement could be taken either as a fatal self-contradiction or as a witty entertainment of the domestic Adversary to whom it refers. Probably it is best understood in relation to Lewis's tacit 'Romantic anthropocentrism' (in Neil Mann's phrase), his conception of the self as an imitation of God, repeating in its more limited way God's process of becoming real (or of making our world real).[70] 'The personality that we each possess we are apt to despise, certainly, because it has so little material power,' Lewis concedes later in the book (in a chapter on 'God as Reality'), but claims 'still without conceit at all or even blasphemy, we have a god-like experience in that only' (*TWM* 375). The difficulties of Lewis's philosophical position in outlining his method seem intractable; his way of defining his 'essential' personality differs from that of his opponents only in his supplementary faith that what emerges from the struggle corresponds to an otherwise apparently inaccessible essence—the summit of the hierarchy he had postulated for 'Joint'. Nevertheless, the route to the kind of values about which he wrote *Time and Western Man* to promote was not ideally through struggle, but through a relationship with the external world revealed by consciousness. This relationship is akin to the 'timeless' nature-mysticism of oriental landscape art and its occidental equivalents—the traditions mentioned in Lewis's 'The Critical Realists' and Yeats's 'Introduction' to *Essays and Introductions*.

A passage from a draft of 'God as Reality' throws some light on this, partly because it did not find its way into the final text. By reason of its reference to one of the 'occidental equivalents' we have mentioned, it also provides a useful opening to our discussion of the fourth major area of dialogue between Yeats and Wyndham Lewis. The passage immediately preceded what we have just quoted concerning the personality as 'god-like', and leads up to it by rejecting the ideology of struggle instilled in us by the 'brutal mindlessness of the capitalist industrial world':

The Moloch of Modern Ideas and its hierophants are a far greater destructive force for *us* than the peaceful courses of the stars and the occasional disquietude of volcanoes or hurricanes. It is not Nature, but they, that is our enemy. Nature is indeed our friend. And Time has brought us round, through its revenges and adjustments, to the point at which we look to Nature, that great, though uncertain, power, for help [—] but to that issue the tradition of our race[,] if nothing else, invite[s] us. It is not the moment to forget that spring of imagination and miraculous fable, pouring everywhere from the valleys of the 'Celtic fringe', which dominated with its beauty and with its noble myths Europe in its most characteristic age since greek antiquity, the post-roman, and catholic, age. . . . We worship, if we worship, still the virgin-goddess, the stars on the ocean, the break-of-day: the natural magic that inspired our earliest beliefs.[71]

Beside this frank avowal of a worship of Nature and its 'magic', the published text's predominantly epistemological commitments can look a little pallid. But, on the other hand, in other contexts, commitment to 'natural magic' can also look like the nostalgic retreat of members of a marginalised class before the new power that has disarmed them. This was not an image Lewis would have wished to evoke in his avowedly revolutionary attack on the Moloch of Modern Ideas.

Lewis's problem also comes from his acceptance of a version of his Adversary's position. Both Alfred North Whitehead and Henri Brémond deploy ideas of Romantic mysticism as part of their 'anti-materialism'.[72] Believing in a version of this himself, Lewis dissociates his mysticism because he believes that theirs is too 'democratic' and would simply lead the hypnotised masses into servitude (*TWM* 181-2) Mysticism is only suited to magicians, priests and artists. For artists it is an essential prerequisite for creation: 'for the production of such a work [as *King Lear*] an entranced condition seems as essential as it was for Blake when he conversed with the Man who Built the Pyramids' (*ibid.* 187). This dissociation makes Lewis's polemical position open to misunderstanding and misrepresentation. Yeats was aware of his difficulty (just as Lewis himself was aware of a similar difficulty faced by Nietzsche)[73] and wrote of it to Olivia Shakespear:

He will have an immense effect—but alas he is so clear the fools will think they understand him and hiss or bray what they have found.

He should have remembered that even the least of the nine hierarchies cho[o]ses to remain invisible—afraid perhaps of those Academy painters (12 Jan 1928, *L* 734).

'Natural Magic' or 'Celtism', then, faces Lewis with a problem that has a double aspect: first, that he appears to be endorsing the quasi-mystical views of those he says he is attacking, and second (which is the other side of the same coin), that he needs to reckon with the political and ideological function of 'Celtism' and its supposed attributes in the modern world. In both of these aspects, Yeats was for Lewis a crucial presence. Similar problems were faced by Yeats himself, of course, in a far more acute form. Celtism was used in defining an Irish identity, so was a great political reality, its mysticism enlisted paradoxically for quite worldly ends. Yeats was inextricably caught up in this—and his work was enriched by the difficulties this caused him. For Lewis, on the other hand, the political enlistment of 'Celtism' was always a doubtful manoeuvre, whether by Matthew Arnold or by Irish Nationalists, and he devoted an appendix of his study of Shakespeare to expounding its purely ideological basis and some of the ethnographic ironies implicit in the Celt—Saxon stand-off.[74] It is the other side of this double problem that receives the richest treatment in Lewis's work, however, for it turns out to involve the same dilemmas discussed in our opening section.

Behind much Modernism there lies the Romantic yearning to reveal the presence of a metaphysical Absolute in the phenomenal world. This is certainly true of Ezra Pound in *The Cantos*, and of T. S. Eliot in his pre-Christian phase (though except in his Hindu-Buddhism, Eliot approached the Absolute largely through the phenomena of culture).[75] In the 'Celtism' of Yeats and Lewis, also, the seer, shaman, or artist in touch with supernatural powers can ideally reveal this Absolute. But Yeats and Lewis were both students of William Blake,[76] and were aware that the revelation of any Absolute worth the name constitutes a definitive evaluation—or a Last Judgement—on the phenomenal world. Lewis quotes F. H. Bradley (himself in some respects a Platonist) on the possibility of such a revelation: 'It would mean a view of the finite from the Absolute's point of view, and in that consummation the finite would have been transmuted and destroyed'.[77] This paradox has its effects on their art in various ways. In early Yeats the vehicle for its expression is frequently erotic frustration, redeemed only by removal from the phenomenal world, as in 'Baile and Aillinn', or by the destruction of the phenomenal world itself. *The Wind Among the*

Reeds is full of this form of erotic apocalypticism, as in such poems as 'Aedh tells of the Rose in his Heart' and 'Mongan laments the Change that has come upon him and his Beloved, and longs for the End of the World' (*VP* 142-3, 153).

Wyndham Lewis appears to have been profoundly ambivalent about this aspect of Yeats's early work. Indeed it is probable that, because of his combined attraction and resistance to it, this work that the early, 'mystic' Yeats produced was more present to Lewis than the later work, despite its less Romantic feel. Lewis paid a generous tribute to the Modernist that Yeats developed into: 'the greater Yeats | Turning his back on Ossian, relates | The blasts of more contemporary fates'.[78] But when Yeats died, Lewis wrote an oddly unsatisfactory and seemingly ungenerous obituary that shows his continuing ambivalence about the early work. He dismisses the final two lines of 'Who goes with Fergus' as 'stuffed' language, and says that they are typical of the 'limp-hand' effect of 60 per cent of the early verse. Nevertheless, he calls Yeats a great poet, and (referring again to the early work, it would seem) agrees with the common opinion that Yeats had written lyrics 'of consummate beauty' that are 'as lovely as anything in English'.[79] Praise of this kind shows precisely why Lewis's tribute must remain unsatisfactory, for Lewis's whole aesthetic is based on the outlawing of such terms as 'consummate beauty', and 'lovely'.[80] Such terms inevitably evoke a middlebrow conception of art as a 'refuge' from 'modern life'. But there is no doubt that certain early lines of Yeats's had actually become part of Lewis's consciousness, to such an extent that he could slightly misquote them at length and at will. During the Second World War, when Lewis was in Canada, earning his living lecturing undergraduates at Assumption College, Windsor, ostensibly on 'Creative Literature', he indulged his reminiscent humour by describing to the students how he and Joyce in Paris before the war could gain entry to cafés at closing time through Joyce's 'crooning' of Verlaine. In the same lecture notes he recalls hearing Yeats recite:

> ARL the words that I utter
> And arl the songs that I wroite
> Must spread out their wings untoiring,
> And never rest in their floight:
> Till they come where your sad sad heart is,
> And sing to you in the noight,
> Beyond where the waters are moving,
> Storm-darkened or starry broight.

Lewis's ostensible purpose is to subject Yeats's verbal music to a quasi-imagist critique such as he must have heard Pound make, but the number of lines he writes down in his notes, clearly from (faulty) memory, show that he is really indulging in forbidden pleasure.[81]

He would have forbidden himself the pleasure early, intent on creating an art and literature to express and criticise the modern world rather than offer a romantic refuge from it. *Tarr*, for example, mounts a determined critique of any identification of erotic desire with metaphysical transcendence, and much of Lewis's work is intent on exposing how what are normally regarded as oases of 'value' in the desert of modern materialism have been invaded and poisoned by precisely those ideologies from which they ostensibly offer a retreat.[82] 'Celticness', as a certain kind of ethnic identity that guarantees authenticity, is a related idea which Lewis is frequently at pains to explode, not only in *The Lion and the Fox*, but also in *Time and Western Man*:

> The romantic persons who go picking about in the Aran Islands . . . or elsewhere, for genuine human 'antiques', are today on a wild-goose chase; because the sphinx of the Past, in the person of some elder dug out of such remote neighbourhoods, will at length, when he has found his tongue, probably commence addressing them in the vernacular of the *Daily Mail* (*TWM* 80-1).

Worse still, the 'shamanistic' aspect of Celtism, the otherworldiness that accompanies communication with occult powers of nature, has been appropriated by modern societies and put to specifically political purposes, according to Lewis. He devotes a whole section of his political analysis of post-First World War liberal-capitalist-democracy, *The Art of Being Ruled*, to an exposition of the political function of the adoption by men of the 'feminine' social privileges of the shaman, which are understandably attractive after the slaughter of so many men in the war:

> The calling of the priest in every nationality offers a convenient refuge from the stress of life to the defeated or quietist vitality. And in some cases the priesthood is in this way a social expedient of great use, extracting from life the practically unfit, and so offering a suitable occupation to people who would otherwise be a drag on the active community. At present the prevalent shamanistic fashion serves a similar purpose.[83]

Lewis is primarily concerned with an 'Anglo-Saxon' context in his social analyses, rather than an Irish one, and in that context, 'shamanistic' behaviour is a defeatist response to the War. Yet he is not above hinting that Yeats's own mysticism has its origin in a similarly defensive reaction of Irish culture to a dominant, imperialist neighbour:

> . . . Joyce and Yeats are the prose and poetry respectively of the Ireland that culminated in the Rebellion. Yeats is the chivalrous embodiment of 'celtic' romance, more of St. Brandon than of Ossian, with all the grand manners of a spiritual Past that cannot be obliterated, though it wear thin, and of a dispossessed and persecuted people. Joyce is the cold and stagnant reality . . . above which that Yeatsian emanation floats.[84]

At any rate, it is into a specifically British context that Lewis introduces a Yeatsian version of the modern 'shaman' in *The Apes of God*.[85] This massive satire, largely conceived in the early twenties, but revised and completed in 1929, provides a tour of the London art-world in 1926, culminating in the General Strike of that year. As we have explained, the book derives from some of the metaphysical preoccupations of 'Joint'. In that theological-metaphysical context, the burden of its title is that modern society has only a small repertoire of imitation 'god-like' roles, owing to its rejection of genuine imaginative and creative artists. For it is in the work of artists that mankind can develop the 'god-like experience' referred to in *Time and Western Man*, and escape the 'Calvinist' determinism of mechanical imitation. As well as caricaturing the social world, and its snobbishly incompetent dealings with the arts, in a more subtle way Lewis brings in versions of the 'Modernism' practised by his contemporaries and rivals, and submits them to the test of making sense of the culture they must reflect. The Modernisms of Joyce, Pound and Proust are those most clearly identifiable (though it must be stressed that none of these figures are subjected to the kind of personal caricature that, for instance, the Sitwells suffer),[86] and Yeats, at least in his younger incarnation, has an important place alongside them. In *The Apes of God* Lewis works through his ambivalence about the 'Celtism' he endorsed in the rejected draft of *Time and Western Man* as a force to resist the Moloch of Modern Ideas.

Yeats's psychic powers are embodied, in *The Apes of God*, in the character of Daniel Boleyn.[87] The association is hinted almost from the character's first appearance. His mentor, Horace Zagreus, is a character of genuine presence but also an exhibitionist and charlatan; Zagreus's patronising relationship to Boleyn is reminiscent of that of a number of Yeats's associates to Yeats. In the past both McGregor Mathers and Aleister Crowley had tried to bully the young Yeats.[88] Since Lewis's most powerful satiric portraits are composites, Mathers's and Crowley's behaviour thus serves as the armature for a disguised satire on Ezra Pound, who had grown arrogant in his dealings with the older poet. Horace introduces Dan to the aged Sir James Follett as the author of 'one most lovely poem'. The epithet may retrospectively remind us of Lewis's praise of Yeats in his obituary, but here it carries its more predictable force, as becomes clear when the first lines of Dan's distinctly fin-de-siècle production are quoted: 'Cynthia do not spoil my hair, | Harp-tongued tigress—Cynthia'.[89] Having effected the introduction, Zagreus directs Dan up a staircase: '. . . No, this way. Tread softly because you tread on my dreams.—Mind the step.' The dreams (of inheritance) are Zagreus's, not Dan's, but the Yeatsian association is still reinforced, just as, in the paragraph after Dan's (scarcely Yeatsian) lines are quoted, they are renewed (again obliquely) by the narrator's description of Dan's action as he considers whether he has sufficient stamina to become a painter: 'He lifted up a pearl-pale hand'.[90]

Dan is 'only nineteen', has recently arrived from Ireland, is virtually inarticulate in company, and, partly because he is proclaimed as a 'genius' by the infatuated Zagreus, is subjected to continuous humiliation as he makes his uncomprehending way round the salons and studios of the London art world. When Dan, at the end of the book, wanders round London trying to escape the attentions of motorists offering him lifts, he has no idea that what is in progress is a General Strike. We see the strike's effects largely through Dan's eyes, and it is clear that, whatever the nature of his 'genius', it is not adequate to a comprehension of life in a modern city. This portrayal of a young *naïf* as the Irishman in mighty London, is not particularly ingratiating. But Dan begins to win the reader's sympathy, for he is at least the only character in the book without affectation or malice. His unworldliness, though it can be exasperating, is that of the young Yeats, as recounted in *Reveries over Childhood and Youth*, and its sequels: repressed emotionality on the brink of tearful expression (mistaken by others for thick-skinned taciturnity), embarrassed incomprehension of his own sexuality, and susceptibility to baffling or frightening visionary experiences.[91]

What clinches the association with Yeats is a 'dossier' compiled by Zagreus to justify his claim of Dan's 'genius' to Zagreus's own 'master', Pierpoint. This is a tale, closely modelled on those in Yeats's *The Celtic Twilight*, of mysterious powers of prophecy granted to the son of a 'gentleman-farmer', Diarmuidh K., 'much addicted to the study of astrology, and the occult works of Cornelius Agrippa'.[92] These powers may not be exploited before the boy's fifteenth birthday, and any question directed to him before that date will result in disaster. Sure enough, virtually on the eve of the promised day, a distraught girl whose lover has neglected to attend to Mr K.'s prized cow, that is about to calve, meets the boy by chance, and cries out across the hedge:

> 'Ah! Master Anthony, alanna, do you know where the black cow has hid herself?' 'Black cow!' said he, 'she is lying dead in the byre.' At the moment his eyes opened wide as if about to start from his head, an expression of terror took possession of his features, he gave one wild cry, fell powerless on his face, and when his wretched father came running to the spot, on hearing of the circumstances, he found an idiot in the place of his fine, intelligent son. (*AG* 479).

According to Zagreus, Dan is fey, has gifts of prophecy that 'have been blasted by some shock in childhood' and has 'become an idiot'. Zagreus believes Dan's powers may be restored.[93] Pierpoint has apparently dismissed Zagreus's theory—as far as he is concerned, Dan is no more than the idiot he seems. But there is good reason to believe that Zagreus's theory about Dan is right, for he has already during the narrative had a recrudescence of a visionary episode first experienced in childhood during the Rebellion of 1916:

> he had had that as a schoolboy in Ireland, when the Rebellion was, the night before the arrest of his father, when he had seen through the pavement (as he had dreamed he was walking) scenery beneath his feet. There was a world that ran through things, like pictures in water or in glassy surfaces, where a mob of persons were engaged in hunting to kill other men, in a battle park, beneath crackling violet stars (*AG* 416-17).

Dan seems to see a park, planted with spikes, and under the surface, blood. The earth cracks, and smoke and thundering fountains burst through. 'Nothing could live thought Dan, or *love* thought he, where he had been looking . . . . He would never look again! Never of his own free will would he look again for years!'

The description of Dan's prophetic vision is quite unlike anything else in *The Apes of God*. It concludes with an image that aptly conveys its own relationship with the art of the 'surface' so rigorously practised elsewhere in the book, one of 'breaking through into something else, as you put your fist through a sheet of paper'.[94] It is a narrative, mythologised version of that Last Judgement in which the veil of matter (akin to the Hindu and Buddhist Maya) is rent and dissolved into the Absolute. Its particular terms and setting cannot but remind of an apocalyptic strain in Yeats's early work that we have so far not mentioned. Alongside the erotic apocalypticism (which Lewis would have dismissed) was another form that was at least partly political. Dan's vision is closely akin to the one embodied in 'The Valley of the Black Pig', a poem in which the speaker has a vision of a coming mythological battle in which (as Yeats explains in the note to the poem published in the first, 1899, edition of *The Wind Among the Reeds*) the enemies of Ireland would be routed.

> A few years before my time, an old man who lived at Lisadell, in Sligo, used to fall down in a fit and rave out descriptions of the Battle; and a man in Sligo has told me that it will be so great a battle that the horses shall go up to their fetlocks in blood, and that their girths, when it is over, will rot from their bellies for lack of a hand to unbuckle them (*VP* 809).

Elsewhere Yeats writes of his talk about war with an old Sligo woman: '. . . the battle of the Black Pig . . . seems to her a battle between Ireland and England, but to me an Armageddon which shall quench all things in the ancestral darkness again . . . .[95]

The significance of this visionary material in *The Apes of God* is not easy to expound. Briefly, Dan's turning his back on it appears to reinforce the impression the reader has that the mysticism of the Irish visionary is inadequate before the reality of modern life. This would not represent Lewis's final judgement of Yeats, it must be added: the character Dan is used, rather, to evoke certain shamanistic powers associated with Yeats and 'Celtism'. And, of course, it is necessary to distinguish between Dan's reaction to his own powers and the use to which 'the greater' Yeats put his own in narrating the blasts of contemporary fates. Judgement of Dan is tempered, also, for although he is incompetent in the modern world, the content of his vision is actually tragically anchored to Twentieth Century realities: the arrest during the night, the blood-soaked ground, the barren landscape and fountains of earth sent up by shell-fire. Encoded into this vision are the Easter Rising and Civil War, the General Strike (through references to a park—Hyde Park, used as a centre for strike-breaking), and, most strikingly, to the First, and future, World Wars. The Yeatsian, and Romantic, conception of the artist as seer is endorsed at this point, though at the same time 'vision' and 'shamanism' are shown not as timeless but as the corollary of specific historical circumstances. Truly 'despised and rejected' by the artistic society of 1926, Dan has that visionary gift that Lewis identified in his endorsement of Celtic 'natural magic' as a vital weapon against the fake-mysticism he identified as the ideology of industrialised 'modernity'.[96] So a vicious circle is suggested: 'the creative myths and dreams of the poets are no longer allowed' in modern industrial culture (*TWM* 35); the threatened visionary therefore retreats willingly into the idiocy to which society consigns him. A silenced Cassandra, he harbours a vision of the destruction that will come to society precisely because it represses his visionary powers. Meanwhile, in a further irony, this society (that has submitted itself to imitative determinism) adopts the stereotype role of the 'artist' as its most comfortable and flattering 'role-model'—though the powers of the true visionaries are too dangerous for it to handle.[97] What *The Apes of God* shows is not, then, that the 'natural magic' of Celtism and Yeatsian vision are obsolete in the modern world, but that, for want of them, the only exit from that world's paralysis is likely to be apocalyptic violence.

'That big Nothing we call God'

This essay has circled around various ideas about types of the 'apocalypse' in the work of Lewis and Yeats. As narrative, that apocalypse takes the form of a Last Judgement in which all is destroyed. As theology, it is the encounter between the finite and God. As metaphysics, it is the dissolution of realism into absolute idealism. As aesthetics, it is the dissolution of conventions of the intellect into pure, abstract sensation. Both Yeats and Lewis are enticed by, yet resist such apocalypses, which necessarily defeat them as artists. When glossing 'The Hosting of the Sidhe' (*YP* 507), A. Norman Jeffares gestures to Yeats's 1930 Diary'

> I think that two conceptions, that of reality as a congeries of beings, that of reality as a single being, alternate in our emotion and in history, and must always remain something that human reason,

because always subject to one or the other, cannot reconcile. I am always, in all I do, driven to a moment which is the realisation of myself as unique and free, or to a moment which is the surrender to God of all that I am. I think that there are historical cycles wherein one or the other predominates, and that a cycle approaches where all shall [be] as particular and concrete as human intensity permits. Again and again I have tried to sing that approach [in 'The Hosting of the Sidhe', 'The Everlasting Voices' and 'To his Heart, bidding it have no Fear' (*VP* 140-1, 158)] . . . and have almost understood my intention. Again and again with remorse, a sense of defeat, I have failed, when I would write of God, written coldly and conventionally. Could those two impulses, one as much a part of truth as the other, be reconciled, or if one or the other could prevail, all life would cease' (*Ex* 305).

The passage recalls that in *Time and Western Man* to which Yeats alludes in a footnote to his discussion of the *Cantos* in 'A Packet for Ezra Pound' (*AVB* 4):

If the contrast is between a conception of the world as an ultimate Unity or the one hand, or a Plurality on the other; if you have, dogmatic and clear-cut, or rather if you could have, on the one side a picture of a multiplicity of wave-like surface changes only, while all the time the deep bed of Oneness reposes unbroken underneath: on the other side the idea of an *absolute* plurality, every midget existence, every speck and grain, unique (for what such 'uniqueness' was worth) and equally *real*, irrespective of any hierarchy of truth at all: then can there be any question that the hypothesis of Oneness is the profounder hypothesis, and must, if it lay thus barely between those two, be the real? But we are surface-creatures only, and by nature are meant to be only that, if there is any meaning in nature. No metaphysician goes the whole length of departure from the surface-condition of mind—that fact is not generally noticed. For such departures result in self-destruction . . . .[98]

Modelled on a fusion of literary genres—the Dialogue of the Dead—and what Yeats had gleaned from séance and tradition of the soul's growth to self-knowledge in after-life, for Lewis, *The Childermass* was one of the narrative vehicles through which the 'self-destruction' of an encounter with the Absolute was thought through, as we have explained in the second part of this essay. That visionary work was originally intended to conclude in Armageddon and chaos. But the book was abandoned until long after Yeats's death, and was transformed and enlarged into a trilogy entitled *The Human Age*, broadcast in dramatised form on the radio in 1955, and published in 1956 and 1957.[99] This also was to end in destruction or Armageddon, but while writing it, Lewis decided to complete the series with a fourth book. Significantly this bears the Miltonic title, *The Trial of Man*, recalling also 'The Soul in Judgement' section of the revised *A Vision*.[100] In *The Trial of Man* a more conceptual judgement would be worked out. He did not finish this, but a draft of the rejected opening was printed as an appendix to the 1966 paperback reissue of Book 3, *Malign Fiesta*. There has been a battle, in which God has overcome Sammael (Satan); now a mysterious 'Stranger' visits the crippled Sammael in hospital. The nurse considers her reaction to Him:

> From her young days she remembered 'Where there is nothing there is' . . . oh, what was it that there was? Something like *this* . . . something which was not zero, as she had always supposed this meant. No—that *nothing* of her early teachers meant somewhere where *nothing* oppressively human was to be found—nothing functional, that loved and hated, nothing that uncomfortably *willed* and wanted—something which *had* everything. But that was the reverse of nothing, was it not?

Sammael confirms the identification of the Stranger: '"I smelled that great absence of guts—that big Nothing we call God".'[101] What the nurse is trying to remember is the completion of the phrase Yeats used as the title of a short story of 1896, 'Where there is Nothing, there is God' (*VSR* 48-54) later re-used in abbreviated form as the title of a play, *Where there is Nothing* (1902), written by Yeats with assistance from Lady Gregory and Douglas Hyde, and subsequently rewritten by Lady Gregory and Yeats as *The Unicorn from the Stars* (1908).

It is not clear which of these interlinked works Lewis has in mind,[102] but the phrase 'Where there is nothing, there is God' takes on an especially mystico-anarchist dimension in Paul Ruttledge's famous sermon to the friars in *Where there is Nothing* (*VPl* 1140). In the final version, Paul Ruttledge has metamorphosed into Martin Hearne, a coachbuilder, seer and visionary, whose 'business is not reformation but revelation' (*VPl* 704). He 'leads' an attack on the local big house, which is plundered by beggars and burnt down. As a result he is shot by constables. As with Dan in *The Apes of God*, his

vision is apocalyptic, but, unlike Lewis's Dan, he embraces destruction. This time his message is contained not in a sermon, but in
speech to his followers. The Heaven he sees is 'continual battle', but

> . . . we shall not come to that joy, that battle, till we have put out
> the senses, everything that can be seen and handled, as I put out this
> candle. [*He puts out candle.*] We must put out the whole world as I
> put out this candle [*puts out another candle*]. We must put out the
> light of the stars and the light of the sun and the light of the moon
> [*puts out the rest of the candles*], till we have brought everything to
> nothing once again. I saw in a broken vision, but now all is clear to
> me. Where there is nothing, where there is nothing—there is
> God![103]

This play was not Yeats's last word on 'Nothing';[104] but it is possible
that his thoughts on this occasion owe something to the Buddhist
concept of Nirvana. As Philip Almond explains, 'Of all the aspects
of Buddhist doctrine with which the Victorians dealt, the question
of the nature of Nirvana aroused the most interest and the most controversy . . . . Ontologically, the central issue in this hotly disputed
question concerned what the attainment of Nirvana meant for the
existence of the previously suffering individual. The majority
opinion throughout the nineteenth century followed the interpretation made by the oldest school of Buddhism'.[105] According to the
Hinayana interpretation Nirvana, essentially, entailed the 'annihila-
tion of the individual . . . literally a blowing-out, as if of a candle'.[106]
In January 1926, writing to Sturge Moore, Yeats recalls a youthful
interest in 'early Buddhism' (*TSMC* 68). The annihilationist view of
the Hinayana school, however, had been challenged by the growth
of Mahayana Buddhism which, fusing with Tibetan shamanism, saw
Nirvana take on 'the bright colours of a paradise . . .'.[107] The same
1926 letter to Sturge Moore shows that, through reading Arthur
Waley, the poet had been introduced to Zen, a Chinese and Japanese
sect of the later school of Buddhism. In the following year Yeats
read Suzuki's *Essays on Zen Buddhism*. Amongst other things Yeats
learnt that 'the Hinayana conception of Nirvana was too limited
and negative, a negation of life rather than an affirmation, with too
great a contempt for the external'.[108] Because Yeats is able to wed
such ideas to Neo-Platonism, a Western tradition of 'Nothing' is
eventually brought into play.

Artistically, the fragment of *The Trial of Man* that survives is a
poor thing, hardly to be compared with the productions of Lewis or
Yeats at their best. But it is quoted here to indicate the continuing

importance of Yeats's thought to Lewis at a time when, his powers failing, he attempted to work through in narrative form some of the fundamentals of his view of life. His first play, *Enemy of the Stars*, questioned the philosophy of the egoist Max Stirner, who 'founded [his] affair on nothing'.[109] In rejecting Bradley's excessively quantitave vision of the Absolute in *Time and Western Man*, Lewis had found himself irresistably articulating its opposite: 'But so, too, on that absolutist, quantitative scale, you arrive at *nothing* which is the only safe and stable thing to be!'[110] Later, like Yeats, Lewis had asked himself 'What is the explanation of it all', and puzzled over how life and its values could issue from 'Nothing'.[111] The 'nothing that is God' had been approached, this century, with something amounting to the prophetic frenzy of Yeats's visionary Martin by various forms of Modernism, in theology and the arts. At the end of his life Lewis was much concerned with pointing out the dangers of these Modernisms.[112] His last completed novel (*The Red Priest*) concerns a theologically Modernist clergyman eager to share his experience of an encounter with God: ' '. . . God is, of course, a terrifying reality. I had thought I knew all about God, and had Him in a pigeon hole. But I met Him at the corner of a street—He entered my mind with a bang, and nearly burst my head open. . . .' ' Only by feeling 'the ultimate next thing to nothingness—to zero', can God be encountered.[113] In his missionary zeal, he breaks other heads, and is himself eventually killed trying to take his message to the ultimate Eskimo in the Arctic (recalling 'the Polar regions of our psychic existence' of Lewis's 1914 formulation). He leaves behind a son, appropriately 'christened' by his widow as 'Zero', since he promises to resemble his father.

The other form of Modernism Lewis was concerned with was painting, though he was by 1951 too close to blindness to see a picture. *The Demon of Progress in the Arts* (1954), which was Lewis's last critical book, was an attempt to counter that form of Modernism deriving from Kandinsky, and discussed in the first section of the present essay. In this Modernism the drive to abolish the 'conventions of the intellect' and break through to some abstract spiritual absolute was paramount. Lewis warns:

> What I am arguing about in this book is that an easily defined limit exists in painting and sculpture, in music, in the theatre, in literature, in architecture, and in every other human art. . . . beyond a certain well-defined line—in the arts as in everything else—beyond that limit there is *nothing*. Nothing, zero, is what logically you reach past a line, of some kind, laid down by nature, everywhere.[114]

When the nurse in the *Trial of Man* fragment rejects the destructive interpretation of Yeats's line implicit in the identification of his 'Nothing' (where God is) with a simple 'zero', Lewis, through her, is belatedly completing his most fruitful dialogue with Yeats and aligning himself with the Zen affirmation of Nirvana. It is indeed a debate apt for the genre of Dialogue of the Dead, but it had begun many years previously—the other side of two world wars, perhaps as early as the publication of *The Wind Among the Reeds* itself, a book Lewis apparently knew with the memory of the gauche adolescent he himself had then been.[115] After such a violent half century, Yeats might well have considered Lewis's quasi-Buddhist or Stoic interpretation of the apparently apocalyptic mantra 'Where there is Nothing, there is God', a fitting end.

NOTES

1. 'Lewis would find the problem he discusses in *The Theaetetus*', Yeats to Olivia Shakespear, 28 March 1927 (*L* 724). There are several references to Plato's dialogue in the finished version of *Time and Western Man* (but none in the incomplete draft published in *The Enemy* in February, which Yeats had been reading). Plato here exposes the inadequacy of the relativist sensationalism of Protagoras—which is what Lewis attempted in relation to such philosophers as A. N. Whitehead and Samuel Alexander. In *The Enemy*, Lewis had already pointed out that Alexander's attempt to support his own views by reference to differences between the supposed Zeitgeists of Plato's era and our own were historically unsound: 'But as everybody knows, and none better than Professor Alexander, the age of Plato swarmed with empirical, sensationalist, philosophers, from Protagoras downwards' (*The Enemy: A Review of Art and Literature* [1927, rpt. ed. David Peters Corbett, Santa Rosa: Black Sparrow Press, 1994], I, 133). Lewis's references to *The Theaetetus* are to Socrates' famous description of a philosopher as someone who 'does not know whether he is a man or some other creature' (generally considered to be a digression from the main argument).

2. Wyndham Lewis, *Time and Western Man* (1927), ed. Paul Edwards (Santa Rosa: Black Sparrow Press, 1993), p. 284, hereafter *TWM*. Yeats's marginalia to *Time and Western Man* and markings, turned-down pages, etc. suggest that he read Lewis's text with care (*YL* 157). Roger Parisious has found further pages which show evidence of Yeats's attentions. We are grateful to him for sharing the results of his research with us. See nn. 42 & 61.

3. *TWM* 37-42, 67-72. On Yeats's misgivings, see Warwick Gould, '*The Unknown Masterpiece*: Yeats and the Design of the *Cantos*' in Andrew Gibson (ed.), *Pound in Multiple Perspective: A Collection of Critical Essays* (London: The Macmillan Press, 1993), pp. 40-92.

4. See Warwick Gould, 'The Unknown Masterpiece', esp. pp. 49-57.

5. Ezra Pound, 'Vorticism' (1914), *Gaudier-Brzeska: A Memoir* (New York: New

Directions, 1970), p. 87. (Pound's ellipsis.)

6. Wyndham Lewis, 'A Review of Contemporary Art' (1915), rpt. *Wyndham Lewis on Art*, ed. C. J. Fox and Walter Michel (New York: Funk and Wagnalls, 1969), p. 63.

7. He is unlikely to have missed its first publication in *Blast* 2 (1915), given Pound's close association with the magazine. Lewis did not republish the essay until 1939.

8. 'Mr Lewis stands, in a paradoxically high-pitched and excited way, for common sense . . .' F. R. Leavis, 'Mr Eliot, Mr Wyndham Lewis and Lawrence' (1934), *The Common Pursuit* (Harmondsworth: Penguin, 1966), p. 243.

9. Interview by 'M. M. B.', *Daily News and Leader* (7 April 1914), quoted in Richard Cork, *Art beyond the Gallery in Early Twentieth Century England* (New Haven and London: Yale University Press, 1985), p. 184. Lewis went on to suggest an analogy between Cubism and Chinese Geomancy, which he followed up in 'Fêng Shui and Contemporary Form' in *Blast* 1 (June 1914), rpt. *Wyndham Lewis on Art*, pp. 41-2.

10. *TWM* 187. In 'Der Vortex—Intensität als Entschleunigung', in the catalogue of the 1996 Hanover and Munich exhibitions *Blast: Vortizismus—Die Erste Avant-garde in England 1914-1918*, ed. Karin Orchard (Hanover and Munich: Ars Nicolai, 1996), pp. 22-38, Hubertus Gassner traces the influence of Hindu cosmogony—especially as mediated through Annie Besant and Charles W. Leadbeater, *Occult Chemistry* (1908)—on, not only Pound's, but also Wyndham Lewis's esoteric thinking and its artistic realisation. Certainly Besant and Leadbeater's earlier *Thought Forms* (London and Benares: The Theosophical Publishing Society, 1905) has memorable illustrations of 'little splotches of colour', 'etherial' and 'cloud-like', as well as more dynamically organised, shapes that anticipate, somewhat, the later Modernist experiments.

11. 'The Credentials of the Painter' (1919) rpt. in Wyndham Lewis, *Creatures of Habit and Creatures of Change: Essays on Art, Literature and Society 1913-1956*, ed. Paul Edwards (Santa Rosa: Black Sparrow Press, 1989), p. 76. This seems to be a more considered expression of Lewis's mature opinion than the slightly uncritical endorsement of spiritualism in the 1914 *Daily News and Leader* interview quoted above, and the strong reaction against spiritualism evident in his 1915 criticisms of Kandinsky: 'Kandinsky's spiritual values . . . seem to be undesirable, even if feasible: just as, although believing in the existence of the supernatural, you may regard it as redundant and nothing to do with life' ('A Review of Contemporary Art', p. 72). Lewis's image, in the 1919 essay, of art as a 'coin', may well be a recollection of the coin demanded by Charon for ferrying souls from this world to the next. For both Yeats and Lewis, art is one of the most important vehicles available for effecting such a crossing.

12. David Hume, *A Treatise of Human Nature* (1739), ed. E. C. Mossner (Harmondsworth: Penguin, 1969), p. 316.

13. Ezra Pound, 'Canto XCIV', *Section: Rock-Drill* (1955), rpt. *The Cantos* (London: Faber and Faber, 1964), p. 673. There is another way that 'Justice' emerges in the *Cantos*, through a 'masculine' direction of the will, cutting through to clean values. Likewise, despite Pound's desire for an immediate language (manifested in his fondness for ideograms, hieroglyphs and pictograms), mind has already saturated his gists, piths and fragments with concepts. To take these two points in turn (and leaving aside the nature of the 'clean values' or 'Justice' the *Cantos* establish): in Pound's work the direction of the will is registered all too often,

as, (in Yeats's words) a 'nervous obsession . . . raging at malignants' (*OBMV* xxv). This assertiveness alternates with the rather *voulu* 'natural' revelations (or with such ineffective syntheses of the two as 'From ploughing of fields is justice'; 'Canto C', *The Cantos*, p. 743); secondly, as Yeats has it in his summary of Wyndham Lewis's quasi-Kantian argument from 'God as Reality' (*AVB* 4n.); see *TWM* 377, quoted below), all rejections of the forms and categories of the intellect 'stop at the conscious mind', which can only function because of such categories in the first place. Since all valuations of nature are possible only in relation to a conscious mind, why attempt an impossible elimination of many of the mind's shaping capacities? The answer to this would tell us a lot about Pound—not all of it to his detriment.

14.   *AVB* 25. Whether Yeats knew the 'equivalent' passage in Hume's *Treatise* (which tended to be neglected in favour of his *Enquiries* until some time after Yeats's death) we do not know. The argument does not depend on such knowledge. It might be significant that Yeats uses the expression, 'overwhelmed by miracle', which could be taken as an implicit gibe at Hume's famous and sceptical 'Essay on Miracles', incorporated into the *Enquiries*.

15.   Lewis's drawings were not really constructed from cubes, though they were certainly governed by 'conventions of the intellect'. Yeats may well have had Pound's own statement about Brancusi's 'ovoids' in mind: 'with the ideal form in marble it is an approach to the infinite *by form*, by precisely the highest possible degree of consciousness of formal perfection; as free of accident as any of the philosophical demands of a 'Paradiso' can make it' (Ezra Pound, 'Brancusi' [1921], rpt. *Literary Essays of Ezra Pound*, ed. T. S. Eliot [London: Faber and Faber, 1954], p. 444). To Yeats, such a statement would have shown Pound damning his own practice out of his own mouth.

16.   Friedrich Nietzsche, *The Complete Works*, ed. Oscar Levy, vol. X, *The Joyful Wisdom ('La Gaya Scienza')* tr. Thomas Common (London: T. N. Foulis, 1910), sect. 354, p. 298.

17.   *VP* 481. Neil Mann notices that the 'Introduction' to *AVB* implies relativism for art, and quotes the Pound translation from Leopardi to which Yeats alluded in the first published version of 'A Packet for Ezra Pound': 'if one wrong note | Strike the tympanum, | Instantly | That paradise is hurled to nothingness.' See his '*A Vision*: Ideas of God and Man' (*YA8* 158-9). The consonance of Yeats's image with Leopardi's supports our treatment of the realms of art and reality as subject to the same epistemological argument. The apocalyptic evocation of 'nothingness' is also notable.

18.   TS. (c. 1924), Wyndham Lewis Archive, SUNY at Buffalo (A2111, B1, F11).

19.   *Ibid*. The direct source of this idea is Henri Bergson's *Creative Evolution*, tr. Arthur Mitchell (London: Macmillan, 1911), p. 15: 'life . . . manifests a search for individuality, as if it strove to constitute systems naturally isolated, naturally closed'. See *TWM* 351 & n.

20.   Yeats allowed a letter to Lewis praising *The Childermass* to be used in publicity for the American edition (see Wyndham Lewis, *The Letters of Wyndham Lewis*, ed. W. K. Rose [London: Methuen, 1963], pp. 182-3) and another praising *The Apes of God* to appear in Lewis's *Satire and Fiction* (London: The Arthur Press, 1930), p. 29.

21.   'I used to meet him at lunch at the Vienna Cafe, and that was in the first decade of the century' (unpub. letter, 12 Mar 1951, Lewis to Allan Wade, responding to

a request for copies of Yeats's letters). We are grateful to Hugh Anson-Cartwright for providing a copy of this letter.

22.   Lewis to Moore, 4 Jan. 1916, *The Letters of Wyndham Lewis*, p. 75. 'Approve' is a word with moral connotations. Perhaps Yeats had views about Lewis's attitude to his parental responsibilities (he had two children by Olive Johnson, supported them financially, but was not otherwise much of a father to them), or his misogyny, which was at its most powerful around 1916. In his entry on Phase Nine in *A Vision*, Yeats notes that 'one finds at this phase, more often than at any other, men who dread, despise and persecute the women whom they love', and records as indicative Lewis's remark to him about Augustus John's 'mistress' (perhaps his wife, Dorelia, whom Lewis disliked), 'She no longer cares for his work, no longer gives him the sympathy he needs, why does he not leave her, what does he owe to her or to her children?' (*CVA* 54).

23.   *YVP1* 290 (answer given on 26 January 1918), and *YVP3* 58, Phase 9. The editors point out that '& passion' is a mistranscription of 'of vision'.

24.   See *Tarr: The 1918 Version*, ed. Paul O'Keeffe (Santa Rosa: Black Sparrow Press, 1990), pp. 298-300. The quotation is from p. 299.

25.   In 'Mr Zagreus and The Split-Man', one of a pair of forerunners to *The Apes of God* published during the early Twenties in *The Criterion*, Zagreus refers to a character named Joint whose role seems to anticipate that of Pierpoint in the novel (Wyndham Lewis, 'Mr Zagreus and the Split-Man', *The Criterion*, II:6 [February 1924], 140). Joint is the eponymous hero of an unfinished satirical narrative dating from this period; sections of this manuscript were edited by Hugh Kenner and published as 'from *Joint*', *Agenda* (Wyndham Lewis Special Issue), VII:3—VIII:1 (Autumn-Winter 1969-70), pp. 198-208. Significantly, among these fragments is 'The Infernal Fair' (a dream episode containing elements of the Dialogue of the Dead, that ancient subgenre of Menippian satura), for in *Blasting and Bombardiering* (1937) Lewis himself identified 'Joint' as one of the sources of *The Childermass* (1967 Calder edition pp 230-1, see also Peter L. Caracciolo, 'Byzantium and Cosmic Man', *Wyndham Lewis Annual* 2 (1995), p. 24, and 'The Metamorphoses of Wyndham Lewis's *The Human Age*; Medium, Intertextuality, Genre' in Ian Willison, Warwick Gould, Warren Chernaik (eds.) *Modernist Writers and the Marketplace* (London: Macmillan, 1996), pp. 258-286, esp. pp. 264-5.

26.   Lewis's 'Joint' notebook in the Carl A. Kroch Library, Cornell, gives a clue to his conception of such a hierarchy:

<u>Hierarchy</u>.   Joint.
                      Bully (super-Joint).
                      X (super-Bully)

<u>Thesis</u>   Indian idea of many lives (actual terrestrial one one only) etc. Progression

                      In life most people live one life to its finish, live more & more mechanically reproducing themselves. Some are capable of including in <u>one</u> life <u>several</u>.
                      Complexity ETC.
                      Bully is a <u>purified</u> Joint. X as a purified Bully ETC.

The higher up the scale of reality (and in this scheme 'X' is the highest), the less determined and finite the character is. The allusion to Hindu cycles of existence shows how close Lewis is here in his thinking to the Yeats of *A Vision*. His schema for 'Joint' (which cannot be taken as definitive) is naturally adapted to satire (in the Jonsonian sense) because satire concerns itself with personalities that are artificially limited; as Zagreus explains in *The Apes of God*: 'To the satirist a thing must present itself as more simple, it must possess a stupid finality, it must be more rigidly contained by its genera, than in fact anything is.' (*The Apes of God* [1930, rpt. Santa Barbara: Black Sparrow Press, 1981], p. 451). *Hereafter AG*. The 'higher' orders of being are less subject to a 'Calvinist' determination. The ultimate, undetermined Unity (God), remains beyond our human horizon, however: 'As we determine ourselves, we negate Perfection, understood as an absolute Unity; it is written, we cannot avoid this cancellation' (*TWM* 372). Lewis was unhappy with the 'Calvinist' implications of some of his ideas, and attempted to subvert them by emphasising that God had 'abdicated', leaving each of us free to determine ourselves within a reality that, if ultimately dependent on God, was an 'extraordinary Aladdin's cave', a 'paradise' (p. 376).

27.   For a passage where both Joyce and Pirandello can be traced, see 'from *Joint*', p. 201: '[Joint] expressed himself as follows. 'If I lie here drivelling like this and allow the author to snapshot this mechanical reminiscent rubbish swishing about in my inane I shall find myself mixed up in people's minds with Mr. and Mrs. Bloom, that obnoxious couple over the road . . . . Dear, dear, sometimes I wish I weren't a character in fiction, but a real person'. Yeats pointed to a connection between *The Apes of God* and Pirandello in his letter of commendation (*Satire and Fiction*, p. 39). Compare also Yeats's relationship with Michael Robartes and Owen Aherne. Yeats continued to be amused about such matters and to Olivia Shakespear on 9 March 1932 commented on the self-judgemental responses of a combative Irish Republican journalist who wrote 'articles in the English press against Ireland' that 'Pirandello and St John of the Cross are strangely mixed up here' (*L* 793).

28.   In the sense that a 'ghost' is more determinate than something living. The installment of *The Apes of God* that Lewis published in *The Criterion* before the book had been separated from the 'Joint' project, is headed with a note by Lewis in which Zagreus (a major character in the finished work) is called 'an important ghost' (p. 124). It was only in the *Childermass* development from 'Joint' that the characters clearly remain ghosts.

29.   The 'metaphysical' dimensions of *The Childermass* (as well as its eventual sequels) and *The Apes of God* are illuminated by Lewis's response to the Great War; the Platonism revealed in these reactions verges on the Manichean. In this fiction the Calvinistic determinism of which Lewis sought to exculpate God resurfaces as the weapon of another Power. See the 1937 memoir *Blasting and Bombardiering* (London: Eyre and Spottiswoode, 1937), pp. 170-7, 193; see Peter L. Caracciolo, '"Carnivals of Mass-Murder": The Frazerian Origins of Wyndham Lewis's *The Childermass*' in Robert Fraser (ed.), *Sir James Frazer and the Literary Imagination: Essays in Affinity and Influence* (London: Macmillan, 1990), pp. 207-231, esp. p. 215; 'Like a Mexith's renowned statue bristling with emblems': Masquerade, Anthropology, Yeats and Pound among Wyndham Lewis's *Apes of God*' in Andrew Gibson (ed.) *Pound in Multiple Perspective*, p. 138; 'Byzantium and Cosmic Man' esp. pp. 26-7. Enlightening on *The Human*

Age is Michael Nath, '"Monstrous Starlight": Wyndham Lewis and Gnosticism', in Paul Edwards, ed., *Volcanic Heaven: Essays on Wyndham Lewis's Painting and Writing* (Santa Rosa: Black Sparrow Press, 1996), pp. 149-67; for a more general commentary see Daniel Schenker, *Wyndham Lewis: Religion and Modernism* (Tuscaloosa: University of Alabama Press, 1992).

30.   Only 'Section I' was published in 1928; Lewis's recalcitrance in completing the work eventually caused an acrimonious split with Chatto and Windus.

31.   Lewis to Moore, 3 September 1928, 'The Sturge Moore Letters', ed. Victor Cassidy, *Lewisletter* 7 (October 1977), p. 21. Traces of this original plan can be discerned in the continuation Lewis wrote in the 1950s, *The Human Age*.

32.   Cf. T. S. Eliot's '*Ulysses*, Order and Myth', *The Dial*, 75 (Nov 1923).

33.   In a typescript passage considerably modified for publication (perhaps through fear of censorship), the Bailiff has one of the dead beheaded for appearing before the court with a prominent erection visible through his clothing. Typescripts of *The Childermass* are in the Library of SUNY at Buffalo. Lewis's miscellaneous notes for the work are at the Carl A. Kroch Library, Cornell University.

34.   Kroch Library, Cornell University.

35.   Walter Michel, *Wyndham Lewis: Paintings and Drawings* (London: Thames and Hudson, 1971), nos M 617-19. All references to Lewis's visual work will be to Michel's catalogue; works with numbers preceded by 'M' are on paper, and those with numbers preceded by 'M P' are oil paintings. For colour reproductions of these images (plates 23-5) and an account of the circumstances of their composition, see Richard Cork, *Wyndham Lewis 1882-1957: The Twenties* (exhibition catalogue, London: Anthony d'Offay, 1984), n.p.

36.   *LE* 47-73, and originally published as an epilogue to Lady Gregory, *Visions and Beliefs in the West of Ireland, Collected by Lady Gregory: With Two Essays and Notes by W. B. Yeats* (1920).

37.   See Peter L. Caracciolo, 'Byzantium and Cosmic Man', pp. 23-29 for an exploration of the parallels between Lewis's work and Yeats's essay, which are too numerous to be coincidental—it was actually Yeats's own description of the region of the dead (supplemented with others) that Lewis's imagination had brought to such vivid life. Note also E. W. F. Tomlin's comment, 'This is the hallucinatory world of Yeats's *Byzantium* and of . . . Eliot's *Waste Land*', *Wyndham Lewis* (London: Longmans, 1955), p. 28. Annotating 'Byzantium', Jeffares (*YP* 601) explicates 'Hades' bobbin' as 'probably taken from the spindle in Plato's myth of Er (*The Republic*, 820)'. Lewis draws upon the same Platonic vision of divine judgement in *The Childermass* (see 'Carnivals of Mass-Murder').

38.   Tomlin, *Wyndham Lewis*, p. 30.

39.   *The Childermass: Section I* (London: Chatto and Windus, 1928), p. 2.

40.   *OED*, entry for 'turnpike', senses I. 2 and II. 8.

41.   'Textual Appendix', *TWM* 523. The quotation is misremembered from Rossetti's 'Sudden Light'. An undercurrent of scepticism remains in this passage, however. Lewis was well aware of Hume's comments on the certainty of the sun rising, and of William James's description of 'mental fire' as 'what won't burn real sticks' (cited in 'The Critical Realists').

42.   *TWM* 267. This quotation follows shortly after the deleted passage in the typescript (at Cornell). According to Roger Nyle Parisious (private communication), Yeats's copy of *Time and Western Man* shows signs of particular attention at this point in the chapter on Spengler (p. 285 in the original edition).

43. The same apprehension perhaps led Lewis to give the Wandering Jew a Gentile name; for tradition has it that the accursed nomad will arrive at the Judgement Seat on the Last Day. According to the rather less anti-semitic version of the mediæval legend the mocker of Christ on the *Via Dolorosa* is a non-Jew.

44. There were other obstacles, see 'Carnivals' p. 223; 'The Metamorphoses' p. 264.

45. *YA8* 163, 165, 169. See also Ron Heisler's discussion of 'Yeats's and the Thirteenth Æon', below pp. 253-64.

46. *TWM* 377. Neil Mann discusses Yeats's God as one of 'Choice or Chance', and quotes Yeats's 1920 note on 'Calvary', in which Michael Robartes declares '. . . when God throws He uses dice that have all numbers and all sides. Some worship His choice; that is easy; to know that He has willed for some unknown purpose all that happens is pleasant; but I have spent my life in worshipping His Chance . . .' (*VPl* 790). The student of Hume will be reminded of his statement in the *Enquiries* where he denies the existence of chance: 'Though there be no such thing as *Chance* in the world; our ignorance of the real cause of any event has the same influence on the understanding [as if there were] and begets a like species of belief or opinion' (*Enquiry concerning Human Understanding*, ed. J. Selby-Bigge [Oxford: Clarendon Press, 1894], Section VI, p. 56; see also *YL* 936). Lewis alludes to this same statement of Hume's in a passage deleted from *Time and Western Man*, quoted more fully below, in our discussion of 'Celtism'; having affirmed a faith in 'Natural Magic', Lewis declares, 'We worship things, or emblems of nature, before the swarming of Time; Chance rather than a God of Law or a God of Science' (quoted in editor's 'Afterword', p. 476; and see accompanying note). It seems probable that the 'fundamental agreement' of Yeats and Lewis went deeper than either of them knew.

47. Lewis to Wade, 12 March 1951. See n. 21.

48. Gladys Anne Wyndham Lewis to Hugh Anson Cartwright (n.d.; we are grateful to C. J. Fox for providing this quotation), and Jeffrey Meyers, *The Enemy: A Biography of Wyndham Lewis* (London: Routledge and Kegan Paul, 1980), p. 157. The drawings that Yeats saw are lost. They may have been bought by Lewis's publisher, C. H. Prentice, according to Mrs Lewis. Lewis invited Prentice to see them in 1930: 'I have a number of pictures (some of *a tower*, a special set) . . . I should like to show them to you . . .' (Lewis to Prentice, 14 October 1930, *Letters*, p. 196).

49. On Yeats's and Lewis's interest in *The Thousand and One Nights*, also see respectively Warwick Gould, 'A Lesson for the Circumspect: W. B. Yeats's two Versions of *A Vision* and *The Arabian Nights*' and the editor's 'Introduction' in *'The Arabian Nights' in English Literature*, ed. Peter L. Caracciolo (London: Macmillan, 1988), pp. 42, 43, 47, 56, 244-73.

50. *Bagdad* (M P38) is generally dated 1927, on the authority of the *Wyndham Lewis and Vorticism* catalogue of Lewis's retrospective at the Tate Gallery in 1956. There is no other evidence that it was painted before 1929; Lewis was not reliable as a dater of his paintings, and *Bagdad* is neither signed nor dated. It may have formed part of a cupboard painted by Lewis: the other panels (M P39-42) are labelled by Moffat, 'Painted in 1929', but they differ in style from *Bagdad*. The painting is in the collection of the Tate Gallery.

51. Wyndham Lewis, *The Caliph's Design: Architects! Where is your Vortex?* ed. Paul Edwards (Santa Barbara: Black Sparrow Press, 1986), p. 20.

52. Andrew Causey, 'The Hero and the Crowd: The Art of Wyndham Lewis in the Twenties', *Volcanic Heaven*, p. 101. See *TWM* 7: 'Contemporary, too, are the building of Alexandria, of Baghdad and of Washington'.

53. Lewis wrote to his publisher during his first visit to New York: 'You can here observe "the neo-barbarism" in full flower. The high buildings are very impressive, especially the later ones "hanging-gardens" style.' Lewis to Prentice, 1 August 1927, *Letters*, p. 169.

54. W. J. Perry, *The Children of the Sun: A Study in the Early Hstory of Civilization* (London: Methuen, 1923), p. 130. A heavily annotated copy of Perry's *The Growth of Civilization* (1924), once owned by the painter-novelist and now in the HRHRC, Austin, indicates how closely Lewis scrutinised this anthropologist's theories during the period in which he was composing the first version of 'Mr Zagreus and the Split-Man'; for Perry's influence on *The Apes of God* see 'Like a Mexith's Renowned Statue' esp. pp. 144-5, 155, n. 61.

55. For a discussion of Lewis's paintings of the thirties in these terms, see Paul Edwards, '"It's Time for another War": The Historical Unconscious and the Failure of Modernism', in David Peters Corbett, ed., *Wyndham Lewis and the Subject of Modern War* (Cambridge: C. U. P., 1997).

56. *The Convalescent* (M P46), *The Tank in the Clinic* (M P77) and *The Mud Clinic* (M P75) were all exhibited in 'Paintings and Drawings by Wyndham Lewis', December 1937, at the Leicester Galleries.

57. Wyndham Lewis, Foreword to catalogue, 1937, rpt. Walter Michel, *Wyndham Lewis*, p. 440.

58. In Walter Michel, *Wyndham Lewis*, p. 26. Note the relation of this picture to M 626 (1927), the title of which translates as 'immortal, therefore the soul') and another drawing with the same title, not in Michel (*c.*1933), reproduced as No. 123 in Jane Farrington, *Wyndham Lewis* (London: Lund Humphries & Manchester Art Galleries, 1980) and (in colour) as Pl. 10 in Seamus Cooney, ed., *Blast 3* (Santa Barbara: Black Sparrow Press, 1984).

59. As Kenner observes, in *ATHANATON* there are 'motifs from naval architecture . . . cross-sections of ships, cunningly metamorphosed into a grinning totem. . . . And hard against this black totem its blanched double, featureless and in profile, suggests some soul-body dichotomy to rhyme with the large dichotomy by which the picture is flanked' ('The Visual World of Wyndham Lewis', p. 26). On the relationship of Lewis's distortions here to the multiforms and similar expressive distortions found in the art of the Celts and other archaic societies, see the following note.

60. Neither Yeats nor Lewis ever visited Constantinople or Greece, but both visited areas of Italy influenced by Byzantium e.g., Venice, Ravenna, Sicily and Rome. Both studied in the British Museum where O. M. Dalton built up a fine Byzantine collection: his *Byzantine Art and Archaeology* (1911; *YL* 461) and *Eastern Christian Art* (1925) are well known. See *NC* 211 & ff. for a compendium of references on Yeats's scholarly sources on Byzantium. Commenting on his exhibits in the Second Post-Impressionist Exhibition (5 October 1912—31 January 1913), particularly *Creation* (M 46, 1912) and *Mother and Child* (M P6, 1912), the *Athenaeum*'s reviewer (who may have talked with Lewis) observes that these pictures are 'detached . . . mathematical . . . powerfully fantastic. . . . We can imagine the arabesques of the Book of Kells sharing with Egyptian sculp-

ture the parentage of such pictures' (*Athenaeum*, 12 Oct. 1912, p. 422). 'The
closest parallel [to Lewis's *Mother and Child*] is with Boris Anrep's con-
temporaneous description of the Russian icon as a nationalist resource for Gon-
charova's saints', notes Lisa Tickner in her 'A Lost Lewis: The *Mother and Child*
of 1912', *Wyndham Lewis Annual*, II (1995), 5, 2. A drawing of the same year,
Russian Madonna or *Russian Scene* (M 83, 1912) shows Lewis's knowledge of
Russian icons. The Yeats circle too became intimate with the arts of more than
just the Orthodox and Ancient Irish Churches. Pl. 9-10 in *YA4* demonstrate
how Sturge Moore's cover for *Responsibilities and Other Poems* (1916) derives
from a design which was based on a page from an early 7th century copy of the
Latin Gospels that 'resembles the Lindisfarne Gospels'; serpentine ornaments
reminiscent of spiral motifs in the *Book of Kells* may be seen. See also *TSMC* 30-6,
48. *Stories of Red Hanrahan and The Secret Rose*, illustrated and decorated by
Norah McGuinness (London: Macmillan, 1927) shows Yeats's absorption in
Byzantine mosaic and old Irish art: see *L* 738 and *VSR* 271-86 & pl. 9-37. Such
syncretism was not unique at this time: Art O'Murnaghan's *The Book of Resurrection* (1922) unites Celtic art and eastern mysticism (see *The Rediscovery of
Ireland's Past: The Celtic Revival 1830-1890* [Thames and Hudson, 1980], p. 120
and plates xxi-xxii). In a postcard to A. H. Fisher (11 July 1931), Sturge Moore
took a purist view of the Byzantine exhibition in Paris in 1931 (Sturge Moore
papers, London University Library); whereas Yeats's spiritualist interests had
led in the previous year to *The Resurrection*'s enthralling synthesis of Buddhist
Noh drama and mediæval mystery plays. See also D. J. Gordon, *W. B. Yeats:
Images of a Poet* (Manchester: Manchester University Press, 1961), p. 81. There is
a distinct 'family resemblance' between the profile stuck on its pole in
ATHANATON and the stylised zoomorphs of the old Irish illuminated manuscripts, though it also recalls an Easter Island statuette in the British Museum.
See Leonhard Adam, *Primitive Art* (Harmondsworth: Penguin, 1940), pl. 41;
also Malcolm Mcleod and John Mack, *Ethnic Sculpture* (London: British
Museum, 1985), p. 48.

61. In *TWM*, Lewis refers to Spengler's historically valid claim that 'the greek statue
     . . . came to life in Byzantium or Alexandria by receiving soulful eyes that
     "entered into" the onlooker' (p. 269). Roger Nyle Parisious informs us that the
     equivalent page in Yeats's copy of Lewis's book (p. 287) shows signs of the
     reader's close attention here. Yeats had already singled out Spengler's reference
     to the drilled pupils of eyes in Roman statues as evidence of the similarity
     between his own and Spengler's theories of cyclical history (see *TSMC* 105).
     Compare also 'the sparkling eye' which Lewis sees as similarly transforming
     Ancient Egyptian art in *The Diabolical Principle and the Dithyrambic Spectator*
     (London: Chatto and Windus, 1931, p. 182). In Lewis's exposition of his theory
     of the comic, 'The Meaning of the Wild Body', it is the eye of a fat man running
     that indicates his detachment from his absurd and clumsy body, and shows that
     he is a person, not merely a *thing* (1927; rpt. Wyndham Lewis, *The Complete
     Wild Body*, ed. Bernard Lafourcade [Santa Barbara: Black Sparrow Press, 1982],
     pp. 159-60). The presence of eyes in *ATHANATON* associates the image not
     only with 'Byzantium', but also with Yeats's 'drilled pupil of the eye [in a
     Byzantine] ivory [which gives] to Saint or Angel a look of some great bird star-
     ing at miracle' (*CVA* 191-92). The ghostly presence in Lewis's picture seems to
     anticipate 'A Bronze Head': 'Human, superhuman, a bird's round eye, | Every-

thing else withered and mummy-dead. | What great tomb-haunter sweeps the distant sky . . . ?' (*VP* 618).

62. Yeats wrote to thank Moore for *The Winding Stair* cover on 7 September 1933 (*TSMC* 177). It is possible that Lewis might have not only seen a draft of Yeats's 'Byzantium', but also might have followed the collaborators' initial ideas. Yeats first suggested (26th September 1930) images that recall Sturge Moore's designs for *Reveries* and *Selected Poems*: 'The Winding Stair, as you will see by one of the poems is the winding stone stair of Ballylee enlarged into a symbol but . . . . [i]t might be a mere gyre—Blake's design of Jacob's Ladder—with figures, little figures. . . . Of course a suggestion of a stone stair might be possible—a hooded figure coming or going, perhaps entering, a mere suggestion of a stair.' By 4 Oct., he had decided to call the book *Byzantium*. On 5 Oct., Sturge Moore noted 'a good number of possible graphic images'. The 'moon-lit dome' of Hagia Sophia, above which float the psychic emanations successively conjured up in 'Byzantium' provided the basis for an initial design (now in the University of London Library; see *YA4*, pl. 9-15). On 5 Oct., Moore is glad to have recently heard from Lewis of Yeats's 'passage through London'. On 8 Oct., making an 'improvement' to his poem and pointing his designer to 'Raphael's statue of the Dolphin carrying one of the Holy Innocents to Heaven', Yeats 'approv[es] Lewis's philosophic attack in his *Apes*: indeed I always approve his philosophy'. On 24 Oct., Moore responds cautiously to Yeats's enthusiasm for Lewis: he agrees that 'many of the situations in his Apes are magnificent inventions and much of the writing is most compelling'. Sturge Moore is 'not sure what the positive tenets of Wyndham Lewis's philosophy are' but 'more or less understand[s] the negative ones, and only deplore[s] the necessity he feels of turning them into a kind of politics in which personal animosity plays a large part'. By 11 Jan. 1931, Moore is 'refreshed' by Lewis's uncritical account of the 'Hitlerites' in Germany (pp. 163-68).

63. Born in Canada, of partly native American (Huron) stock, or so the family gossip went, and with his long-standing interest in Cave art, Polar and Steppe culture, Lewis was, as might be expected, drawn to the so-called 'X-ray' style (developed by the early hunters) in which the animal's internal organs were displayed. Originating 'in the prehistoric rock pictures . . . in Scandinavia and Siberia, the X-ray style has continued in use as late as this century in the ornamental art of native Siberian hunters . . . and in America among the Eskimos and Indians of the North-West. . . . The magic rites which are practised among the Ojibwa (Chippewa) people of the northern U.S.A. and Canada include the drawing of images 'in the X-ray style', and can still be observed . . . . The same tendency towards abstraction . . . already noticed in the Siberian rock pictures can be followed in X-ray images found in India, Malaya and western New Guinea, [Australia].' Andreas Lommel, *Landmarks of the World's Art: Prehistoric and Primitive Man* (London: Paul Hamlyn, 1966), pp. 71-2. A succession of books on this subject appeared in the late twenties: Franz Boas, *Primitive Art* (Cambridge, Mass.: Harvard University Press, 1927), G. Boroffka, *Scythian Art* (1928) and Mikhail Rostovtzeff, *The Animal Style in South Russia and China* (Princeton: Princeton University Press, 1929). Sturge Moore's use of the X-ray style most probably derives from Lewis's example.

64. It would seem more than likely that *ATHANATON*, a pen and ink gouache (10 x 11in), was one of the new works which the poverty-stricken Lewis remembers

having had to complete on a chair for want of an easel. See letter to Sidney Schiff, 21 May 1933, (*Letters*, p. 213).

65.   At least two other of Lewis's thirties pictures have Yeatsian connections. *The Siege* [later retitled *The Surrender*] *of Barcelona* (1936; M P61) may reflect Sturge Moore's design for *The Tower*. Lewis's massive walls and forts in the fore- and middle-ground of the picture are as without crenellation as Thoor Ballylee is revealed to be in that design. A 1938 watercolour, *Fann Macuil, the Great Irish Giant, Waiting for Far Rua* (M 901) is a mocking homage to Yeats.

66.   See 'Byzantium and Cosmic Man', pp. 25-6. Yeats returns to the theme in 'News for the Delphic Oracle' (*VP* 611-2).

67.   As his lecture-notes, quoted on page *check*, confirm. See Wyndham Lewis, *America and Cosmic Man* (London: Nicholson and Watson, 1948), Chapter 20 (the introduction to Part Two, in which Lewis discusses his hope for a renewed global civilization). Lewis's thirteen-paragraph chapter seems to acknowledge Yeats's eloquent experiment with the sonnet and sequence forms in 'The Second Coming'. See the discussion in 'Byzantium and Cosmic Man', p. 28.

68.   See Walter Michel, *Wyndham Lewis*, ch. 6, and Robert Stacey, '"Magical Presences in a Magical Place": From *Homage to Etty* to *The Island*', in Catherine Mastin, Robert Stacey and Thomas Dilworth, *'The Talented Intruder': Wyndham Lewis in Canada, 1939-1945* (Catalogue of exhibition; Windsor, Ontario: Art Gallery of Windsor, 1993), pp. 107-54. In his discussion of *The Island* (M P104, 1942), Lewis's major imaginative oil of the forties, Stacey discusses suggestions that the island depicted is modelled on Böcklin's *Die Toteninsel*.

69.   Wyndham Lewis, *The Human Age: Book 2, Monstre Gai; Book 3, Malign Fiesta* (London: Methuen, 1955), pp. 370-3.

70.   Philip Head, in an unpublished paper delivered at the Wyndham Lewis conference held at the University of Hertfordshire, 25 May 1996, 'A Tale of Two Critics: Wyndham Lewis and Sir Herbert Read', argues convincingly that Lewis, despite his professed 'classicism', was more truly in the English Romantic tradition (particularly of Coleridge) than the more publicly pro-Romantic Read.

71.   Draft of p. 375, Textual Appendix, *TWM* 527. Lewis's statement (quoted above, n. 53) that he worships a 'God of Chance' immediately follows this passage.

72.   Lewis attacks Whitehead's *Science and the Modern World* (Cambridge: Cambridge University Press, 1926) and the Abbé Brémond's *La Poésie pure* (Paris: Bernard Grasset, 1926) in *TWM*.

73.   See the chapter, 'Nietzsche as a Vulgariser' in Wyndham Lewis, *The Art of Being Ruled* (1926) rpt., ed. Reed Way Dasenbrock (Santa Barbara: Black Sparrow Press, 1989).

74.   Wyndham Lewis, *The Lion and the Fox: The Role of the Hero in the Plays of Shakespeare* (London: Grant Richards, 1927; *YL* 1123).

75.   On Eliot's long-standing and complex debts to Buddhism see: T. S. Eliot, 'The Use of Poetry and the Use of Criticism' (1933) in *Selected Prose*, ed. F. Kermode (London: Faber, 1975), p. 83; Stephen Spender, *Eliot* (London:Fontana, 1975), pp. 26-7; P. S. Sri, *T. S. Eliot: Vedanta and Buddhism* (Vancouver: Vancouver University Press, 1985); P. L. Caracciolo, 'Buddhist Typologies in [the Marlow Cycle] and their contribution to the Modernism of Jacob Epstein, Wyndham Lewis and T. S. Eliot' in *Conradian* XIII (1988), pp. 67-91. T. S. Eliot's work, until it sought the backing of theology, constituted a continuous judgement by the Absolute upon itself.

76. Lewis's interest in Blake probably came from his connection with the Laurence Binyon and Sturge Moore circle, in whose company he met Yeats at the Vienna Café. Moore's study of Blake and Flaubert, *Art and Life*, was published in 1910 (London: Methuen).

77. F. H. Bradley, *Appearance and Reality* (2nd ed., 1902), quoted in *TWM* 419; Bradley is called a Platonist in Angela Elliott's Introduction to Part VI of Anna Baldwin and Sarah Hutton, edd. *Platonism and the English Imagination* (Cambridge: C. U. P., 1994), p. 278. Bradley was a Platonist in being an idealist, but the immediately influential predecessor in his case was Hegel, as Dennis Brown recognises in describing him as a Neo-Hegelian in his contribution to *Platonism and the English Imagination* (p. 306).

78. Wyndham Lewis, *One-Way Song* (1933), rpt. *Collected Poems and Plays*, ed. Alan Munton (Manchester: Carcanet, 1979), p. 58.

79. Wyndham Lewis, 'W. B. Yeats' (1939) rpt., *Creatures of Habit and Creatures of Change*, p. 285.

80. At the end of the obituary, Lewis attempts to apply a 'tougher' vocabulary to a commendation of Yeats's work, but not many readers will find the new formulation more satisfying: 'The fact is that in a certain mood I *do* respond to Maeterlinck, even to an Irish brogue. And Yeats *has* given me a sort of kick: a kind of soft, dreamy kick. I am obliged to him.' (*ibid.*, p. 286.)

81. 'Creative Literature', (1943-44) unpublished manuscript lecture notes in the Carl A. Kroch Library, Cornell (Box 50). It seems unlikely that Lewis actually heard Yeats recite these particular lines, since the poet did not choose to reprint them after their first appearance, under the title 'Where my Books go', in the children's book *Irish Fairy Tales* (London: T. Fisher Unwin, 1892), p. v. The first two lines should read *'All the words that I gather, | And all the words that I write'* (*VP* 739). Possibly Lewis misremembered the lines from his own childhood reading; he was ten years old in 1892. He also misquotes from *The Wanderings of Oisin* and 'The Song of the Wandering Aengus'. In another lecture (on visual art; 1944, Box 19), he mangles 'Aedh tells of the Rose in his Heart'. Evidence of Lewis's relaxed mood on the occasion of these lectures is provided by his similar quotations of lines from Joyce's poems (of which he officially disapproved), 'Bahnhofstrasse'—slightly misremembered—and, from 'Alone', 'The shore-lamps in the sleeping lake | Laburnum tendrils trail', lines which he praises for their visual image. In Box 24 of Cornell's Lewis collection, there is a transcription by Mrs Lewis from the 'back of T. E. Lawrence letter' of a note on 'Baile & Ailleen' [*sic*], along with a quotation from *The Celtic Twilight* concerning the absence of conventional moral perspective in Celtic beliefs. Lewis strongly approved of this non-moral attitude. The same passage was included in the draft of a section of *The Lion and the Fox* devoted to the contribution of 'race' to Shakespeare's personality (this section was cut and relegated to an Appendix in the published edition): 'Mr Yeats, in his beautiful random essays, *The Celtic Twilight*, reproaches the scottish partner in the 'celtic' combination with brutalizing the fairies . . . . On the moral question, Mr Yeats writes as follows: 'In Ireland we hear little of the darker powers, and come across any who have seen them even more rarely, for the imagination of the people dwells rather upon the fantastic and capricious, and fantasy and caprice would lose the freedom which is their breath of life, were they to unite either with evil or with good.' (Bound typescript of *The Lion and the Fox*, Buffalo, *c.*1923-24). The quota-

ation is from the opening paragraph of 'The Sorcerers'; Lewis also paraphrases one of the stories from 'A Remonstrance with Scotsmen . . .' (*Myth* 37-40, 106-9).

82. For a discussion of this aspect of Lewis's work, see Peter Nicholls, *Modernisms: A Literary Guide* (London: Macmillan, 1995), pp. 182-87.

83. *The Art of Being Ruled*, p. 267.

84. *TWM* 75. For a perceptive discussion of Lewis's analysis of the interaction of Modernism and nationalism in an Irish context, see Emer Nolan, *James Joyce and Nationalism* (London: Routledge, 1995), pp. 11-13.

85. See, however, Scott W. Klein, *The Fictions of James Joyce and Wyndham Lewis: Monsters of Nature and Design* (Cambridge: C. U. P., 1994), pp. 139-143, for a discussion of the way *The Apes of God* lays bare both the futile nationalist rivalries and the hollow claims of a central Britishness inherent in the cultural politics of the period in Great Britain.

86. Ratner is not, as is frequently thought, a caricature of Joyce, but is modelled on John Rodker, and his writing parodies Rodker's 'Joycean' *Adolphe*. To that extent his inclusion makes a contribution to the dialogue with Joycean Modernism in the book. Jeffrey Meyers repeats the long-standing misidentification in *The Enemy: A Biography of Wyndham Lewis*, p. 180, and adds a new one of his own: 'Lewis also provides a shrewd, ironic vignette of Eliot as the prim, supercilious American, Mr. Horty' (p. 177)—who appears in *AG* 289, 293, 295 and 307. Lewis's notes and diagram of the seating arrangements for the 'Chez Lionel Kein' section of *The Apes* show that Robert Horty represents 'R. Mc.C.', whom we take to be Robert McAlmon. Eliot makes no appearance in the satire, and his version of Modernism seems not to be encoded within it (except indirectly in discussions of the possibility of 'impersonality' in art) either. Lewis's notes are at Cornell, box 3.

87. See P. L. Caracciolo, 'Like a Mexith's renowned statue', pp. 134-36.

88. To Lewis's eyes did Yeats seem to be asking for trouble? Lewis saw the principal so-called 'revolutionary' tendency of his day as being 'that of a return to earlier forms of life' and he targets 'the Naughty Nineties' (see *TWM*, ch. 8); about much the same time, Yeats appears to have felt that the aesthetic ideals and thematic interests of the 1890s were far from dead; a letter of 1928 finds the poet confiding, 'in some curious way—Edith Sitwell to witness—we have returned of late to mood of the nineties', and indeed he welcomed this return. Not only did Yeats defend Sitwell's *Gold Coast Customs* against Lewis's attack (see his letter of commendation of *The Apes of God* to Lewis, September 1930), but he also included six of Sitwell's poems in *OBMV*. See Stephen Regan, '"Oil and Blood": Yeats's Return to the Nineties', *YA7* 194-9.

89. *AG* 40 and 126. Note Yeats's judgement of his own juvenile compositions: 'My lines but seldom scanned, for I could not understand the prosody in the books, although there were many lines that taken by themselves had music' (*Au* 66).

90. *AG*, pp. 42 and 127. The Yeatsian allusions are to 'Aedh wishes for the Cloths of Heaven' and 'Aedh gives his Beloved certain Rhymes', from *The Wind Among the Reeds* (1899): see *VP* 157-8; 176).

91. For Yeats's account of these aspects of himself, see *Au* 11-13, 26, 29 and 78.

92. *AG* 478; a connection with Yeats's uncle, George Pollexfen, might be intended; see 'Like a Mexith's renowned statue', pp. 134-6.

93. *AG* p. 480. Compare the note to 'The Hosting of the Sidhe': 'One hears many stories of the kind, and a man whose son is believed to go out riding among

them at night tells me that he is careless about everything, and lies in bed until it is late in the day. A doctor believes this boy to be mad. Those that are at times "away", as it is called, know all things, but are afraid to speak. A countryman at Kiltartan says, "There was one of the Lydons—John—was away for seven years, lying in his bed, but brought away at nights, and he knew everything; and one, Kearney, up in the mountains, a cousin of his own, lost two hoggets, and came and told him, and he knew the very spot where they were, and told him, and he got them back again. But *they* were vexed at that, and took away the power, so that he never knew anything again, no more than another"' (*VP* 801; see also *YA10*, 3-32).

94.   *AG* p. 418. Lewis's aesthetic of 'surfaces' is expounded in *Satire and Fiction* and *Men without Art* (1934) rpt., ed. Seamus Cooney (Santa Rosa: Black Sparrow Press, 1987).

95.   *Myth* 111. There are some further parallels between Dan's experiences and a vision of the Last Judgement that Yeats himself had had a quarter of a century earlier, a dream memorable both for its serio-comic nature and the elegant circumstances of its publication. The Apocalypse seemed about to take place in a modern metropolis resembling Paris; the dreamer travelled in 'a brake' from an affluent *quartier* to a poor area where the workers had abandoned their labours; next he found that the public was called upon to curse (thus increasing the likelihood of the damnation of) a seller of patent medicines. The possibility that the end is not nigh is raised—in which case the vendor would be compensated: the after-effect of the dream was fear. In *The Apes of God* the 'fulfilment' of Dan's apocalyptic vision is the General Strike of 1926: hardly Armageddon. See 'A Dream of the World's End', *The Green Sheaf*, No. 2 (1903), 6-7.

96.   Later Lewis returned to the idea of the Yeatsian visionary fool in order to convey a sense of the dawning 'truth' about contemporary politics. Launcelot Nidwit reaches an understanding about the Spanish Civil War through 'séances', in Lewis's anti-war pamphlet, *Count your Dead: They are Alive! Or, A New War in the Making* (London: Lovat Dickson, 1937). These are reminiscent of the manner in which Yeats and his wife collaborated in producing *A Vision*. See 'Byzantium and Cosmic Man', pp. 25-6. Lewis re-read Yeats's *Autobiographies* in 1937 when preparing to write his own autobiography, *Blasting and Bombardiering*. His somewhat disobligingly annotated copy of *Dramatis Personae* is in the Kroch Library at Cornell. He discusses Yeats's and George Moore's biographical treatment of each other in *Blasting and Bombardiering*, pp. 10-11.

97.   See Wyndham Lewis, 'The Politics of Artistic Expression' (1925) rpt. *Creatures of Habit and Creatures of Change*, p. 119: 'When you see *art coming over into life* as it were, you know at once, then, what is likely to happen. In this respect things have never looked blacker than they have today. For everywhere the material of tragedy is forsaking the stage and descending amongst the audience.'

98.   *TWM* 377. Yeats avers 'all such rejections stop at the conscious mind' (*AVB* 4n.).

99.   Wyndham Lewis, *The Human Age*: Book 2, *Monstre Gai*: Book 3, *Malign Fiesta* (London: Methuen 1955) and *The Human Age*: Book 1, *Childermass* (London: Methuen, 1956). See D. G. Bridson, 'The Making of "The Human Age"', *Agenda* (Wyndham Lewis Special Issue), pp. 163-71. See also 'The Metamorphoses of *The Human Age*', pp. 258-86.

100. The original title was even more Yeatsian. Responding promptly to a letter from Lewis dated 26 January 1955 that had announced a new name for his super-

natural sequence (*Letters*, p. 559), on 27 January 1955 his publisher, J. Alan White, welcomed *The Human Age* as an 'excellent' general title and looked forward to, inter alia, Book 4, 'The Judgement'. We are grateful to C. J. Fox for sharing with us this information, the result of research in the Cornell Wyndham Lewis archive.

101. Wyndham Lewis, *Malign Fiesta* (London: Calder and Boyars, 1966), pp. 218-19.

102. For a discussion of their apocalyptic, specifically Joachimist dimension, see Marjorie Reeves and Warwick Gould, *Joachim of Fiore and the Myth of the Eternal Evangel in the Nineteenth Century* (Oxford: Clarendon, 1987), pp. 250-61).

103. (*VPl* 708-9). There is a strong possibility, so far overlooked, that this play may have influenced Lewis's *Enemy of the Stars*, first published in *Blast* 1 (June 1914). The visionary in this play abandons normal life to work in his uncle's wheelwright's shop, in order to overcome the inauthenticity of human existence.

104. See Warwick Gould, '"What is the explanation of it all?": Yeats's "Little Poem about Nothing"', *YA5* 212-213. This quatrain of May 1938 is, as Deirdre Toomey has demonstrated, 'an unorthodox contribution to a tradition of poems upon Nothing which go back at least to the early Middle Ages'. See Deirdre Toomey, '"What is the explanation of it all?": Something and Nothing', *YA9* 309-312.

105. Philip C. Almond, *The British Discovery of Buddhism* (Cambridge: Cambridge University Press, 1988), pp. 102-110.

106. Horace H. Wilson, 'On Buddhaa and Buddhism', *The Journal of the Royal Asiatic Society of Great Britain and Ireland*, 16 (1856), pp. 229-65, esp. p. 256.

107. Almond, *The British Discovery of Buddhism*, pp. 106, 110.

108. Mathew Gibson, '"What Empty Eyeballs Knew": Zen Buddhism in "The Statues" and the *Principles* of *A Vision*', (*YA11* 141-55). The affinities betweenthe relation of the Buddhist Wheel of Life to Nirvana and that of Yeats's cycles to the *Thirteenth Cone* are compatible with the sources explored by Ron Heisler (sss *infra*, pp. *check*), since Mani recognized Buddha as a 'revealer'. See Kurt Rudolf, *Gnosis* (Edinburgh: T. & T. Clark, 1983), p. 132.

109. 'Ich hab' Mein Sach auf Nichts gestellt', the first line of Goethe's poem, 'Vanitas! Vanitatum vanitas!' is the first heading and final sentence of Stirner's influential *Der Einzige und sein Eigentum*, translated by S. T. Byington as *The Ego and His Own* (London: A. C. Fifield, 1912).

110. *TWM* 375. Compare a note in Lewis's *Childermass* papers (f. 132), now at Cornell (and quoted, *TWM* 596 [note to p. 377]): 'Diversity is of the essence of individuality. The more diversity nature can contrive, the intenser the individualism produced. Every retreat from that exclusiveness is a step towards a Unity that is strictly Nothing.' One of these extremes or parameters is the equivalent of Yeats's cycle 'where everything would be as particular and concrete as human intensity permits of'; the other equates with the 'surrender to God [that is, to 'Nothing'] of all that I am' (see above p. 138).

111. Most extensively in the 1935 novel (published 1937), *The Revenge for Love*, where the source of value, founded on a 'nothing' that recurs incessantly throughout the text, is Margot's irrational attachment to a clowning Spanish dwarf/baby that claims her as its mother (a kinship she will not deny). See Paul Edwards, 'Signifying Nothing: *The Revenge for Love*', *Enemy News*, No. 15 (Winter 1982), p. 22.

112. There is no space here to consider Lewis's treatment of Sartre and *le néant* in *The Writer and the Absolute* (London: Methuen, 1952), but, for illuminating surveys of the impact of 'Nothing' on modern thought and the arts, see Maurice Tuchman's scholarly collection on *The Spiritual in Art: Abstract Painting 1890-1985* (Los Angeles County Museum of Art, 1986) and George Steiner's *Real Presences: Is there Anything in What We Say?* (London: Faber and Faber, 1989).

113. W. Lewis, *The Red Priest* (London: Methuen, 1956) pp. 107 and 109.

114. W. Lewis, *The Demon of Progress in the Arts* (London: Methuen, 1954), p. 32.

115. 'I remained, beyond the usual period, congealed in a kind of cryptic immaturity. In my social relations the contacts remained, for long, primitive. I recognized dimly this obstruction: was conscious of gaucherie, of wooden responses—all fairly common symptoms, of course.' Wyndham Lewis, *Rude Assignment: A Narrative of my Career up-to-date* (1950), rpt. as *Rude Assignment: An Intellectual Autobiography*, ed. Toby Foshay: Santa Barbara: Black Sparrow Press, 1984), p. 126.

We should like to acknowledge the assistance afforded us in the research for this essay by Small Personal Research Grants awarded to each of us by the British Academy. Thanks also to David McLintock for assistance with German, to the RNIB and Michael Higgins.

Staging *The King's Threshold*

Richard Allen Cave

THE DISCOVERY BY COLIN SMYTHE of a stage design (Plate 4) by Yeats himself for the first production of *The King's Threshold* prompts a reconsideration of this early and much revised play.[1] It is a play that has excited little commentary over the years: critics of Yeats's drama tend to give it honourable mention in passing; Peter Ure and S. B. Bushrui are virtually alone in devoting to it entire chapters in their published criticism.[2] The problem perhaps lies in the extent and complexity of the revisions Yeats felt it necessary to make to it: it certainly is the play where Yeats seems least confident of what he is doing both thematically and theatrically, and many years passed before it reached its final form as recorded in the *Collected Plays*. There is some truth in Ure's judgement that '*The King's Threshold* is, in the best sense, an amateur play and almost the last play by Yeats of which this could properly be said'.[3] 'Amateur' was, interestingly, the word used by Max Beerbohm of the whole company of Irish players when he commented in his column in the *Saturday Review* on the visit to London by the Irish National Theatre Society on the occasion in 1904 when they first played *The King's Threshold* in the metropolis. 'One could not object to them,' he wrote, 'as to the ordinary amateur' and substantiated this judgement by describing their style as offering an 'oasis' in what had otherwise been for some weeks in his experience a theatrical desert.[4] The performance may have been different, special; but he still found it necessary to qualify the work as *amateur*. Was this because the production demonstrated an uncertainty of aim?

Noticeably Beerbohm writes more warmly of the acting than of the play; and indeed he was but one of several critics to complain that *The King's Threshold* lacked action. A. B. Walkley in the *Times Literary Supplement* considered it 'really a procession of supplicants' in which 'typical personages follow one another beseeching the poet to eat and drink'[5]. William Archer agreed: 'Incidents succeed one another in careful and logical gradation but have no complexity of interrelation. They form a series not a system' (*CL3* 561 n. 2). Perhaps the review that rankled most with Yeats was that in the *Daily Telegraph* which described him as decidedly wanting in a sense of theatre and concluded with the opinion that '*The King's Threshold*, doubtless, would make excellent reading . . . but its dramatic qualities . . . are scarcely discernible' (*ibid.*). Yeats tried at first to defend the play to Clement Shorter on the grounds that 'the interest of a poetical drama must always be a poetical interest, and if one doesn't care for poetry poetical drama is somebody else's game. It must be dramatic, but in its own way'. Earlier in the letter he had described that 'way' as sustaining the play 'in a world of vast sentiments' (*ibid.*). Implicit in that comment one can detect the reasons why critics found the play in performance monotonous and predictable: *The King's Threshold* in its first performed version showed a sad want of tonal variety. However a few weeks later when the play was to be revived for a 'conversatione', Yeats set about considerably revising whole sections of it creating new scenes especially for the Mayor of Kinvara to add 'energy', dramatic interest and variety. He went through the text 'line by line with William Fay', intent on improving it in a manner possible only 'when one has the actors under one's eyes' and created a new episode involving the Mayor, the Cripples and Seanchan's former servants 'which works itself up into a tumult of voices which are suddenly silenced by the entrance of the Court'.[6]

If it was the dramatic structure and the playing that elicited comment from the London reviewers, it was more usually the theme and the design which Irish critics chose to write about the previous autumn. Anticipating the opening of the play on October 8, 1903, Yeats had written in the September issue of *Samhain* announcing his

new work and describing it as 'founded on the old story of Seanchan
the poet, and King Guare of Gort'; but he warns that there is a significant change in his treatment of the material: 'I have seen the
story from the poet's point of view, and not like the old storytellers,
from the King's' (*Ex* 102-3). Though Yeats writes of '*old* storytellers', the likeliest source which would have been familiar to the
majority of his audience was Lady Wilde's tale 'Seanchan the Bard
and the King of the Cats' from *Ancient Legends of Ireland* (1887).[7]
This is a farcical yarn in which Seanchan pretends to be disgusted
with the food proffered to him by the King and goes on a hunger-
strike to shame him, because privately he is sulking out of envy for
the superior quality of life, the rich dress, and the privileges experienced by the nobility at Guaire's court. None of the characters in
the story is particularly admirable and laughter at the comedy keeps
the reader quite distanced from them all.

Clearly at this stage of his career Yeats was not happy with this
debased image of the poet and his vocation. The shift in focus he
writes about inevitably introduced a change of tone, as is implicit in
that phrase about a 'world of vast sentiments' which Yeats penned
to Clement Shorter. A. E. Malone writing retrospectively about the
play guessed Yeats's agenda:

> He [Yeats] had been conducting a strenuous agitation in favour of
> the artist in the national life, but no change had been effected in
> public opinion. The claims of the artist were challenged by the
> politicans and the moralists, and in this play no room was left for
> doubt as to the place which Mr. Yeats demanded for the artist in the
> life of the nation. That the topicality was deliberate is indicated by a
> note which the poet appended to the play in 1911. The play, he
> says, 'was written when our Society was beginning its fight for the
> recognition of pure art in a community of which one half is buried
> in the practical affairs of life, and the other half in politics and a
> propagandist patriotism'.[8]

Arthur Griffith, writing in *The United Irishman*, clearly perceived
Yeats's agenda too; and would have none of it. The play was, he
argued, beautiful but unconvincing:

> If the poet desires, as Mr. Yeats's poet desired, to sit at the King's
> table, and feast at the King's expense, it is right he should obey the
> King's law. But this Mr. Yeats would not have him do. He would

have him accept Caesar's wages without rendering Caesar obedience, and would deem it virtue in him that he refuses to do so. We are firm believers in the freedom of art, but if the artist lusts after place and power, it is reasonable he should pay the price by relinquishing some of that freedom. When the homage rendered to art ceases to be voluntary, it ceases to be sincere, and it was that insincere homage that Seanchan, who no doubt had been corrupted by too plentiful red ale and tender swineflesh and purple and fine linen, was after. As we watched the play, our sympathy went out to the honest soldier who wished to put his sword into the selfish old man who lay on the King's steps intimidating where he could not convince, contending for a soft life in a King's bosom instead of an eternal one in a people's heart. We hold it a pity that King Guaire did not hang Seanchan. Had he done so, Art would have been for all time his debtor.[9]

The verdict was cruelly expressed (within fifteen months Yeats was calling Griffith's bluff in shaping the dramatic movement towards the founding of the Abbey Theatre as a *national* enterprise); but a reading of the first published versions of the play make it apparent how such an interpretation was possible.

Yeats saw the play very much as a vehicle for the central actor, had indeed written the part of Seanchan with Frank Fay firmly in mind and he took pains before rehearsals began to ensure that Fay fully appreciated the demands it would make on his stamina and vocal resources. Even so, that first version does not give the actor much help: the part can read as querulous and intemperate, as Seanchan castigates or belittles everyone who seeks to persuade him to end his fast. In defending the work of the Irish Literary Theatre Yeats recalled how 'Euripides once made hostility enthusiasm by asking his playgoers whether it was his business to teach them or their business to teach him'.[10] The didactic impulse in *The King's Threshold* is perhaps too strong, too directive; its nature as allegory or parable results in a decidedly closed ending (Guaire learns his lesson and restores Seanchan to his former privileges) where *Cathleen ni Houlihan* and *The Hour-Glass* have more enigmatic conclusions which leave audiences to make their own choices of interpretation.

The problem is that the ending of *The King's Threshold* does not sit comfortably on the rest of the play: the King is showed as every bit as intransigent as Seanchan but for the sake of the ending he suddenly and inexplicably capitulates (in that sense there is no *learning* of a lesson, no process of change). The whole movement of the drama with its battle of two intractable wills requires a different ending; and Yeats knew it ('I had originally intended to end the play tragically').[11] But he agreed for a friend's sake—was that friend, perhaps, Lady Gregory?—to resolve the action peacably; and the play was not given its present tragic conclusion till 1922, which leaves Seanchan dead, the King shamed, and the issue of principle challengingly unresolved, since the moral victory Seanchan has won has cost him his life.

It is not surprising that a tragic ending should be felt to be appropriate: Yeats confided to Frank Fay that the play 'is constructed like a Greek play' (*CL3* 413, 8 August, 1903). Within a few days he wrote sending some revisions to the original typescript, adding that he wanted 'the whole opening of the play done in a grave statuesque way as if it were a Greek play' (*ibid.* 417, 14 August, 1903). Significantly by the same post he wrote also to Gilbert Murray, whose translations of some four plays by Euripides were currently in the process of being staged by Granville Barker at the Royal Court Theatre, informing him that *The King's Threshold* was virtually finished and promising to send a copy as soon as possible; he stated the intended dates of performance and urged Murray to come and see it (*ibid.* 418). Clearly Greek tragedy with its implacable progress towards a destined conclusion was Yeats's model throughout the composition of the play: Euripides' preferred dramatic structure would appear to be episodic like Yeats's play, though a closer thematic parallel amongst the extant classical tragedies would be Aeschylus' *Prometheus Bound* where a victim of tyranny, who is suffering for giving to mankind fire and the creative arts, is approached by a series of visitors intent on either sympathising with him or persuading him to desist in his rebellion and submit to Zeus's power.[12] The question remains why Yeats lacked the courage of his convictions and delayed giving the play its required ending till actual political circumstance (the hunger strikes of the suffragettes and later of Terence MacSwiney) set him ready examples.

Laying the burden of responsibility on a 'friend' would seem a little unjust (though Lady Gregory's collaborative hand in Yeats's dramatic work was still strong at this time); it would seem that he is on sincerer ground in admitting that he was all too well aware that 'a tragic effect is very fragile and a wrong intonation, or even a wrong light or costume will spoil it all'.[13] In 1903 Yeats had still a great deal to learn about controlling and directing audience response and he had but recently had the experience of hearing audiences, stimulated to laughter by the opening passages of dialogue in *Cathleen ni Houlihan*, continuing their mirth after the appearance of the Old Woman, when he had wished to shift the drama on to another plane of reality and an appropriately elevated tone with her entrance. With his next plays, *On Baile's Strand* and *Deirdre*, he was to begin to experiment with deploying moments of black or bitterly sardonic comedy at the very moment of the tragic crisis, as if to forestall an audience's reaction to heightened emotion that might be of the wrong tenor. Increasingly over his career as playwright Yeats was to discover how to heighten the tragic climax by offering it in startling juxtaposition with a belittling or absurdist moment of comedy; but that masterful control of tone was the mark of his maturity. It would have been a daring and unparalleled departure for him creatively in 1903, though with the revisions he embarked on in 1904 (seemingly in response to his London critics) he began to introduce elements of comedy and satire into *The King's Threshold* to achieve a greater tonal variety.

Yeats's other worries concerning the potential distraction of some detail in the lighting or a costume, if accurate reflections from 1922 of his thinking in 1903, show his growing preoccupation with the need for a complete presentational unity in staging a play. The remark about lighting and costume may indicate also a longstanding dissatisfaction with the first production of *The King's Threshold*, for which he had considerable expectations which were not in the event realised. It is within this larger context of expectation that the newly discovered design by Yeats for a setting for *The King's Threshold* should be read. What is not immediately apparent is when precisely Yeats made the design. The letter quoted above to Frank Fay about the role of Seanchan continues with a request:

> I wish very much you could send me the right measurements for a curtain . . . I want to get it embroidered if I can. I look upon it as part of the staging of Seanchan [*The King's Threshold*] for there is to be a prologue spoken by Mr Russell in the Wise Man's dress. I want the dark dress and the dark curtain to fix themselves on the minds of the audience before the almost white stage is disclosed. If I cannot get the measurements by Monday it may be too late, as the designer who is now here is going away.[14]

The identity of the designer is not known; but the likelihood, since Yeats was writing from Coole Park, is that he had Robert Gregory in mind who had assisted with the designs for *The Hour-Glass*, staged earlier that year and who was to design the setting for *On Baile's Strand* for the opening of the Abbey in 1904. The design being referred to here, however, is for a front curtain only. Earlier in that same letter Yeats makes Fay a promise:

> I am sending your brother Seanchan [the play in typescript] today. . . . If I can get them done I shall send at the same time *the maps of the more important positions* (*ibid*. 413, emphasis added).

Are these perhaps the recently discovered sketches? They comprise a 'front view' and floorplan, making it clear where certain stage-objects, properties and characters are ideally to be situated. When one compares the 'front view' with one of the surviving photographs of the first performances, such as that reproduced as Plate 14 in *Images of a Poet*,[15] it is apparent that Yeats's design was realised on the stage of the Molesworth Hall quite precisely. A possible difficulty remains: Yeats speaks in that same letter to Fay of the brilliant effect of an 'almost white stage' suddenly revealed after the dark prologue, which he envisaged (to judge by the printed text) as lit merely by 'a guttering candle' held in 'a brass candlestick' by the actor (*VPl* 313), whereas the design refers specifically to 'flies (grey cloth like hangings[)]'. Did some change of decision occur regarding the colour of the curtains because white was found to be highly impractical? The photographs suggest that the curtains were uniformly light-to-mid grey. A closer look at the sketch makes one ponder whether Yeats was aiming for a yet more complex effect than was finally implemented. Ought we perhaps to read the sketch with *both* colour schemes in mind? Yeats has made no effort to indicate either by shading or by annotation that the main curtains crossing the stage at the rear were to be the same colour as the suspended hanging from the flies (he merely notes that gaps should be left to create '3 entrances through curtain' or, as noted on the floorplan, '3 splits in curtain for entrances'). In practice curtains and hangings clearly were of one colour. But was his initial intention to differentiate between the main curtains and the short suspended hangings so that with the two widely spaced pillars he would achieve a stylised image of a raised portico without resorting to any cumbersome and expensive solid structures? This would certainly be in line with Yeats fast-developing distaste for traditional kinds of painted scenery, which a built setting would certainly entail.

The issue of the portico in relation to the lay-out of the rest of the stage is worth dwelling on. What is not clear from the sketch is whether Yeats intended that the curtains should extend round the two sides of the stage to create a box-type set of relatively taut curtaining (such as was used for *The Hour-Glass* previously that year and would be deployed by Gregory later for both *On Baile's Strand* and *The Shadowy Waters*). Again the photographs show that this occurred in practice and indeed there are balancing curved lines to stage-right and to stage-left at the front near the sketched frame which may be a crude attempt to indicate angled tabs or that the curtained walls were to be turned into the wings at these points to effect what is labelled 'entrance' on each side. What the sketch does not reveal, but which is evident from the photographs is that a rough floor-covering was used that seems (so far as a monochrome image allows one to judge) of an identical colour with the curtains. Again Yeats makes no attempt to colour in the flooring of either design in the way that he has shaded in the pillars and the suspended hangings. What we have here is a simple staging that permits of five separate points of entry, suggestive of entrances either from the palace or from the countryside. All this may be supposed from a close reading of the stage directions for the play; there is reference both in the directions and the dialogue to the steps on which Seanchan is first seen reclining and the design provides for these; also prescribed are 'a table or litter in front of steps at one side, with food on it, and a bench' which are again present in both sketches. What the directions at no point indicate is the portico; we are informed at the play's opening that the action is set on 'Steps before the Palace of King Guaire at Gort' and that at the start the King is to be seen 'on the upper step before a curtained door'.[16] The stylised portico is how Yeats chose to evoke a palace.[17]

For all its simplicity, the image is replete with theatrical resonances. Appropriately, given Yeats's intention that *The King's Threshold* should imitate the structure of classical tragedy, the setting evokes at once the form of the Greek theatre with the central elevated entrance (the *skene*, a facade with three doorways) and upper stage leading by a flight of steps down to a larger playing space, the *orchestra*. It is to be noted with regard to this suggestion of a Greek theatre space that, when in the summer of 1910 Yeats was in possession of the set of model screens given to him by Edward

Gordon Craig and was experimenting with various arrangements of them to suit existing plays in the Abbey repertoire, he chose for *The King's Threshold* to preserve the structural arrangement depicted in the sketch and already in use.[18] Instead of curtains there is now an arrangement of screens with a single entrance at the summit of a flight of three steps; but otherwise the constituent elements of the setting remain the same as in Yeats's initial sketch of 1903 with one notable exception. He had been exploring in floorplans for several plays (*The Land of Heart's Desire, Deirdre, The Deliverer* by Lady Gregory) with settings either constructed on the diagonal or deploying pairs of diagonals converging to create a centrally placed corner to give a sense of architectural solidity and to enable him to experiment with angled lighting effects creating pools of shadow and rhythmic patterns of light and darkness. The sketched design for *The King's Threshold* (see Plate 5) follows this format by turning the original palace structure through an angle of some 30-40 degrees and moving it over to stage right; high screens suggesting a palace wall are situated along the stage-left side of the steps; this configuration of screens then turns through 90 degrees, leading off into the wings; a downstage square, tower-like arrangement of equally high screens on the left creates two entrances to either side of it of more impressive dimensions than the original (1903) gap in the curtained wall of the box set and effectively blocks off the audience's view into the wings here; their view to stage right is blocked by a high screen placed against the proscenium wall and angled straight up-stage. This simple readjustment of the original design creates a remarkable atmosphere of grandeur. In the marginal annotations to the floorplan Yeats makes a further observation: 'The three doors in shadow leaving L[eft] of stage bright might do Oedipus'. Over a period from 1909 to 1911 Yeats revived his scheme for staging Sophocles' *Oedipus Tyrannus*, hoping to attract the actor, Murray Carson, to play the title role with the Abbey company.[19] What is of significance for my immediate argument is Yeats's suggestion that the very same set under different lighting states might be used for both his play and Sophocles'.

But the theatrical references do not stop at the Greek theatre. The particular stylised form that the representation of the portico takes using the dark hangings and the two pillars is immediately evocative of the penthouse of the Elizabethan stage, an image which is further strengthened by the pronounced forestage beneath it. Such a representation of the Renaissance stage of Shakespeare's day was at the turn of the century brought to the attention of English theatregoers by the work of William Poel and his Elizabethan Stage Society. Poel (1852-1924) began staging the plays of Shakespeare and his contemporaries on a fit-up stage that reproduced much of what was known at his time of the design of Henslowe's Fortune Theatre, which opened in Cripplegate in 1600. Shaw for one was deeply impressed by Poel's achievement, championing his work repeatedly in his reviewing for *The Saturday Review* (Poel was to play Keegan in the Royal Court production of *John Bull's Other Island* in 1904); Yeats had attended the opening performance of Poel's revival of his production of *Everyman* at the St. George's Hall in 1902; and Harley Granville Barker, the actor-director, who had played the roles of both Richard II and Edward II for Poel and whose own productions of Shakespeare later owed much to Poel's inspiration, was a regular attender at Yeats's Monday evening gatherings in London (he was present along with Miss Horniman at the first reading of *The King's Threshold* on May 4, 1903); Poel himself was to lecture on 'the Elizabethan Playhouse' by Yeats's invitation at the Abbey on November 21, 1907. That Yeats's sketched design for *The King's Threshold* in 1903 should suggest a stylised representation of the Renaissance stage cannot be accidental, given the theatrical milieu in which he was moving in 1903.

Repeatedly in his writings about theatre before the establishing of the Abbey in 1904 Yeats refers to classical Greece and Elizabethan England as two of the great ages of Western theatre (along with Calderon's and Racine's stages in Spain and France and the contemporary situation in Scandanavia). He contends that 'it is only at the awakening [of the impulse to create theatre]...that great numbers of men understand that a right understanding of life and of destiny is more important than amusement' and goes on to define that 'right understanding' by arguing that 'in London, where all the intellectual traditions gather to die, men hate a play if they are told it is literature, for they will not endure a *spiritual superiority*' (*UP2* 199, emphasis added). Theatre at its best in Yeats's view is educative and spiritual. I have argued above that Yeats's aim with the play was didactic: to impress on audiences an awareness of the proper role of the artist (poet and dramatist) in relation to his or her society. Reading Yeats's design for the first staging of *The King's Threshold* in the way that I have just suggested is to see how even in visual terms it is asserting a cultural agenda: Yeats is confidently inviting the audience to experience his play in performance as situated within a tradition of staging that embraces the Greek and the Elizabethan in its representational simplicity. Irish audiences are to realise how by virtue of Yeats's art and artistry they are poised at a moment of significant 'awakening'. (Such a reading would seem to make a tragic ending to the action even more imperative.)

It was an ambitious agenda. In the event, however, the element of design to attract attention was the costumes; and they were the work of Annie Horniman. Prior to the opening of the performance Yeats was enthusiastic about her work. There is more than a touch of egoism behind his remark to Frank Fay: 'with the beautiful costumes that are being made for it [*The King's Threshold*] I should make something of a stir' (*CL3* 413, 8 August, 1903). This euphoria continued into early October when he wrote to Lady Gregory from Dublin about the progress of the production: 'The costumes are extraordinary [sic] beautiful. The fame of them is going abroad and I think is helping us a good deal' (*CL3* 438). The critic for *The Daily Express* was suitably impressed: 'The colour-scheme was conceived with great taste, and the individual dresses were well-designed'.[20] But the comments of Tom Kettle printed in *New Ireland* give pause for thought:

> . . . the costumes of King Guaire and his Court were of a richness almost barbaric. The cut and colour of each garment was adjusted, I understand, to a scheme marvellous in its emotional and symbolic value, and beyond the capacity of any but a society journal to record.[21]

There is a sting in the tail of this seeming praise with that final reference to a society journal; the implication is that the sumptuousness was far from fitting for either the saga world of the play or the seriousness of Yeats's purpose. Society journals were prone to review the dresses made by fashion houses for upper class comedies by the likes of Wilde staged at theatres such as the St. James's or the Haymarket in London. This was hardly in line with Yeats's agenda in staging *The King's Threshold* or with the principles underlying the founding of the theatre movement.

While Yeats remained loyal to Miss Horniman, who had personally met the cost of the costumes ('Miss Horniman has to learn her work however and must have freedom to experiment' he wrote to Fay [*CL3* 528, 20 January, 1904]), he nonetheless must have felt the barb of remarks like Kettle's deeply. When it came to designing costumes for *On Baile's Strand* and Miss Horniman again proffered her aid Yeats had to be a model of tact: 'I have written to Miss Horniman,' he informed Lady Gregory, 'suggesting as delicately as I could that there ought not to be gorgeousness of costume' (*ibid.* 530.). And Yeats felt it necessary to reassure Frank Fay that his scheme for the setting was not what was at fault: 'I do not think the greys [i.e. the hangings and curtains] kept the people [in *The King's Threshold*] from standing out, though there were other defects—too many colours & so on' (*ibid.* 528). A glance at the photograph of the cast line-up for the production, which is reproduced in *Images of a Poet*, shows a total lack of any design principles behind Miss Horniman's scheme; the costumes are overladen with obtrusive detail to create a comic mix of period styles which gives the impression of Edwardian charades or of operetta; the actors so clad appear uncomfortable, amateurish and lacking in dignity.

In May 1914 Lady Gregory and Yeats were to commission new costumes from Charles Ricketts for a revival of the play in London. One can detect an evident relief behind Yeats's letter thanking the designer for his work in a manner that suggests that painful old memories still rankled:

> I think the costumes the best stage costumes I have ever seen. They are full of dramatic invention, and yet *nothing starts out or seems eccentric*. The Company never did the play so well, and such is the effect of the costumes that whole scenes get a new intensity, and passages or actions that had seemed commonplace became powerful and moving.[22]

Ricketts by 1914 was, of course, designing for a rather different play from that for which Miss Horniman originally provided the costumes. Revisions in April 1904 and again in 1905-6 had in part re-structured some of the scenes and wholly changed the tone of others; a sharply satirical treatment of characters such as the Mayor and the Cripples had replaced what was at first a rather flat handling of these roles. This had effected a major change in the play in that it helped focus an audience's attention more on the thematic concerns of the play than on its episodic narrative structure. Through the satire Yeats can now carefully discriminate between different levels and degrees of selfhood: Seanchan's zealous adherence to his principles as honouring the dignity and status of his vocation as poet is defined against the King's obsession with his authority, the courtiers' varying types of self-centredness, the Mayor's gross self-importance, Brian's selfless but blind devotion to his master and Fedelm's apolitical but care-worn passion. The theme of the play is now wholly inhabited imaginatively by Yeats and its didactic intentions are more discreetly handled and subsumed within the dramatic artistry. The sense of Seanchan as an outsider within his society is powerfully realised by psychological means; his commitment to his status as poet is now experienced through these patterns of contrast as absolute; there is an implacability driving on the action now, which would make the final revision of 1922 giving the play a tragic conclusion an utter necessity.

Throughout all these revisions and revivals one aspect of the play remains constant: Yeats's original scheme for the setting. Evidence that in performance it proved a perfect playing space for the drama is to be found in the response of Joseph Holloway to the opening night: it was in his view 'a thing of exceptional beauty to the eye and ear'.[23] In drawing attention to the visual quality of the performance, Holloway was not, however, referring to Miss Horniman's costumes but rather to a feature of the direction: 'the grouping, considering the limited space at command, was remarkably effective' (*ibid*). It is puzzling at first in studying Yeats's sketch to gauge why he included only three steps rising from the forestage to the portico, if he wished to give prominence to the largely prone figure of Seanchan. But a further entry in Holloway's diary, made after he had attended a rehearsal on October 2, adds a feature to the design which the sketch cannot make apparent: 'The Society is going to a lot of trouble over the proscenium, and intend to have a raking stage'.[24] As the auditorium of the Molesworth Hall was not raked, then the stage floor must needs be so to allow the range of the audience an uninterrupted view of the performance. This was considerate respecting an audience's need for clear sight-lines; but the device of raking the floor, conjoined with the deployment of the stepped setting, also allowed Yeats the means of attempting a new kind of experiment with stage space.

From his earliest plays Yeats had inventively exploited the relation between the actual playing space and the off-stage space. Doorways are central within the necessary features of the design-schemes for these works because as thresholds they are invested with considerable dramatic power as points of intersection between different planes of reality. As in many a Greek tragedy, entrances and exits in Yeats's plays are in consequence more than merely functional. The whole action in *The Land of Heart's Desire* and in *Kathleen ni Houlihan* turns on whether the Fairy Child or the Old Woman will be invited to enter the cottage-room which is the stage-space. Their entrances will effect some radical psychological changes within that apparently normal environment. The doorway in *The Hour-Glass* admits both Fool and Angel to disconcert the Wise Man's championing of reason; later it becomes the focus of his anguish as he waits in desperate expectation for it to admit but one individual who believes in God whose arrival would bring about his salvation. In *On Baile's Strand* guarding the threshold is an anxious preoccupation for Conchubar; despite Cuchulain's scorn, the women are summoned to perform a ritual enchantment to bind the hero to respect that entrance and all that it signifies. Our focus of attention is relentlessly drawn to that doorway as the site of the tragedy, for it is here that Connla will enter thereby transforming that threshold into a test of Cuchulain's fidelity to his oath and a trap from which he will get free only at the cost of his sanity. Stage space is invested here with a potent dynamism because it has been deployed as an integral part of the total dramatic conception.

In these four instances Yeats is working with what one might term lateral space, seen and unseen; but *The King's Threshold* as the sketch makes abundantly clear is a new departure. The play is fundamentally about power relations and dominance; and by using for the first time a split-level stage linked by a short flight of steps, Yeats can begin to examine the dynamic potential of height and depth within the playing space. Significantly Seanchan is to be situated at a mid-point on the steps between the royal and courtly characters, who descend to him from above out of the palace from which on King Guaire's order he has been expelled, and the forestage inhabited by commoners, his betrothed (Fedelm), his students and servant(s), the Mayor and the cripples, a world where his calling as poet makes him a significant outsider, by giving him an elevated status. It is Seanchan's ambition to compel the King to invite him up into the portico and thence into the palace; so off-stage space again carries symbolic and psychological resonance. But the action moves inexorably in the opposed direction, as Seanchan progresses painfully from what is designated on the sketch as his first position to what is determined as his last (on the floor by the bench on the forestage) with all that that movement symbolically signifies to both the court and the people. Even the visual dynamic insists on a tragic conclusion.

An elevated position within the stage-picture generally carries connotations of power; but so too does a figure who is absolutely still, particularly if everyone else is moving. Yeats creates great tension in *The King's Threshold* by setting in opposition these two dramatic devices which generally command attention and endow the characters so treated with a notable authority. Seanchan's strength and command come from within, whereas the power of the King and his courtiers is temporal and physical, expressed in terms of their spatial relations with others. The poet inhabits stillness; the court is given solely to activity. His prone body challenges and subverts their authority by compelling them not only to descend but, humiliatingly, to bend to his level if they wish to converse with him and so disturb his contemplation. This is a thrilling dramatic evocation of rebellion because totally unpredictable (far different from the active animosities and rhetorical posturing of the Seanchan in Lady Wilde's tale). If Seanchan moves, it is only by virtue of another's agency, as when the Monk, seeking to free himself from the poet's grasp, drags him across the stage. How people choose to bend to Seanchan defines their nature and their psychological purpose in approaching him. The nature of the setting begins radically to control many other features of the performance and would, if followed through sensitively by a director, make for a subtle but richly allusive (because heavily *signified*) acting style.

Such subtlety would suppose an audience capable of *reading* a performance with attention to the symbolic resonances within details of how the actors were disposed about the playing space; the stage picture before them would have its pictorial and aesthetic interest, but it is to be read predominantly as indicative of the shifting power relations between the characters. This of course requires that spectators have their awareness concentrated on the spatial dynamics of the performance; but clearly in that initial production of 1903 it was the costumes with their flamboyant display of colour and patterning that obtruded on the audience's attention. (It is noticeable that Ricketts' costume designs of 1914 while characterful deploy natural dyes in the colour-scheme: russets, ochres, greens.) It is hardly surprising, therefore, that Yeats and Fay should have been anxious to curb Miss Horniman's inventive ways with colour when it came to her designing the costumes for *On Baile's Strand* a few months later. Deploying stage space in this unusual way was a wholly new departure for Yeats and his immediate command of the technique (charging the use of space and especially its vertical dimension with political connotations) is impressive. But it was not a technique he was to return to and examine further till much later in his career with the opening scene of *The Player Queen*, and the positioning of the ghosts in *Purgatory*, where in both instances he seems more preoccupied with creating a degree of detachment of the figures situated above from those moving below rather than with defining differences of status and political authority.

To judge by the comments of reviewers in Dublin and London, audiences in 1903 were not equipped to deal with the innovative demands of Yeats's scenic stagecraft in *The King's Threshold*; conditioned by contemporary conventions of design and of performance they accepted the design elements as of background interest (always excepting those garish costumes) and read them simply as functional and pictorial. They did not see the organic unity that underpinned the whole event as a consequence of the careful relation Yeats had created between theme and design. As so often with Yeats's inventions in the theatre, the time was not yet ripe to appreciate his originality. The newly discovered sketch of Yeats's design for *The King's Threshold* reveals a hitherto unsuspected point of development in the playwright's process of discovering himself to be (in the fullest sense of the term) a man of the theatre. Already those organising principles are at work here which seek to create a unity out of the constituent literary and theatrical components of drama: principles, normally seen as characteristic of his later plays, that are sensitive to the symbolic and poetic qualities that can be invested in all aspects of a performance and which ideally require spectators to be not purely receptive but vital and creative in their response to that performance. *The King's Threshold* is often dismissed, as we have seen, as a rather amateurish product. The sketched design invites a reappraisal of both play and production as altogether more sophisticated than this somewhat derogatory term suggests.

NOTES

1.   The design was found in the Houghton Library, Harvard University.

2.   See Peter Ure, *Yeats the Playwright: A Commentary on Character and Design in the Major Plays* (London: Routledge & Kegan Paul, 1963), Ch. 2, and Suheil Badi Bushrui *Yeats's Verse Plays: The Revisions, 1900-1910* (Oxford: Clarendon Press, 1965).

3.   *Yeats the Playwright* p. 31.

4.   Max Beerbohm: 'Some Irish Plays', *Saturday Review* (April 9, 1904), pp. 456-7.

5.   In an anonymous review, the *Times Literary Supplement* (1 April, 1904), p. 102.

6.   *CL3* 580. The letter is dated 15 April, 1904; the *conversazione* took place on 26 April. Virtually the same words to describe his endeavours were used by Yeats the following day in a letter to Lady Gregory to justify his claim that as a result of the revisions the play is now 'much stronger' (*ibid*. 581-2).

7.   Yeats's principal influence, however, was Edwin Ellis's *Sancan the Bard*, a verse-drama published in 1895; but this was not widely read. Yeats introduced far more visitors to Seanchan hoping to stay his fasting than Ellis deploys and significantly Yeats makes his final visitor Seanchan's betrothed, Fedelm, rather than as in Ellis a slave-girl with whom the poet falls rather implausibly in love. Ellis's play ends happily with the restoration of Seanchan's status as does Yeats's *The King's Threshold* in all but its final version.

8.   A. E. Malone, *The Irish Drama* (London: 1929; re-issued London and New York: Benjamin Blom, 1965), p. 138.

9.   Arthur Griffith, 'All Ireland', *The United Irishman* (17 October, 1903), 1.

10.   W. B. Yeats, 'The Irish Literary Theatre, 1900' (*UP2* 199). See also his stated belief in the essay 'An Irish National Theatre': 'Literature is, to my mind, the great teaching power of the world, the ultimate creator of all values, and it is this, not only in the sacred books whose power everybody acknowledges, but by every movement of imagination in song or story or drama that height of intensity and sincerity has made literature at all. Literature must take the responsibility of its power, and keep al its freedom . . .' (*Ex* 117). The essay was originally published in *Samhain* in 1903.

11.   See 'A Note on the new end to *The King's Threshold*' in W. B. Yeats, *Seven Poems and a Fragment* (Dundrum: Cuala Press, 1922).

12.   Robert Lowell, in his adaptation of Aeschylus' play, chooses to present it as a debate about the role of the artist in society.

13.   W. B. Ycats, 'A Note on the new end to *The King's Threshold*', *Seven Poems and a Fragment* (Dundrum: Cuala Press, 1922).

14.   *CL3* 413-4. The prologue was eventually abandoned as the casting of the play required the full strength of the company, though not before Yeats had explored the possibility of Willie Fay, who was to play the Mayor of Kinvara, wearing a red dressing-gown over his Mayor's costume in order to deliver the opening sardonic speech. The Wise Man is the central character in Yeats's play, *The Hour-Glass*, which had been staged on 14 March, 1903; the setting and costumes for this production were designed by Sturge Moore from an idea and sketch by Robert Gregory.

15.   D. J. Gordon, *Images of a Poet* (Manchester: Manchester University Press, 1961), p. 69.

16.   *VPl* 257. There are no substantive changes to the stage directions in the various published texts of the play.

17.   There is one detail in the 1903 design which is misleading and that is the line denoting the front of the stage which seems to include footlights by virtue of the small crenellations. The production actually caused some stir because the company disposed of the footlights customary in contemporary theatrical practice in favour of a different style of lighting inspired by Edward Gordon Craig. Holloway offers the most detailed account of this aspect of the production: 'No footlights were used, but two limelights—one at either side of the stage—and

one from the back of the hall, were substituted' (*Joseph Holloway's Abbey Theatre*, eds. Robert Hogan and Michael J.O'Neill [Carbondale and Edwardsville: Southern Illinois University Press, 1967] p. 26). Limelight made for a remarkable brilliance, which would have emphasized the simplicities of the setting and defined the actors with great clarity. It would also have created a steady state rather like the permanent white light that Brecht delighted in for his productions. In other words there was little attempt at pictorial illusion of the kind generally preferred at this date. The crenellated line, suggesting the presence of footlights, continued to be Yeats's way of designating the front of the stage even when he was planning settings while using Craig's system of screens where no footlights were actually to be deployed. Indeed footlights were anathema to Craig and Yeats.

18. Yeats's sketch for a groundplan of a setting for *The King's Threshold* using the Craig system is reproduced in Liam Miller, *The Noble Drama of W.B.Yeats* (Dublin: The Dolmen Press, 1977), p. 158.

19. Though eventually Murray backed out of the plans, Yeats still pursued the idea and with particular vigour after Nugent Monck came from the Maddermarket Theatre in Norwich to direct plays at the Abbey late in 1911. Monck was by general agreement one of the few directors at the theatre who discovered how to use the Craig screens with a truly inventive awareness of their scenic potential. Monck began rehearsing *Oedipus* with the B company (the main company was touring in the States) immediately on his arrival in Dublin; this work never came to public performance, however.

20. Cited in Robert Hogan and James Kilroy, *Laying the Foundations:1902-1904* (Dublin: The Dolmen Press, 1976). p. 72.

21. *Ibid.* p. 72. Thomas (Tom) Kettle (1880-1916) was a well-known Dublin poet and economist, and friend of James Joyce. He became Nationalist MP for East Tyrone in 1906 and Professor of National Economics at UCD in 1909. He protested that both *The Countess Cathleen* and *The Playboy of the Western World* were misrepresentations of Ireland, but he was a supporter of the Literary Revival. He died at Ginchy, on the Somme.

22. *L* 587 (emphasis added). The letter is dated 11 June, 1914. A detailed discussion of Ricketts's costume designs for *The King's Threshold* can be found in Richard Allen Cave, *Charles Ricketts' Stage Designs* (Cambridge: Chadwyck-Healey, 1987), pp. 54-8. The discussion also refers to the designs made at the same date for *On Baile's Strand* and Synge's *Deirdre of the Sorrows*. What is of note is Ricketts' technique in all the designs for *The King's Threshold* of taking what is a heroic style and slightly exaggerating it to achieve a satirical effect. There is considerable wit in the style but not at the expense of Yeats's artistry.

23. *Joseph Holloway's Abbey Theatre*, p. 26.

24. Cited in Robert Hogan and James Kilroy, *Laying the Foundations: 1902-1904* (Dublin: The Dolmen Press, 1976), p. 70.

Noh, Fenollosa, Pound and Yeats—Have East and West Met?

Masaru Sekine

THERE IS STILL a huge gap between East and West,[1] and this essay will glance at its causes, by tracing the efforts of Fenollosa, Pound and Yeats to bring Noh drama to the West in works created some eighty years ago. I hope my analysis may provide some clues to the problem they faced and also a possible way to transcend it.

In his introduction to *'Noh', or Accomplishment* Ezra Pound wrote 'It may be an exaggeration to say that he [E. Fenollosa] had saved Japanese art for Japan, but it is certain that he had done as much as any one man could have to set the native art in its rightful pre-eminence and to stop the apeing of Europe'.[2] This is by no means an exaggeration. During the frantic westernization of Japan in the Early Meiji period (1868-1912), after two and half centuries of isolation from the rest of the world under the Tokugawa shogunate, Fenollosa was appointed as a professor of politics and philosophy to help the country with its westernization programme, by educating elite young Japanese at Tokyo University in 1878. Fenollosa, soon after his arrival in Japan, was attracted to its traditional art, and realised that it was in danger of becoming extinct. He was fortunate to have influential friends around him to assist his quest for the essence of Japanese aesthetics. Baron Kaneko, who studied at Harvard at the same time as Fenollosa and became friends with him on his arrival in Japan, recommended that he learn Japanese art from his own student, Nagao Ariga of Tokyo University. Baron Kaneko, himself, took Fenollosa to the residence of his former feudal lord, Duke Kuroda, to show him his collection of Japanese masterpieces. Thus Fenollosa was introduced to Japanese art.

Fenollosa was a quick learner and, a few years later, appointed as a commissioner of art at the Royal Household, he was officially sent to Kyoto and other Kansai areas to investigate Japanese art forms with some of the Japanese art historians. Among them was Kakuzo Okakura, a former student of his, who later became his strongest ally in defending Japanese Art. Fenollosa met talented and trained Japanese painters, such as Gaho Hashimoto and Hogai Kano, who had, by then, taken up the style and techniques of European oil painting in order to make a living, since nobody bought Japanese paintings at this time. Indeed, priceless traditional art treasures were, then, being sold for almost nothing. Fenollosa later moved from the university to the Ministry of Education, to start an Art College in Tokyo mainly to teach Japanese arts. Fenollosa and Okakura were allioed in their attempt to win over some of the committee members who were pro-European arts and had tried to stop their venture. Okakura later became the president of this Art College, though it was Fenollosa who had successfully persuaded the Minister of Education, Count Mori, to found it.

Despite his incomparable contribution to the restoration of Japanese Art, Fenollosa had to leave the country almost immediately after Okakura was appointed as President of this newly born Art College. Fenollosa seemed to have thought he was going to succeed the first President, Shin Hamao, as he was performing the role of Deputy. What Fenollosa did not realize, however, was that he was in fact employed first by the University of Tokyo, and secondly by the Ministry of Education, with renewable contracts for two years and then for five years. He was one of those foreigners employed to teach Japanese youth various aspects of European science and technology as a part of the government general plan for westernization of the country. They were employed at exceedingly high salaries, and the new Government later found that it could not keep paying out such huge salaries. The Government had, in any case, planned to replace these expensive foreign professors and technicians with their own Japanese students in order to cut costs. The

Tokyo Art College was given a very small annual budget and must have found it impossible to keep paying Fenollosa his original salary. Another reason for his departure was Fenollosa's language problem: he did not speak Japanese well. When he introduced western methods of teaching,[3] instead of using the traditional Japanese methods (basically teaching through repetition for days, months, or even sometimes years), he was unable to explain his own method in Japanese.

It also was a disadvantage that Fenollosa could not paint himself. Consequently he started losing his students. It was ironic that Fenollosa had to leave Japan just at the time when he had been the person mainly responsible for founding an Art College to promote Japanese Arts. In effect, he was merely a catalyst. Once his main mission had been accomplished, he became a burden. And so he went back to the United States, to became Curator of the Asian Art Department of the Boston Museum of Fine Art. During his first stay in Japan (1878-1890), Fenollosa's achievements had been immeasurable, and, without his devotion, Japanese art would certainly not have recovered so quickly from the devastating humiliation of being overwhelmed by the rapid infiltration of western ideas and techniques. Fenollosa, then, was not successful as a teacher of Japanese art, but he certainly saved Japanese art, and made the world aware of the existence of this ultra refined and sophisticated tradition. Indirectly, long after his death, his influence helped to promote and thus to save the uniquely beautiful complexes of architecture and gardens of two historic capital cities of Kyoto and Nara, from complete destruction by Allied bombing; thus preserving the essence of Japan's cultural heritage.

Fenollosa stayed in Boston for six years (1900-1906). Compared with his life in Tokyo, where he had lived as one of the capital's celebrities, being constantly asked to evening parties of Japanese aristocrats and foreign diplomats as well as to the ceremonial events at Court, Fenollosa now had a rather tedious life, cataloguing the art collections he had brought from Japan.[4] His love affair with his secretary, his subsequent divorce from his first wife and re-marriage caused a scandal in the quiet, conservative Boston community. His love of Japanese arts, combined with the scandal, made Fenollosa decide to go back to Japan. Things, however, did not go well as he had hoped they would. He was rejected by Tenshin Okakura (as Kakuzo Okakura was known after he achieved fame), and could not get back to teaching at Tokyo Art College, where he was no longer needed, so he had to be content to teach English at a high school in Tokyo. During his subsequent four years in Japan, Fenollosa's life was not as distinguished as it had been before, however he was paid well enough to be able to travel to the ancient capitals of Nara and Kyoto with his second wife. This rather quiet time gave him a greater opportunity to learn more about Japanese culture. He resumed taking lessons from Minoru Umewaka in Noh singing and dancing.

Fenollosa also took his student to lessons from Minoru Umewaka and his son, Takeyo, as he still needed someone to translate the Noh plays he was learning. He wrote down in notebooks the texts of plays he had learned and also those he saw performed on stage in Tokyo. These notes were handed over to Ezra Pound, for publication after his death, by Fenollosa's widow, Mary McNeil Fenollosa. Though the credit for the translations was given to Fenollosa, it was his student Kiichi Hirata[5] who had actually produced the first version of those translations for him. The translation of Noh plays is a virtually impossible task for anyone, at any time, for the texts are like tapestries woven with different colours and different types of threads, and they are not always consistent. They are more difficult to translate than, say, Shakespeare (into Japanese or other non-European languages). The Noh texts were mostly written in the late fourteenth century in verse and prose (mainly the spoken part), and their language is too ancient for modern Japanese audiences to understand fully. Though Japan was a homogeneous country, and the Tokugawa shogunate basically froze all changes, the ancient language was not fully open to Fenollosa's assistant, and he failed to comprehend them fully.

Comparative examination of a specific Noh text, that of *Nishikigi* shows how it was translated by Fenollosa and his student, how it was edited by Ezra Pound and finally how it was adapted by W. B. Yeats. Through this analysis, I will trace how this play had been westernized in Pound's edition and how Yeats westernized it still more in *The Dreaming of the Bones*. Mary McNeil was herself a writer, and had read Pound's work on Chinese poetry. Impressed by this, she decided to trust him to do the editorial work of Fenollosa's translations of Noh plays.[6] Pound immediately started working on this project, while he was at the same time working for Yeats as a personal secretary at Stone Cottage in Sussex, during the winters of 1915 and 1916. Mrs Fenollosa had given Pound £40, plus all the benefits which might accrue from the proposed publication, for undertaking this arduous task. His knowledge of Noh was extremely limited when he took on this project. Neither, indeed, had the supposed translator, Fenollosa, understood archaic Japanese sufficiently for this complex task. And his Japanese student had not had a full command of English, though he did have a passionate drive to write down and edit these mysterious literary treasures of Japan. I propose to examine first the three texts from the point of view of religion, second from the point of view of poetry, third from the point of view of languages, and finally from the point of view of aesthetics.

Before he began translating Noh plays, Fenollosa had studied Buddhism in Japan and become a Buddhist of the Tendai sect, taking the Buddhist name of Teishin-koji, given to him by Keitsu Sakurai, a renowned monk. He was also given the Buddhist name of Setsushin-koji, and was at the time friendly with Tenshin Okakura. In an article on Noh he wrote

> . . . In the fifth century before Christ the Greek drama arose out of the religious rites practised in the festivals of the God of Wine. In the fifteenth century after Christ, the Japanese drama arose out of the religious rites practised in the festivals of the Shinto gods, chiefly the Shinto god of the Kasuga temple at Nara . . . (*NOA* 101-2).

Here, Fenollosa compared the origins of Noh with those of Greek plays. But in this short quotation, there are two mistakes. The first is the date given for the rise of Noh. It had already been performed for the Shoguns and aristocrats before the fourteenth century, but it is believed to have been perfected in the latter part of that century. Ze-Ami, was performing at the Imagumano kanji-kogyo (a fund raising public performance for a temple) in 1372, where he was spotted by Yoshimitsu, the third shogun of the Ashikaga. The young Noh actor was then twelve and the shogun was eighteen. It was in Ze-Ami's time that the Noh made a remarkable progress in refinement and sophistication, as Ze-Ami and other Noh actors desperately tried to meet the aristocratic tastes of their powerful patron.

The second mistake is the statement that Shinto divinities chiefly were worshipped in Noh performances. Noh was not exclusively Shinto, Buddhist divinities were also evoked. In this article, Fenollosa did not distinguish between shrines and temples; the former were for Shinto gods and the latter for Buddhist. Later Fenollosa compared Greek plays, Shakespeare and the Noh, and there stated, contradictorily, that the Noh arose from both Shinto and Buddhist worship. He was not able to give a clear idea of the religious aspect of the Noh even in this introductory article. In fact, it is confusing, as Shinto and Buddhism are often merged both in their forms of worship and also in Noh drama. For example, in the play *Uneme*, *Myojin*, who is regarded as a Shinto god, was given another name *Bosatsu*, the name of a Buddhist god.

Nishikigi is a play which clearly demonstrates the supreme power of religion. *Waki*, the supporting role, is a travelling monk, not a priest. After an introductory song of *shidai*, he himself announces that he is a travelling monk. He goes to the far North of Michinoku, searching for enlightenment. There he attracts a couple of ghosts, who are disguised as a village man and woman. In Shinto, this is impossible, since belief about death and the after-life of human beings is not compatible with the existence of ghosts. After death, a man is believed to go back to the world of deities, is given the after name of such and such *mikoto*, symbolising the state of being a deity. There is no concept of heaven and hell in Shinto. Consequently, in Shinto the existence of ghosts is denied.

The ghosts in this play need to have the monk's prayers in order to get released from their earth-bound status. They show the monk a local product of *hosonuno*, narrow cloth, and *nishikigi*, a symbol of love, used in courtship in this region. These objects make the monk curious, and he can not help asking questions of the couple about this narrow cloth and the symbol of love. They tell him a well known tragic story of a foiled courtship, referring to both of these symbolic objects. The *hosonuno* cloth does not have enough width to make a kimono. If it did, the kimono would not overlap in the front. This, in courtship, symbolised a one-sided love, as the lovers' breasts would never meet.[7] *Nishikigi* is an ornate branch of a tree to be placed at the door of the house of a lady a man is courting. If she takes the symbol into the house, it is a sign that he can visit the woman. If she does not, his courtship is unsuccessful. The couple succeed in getting the monk interested enough in their tragic story to ask them to take him to the grave mound where the legendary lover was buried. He had placed a thousand love tokens at his love's house without any success, and he died of despair. When they arrive at the grave mound, the ghostly couple disappear into the mound. The monk decides to stay there with his followers, and to pray for them during the night.

The *schema* of this play might be compared to the restrictions of traditional western religious art, in which even great painters were constrained by an established iconography and programme, although individuality might be expressed in the depiction of a landscape background. Writers of Noh plays could not escape from such frameworks as the one seen in this play.

In this first part of *Nishikigi* there are not many direct references to Buddhism; consequently there is only one part to examine. It is at the beginning of the play: after the *waki* sings an introductory song of shidai, and announces that he is a travelling monk.

Noh: *Korewa shokoku ikkenno so nitesoro (N 1)*

Fenollosa: This is a priest who (is taking) a glance at each of many provinces.[8]

Pound skipped this part, perhaps unaware of the stage convention of the Noh theatre. In the second part, there are many direct and indirect references to Buddhist gods, to the monk and the power of prayer. In the works of Fenollosa and Pound we can see some extensive confusion. After the intermission, while waiting for the appearance of the *shite* and *tsure*, the monk, with his disciples, sings a short piece called machiutai with his disciples, announcing that they will give a service for the spirits of the dead.

Noh: *koe bu[tsu]jioya nashinuran (N 8)*

Fenollosa: perhaps I had better perform a voice service to Buddha (*FN* 82)

Pound: I will do service to Butsu (*NOA* 139)

Butsuji is a ritual of Buddhism, and the service is dedicated to the dead so that they will ascend to Heaven. The monk will seek the power of Buddha in his prayer to save the suffering spirits. The monk says his prayer aloud (Fenollosa called this 'a voice service'). As for Pound's translation, 'Butsu' could be merely a sound to European readers. It is hard to determine where Pound got this word from—perhaps from the original Noh play, in which case he was not aware of its meaning. A Chinese character is used for the word, *butsu*, and it can be also read as *hotoke*, meaning the dead. Here

Fenollosa's translation was wrong, and, as for Pound's, it did not make any sense at all.

The confusion of Fenollosa and Pound becomes more obvious in the following part of *tsure* (a companion to the main character, the *shite*).

Noh: *Ikani, oso. Ichiju ichigano nagareo kumumonono enzoto kikum-noo....* (*N* 8).

Fenollosa: How! O, priest! Beyond the fact that I hear that even to dip up(water) from (the shadow) the same tree (falling on) the same river (is) just the karmic cause from some other life, ...(*FN* 83).

Pound:　Aïe, honoured priest!
　　　　You do not dip twice in the river
　　　　Beneath the same tree's shadow
　　　　Without bonds in some other life. (*NOA* 140)

In the case of Fenollosa's version, it may be that his interpreter did not know the meaning or the source of the phrase *'ichiju ichigano nagare'*. Otherwise it was Fenollosa who chose not to include the religious implication here. This phrase is from *Seppomyogenron*,[9] a medieval Buddhist text in two volumes, and is abbreviated from *'ichijunomotoni yadori ichigano nagareo kumumo'* i.e., 'staying under the same tree and drinking from the same river', which implies that their chance meeting was not really accidental, but that they are destined to meet from some kind of relationship they had in their previous world (*tashoono enzokashi*). Fenollosa tried to follow the more complicated religious implications in his translation, while Pound, in the next speech by the *shite*, revealed that he was not even trying to make sense out of Fenollosa's translation (which is decidedly hard to comprehend).

Noh:　*Niseto kanetaru chigiridanimo sashimo mitoseno hikazu tsumoru nishikigino aigataki norino chiguno arigatasayo* (*N* 8-9).

Fenollosa:　even, even the love promise, which has to do with two worlds, even for that having become three years, the number of these days heaping. O, how thankful is this

mysterious meeting the law which (meeting) it is difficult to
have by this nishikigi (*FN* 84).

Pound: A service that spreads in two worlds,
          And binds up an ancient love.
          That was stretched out between them.
          I had watched for a thousand days.
          I give you largess,
          For this meeting is under a difficult law (*NOA* 140).

In Buddhism, marriage is believed to last for two lives. Thus, if a
couple is married in this world, they will be married again in the
next. What the line means here is that though a marriage is a
promise for two lives, the couple could not get married in this life
despite the fact that the man had sought to do so for three years.
Now, however, because of the monk's prayer, they can be happily and gratefully united in the next world, since they had been
destined, by karma, to be a married couple. Fenollosa lost the
track here. Pound, working from Fenollosa's confusing translation, lost his comprehension of the plot, and began to invent his
own version. Each time Fenollosa came to a sentence or phrase
with religious implications, he became uncertain. That is because
his translators were, though intelligent, not well versed in
Japanese cultural tradition, and were more interested in learning
English. Where Fenollosa was not certain, Pound was completely
lost, and invented sentences and phrases out of his imagination to
continue the story.

Noh: *Shinnyono tamawa izukuzoya motometakuzoya oboyuru* (*N* 7).

Fenollosa: As for the jewel of tree appearance, where indeed is it?
(*FN* 78-79).

Pound: 'While the frost's lying here on the road.
          Who'd tell you that now?' (*NOA* 138).

Fenollosa and his translators did not realise the implication of *'shinnyono tama'*, and interpreted it as a dew from a tree, which, like a
jewel, shines beautifully in the morning sun, but they completely
failed to see that this very phrase meant enlightenment. However,
the only religious word neither of them failed to understand was

'naraku', meaning hell, as the concept appears to be almost universal.

The Noh was a poetic theatre for an aristocratic audience until the end of the Tokugawa shogunate (1868). Yeats became immediately interested in this Japanese theatre. He was hoping to revive the Irish poetic heritage through the theatre, although he knew that reviving Ireland's cultural identity through verse-drama could limit his audience. Inspired by the Noh, Yeats wrote *Four Plays for Dancers*. Though he based *The Dreaming of the Bones,* the third of the series, on the Noh play, *Nishikigi*, there are not many resemblances between his play and its source in the use of poetry, and there are strong reasons to doubt that Yeats ever understood the Japanese poetic forms, *waka* and *renga*, from Fenollosa's and Pound's versions of Noh plays. It must in any case have been almost impossible to envisage the original poetry from their work. Japanese is a syllabic language, and does not rhyme. *Renga* poems start with five, seven, five, syllables and can go on to any length by repeating sets of seven, five syllables. When a *renga* poems concludes, it ends with double sets of seven syllables, whereas *waka* has fixed sets of syllables of five, seven, five, seven and seven. So *waka* has thirty one syllables in all.

The Noh is like an opera in many ways, though the outcome on the stage is altogether different. In the Noh, as in opera, characters have speaking parts and also singing parts. Speaking parts are written with plain language, and the singing part in verse (basically a renga type of poetry with sets of seven, five syllables). Into these spoken and sung parts, *waka* poems are blended, sometimes in full, and sometimes as partial quotations. Translation of these Japanese poems is at any time virtually impossible, as feelings and emotions attached to the words can evaporate when the poems are put into other languages. However there always is some one such as Professor E. A. Cranston, of Harvard University, who challenges the otherwise impossible tasks of translating those complex *waka* poems.[10]

However, unfortunately there were no such translations available at Fenollosa's time. Fenollosa and his interpreters did all they could to save the flavour of the original poetry. They even tried to translate, for example, *'makurakotoba'* (an introductory part to the poem proper). These introductory words and phrases are often irrelevant to the content of the poem; they are used to bring out certain crucial words in the poem, and at the same time to create an appropriate atmosphere before the poet expresses his thoughts or feelings. But sometimes the introductory part and poem proper can harmonise, when *'makurakotoba'* evokes images of some natural phenomenon—a storm, high waves, wilderness or rushing mountain streams—and can then coincide with the feelings to be projected later in the same poem.

> *Seohayami iwanisekaruru takigawano* [*makurakotoba* = introduction]
> *waretemosueni awantozoomoo*[11]

> So swift the rapid,
> plunging stream sweeps round the rocks
> That seek to block:
> In the end to meet again,
> My love, though parted now.[12]

The introductory part provokes an image of a fast running mountain river hitting the rock in the middle of a stream and splashing water. This image is traditionally associated with the feeling of lovers facing a separation. The rock in the middle of the river symbolises some obstacle, such as commitment to the service to the emperor, which causes their separation. But the stress, here, is the latter half of the poem; the expression of their strong wish to be eventually re-united. The other tricky technique used in Japanese poems is a pun. Of course, this is not confined to Japanese poetry alone, for puns are common to poetry of East and West. In translation, however, they pose problems.

Poetic expression and vocabulary are not easy to translate. Fenollosa and his interpreter missed a few of them in *Nishikigi*, such as *'hatate'* and *'yukiomegurasu'*. Fenollosa translated *'hatate'* as 'the banner bomb of clouds', while Pound cut off the implication and simply edited it as 'no other man's flag in my hand , no more than a cloud has'. Pound completely missed the point here, as the original Japanese text meant the clouds are being blown off, just like banners in the wind. The stress is on the cloud, since the banners do not have any relevance to the play. When it comes to the latter example, Fenollosa translated it, without being able to drop the literary meaning, as 'O how glorious are this sleeves of the dancer which seem to sweep in whirl of snow'. Pound edited it as 'how glorious the sleeve of the dance. That are like snow whirl'. Pound's editorial work is better than Fenollosa's translation. The snow here implies only visual serenity, purity and beauty. It simply means that the dance is glorious, and nothing to do with actual images of snow, such as 'snow whirl'.

In *Nishikigi*, sixteen *waka* poems were quoted in full, or in part from earlier anthologies of *waka* poems, and a part of a Chinese poem was also quoted to decorate and strengthen the plot. Four *waka* poems by Narihira Ariwara are quoted from *Kokinshu*, an anthology of *waka* poems.[13] Narihira had been one of the best-known love poets in the royal court in the Heian period. Since this play was about a sad love relationship, it is understandable that Ze-Ami included four of Narihira's poems. Because the location of the play is in far North of the Michinoku region, some poems, chosen by Ze-Ami, are directly linked to this locality. All those *waka* poems became a nightmare for the interpreter, the translator and finally the editor.

Let us examine how some of them were used in the play, and how they were translated and finally edited. The first waka poem Ze-ami quoted was by Tooru Minamoto, and was in the *Kokinshu* waka anthology. Ze-Ami changed the last seven syllables to five syllables— into a 'renga' type—as he put two poems together to run on one after the other. But as for the second poem, he merely used the middle section of the poem to fit into the story proper.

Noh (waka): *Michinokono Shinobumojizuri tareyueni*
                                midaresomenishi warekarato[14]

Fenollosa: 'My fault', who am beginning to be tangled—for whom (just as) the grass pattern of shinobu cloth in Land's End (are tangled), (*FN* 60-61).

Pound: Tangled, we are entangled. Whose fault was it, dear? tangled up as the grass patterns are tangled in this coarse cloth (*NOA* 132).

Cranston: Random-patterned cloth
             Of Shinobu in the Northland
             Not for some other
             Began in me the adadon
             That imprints with wild desire. (tr. E. A. Cranston)[15]

The first two sets of five and seven syllables are pillar words, which were used to introduce the first word of the third set. This waka simply means, 'who is causing the confusion in my thought like the pattern on *shinobumojuzuri* (kimono)?', (i.e., certainly not because of my amorous nature). This poem is evoking love-sickness in a subtle way, and, embellished by those pillow words, it brings in an element of romantic nostalgia attached to this remote corner of Japan (where aristocrats from the royal court would not dream of going). Also the textiles of the region add something unique and exotic, just as impressionist painters adopted Japanese wood block prints to add something different and mysterious to their work. When the word 'tangled' was used, it meant the entangled relationship of a man and a woman, but in the original text it meant entangled thoughts.[16]

Noh (waka): *Nishikigiwa tatenagarakoso kuchinikeri* (*N* 5)
                     kyoonohosonuno muneawajiyato[17]

Fenollosa: As for nishikigi, in the fact of its continuing to be set up, it has decayed. So it seems narrow cloth of kefu will not meet across the heart (*FN* 72).

Pound: At last they forget, they forget.
                   The wands are no longer offered,
                   The custom is faded away.
                   The narrow cloth of Kefu
                   Will not meet over the breast (*NOA* 136).

Cranston: My brocade sticks stand
                   Undisturbed where I set them
                   Rotting away
                   The new cloth of Kefu
                   Meet not at the breasts—nor we?

It will be obvious from these quotations that neither Fenollosa or Pound realised that they were going over an independent *waka* poem, inserted by Ze-Ami. This poem combined two separate legends, one of *nishikigi* and the other of *hosonuno*. Ze-Ami combined the legends in this play, focusing on the poem. The literal translation is that *Nishikigi* starts decaying even while it is being set up: [a kimono made of] *hosonuno* of *kefu* is not wide enough to double cross in the front. This actually means that the man's courtship keeps failing because of the woman's constant refusal and thus they will not be able to hold each other in a close embrace.

The other use of poetry is to create atmosphere on stage and to emotionally mobilise the audience by quoting telling sections from well known waka poems. This is almost as effective as quoting a whole waka, and on some occasions it can be more effective, because it does not hinder the course of the plot. In *Nishikigi*, there are nine partial quotations of seven syllables of a set of seven, five syllables. Fenollosa was perhaps not aware of quotations of this kind, and it was impossible for Pound to detect any of them from his notebooks of translations.

Pound ignored Fenollosa's notes on stage movements and musical transcripts of Noh plays, as they were sketchy and would not give sufficient guidelines for a reader to visualise a total performance. The Noh is a traditional theatre, and each of its five schools has its own stage directions for all the plays in its own repertoire. Usually a play has only one set of stage directions with some partial variations. Noh actors are not allowed to invent or improvise new ways of acting at all. They have to follow detailed descriptions of stage directions developed for those plays at the time of Ze-Ami, and also at some time later. But in the Tokugawa shogunate, all stage directions were made traditional and no one was allowed to challenge them in response to the shogunate's policy of respecting and preserving traditions intact, in their efforts to consolidate power, and to freeze and stabilise society. Such stage directions were treasured and guarded by the head of each school as its secrets, and Fenollosa did not have access to them. These stage directions were called 'katatsuke', and what Fenollosa wrote down in his notebooks was something far from them. A Noh actor needs more than ten years of hard training to become a professional, and to be able to use these 'katatsuke'.

Pound limited the musical scores for publication. In the first publication for the Cuala press, Pound had omitted the music of *Hagoromo*, but included it in an appendix to *Noh, or Accomplishment* (pp. 257-68). Once re-scored for western performance, this music became totally different. It can be played on the piano or any other European instrument, but then does not sound like the music in a Noh play. In Noh there are two types of singing; one weak form and one strong form. As these employ different types of voice production, they cannot be simply represented by western musical signs such as *pianissimo* or *forte*. Some weak form of singing needs to be sung forcefully and some of the stronger form needs to be sung gently. Further, the musical scale used in the Noh theatre is not absolute, like western music, and it varies according to the age and sex of the character. Even the same character changes the tone of the singing voice according to the mood at the time. This means, even though the starting key is suggested to be *jo*, meaning high, this high tone can vary to such a great extent that *jo* for an old woman can be lower than *ge* (low) for a young woman. And also, in Noh singing, voice production is different; when the key changes, a Noh actor's voice tends to go up gradually. He does not hit the right key immediately.

There are other things which are unique to the Noh, such as its glorious costumes and masks. Fenollosa gives only a brief general account of these in *Noh, or Accomplishment* and *The Classic Noh Theatre of Japan*. He does not specify the costumes or masks for *Nishikigi* or any other plays. In the Noh they are specified as follows:

> *Mae-shite* (man) *hitamen* (no mask), yellow collar, *mizugoromo* (kimono) & *shiro ookuchi* (baggy trousers), *suki-suho* (over gown), *otoko oogi* (man's fan) *nishikigi* (to be carried in his hand)

> *Nochi-shite* (ghost) mask, *awaotoko* or *kaishi*, *kurokashira* (black haired head gear) hairband in black with gold, plain collar, *mizugoromo* (kimono) & *hangiri* (baggy trousers), *hohi* (gown), *shura-oogi* (a fan which symbolises purgatory or hell)

> *tsure* (woman) mask, *tsure*-men, *katsura* (wig), *beni-iri-katsuraobi* (belt), red collar, *surihaku*, *beni-iri-karaori*, *hosonuno* (to be carried over an arm)

> *waki* (monk) *kaku-boshi* (acquire cap), purple collar, plain *shinonome* & no baggy trousers, black fan, *juzu* (rosary) (*N* iv).

The *waki* has two or three accompanying monks with him, and they are given the same instruction for their costumes. The stage directions also say that the lead in the first part should carry a *nishikigi* in his right hand and that the *tsure* (woman) should carry a *hosonuno* over her left arm. As for music, Fenollosa was right to say the principle of *ying* and *yang* was applied in Noh music: first seven syllables for *ookawa* (big drum) for *yang* and the following five for *kotsuzumi* (small drum) for *ying*. But for practical reasons, twelve syllables were distributed into eight beats. *Ookawa* takes charge of the first four beats and *kotsuzumi* the latter half. Fenollosa had lived in Japan and saw many performances and learned the Noh from the

Umewaka family, so he did have a broad experience of Noh. However Pound had never been to Japan, nor had he ever seen a Noh play, so he did not know anything about these detailed arrangements. It is not justifiable to blame Pound for reducing Fenollosa's translation to mere literature, simply because Fenollosa did not give enough information or consistent explanations of stage movements and music, costume and other theatrical elements.

From the comparison of these three texts, major difficulties in understanding and translating Noh into English caused by the differences in religions, poetry and also music become obvious. Straight conversational parts of the Noh play, *Nishikigi*, were translated by Fenollosa with ease, but those parts involving concepts of Buddhism and traditional forms of Japanese poetry were not so easily done. Fenollosa was a Buddhist convert, and yet he did not fully understand the religious implications of the Noh texts. As for Pound, he did not show any understanding of religion in his editorial work. Religion as personal belief is not easily changed, linked as it usually is to ethnic background. Faith and beliefs are the last things one wants undermined by other religions. Pound might have been inhibited by ambiguous references to Buddhist teachings which Fenollosa had preserved from the original text.

Waka poetry is the briefest literary form for expressing one's ideas and feelings. Consequently, each word carries great deal of significance. The shorter the poetic form is, the deeper the reader has to dig in for hidden meanings and implications. When it comes to translating such short poems, it can seem impossible to find a word of one's own language which can replace a word of the original language. That is because each word chosen by a poet carries cultural, historical, religious and customs of its country. As noted above, it is the same with Japanese music which, when re-scored, loses everything except an accurate melody and is a completely different thing. Even accuracy is in doubt, as the music, made not the singing voice, but by a flute and drums cannot be transcribed simply. There is thus no musical sound like the Noh music in Western music. A BBC crew once tried to record the music of the Noh, but the recording technician could not believe that each time the flute or a drum was played, the high pitched sound went beyond the recording capability of his machines. Advances in technology will make it possible to communicate such sounds some time in the future.

W. B. Yeats read Pound's editorial work, and gave him suggestions, most of which Pound rejected.[18] They included suggestions such as 'ornate' to 'painted', 'void' to 'empty', 'largesse' to 'thanks' and 'tryst' to 'marriage' (*YA4* 133-37). These suggestions show that Yeats was more objective, and was trying to make the work plain and easy to understand. Pound refused the suggestions, because, it would seem, he wanted to retain some generally mystic feeling throughout the play. Some of the suggestions Yeats made should not have been ignored. He pointed out that, in the following quotation, that 'them' is not clear and also suggested a full stop after 'sunset'.

Noh: *Geniya nanomiwa iwashirono matsuno kotonoha torioki*
            yuhino kagemo nishikigino yadorini izaya kaeran (N 5).

Fenollosa: Indeed as for the (love) name only, having bound
            together the word-leaves of the pine trees of Iwashiro,
            (Which speaks those names), as it is now the image of
            the evening sun. We shall return (come, let's go) to
            our lodging of nishikigi (*FN* 73).

Pound: A tale to bring shame on the gods.

            Names of love,
            Now for a little spell,
            For a faint charm only,
            For a charm slight as the binding together
            Of pine-flakes in Iwashiro,
            And for saying a wish over them about sunset,
            We return, and return to our lodging.
            The evening sun leaves a shadow. (*NOA* 136-7)

Fenollosa first got confused over the puns in these poetic lines and did not make their meaning clear, so Pound took the liberty of completely inventing this section to link this part of the story to the rest. The original text means that they have said their names and would like to look forward to the next meeting, and that, since it is already evening, the sun is casting a shadow on their lodging (the mound) of *Nishikigi*, and then they should go back there. There was no way Yeats could tell what the original text was like from their works, but he somehow knew Pound's editorial work was not sufficient .

Yeats's own version of Noh plays, *Four Plays for Dancers* (*At the Hawk's Well*, *The Only Jealousy of Emer*, *The Dreaming of the Bones* and *Calvary* did not have a big commercial success, nor did they make a great impact on English literature, but they certainly became a landmark for combining European thought with Japanese tradtional Noh theatre. *The Dreaming of the Bones* is Yeats's adoption of *Nishikigi*, and is the most succesful of his four attempts. The structure of the play is very similar to that of a dream play of the Noh, although all religious aspects of Noh were eliminated in Yeats's version. The *waki* in a Noh play is normally a monk who has religious power to save suffering spirits, but in this play of Yeats's it is the Young Man who fled the Post Office after the Easter Rising to whom Yeats give the power to save suffering spirits by setting a condition. The couple this Young Man encounters in the hills on the border of Clare and Galway are the ghosts of Diarmuid and Dervorgilla who had brought the Normans into Ireland seven hundred years before. The Norman invasion of Ireland began the subsequent British colonialisation of this island. The ghost of Dervorgilla almost succeeds in persuading the Young Man to forgive them. The condition set by Yeats for the release of the earthbound spirits was to get some one of their race to say 'I forgive them', which is very like the prayer of a monk in the Noh play. The couple could have been saved from their purgatory, but Yeats could not allow the Young Man to utter his forgiveness, something which is understandable since this Young Man narrowly avoided being shot by the British soldiers during the Rising and will yet be shot if he is caught. In *Nishikigi*, the ghost couple are saved, while, in Yeats's *The Dreaming of the Bones*, they are not. Despite such fundamental differences, the climax of *The Dreaming of the Bones* seems to share the aesthetics of Noh drama, which is described by the symbolic term *hana* (flower).

Young Man. You speak of Diarmuid and Dervorgilla
   Who brought the Normans in?

Young Girl.   Yes, yes, I spoke
   Of that most miserable, most accursed pair
   Who sold their country into slavery; and yet
   They were not wholly miserable and accursed
   If somebody of their race at last would say,
   'I have forgiven them'.

Young Man.   O, never, never,
   Shall Diarmuid and Dervorgilla be forgiven.

Young Girl. If some one of their race forgave at last
   Lip will be pressed on lip. (*VPl* 772-3).

The intense appeal by the Young Woman and also the desperate dance by the ghost couple reveal their unconsumable passion. The rejection by the Young Man adds sorrow to the scene, and sorrow, Ze-Ami says, is very effective in creating *hana* on the stage. I have elsewhere observed how Ze-Ami' manages such effects e.g., in

Usugirino magkinohanano asajimeri akiwayubeto tarekaiikeri.

This *waka* poem can be translated as

What a beautiful sight of wet flowers in the hedge on a misty morning. Who said Autumn is best in the evening.

which suggests that while 'flowers may be marvellous on their own, the subtle effect of faint mist may make them even more exquisitely poetic. The effect of dew upon flowers, like that of sorrow upon a fine face, suggests an additional spiritual finesse, and proves still more captivating than ordinary flowers, ordinary beauty'.[19]

Yeats, then, did not follow the tradition of the Noh in his plot and theme, but he did succeed in creating the essence of Noh aesthetics. While working in the reading room of the Beinecke Library, Yale University, I saw an example of perfect harmony of European Architecture and Japanese aesthetics, just in front of me, out in the courtyard. The architect was Gordon Burnshaft and the sculptor was Isamu Noguchi. There was no original Japanese material (rocks and water, trees and bamboos); all that was used was marble. Yet this courtyard gave the kind of serenity and peace only rarely found in old gardens in ancient Japanese cities. Fenollosa's and Pound's work in introducing the Noh to the West was significant, and Yeats's attempt to adopt the Noh was courageous and to some extent successful to some extent. To bring the theatre of East and West into total harmony, such as that seen in the symbolic fusion of the Beinecke Library courtyard, one would need to extract and to verify their genuine and simple essences, before creating a powerful dramatic piece, which could be universally appreciated. Such a play would transcend local and trivial creative conventions, to produce a work of universal spiritual value.

NOTES

I am very grateful to Professor E. A. Cranston, Harvard University, who arranged my visit to Harvard, helped me with *waka* poems and gave me permission to quote his translations of poems; to the Fulbright-Japan USA Educational Commission which made my research financially possible and also the Beinecke Library, Yale University, which provided me with invaluable research material from the Yale Collection of American Literature. He has recently published a massive book of a complete translation of Manyoshu, the oldest anthology of Japanese poems.

1. Oh, East is East, and West is West, and never the twain shall meet,
    Till Earth and Sky stand presently at God's great Judgement Seat;
    But there is neither East nor West, Border, nor Breed, nor Birth,
    When two strong men stand face to face, though they come from the ends of earth!.
        (Rudyard Kipling, 'The Ballad of East and West', 1889).

2. London: Macmillan, 1917, p. 3. Hereafter *NOA*. Later republished as *The Classic Noh Theatre of Japan*. The plays in these volumes were first published in *Certain Noble Plays of Japan: From the Manuscripts of Ernest Fenollosa,* chosen and finished by Ezra Pound, with an introduction by William Butler Yeats (Dublin: Cuala Press, 1916).

3. Bunsaku Kurata (ed.), *Fenollosa to Meiji Bunka* (Japanese) Shinichi Kurihara (Tokyo: Rokugei Shobo, 1968), p. 425.

4. *Ibid* p. 448.

5. Hirata graduated from Koto-Shihan-Gakko in 1889, and became an English teacher at its junior school.

6. See Yoko Chiba 'Ezra Pound's Versions of Feollosa's Noh Manuscripts and Yeats's Unpublished "Suggestions and Corrections"' (*YA4* 121-44 at p. 121 & n. 4.

7. Ze-Ami, *Nishikigi,* ed. Sakon Kanze XXIV (Tokyo: Hinoki Shoten, 1985), p. 5. Hereafter *N*.

8. Fenollosa's Notebook p. 59. The Beinecke Library, Yale University, YCAL MSS Box 93 Folder No. 3410. Hereafter *FN*.

9. *Seppomyogenron*(Japanese), ed. Entsu in the 5th year of Kanbun.

10. See n. 1.

11. Ex-Emperror Sutoku, *Shikashu* VII:229. One of the Ogura Hyakunin Isshu.

12. Translated by Professor E. A. Cranston.

13. *Kokinshu,* edited by Kino Tsurayuki, Kino Tomonori, Ooshikoshino Mitsune and Minobu Tadamine in 914.

14. *N* 1-2 (Originally *warekaranakuni* in the poem by Minamoto tooru (822-895).

15. Yeats was very impressed by Pound's version of this passage which he quotes in his discussion of the play in 'Swedenborg, Mediums and the Desolate Places' (*LE* 70).

16. The main poem in this play was written by Noin-Hoshi, and was included in *Go-Shuishu* waka anthologies. *Go-Shuishu* was edited by Fujiwara Michitoshi in 1086.

17. Originally *muneawajitoya*. *Noin-hoshi Shu* 127, Real name was Tachibana Nagayasu (988 - ?), one of the thirty-six best poets in the Heian period (?- 1192).
18. See Yoko Chiba, *YA4* 121-44. The suggestions and corrections are in the Pound Archive, Beinecke Library, Yale Universty, YCAL. Box 137 Folder No. 5591.
19. see my *Ze-Ami and His Theories of Noh Drama* (Gerrards Cross: Colin Smythe, 1985). p. 151.

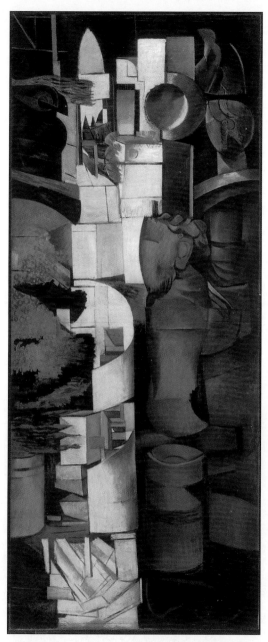

1. *Bagdad* (1927), oil painting by Wyndham Lewis.

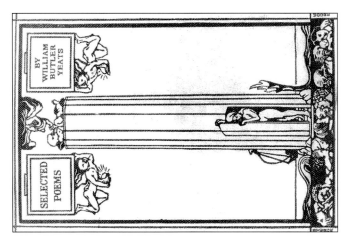

3. Cover design for Yeats's *Selected Poems*
   (New York: Macmillan, 1921).

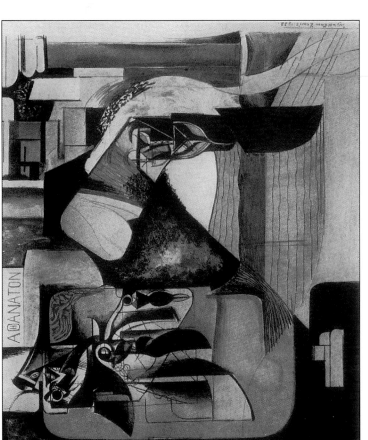

2. *Athanaton* (1933), pen, ink and gouache
   by Wyndham Lewis.

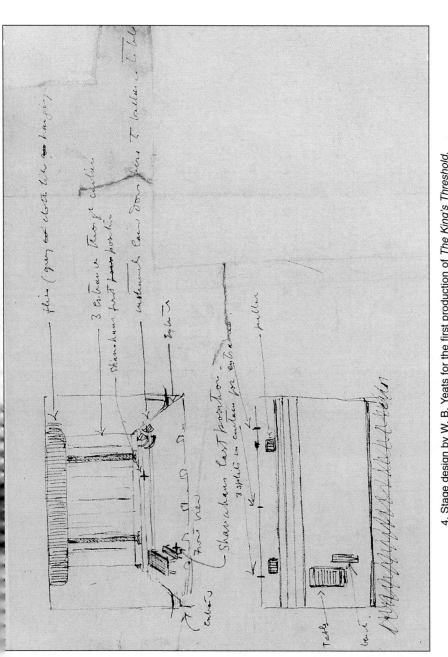

4. Stage design by W. B. Yeats for the first production of *The King's Threshold*.

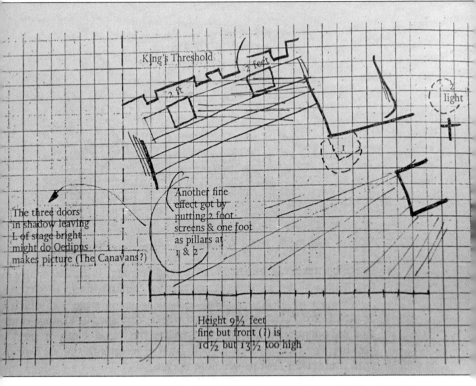

In the image, the following handwritten text appears:

King's Threshold

2 feet

2 ft.

light

Another fine effect got by putting 2 foot screens & one foot as pillars at 1 & 2

The three doors in shadow leaving L of stage bright might do Oedipus makes picture (The Canavans?)

Height 9½ feet fine but front (?) is 10½ but 13½ too high

5. Liam Miller's transcription of p. 23 of W. B. Yeats's 'Scene Notebook', in his *The Noble Drama of W. B. Yeats* (Dublin: Atlantic Highlands, N.J., 1977).

6. and 7. (below and opposite) John Butler Yeats's marginalia and drawings in a copy of *The Wanderings of Oisin and Other Poems* (1889).

Beneath the sheltering shadow of Thy Church;
And Thou shalt bend, enduring God, the knees
Of the great warriors whose names have sung
The world to its fierce infancy again.

The mist-drops hung on the fragrant trees,
And in the blossoms hung the bees.
We rode in sadness above Lough Laen,
For our best were dead on Gavra's green.
The stag we chased was not more sad,
And yet, of yore, much peace he had
In his own leafy forest house,
Sleek as any granary mouse
Among the fields of waving fern.
We thought on Oscar's pencilled urn.
Than the hornless deer we chased that morn,
A swifter creature never was born,
And Bran, Sgeolan, and Lomair
Were lolling their tongues, and the silken hair
Of our strong steeds was dark with sweat,
When ambling down the vale we met
A maiden, on a slender steed,
Whose careful pastern pressed the sod
As though he held an earthly mead
Scarce worthy of a hoof gold-shod.
For gold his hooves and silk his rein,
And 'tween his ears, above his mane,
A golden crescent lit the plain,
And pearly white his well-groomed hair.
His mistress was more mild and fair
Than doves that moaned round Eman's hall
Among the leaves of the laurel wall,
And feared always the bow-string's twanging.
Her eyes were soft as dewdrops hanging

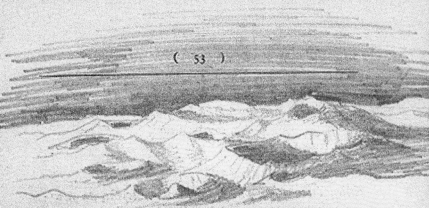

TIME AND THE WITCH VIVIEN.

*A marble-flagged, pillared room. Magical instruments
in one corner. A fountain in the centre.*

Vivien (looking down into the fountain). Where
  moves there any beautiful as I,
Save, with the little golden greedy carp,
Gold unto gold, a gleam in its long hair,
My image yonder? (*Spreading her hand over the
  water.*) Ah, my beautiful,
What roseate fingers! (*Turning away.*) No; nor is
  there one
Of equal power in spells and secret rites.
The proudest or most coy of spirit things,
Hide where he will, in wave or wrinkled moon,
Obeys.
   Some fierce magician flies or walks
Beyond the gateway—by the sentries now—
Close and more close—I feel him in my heart—
Some great one. No; I hear the wavering steps
Without there of a little, light old man;

8. John Butler Yeats's marginalia and drawings in a copy of *The Wanderings of
Oisin and Other Poems* (1889).

A GROUP at last night's meeting of the Oxford University English Club, when Mr. W. B. Yeats read and spoke about his poems: Mr. Derek Palmer, the Rev. Montague Summers, Mr. J. G. Greenlees, Mr. W. B. Yeats, Miss Allison-Brown, and Mr. W. R. Rumbold.

9. Yeats with Members of the Oxford University English Club, *Oxford Mail*, 6 June 1933.

a very wonderful place, with Roman walls 18 feet high, running in a squar[e]
all about it, + a little amphitheatre inside, all neat and trim; + a
beautiful brook, running in a concreted channel, just outside the walls, [a]
fine sight. You'd ought to have had the Romans down to the Gara, to conce[?]
that channel; for surely it would have added to the ease of our sports ther[e]

I am aweary. I was up till 2 this morning, + got out of bed at 6.
You must forgive a dull note

With very kind regards to Mrs Yeats.

Yours [...]

John Masefield.

When a sunset's clear, and as red as fore,
a Liverpool clipper makes Baltimore
When a sunset's foul in a bank of black
a Liverpool clipper has to put back
Sing Tooral ooral looral.

[row of drawn symbols / code]

what are the symbols
for Whydah + Kreek, I always confuse them. + What is X

10. Undated letter from John Masefield to Jack B. Yeats, partly in code.

Yeats and the Ghost of Wordsworth

Maneck H. Daruwala

After what I have said, Mr. Wordsworth will not be flattered by knowing that Blake deems him the *only poet* of the age, nor much alarmed by hearing that Blake thinks that he is often, in his works, an *Atheist*. Now, according to Blake, Atheism consists in worshipping the natural world, . . . Dante and Wordsworth, in spite of their Atheism were inspired by the Holy Ghost. Indeed, all real poetry is the work of the Holy Ghost, and Wordsworth's poems (a large proportion, at least) are the work of Divine Inspiration. . . . in general Blake loves the poems. What appears to have disturbed his mind, on the other hand, is the Preface to 'The Excursion.' He told me six months ago that it caused him a stomach complaint that nearly killed him (Letter from Crabb Robinson to Dorothy Wordsworth, quoted in *WWB1* 147-8).

BLAKE'S REPORTED REACTION TO WORDSWORTH, though well on the road to excess and somewhat unorthodox in its reasons, was not an atypical one. Wordsworth was too original and too influential a poet not to evoke strong reactions from his contemporaries and the perceived contrast between the two Wordsworths too great to ignore: 'thou leavest me to grieve, | Thus

197

having been that thou shouldst cease to be' (Shelley, 'To Wordsworth'). Yet, sometimes poets who came to mock—such as Byron—stayed to steal.

Yeats's reaction to Wordsworth is somewhat like Blake's without the extremes. It involves the usual Romantic or late Romantic complaint: he was a lost leader, an original and revolutionary poet turned Victorian moralist and rhetorician; but Yeats also shares Blake's irritation at Wordsworth's naturalism, if not for Blake's reasons. To Yeats, who once called Wordsworth 'that typical Englishman' (*E&I* 520), this may have seemed an exaggerated form of an English defect. Dorothy Wellesley records his complaint: 'Why can't you English poets keep flowers out of your poetry?' (*LDW* 190)

The passage which Blake could not stomach was the marvellous and somewhat Blakean opening of the Prospectus to *The Excursion* (1814), originally the final part of the 1798 'Home at Grasmere'. E. J. Ellis and Yeats quote an extended passage from Crabb Robinson who mentioned that Blake was alarmed by the passage about passing 'Jehovah—with His thunder, and the choir | Of shouting angels' unalarm'd (I:144). Crabb Robinson noted: 'I tried to explain this passage in a sense in harmony with Blake's own theories, but failed, and Wordsworth was set down as a Pagan, but still with high praise, as the greatest poet of the age' (*WWB1* 144). According to Crabb Robinson's letter to Dorothy Wordsworth, Blake wanted to meet William Wordsworth in any case, and kept an open mind: 'Mr. Wordsworth is a great man. Besides, he may convince me I am wrong about him. I have been wrong before now' (*WWB1* 148).

Yeats, in his own fashion, was to re-stress Wordsworth's internalization of 'All strength—all terror', of Chaos, and Erebus and heaven, knowing that none of these 'can breed such fear and awe | As fall upon us often when we look | Into our Minds, into the Mind of Man—| My haunt, and the main region of my song' ('Prospectus' 38-41). Yeats asks: 'Why should we honour those who die in the fields of battle? A man may show as reckless a courage by entering into the abyss of himself'.[1] Yet Wordsworth is not usually numbered among the predecessors he created. Yeats continually reminded his readers of his belatedness, and his relations with Blake and Shelley, Keats, Coleridge, and even Byron have been stressed. Yeats's attitude to Wordsworth is notorious. George Bornstein sees Yeats as influenced by his father who 'abhorred Wordsworth': 'Unlike his volatile changes towards other Romantics, Yeats with only rare exceptions persistently denigrated Wordsworth. This Romantic was doomed to be a perpetual foil to the virtues of the others in the world of Yeats criticism'.[2]

In 'Art and Ideas' Yeats cites D. G. Rossetti's 'dislike of Wordsworth' and his reaction against 'the pedantic composure of Wordsworth' as an example of the inclinations of a 'school' or group of artists whom he claimed later as models for his self and his aesthetic at the time (*E&I* 351). Yeats at first contrasted Wordsworth's dross with the purer imagistic ore of Keats and Shelley as seen by Hallam. Wordsworth had been 'the one great poet who, after brief blossom, was cut and sawn into planks of obvious utility' (*Au* 235). Having finished *The Excursion* and begun *The Prelude*, Yeats writes of Wordsworth:

> He strikes me as always destroying his poetic experience, which was of course of incomparable value, by his reflective power. His intellect was commonplace, and unfortunately he had been taught to respect nothing else. He thinks of his poetical experience not as incomparable in itself but as an engine that may be yoked to his intellect. He is full of a sort of utilitarianism and that is perhaps the reason why in later life he is continually looking back upon a lost vision, a lost happiness.[3]

This may not be quite fair to the poet who repeatedly stresses that certain joys and experiences become valuable inspiration precisely because they began as aimless joys or in wandering as clouds which go where the wind takes them. We are told that Yeats's attitude to Wordsworth was probably not sweetened by the irritation of having him held up as a good example. Phillip Marcus links this animosity to Yeats's antagonism towards Edward Dowden and John Eglinton. Dowden, whose seven volume edition of Wordsworth Yeats set himself to read in 1915, was 'withering in that barren soil' of Ireland (*Au* 235); and Eglinton—who later modified his position—praised what he saw as the philosophic or 'Wordsworthian' kind of poetry over the aesthetic turn toward a tradition of 'old faiths, myths, dreams'.[4]

In *Per Amica Silentia Lunae* Yeats remembered 'Wordsworth withering into eighty years, honoured and empty-witted' (*Myth* 342). Yet both poets are, as Bornstein points out, poets of memory and of 'autobiographical self-confrontation'.[5] Yeats sought to remake himself continually as he believed that Wordsworth did not.[6] Patrick Keane argues for the ideological influence of the revolutionary books of the 1850 *Prelude* which he tells us 'Yeats read . . . with particular care'[7] while Michael Baron's 'Yeats, Wordsworth and the Communal Sense: the Case of "If I were Four-and-Twenty"' is a sophisticated and complex analysis of Yeats's recreation of Wordsworth, particularly in his prose (*YA5* 62-82). The general trend of earlier criticism had been that Wordsworth's influence on Yeats was as indirect as it was extensive. He influenced Yeats through the tradition of the great ode and the 'greater romantic lyric,' through the poetry of memory and juxtaposed visions, through the figure of 'the Solitary,' through Shelley, and Keats and Arnold and just about every successor who reacted to him. Harold Bloom, who has been most enlightening on Yeats's Romantic influences—including Wordsworth—once went so far as to say that

> There is no direct influence whatsoever of Milton or Wordsworth upon Yeats, but the single poem that most affected his life and art (and Browning's as well), is Shelley's *Alastor*, and the line leading to *Alastor* and its remorseless version of Romantic quest goes from *Il Pensoroso* through Wordsworth's *Excursion*.[8]

And Yeats certainly seems to have contributed deliberately to this estimate, often contrasting himself with Wordsworth, as in 'A General Introduction to my Work'.

> I discovered some twenty years ago that I must seek, not as Wordsworth thought, words in common use, but a powerful and passionate syntax, and a complete coincidence between period and stanza (*E&I* 521-22).

Yeats and Pound read Wordsworth in Dowden's edition in January and February 1915 at Stone Cottage (*CL3* xxviii), as 'a duty to posterity'.[9] 'To a Young Beauty', composed after this reading, is a perfect example of the pursuit of a passionate syntax and a rejection of the favourite Wordsworthian commonness: 'You may, that mirror for a school, | Be passionate not bountiful | As common beauties may' (*VP* 335-6). It is therefore paradoxically appropriate that the poem seems to have been modelled on a specific poem of Wordsworth's. Pegasus is a gift horse: the influence may not have been advertised, but it seems to have been extensive and might have been conscious. In any case, it suggests a deeper saturation in the rhythms and rhymes of Wordsworth's poetry than we tend to ascribe to Yeats.

II

A poetical passage cannot be understood without a rich memory (*E&I* 227)

'To A Young Beauty' and 'To A Young Lady Who Had Been Reproached For Taking Long Walks in the Country'[10] are both 'advice' poems to young women. Writers of such verse were often concerned with the proper social virtues and womanliness or offered the traditional advice to young virgins 'to make much of time'—occasionally with the author. Time is the natural subject of an advice poem, a subject about which an older adviser may safely claim to know something more—Herrick's 'To the Virgins, to Make much of Time' is ostensibly practical. Wordsworth's and Yeats's subject is also time—but their poems are about individual women, and the advice they give ultimately goes against the grain of social orthodoxy.

To A Young Lady, Who Had Been Reproached For Taking Long Walks in the Country

Dear Child of Nature, let them rail!
—There is a nest in a green dale,
A harbour and a hold;
Where thou, a Wife and Friend, shalt see
Thy own heart-stirring days, and be
A light to young and old.

There, healthy as a shepherd boy,
And treading among flowers of joy
Which at no season fade,
Thou, while thy babes around thee cling,
Shalt show us how divine a thing
A Woman may be made.

> Thy thoughts and feelings shall not die,
> Nor leave thee, when grey hairs are nigh,
> A melancholy slave;
> But an old age, serene and bright,
> And lovely as a Lapland night,
> Shall lead thee to thy grave.[11]

Wordsworth's is an anti-advice advice poem which advises the young woman to ignore her 'rail[ing]' critics and do exactly as she pleases. The very first line of the poem identifies the poet with the young woman and not with 'them'. Usually associated with Dorothy Wordsworth (though sometimes with Joanna Hutchinson) the poem was written perhaps in 1801 and was published in the *Morning Post*, 12 February 1802. Dorothy Wordsworth had responded to a reproach from her Aunt Crackanthorpe, in a letter dated April 21, 1794.[12]

> I am much obliged to you for the frankness with which you have expressed your sentiments upon my conduct and am at the same time extremely sorry that you should think it so severely to be condemned. . . . I cannot pass unnoticed that part of your letter in which you speak of my 'rambling about the country on foot.' So far from considering this as a matter of condemnation, I rather that it would have given my friends pleasure to hear that I had the courage to make use of the strength with which nature has endowed me, when it not only procured me infinitely more pleasure than I should have received from sitting in a post chaise—but was also the means of saving me at least thirty shillings.[13]

The letter strenuously defends the emotional and intellectual delight Dorothy Wordsworth has discovered in nature, knowledge and a measure of independence: 'I derive not only much pleasure but much improvement from my brother's society. I have regained all the knowledge I had of the French language I had some years ago, and have added considerably to it. I have now begun Italian . . .' (pp. 52-3). So much of wisdom depends on knowing what advice not to take; a young woman who can argue so compellingly about not only paradise but French regained would seem to need little defending. The intensity of the response may suggest how important—and how threatened—this independence was, and how crucial to both sister and brother.

It may be that Wordsworth was defending both his sister and himself: the implication of his poem is that the issue was not so much a matter of safety as propriety. Certainly Dorothy Wordsworth with her gypsy tan seems closer to the poem's image of a healthy shepherd boy (compare Louisa—'ruddy, fleet and strong'—in the companion poem) than to the pale ladies of nineteenth century fashion and fiction. In 1794 Dorothy Wordsworth was about twenty-two, her brother twenty months older and recently returned from France. Both made a habit of being reproached by older relatives—who were not pleased when they set up house together the following year. So it may be natural that there is no admonition to the young woman to do anything except follow her own impulses—the rest will come naturally. The poem seems to support a rebellion against 'adult' interference and the conditionings of femininity.

Yeats's debt to this poem for 'To A Young Beauty' shows both the influence of a poet he consistently criticized and how he transformed earlier Romanticism. Yeats's poem is also occasional, intimately related to his own situation as a poet as well as to the young woman's. He is however cast in an avuncular role.[14] 'To A Young Beauty'—invokes in its title a traditional, perhaps ironic, chivalry. Wordsworth's title establishes his occasional context, but his use of 'lady' also heightens the ambiguity of the concept in this poem: there are society ladies and natural ladies; and then there are women.[15] His young lady takes long walks and is reprimanded, Yeats's just is—a young beauty. The poem seems to suggest that her beauty and inexperience present special distractions or temptations. She is a fellow artist and might be a muse—since the speaker is beauty's servant. He is, apparently, a self-proposed model, yet the poem's undertone—'be clever sweet maid'—is unorthodox, especially as the cleverness he demands is not that of a professional *ingénue*.

The central subject of both poems is a somewhat wild young woman and her freedom. The parallels between the two poems, in theme, handling, and substance, as well as in form and structure, in rhythm and rhyme scheme extend to similarities of alliteration. Each poem follows a similar three part division, indicated by the stanza breaks. The first stanza presents the 'problem', the young woman and her freedom. The second stanza deals with the poetic ideal, the potential, in each case a 'divine' young woman. The final stanza deals with the end of life in terms of the wages of the pursuit—of Nature in Wordsworth, of Art in Yeats.

The shared stanza form is also that of Wordsworth's 'Three Years She Grew' and of 'I Met Louisa'. Each poem has three predominantly iambic six-lined stanzas rhyming aabccb with identical arrangements of line length: 4,4,3,4,4,3. The first stanzas even share an exact rhyme 'see' and 'be' in Wordsworth, 'free' and 'company' in Yeats (and a half rhyme); the second stanzas again have similar rhymes : 'cling' and 'thing' in Wordsworth, 'trim' and 'cherubim' in Yeats, and similar terminal vowel sounds: 'fade' and 'made' in Wordsworth, 'may' and 'Beauvarlet' in Yeats. The first and third stanzas of each poem have a long pause in the middle—a semi-colon or colon at the end of the third line; the equivalent pause in the second stanza of each is only a comma. The stanza is not in itself unusual enough to be evidence of anything, but the formal handling of each stanza and the thematic parallels seem too close to be accidental. The beginnings are similar addresses to the young woman. The opening line of Yeats's poem, in its manuscript form[16] attempted to capitalize 'fellow' rather as in 'Dear Child of Nature'. Both poems involve a journey and are organized around dualities. Wordsworth's poles imply 'them' and 'us', a conventional lady and nature's 'Lady' or 'Child' or 'Woman', melancholy slavery and aged loveliness in nature. Yeats's dualities and stanzas are arranged around figures: Jack and Jill versus good company, the cherubim of Beauvarlet versus Ezekiel, the company of fools versus that of Landor and of Donne. The 'green dale' of Wordsworth's first stanza becomes the hill of Yeats's; the 'babes' of Wordsworth's second stanza, associated with the divinity of the 'Woman', become the cherubim of Yeats's.

Each poem challenges a current feminine ideal to redefine an ideal (and 'unfeminine') woman. Each poem looks back to a pre-Christian heritage of female joy, of natural passion and freedom associated, especially in Wordsworth's poem, with the worship of a pagan goddess rather than a Christian god. And each ideal image also represents an ideal of the imagination or the aesthetic world. Wordsworth uses the image of a free woman ('how divine a thing | A Woman may be made') to suggest an ideal of the liberated human imagination in its interactions with nature. And Yeats, taking for models old Ezekiel's cherubim—who have a long ancestry preceding Ezekiel—not those of Beauvarlet, chooses a female ideal of strong and independent beauty over the prettiness and docility of the current feminine one—and the popular image of the cherub. Each poem begins with an address that suggests kinship with the subject and characterizes the poet as well as her: Yeats is an artist,

Wordsworth himself a child of nature. Each opening also establishes the central contrast between the poets:

'Dear Child of Nature, . . .'
'Dear fellow-artist, . . .'

Wordsworth's 'Young Lady' is a child of Nature, Yeats's—he hopes—a child of Art. Wordsworth, turns away from the social respectability ('let them rail') to the imagery of natural shelter, 'a nest in a green dale' and to human ties, young and old, to pleasures not restricted by gender—these are terms that Michael might appreciate as well as Dorothy Wordsworth. All of Wordsworth's interiors—'a nest in a green dale', 'harbour', perhaps a 'hold', and finally even the 'grave'—are also natural exteriors. Yeats's poem seems to open with the aunt's point of view—'why so free'? It is also a sociable poem, and his shelter, appropriately enough, is not a natural one, and it comes at the end of his poem: 'And I may dine at journey's end | With Landor and with Donne'. Typically, Wordsworth turns to Nature, Yeats to the fineness of human nature.

In Yeats's first stanza Wordsworth's idyllic dale becomes the nursery rhyme slope of Jack and Jill headed for a fall which reverses Lucifer's, being caused by herding with the multitude—the 'tragedy' of an *un*aspiring mind. Both poems denounce a selected group, though neither is anti-social, and in fact, each praises friendship. Wordsworth celebrates the somewhat traditional ties of 'Wife and Friend' in the first stanza, of a mother (although like a shepherd boy) in the second, Yeats well chosen 'companions' and the society of artists—suggesting that the common path for young women may be the worst possible one. The company she keeps—or should in Yeats's poem—is the subject of the fourth line of each poem.

Wordsworth's young woman is to be Nature's child (as is Lucy): to develop in Wordsworthian nature is to develop in one's own natural directions unfettered by destructive social regulation. At the end of 'Tintern Abbey' the poet sees his past in his sister's present, in the light of her 'wild eyes'. (Yeats, in 'To A Young Beauty' offers himself as a model more overtly.) Here, her own past, like the poet's, is the literal beacon for her future—and that of others: 'Where thou, a Wife and Friend, shalt see | Thy own heart-stirring days, and be | A light to young and old'. Here, as in 'Tintern Abbey', the poet foresees for her not the premature death of some of the 'Lucy' lyrics, but a lucent future.

Yeats's poem begins with an address to a fellow artist, and also in his case, to a young woman with whom he is emotionally involved. Iseult Gonne, Maud Gonne's daughter, proposed to Yeats in 1915; and whatever the proposals and counter-proposals and refusals that followed when Yeats became a prospective lover, they remained friends; Yeats encouraged and supported her career—nor was this, of course, the only poem he wrote her. Perhaps, as he suggests in another poem to Iseult Gonne, he had little expectation of being heeded. 'But I am old and you are young, | And I speak a barbarous tongue' ('Two Years Later' *VP* 313).

Stephen Parrish's invaluable edition of the manuscripts of *The Wild Swans at Coole* presents the earliest known manuscript of 'To A Young Beauty'—already in an apparently advanced stage of composition or revision—and dated 'Jan 27 1918'. Apart from the changes in punctuation and the spelling of Beauvarlet, the major later revision is in the last stanza. (All the versions of this stanza pick up, I think, Wordsworth's suggestion of a journey and the beautifully prolonged l's of his last lines.) The last two lines—'That not a fool can call me friend: | And maybe at the journey's end | Ill take my meals with Donn'—are revised at the bottom of the page: 'That maybe I at journeys end | May clink a glass with Donne.' The final version, 'And I may dine at journey's end | With Landor and with Donne' accommodates the well-known allusion to Landor's 'I shall dine late; but the dining-room will be well-lighted, the guests few and select' from his dialogue 'Archdeacon Hare and Walter Landor' (*YP* 556; see also *CL2* 165 n. 2). Landor, who 'strove with none for none was worth my strife,' is an appropriate companion for a speaker who won't suffer fools gladly.

'To A Young Beauty' strikes a balance between egalitarianism ('Dear fellow-artist') and lecturing. And it suggests that the creation of the self and of 'the heroic discipline of the looking glass' (*E&I* 270) is shared by young woman and middle-aged man alike. Nor was this Yeats's last word on the subject. In a poem such as 'Owen Aherne and His Dancers' Yeats celebrates the young woman's wildness and freedom as well as her inclination to choose a young lover.

Yeats's address to her as 'Dear fellow-artist' begins with the description of a false freedom, and with a problem created, as in Wordsworth's poem, by 'society'. Wordsworth's solution is 'let them rail', and a fidelity to Nature and natural freedom and wildness, to that 'recklessness' whose Yeatsian version is 'sprezzatura'. Yeats's is also a recovery of self—by a return to art. Here truth to Art and Beauty is truth to oneself, involving passion and discipline.

But just as Wordsworth's young woman seems born to Nature and natural freedom, Yeats suggests that this young girl is born 'to keep in trim | With old Ezekiel's cherubim'. Wordsworth's second stanza directly challenges the social constrictions and pallors of ladyhood: 'There healthy as a shepherd boy. . . ' and the third freedom from the emotional and intellectual repressions of domestic slavery and its narrow dependencies. Old age was never lovlier:

> Thy thoughts and feelings shall not die,
> Nor leave thee, when grey hairs are nigh,
> A melancholy slave;
> But an old age, serene and bright,
> And lovely as a Lapland night,
> Shall lead thee to thy grave.

The second stanza of each poem is about the ideal—and an ideal woman. Neither is in the unconditional present. Wordsworth's is about what shall be, Yeats's what should. Both poets challenge and redefine the current feminine ideal, Yeats by contrasting the fierce beauty of old Ezekiel's cherubim with the softer, languid ideal, and Wordsworth by cutting across conventional class and gender lines, setting up the contrast between the pale, domesticated ideals of femininity, which he suggests create melancholy slaves, and the tanned, exuberant health or gusto of his natural wanderer. Nor is this preference restricted to depictions of his sister. His ballads, of course, are full of tall, wild-eyed women, and a later poem written for Mary Hutchinson presents a similar ideal, not a fawning bundle of sweet attractive graces but an image of 'free' physical movements and 'virgin-liberty':

> . . . Endurance, foresight, strength, and skill;
> A perfect Woman, nobly planned,
> To warn, to comfort, and command;
> And yet a Spirit still, and bright
> With something of angelic light. (1804, Dowden ed., 94-95)

Like the 'Young Lady' she is light associated, like her and Yeatsian cherubs, she is 'divine' and 'angelic'—but not too angelic. Even in a much later poem to Mary Hutchinson, Wordsworth begins with the angelic image only to repudiate it:

> Let other bards of angels sing,
>   Bright suns without a spot;
> But thou art no such perfect thing:
>   Rejoice that thou art not! ('To ——,' 1824)

And in 'She was a Phantom of Delight' she has the crucial association with joy and exuberance of imagination and body: 'A dancing
Shape, an Image gay, | To haunt, to startle, and way-lay' (2, 94). In
'To A Young Lady' Wordsworth's subversive young woman is
'healthy as a shepherd-boy | And treading among flowers of joy'.
And, in this context, she is the embodiment of Nature, the inheritor
of a pagan 'joy' or 'pleasure'. 'Joy' or the 'supreme principle of
pleasure' as he calls it in the famous preface, is the root of all life and
creativity as he sees it, and in this poem exuberance is beauty, a
word never overtly mentioned, in contrast to Yeats's poem. And
Wordsworth's young woman herself is the potential ideal, though
'made' not drifted into. Stanza two merges natural, aesthetic and
divine ideals.

> Thou, while thy babes around thee cling,
> Shalt show us how divine a thing
> A Woman may be made.

She is both child of nature and potential mother goddess here. In
fact, in recalling 'how divine a thing | A Woman may be made', the
poem suggests the traditional triple aspects of the Great Goddess—maiden and mother and crone. The three stanzas of the poem
seem to correspond to this triple succession. The poem opens with
the maiden, moves on to an image of maternal power and divinity
without any loss of natural wildness or suggestions of destructive
patriarchal restraint and ends with the aspects of the goddess in her
third phase: old age, death, wisdom, night, and the icy beauties of
winter (as the Scandinavian Hel she ruled the underworld). Yeats
seems to pick up and modify this in the three stages of his poem: the
first stanza touches upon childish things and nursery rhyme associations, the second on passionate beauty, the third on old age and
journey's end.

In the usual Wordsworthian context, as the stages of 'Tintern
Abbey' suggest, there is delight and animal pleasure in the closeness
to nature—pursued for its on sake, without thought of profit. Yeats
denounced Wordsworth for what he saw as his utilitarianism. But it
is typical of Wordsworth that it is the lack of a profit motive that

accumulates a treasure for the future; this is a subject that also permeates Dorothy Wordsworth's poems—the woman's memory will recreate that joy when she looks upon this landscape in which she sees herself and all her associated happiness. The poem is inevitably about the imagination which sees absent things as though they were present—a major emphasis of the famous 'Preface' as well as of the *Lyrical Ballads*. And here, unlike in the 'Immortality Ode', there seems no great distance between *seeing* and *being*, between seeing delightful days and being joyful and 'healthy as a shepherd-boy'. Unlike the great ode or even 'Tintern Abbey', this is a poem of gain with little loss, and without that insistence on compensatory consolation which Yeats could not—and would not—share with Wordsworth. The landscape *is* her youthful joy, an animal joy which does not pass away when she acquires a family. In this she can be contrasted with the poet of 'Tintern Abbey' and the Ode who has to reconcile himself with philosophy to the loss of dizzy raptures and animal pleasures.

Much early Romantic poetry is concerned not with nature but with the human mind in nature; later Romantic poets such as Yeats stress the anti-mimetic and inward movement. Wordsworth's emphasis on art is submerged, while Yeats stresses human nature in an aesthetic world. It is possible that Wordsworth is trying to reassure a specific young woman that being wife or a mother was not necessarily incompatible with companionship or freedom—or necessarily a form of melancholy domestic slavery. Yeats was ultimately to lament Iseult Gonne's submersion in domesticity and Yeats's young girl is not associated with dependent infants or with the seasonal—or currently fashionable—beauty but with the divinity of old Ezekiel's cherubim. Yeats's emphasis is on the discipline that precedes spontaneity, and the discipline of the looking-glass:

> You may, that mirror for a school,
> Be passionate, not bountiful
> As common beauties may . . .

The association of the passage that follows is not only with the cherubim of the book of Ezekiel recalling the chariot, the fire and the spirit of god, but with their ancestry.[17] Yeats insisted, in his interpretation of 'And did those feet', that Blake's chariot of fire was a chariot of the imagination. The antithesis in 'To A Young Beauty' seems to be not only between two kinds of cherubim but between two antithetical kinds or 'schools' of art, represented by two artists who were contemporaries, although they belong to different worlds— William Blake and Jacques Firmin Beauvarlet, both painters and engravers.[18]

Of Blake, Yeats had written in 1897: 'He announced the religion of art, of which no man dreamed in the world he knew' (*E&I* 111). True art is 'expressive and symbolic . . . False art is not expressive, but mimetic, not from experience but from observation, and is the mother of all evil . . .' (*E&I* 140). According to this definition, the fashionable reproductions of Beauvarlet would be doubly 'false', being imitations of imitations. 'You may, that mirror for a school, | Be passionate, not bountiful | As common beauties may'. In this Blakean and Yeatsian context, 'bountiful' and 'common' may be applied to an artist like Beauvarlet, a representative and an imitator of the currently fashionable. In contrast, the importance of passion amounts to an obsession with Blake. And certainly the contrast in this poem, light as it is, is between a beauty that is fashionable, soft and pliable and a beauty that is passionate, and above all, independent. It recalls the contrast in 'The Old Age of Queen Maeve' between strong, proud and fierce beauty (such as that of Maeve or the ancient cherubim) and 'soft beauty and indolent desire' (*VP* 181) which Yeats saw as the current feminine ideal. The smiling, roccoco *putti* of popular conception, pink, reduced in scale, and sporting vestigial wings, are, even armed with bows and arrows, frothy and unthreatening. Few readers of Ezekiel would characterize the fearful, four-winged myriad-eyed, man-, lion-, ox- and eagle-faced supporters of the throne of God as 'cute,' or with any other adjectives applicable to a later *putto*. Blake's Cherubim may have negative associations for most readers, but they, especially the Covering Cherub, play a central role in Ellis and Yeats's three volume *The Works of William Blake*.[19]

Yeats's insistence of being passionate not bountiful is exquisitely appropriate, given the mingled sexuality and passionate excess apparently embodied by ancient cherubim. In suggesting that his 'fellow-artist' was born to keep in trim with 'old Ezekiel's cherubim' he may—like Wordsworth—be reclaiming an old female heritage. Yeats's 'heaven' in 'To A Young Beauty,' populated by Landor and Donne, is no fool's paradise, and seems to stress what he quotes from Blake in 'Blake's Illustrations to Dante':

'Men are admitted into Heaven not because they have curbed and governed their passions, but because they have cultivated their understandings. The treasures of Heaven are not negations of passion, but realities of intellect, from which the passions emanate uncurbed in their eternal glory. The Fool shall not enter into Heaven, let him be ever so holy. Those who are cast out are all those who, having no passions of their own, because no intellect, have spent their lives in curbing and governing other people's by the various arts of poverty and cruelty of all kinds . . .' (*E&I* 137-8)

As in Yeats's poem, heaven or art is the wages of beauty:

> Mere sympathy for living things is not enough, because we must learn to separate their 'infected' from their eternal, their satanic from their divine part; and this can only be done by desiring always beauty, the one mask through which can be seen the unveiled eyes of eternity. We must then be artists in all things, and understand that love and old age and death are first among the arts. (*E&I* 139)

It is characteristic of Yeats to have turned a poem inspired by Wordsworth into a praise of Blakean art. Passion is a subject on which Yeats repeatedly quotes Blake, a word he repeatedly associates with Landor and with Donne. But Yeats's poem uses the critical vocabulary of Wordsworth as well—and 'passion' happens to be one of Wordsworth's favourite words. That said, a poem which rolls Jack and Jill, Landor, Donne, and 'old Ezekiel's cherubim' so cavalierly into one ball suggests a certain lightness of touch and of heart.

The last stanza is the most moving part of each poem. For Wordsworth, the woman remains the central subject of each stanza. Yeats, also seeing the woman as parallel to himself, a fellow-artist, turns directly to himself in the last stanza. Wordsworth's stanza begins with 'Thy,' Yeats's with 'I'. Both final stanzas deal with the coming of death, though in the first case it is the woman's, in Yeats's poem, the poet's own; but Wordsworth's is the dazzling natural beauty of 'an old age serene and bright, | And lovely as a Lapland night,' and Yeats's a paradise of art. Wordsworth's concerns the self in nature, Yeats's a more social end, though it may be that what Wordsworth calls simply 'thoughts and feelings' Yeats calls 'passion' and intellect'—the dominating ideals of 'To A Young Beauty.' Wordsworth's end is an illuminated beauty, Yeats's a hope that 'I *may* dine at journey's end', balancing arrogance and humility. And Yeats's attack on Wordsworth's consolatory stance is relevant here. Yeats's final stanza seems a direct challenge to Wordsworth's: 'I know what wages beauty gives, | How hard a life her servant lives, | Yet praise the winters gone.' And yet, while Wordsworth's poem leads us to the bleak word 'grave', Yeats's ends with a hope of immortality.

The poems have different ideals, but both may be defined as 'divine' ones—though Wordsworth uses the word, and Yeats deals more obliquely with cherubim. The natural features of Yeats's poems—the nursery rhyme hill and the winters gone—are metaphors as well. But what Yeats saw as 'the indolent fascination with Nature' (E&I 122), Wordsworth saw as dizzy ecstasies. Wordsworth's winterscape and his marvellous Lapland night to come become the difficult winters gone of a poet's life. Wordsworth was about thirty when he wrote the poem and his 'old age', still in the future, is visualized in terms of an ideal other. Yeats, however, was middle-aged, though old enough—and cheerful enough—to praise the winters gone. Wordsworth's ending is powerfully moving, and the last three lines are justly celebrated. His old age is a gorgeously illuminated Arctic night, the auroras of winter (in keeping with the light images of the poem) leading to the grave; Yeats's a tentative journey's end, companionable, sociable, a modern aesthetic feast—not Valhalla but dinner with Landor and with Donne.

Wordsworth, like Coleridge, was steeped in the literature of travel and exploration, and this Lapland night, like the Ancient Mariner and the albatross, may well have emerged out of Wordsworth's fascination with the literature of travel—and from some of the same sources.[20] In Wordsworth's time polar exploration was both an exciting new reality and an ancient tradition. Lapland was both an inaccessible world and a reachable reality. Mary Wollstonecraft notes, in a letter from Sweden, written in 1795 and published in 1796:

> Nothing, in fact, can equal the beauty of the northern summer's evening and night; if night it may be called that only wants the glare of day, the full light, which frequently seems so impertinent; for I could write at midnight very well without a candle. I contemplated all nature at rest; the rocks, even grown darker in their appearance, looked as if they partook of the general repose, and reclined more heavily on their foundation.[21]

This is certainly similar to the 'serene and bright' world delivered by Wordsworth's poem, an old age without the disadvantages of ageing. Lapland, even to the nineteenth century imagination, could be Heaven or Hel(l). Lapland is a place in the mind—it is more than an aggregate of the portions of the countries it covers geographically. The name itself apart from the beauty of its sound, suggests in English a land of dreams and sleep— among other things. ('Lovely as a Danish/Swedish night' would simply not be the same thing.) The last three lines of Wordsworth's poem manage to evoke a dazzlingly rich imaginative association of winter, ice and northern lights without directly mentioning any of those things. A Lapland night may be a season. This is a world where 'the idea that the sun "rises in the east and sets in the west" simply does not apply'.[22] The Arctic has sunless winters and nightless summers, nights where the sun does not rise and the moon does not set (the possibilities, for the poet of benevolent moon of *Tintern Abbey* or Book Fourteen of *The Prelude* would seem to be endless); where the twilights are long and the stars pass by and starlight and moonlight are reflected by the ice and snow. Wordsworth's poem makes no reference to winter, but hints at a world—and a Nature—very different from that of an English dale. When Wordsworth makes Lapland accessible—even, by comparison, as a state of mind—he also reflects his own hope for an ideal harmony between varieties of nature and human nature as he knows them. A Lapland night presents a carte blanche for the imagination.

Textual discovery, biography and criticism since Yeats's time have given us a more subtle and complex understanding of the griefs and losses of Wordsworth's later life. Wordsworth's poetry depends on the heritage of joy and the interactions of pleasure on which he dwells in 'To A Young Lady', so that perhaps personal unhappiness may have both stimulated and disabled his inspiration. Yeats would have agreed that the life of the poet cannot be kept from the poems, but a poet's engagement is finally with the words. And although politics and biography may have played their parts, Yeats's quarrel with Wordsworth is ultimately with words; as is his reconciliation. Yeats profited, in a literary sense, from his reading of Wordsworth, even if it was a quarrel. Yeats's Wordsworth may not be anyone else's Wordsworth. The relations of poets may be like other passionate relationships: each an 'imagined image brings | And finds a real image there' (*VP* 388)—except that there might be no 'real' images. And each poet might also have agreed that writing well is the best revenge.

III

It may be that critics have taken Yeats's own evaluation of the relationship with Wordsworth at face value, yet Yeats's attitude towards
Wordsworth, though often very negative, is mixed. As critics have
suggested, Yeats, who was constantly renewing himself, did not wish
to identify with the ageing Wordsworth: but even the sense of disappointment or betrayal that poets such as Shelley and Browning
felt was rooted in admiration. Yeats's hostility goes beyond
Romantic stereotyping. It is not that Yeats never praises
Wordsworth, it is that he consistently manages to make the praise a
preface to blame, as when he calls Wordsworth 'the one great poet
who, after brief blossom, was cut and sawn into planks of obvious
utility' (*Au* 235). There are exceptions, as in 'Art and Ideas' where
Yeats, criticizing Wordsworth turned moralist insists: 'Wordsworth
had not less genius than the others—even Hallam allowed his
genius' (*E&I* 348). But Wordsworth, who had once fought that 'dry
eighteenth-century rhetoric' (*E&I* 510) which Yeats had hated as a
young man, was himself identified with the 'Victorian rhetorical
moral fervour' (*E&I* 497) against which Yeats's generation was in
revolt.

Yeats's attitude to Wordsworth is no more predictable than his
attitude to Keats or Shelley (although he attacks Shelley for their
similarities and Wordsworth for their differences). While he
generally denigrates the later Wordsworth, he sometimes talks of
the earlier poet, fallen away from. The Wordsworth Keats sees as
the prime example of the egotistical sublime, Yeats classes with men
'like Coleridge, like Goldsmith, like Keats', who 'have little personality . . . little personal will, but fiery and brooding imagination'
(*E&I* 329). Yeats's description of John Synge suggests a parallel to
Wordsworth: 'He was a drifting and silent man full of hidden passion, and loved wild islands, because there, set out in the light of
day, he saw what lay hidden in himself' (*E&I* 330). Synge's search for
a fresh language among 'common' people was not so unlike
Wordsworth's, and his Deirdre is Nature's child, modelled after
Wordsworth's Lucy, especially in Act I of the play. Even Yeats's
praise of Synge in 'In Memory of Major Robert Gregory' is cast in
Wordsworth's vocabulary, speaking as it does of a man coming at
nightfall 'Upon a race | Passionate and simple like his heart'. It was
not until after Synge's death that Yeats discovered his friend's

admiration for Wordsworth. Yeats wrote, in 'A Memory of Synge' (1924), 'I had not known of his passion for Wordsworth, and to know it completes the image' (UP2 437).

I do not suggest that we should exaggerate the affinities between Yeats and Wordsworth. The contrasts still remain overwhelming. Wordsworth's much elaborated 'nakedness,' his aversion to certain kinds of myths, to gods and goddesses—with one exception, Nature—certainly sets him apart from Yeats, as does, above all, his attitude to nature. There remain however parallels between the poets which have not been discussed extensively. This includes a sympathy, in Yeats's case sometimes an empathy, for outcasts and so called 'common' people. Wordsworth's challenge is to the upper classes, Yeats's to the middle—both claim identity with the peasant, the outcast, the beggar, and the tramp. The leech gatherer guided by 'choice and chance', a favourite Yeatsian expression as well, is one example, and to Yeats 'the "Leach Gatherer"' was 'great lyric poetry' (Observer 17 Feb., 1918, UP2 430). Crazy Jane with her witch like ways: 'Bring me to the blasted oak | That I, midnight upon the stroke, | . . . May call down curses on his head', is not unlike a sexual version of Goody Blake, and Harry Gill has much of the self-satisfied righteousness of the Bishop. Neither representative of male authority can outwit a witch. Wordsworth provides a list of characters comparable to Yeats's fleabitten beggarmen, or Tom the lunatic or wanderers, tramps and beggars 'mad as the mist and snow'. Perhaps the Saint and the Hunchback or Hic and Ille or the wanderers of 'The Phases of the Moon' owe something to 'Resolution and Independence' and the passages about veterans and wanderers in The Prelude. It is at Yeats's own direction that we tend to associate the rhyme-maddened men of 'The Tower' (who take 'the brightness of the moon | For the prosaic light of day,' so that 'one was drowned in the great bog of Cloone') with a purely Irish glamour and background, and never with Betty Foy in her terror that Johnny may be tempted 'To hunt the moon within the brook' (I, 296).[23]

Yeats's transformations of Wordsworth are radical in spirit—often more so than Byron's of Wordsworth. Even a great and sophisticated later poem like 'The Wild Swans at Coole' may owe something to its famous predecessors, 'I Wandered Lonely As A Cloud' and 'Resolution and Independence' (Dowden ed., II, 97-98, 119-124), and the parallels are even more obvious in the manuscripts of the poem. The poet 'gaze's, beside the lake beneath the trees at a sight that delights men's eyes. (In the manuscript counting the swans seems as important to Yeats as establishing the number of feeding cattle seems to have been in William Wordsworth's poetry—or in Dorothy Wordsworth's journal.) Swans are not leeches, but in the manuscript version the speaker moves like the Leech-gatherer ('From pond to pond, he roamed, from moor to moor'):

> 'The grey lake lanes are hard under foot
> From-shore-to-shore-I-go
> In [? ?] I go
> Among-the-grey-rocks-I-go
> From-rock-to-rock-among-the-grey-lake lanes
> And-number-the swans'.[24]

In the published version the 'woodland paths are dry', the water 'brimming' and '[u]nder the October twilight' it '[m]irrors a still sky'; Wordsworth's poem spoke of 'a pool bare to the eye of heaven.' Like the leech-gatherer the speaker of Yeats's manuscript has 'grown old' (ll. 16-17) but the swans have not: 'their bodies are not old' (*VP* 322-3, ll. 18-19). Wordsworth's poem begins the morning after the rain; in Yeats's manuscript 'The autumn rains have not begun', the paths are dry, it is evening.[25] Yeats's speaker goes 'Indolently' to number the swans, recalling a younger, happier time.[26] Perhaps this reverses Wordsworth's poem, with its young speaker, its single old man (with his dwindling leeches), and its pleasant season:

> I heard the woods and distant waters roar;
> Or heard them not, as happy as a boy:
> The pleasant season did my heart employ:
> My old remembrances went from me wholly;
> And all the ways of men, so vain and melancholy.
>
> But as it sometimes chanceth, from the might
> Of joy in minds that can no further go,
> As high as we have mounted in delight
> In our dejection do we sink as low;

The ecstasy of Wordsworth's poem is reserved for Yeats's swans: 'All suddenly mount' (*VP* 322). The swans 'scatter wheeling in great broken rings,' while the leech gatherer's rings are writ in water: 'he the pond | Stirred with his staff' . . . Both are meditative poems about the drift of consciousness (the old man's voice is like a stream), and the initial stillness of Wordsworth's pool and Yeats's 'still sky' are vividly disturbed. In the end the swans and the leech gatherer are still with us but each poet's consciousness has drifted; 'in my mind's eye I seemed to see him pace | About the weary moors continually, . .'; 'Among what rushes will they build | By what lake's edge or pool | Delight men's eyes when I awake some day | To find they have flown away?' (*VP* 323).

IV

Poets construct their origins as narrative, sometimes as fiction. Yeats's prose gives a version of his attitude to Wordsworth somewhat different from that which his poems suggest, and criticism may have depended too much—or too exclusively—on the prose map of their relationship, on the teller, rather than the tale. Yet the prose itself suggests some subversive affinities. Among the things they did share was a distrust of abstract theory accompanied by a tendency to abstraction; Wordsworth, having written—with the more philosophical Coleridge—the famous Preface, claimed that he 'never cared a straw about theory,' not entirely unlike Yeats, who having presented his readers with *A Vision*, added the airy declaration comparing its ideas to cubes in abstract art (*AVB* 25) which so aggravated some of his critics. Both poets thought at length about politics and read extensively, yet both distrusted 'bookishness'. Yeats's 'The Scholars' and 'Another Song of A Fool' may be compared to Wordsworth's 'The Tables Turned' and 'Expostulation and Reply' as well as his Matthew and butterfly poems. No more than Wordsworth did Yeats entertain the 'foolish hope of reasoning' (to use Wordsworth's phrase from the 'Preface' to *Lyrical Ballads*) a reader into a liking for certain poems. And like Wordsworth in the 'Preface', Yeats, as 'The Fisherman' suggests, saw himself as a man who had to shape and create the taste and the audience by which he was to be judged. The interaction of thought and feeling, passion, memory and pleasure, are common obsessions with both of them; 'Speech intensified by passion' may be summed up as a definition of poetry either poet might have given, passion being Yeats's favourite word as well as Wordsworth's. And the emphasis on speech—and the ear—is typical of both poets, although not unusual, especially among Romantics; and Synge and Wilde, as dramatists, say similar things.[27] Yeats claimed in 1937: 'I have spent my life in clearing out of poetry every phrase written for the eye, and bringing all back to syntax that is for the ear alone' (*E&I* 529), and much of his expository prose concerns itself with the oral tradition. The stubbornly-felt differences were equally important to self-definition: the 'language to my liking' was discovered not in Wordsworthian 'words in common use' but in 'a powerful and passionate syntax' (*E&I* 521-2), and 'common' is elsewhere used to disparage 'Wordsworth, shuddering at his solitude, [who] . . . filled his art in all but a few pages with common opinion, common sentiment' (*AVB* 134). Yet, late in life, in 'Modern Poetry', his definition of poetry is astonishingly Wordsworthian, even to its glorification of 'common': 'A poem is an elaboration of the rhythms of common speech and their association with profound feeling'(*E&I* 508).

Yeats's quarrel with Wordsworth may have been enduring. It may not have been a lover's quarrel. But, in the light of the extensive parallels of form and substance, it seems difficult to believe that Yeats's 'To A Young Beauty' was not a reaction to Wordsworth's 'To A Young Lady.' A world where a walk in an English dale leads to something like a Lapland night, where an Irish poet may dine with his English ancestors, is a geography of imagination and unfulfilled desire. In such a world, or beyond its *Meta Incognita*[28] perhaps, Yeats may well be dining at journey's end '[w]ith Landor and with Donne'—and with all the Wordsworths.

NOTES

1. Then unpublished, quoted in Richard Ellmann, *Yeats—The Man and the Masks* (London: Macmillan, 1948; N.Y.: Dutton, n.d.), p. 6. I am grateful to Phillip L. Marcus for his valuable advice concerning this essay.

2. George Bornstein, *Transformations of Romanticism in Yeats, Eliot, and Stevens* (Chicago: University of Chicago Press, 1976), p. 45.

3. *L* 590. See also Patrick J. Keane's *Yeats's Interactions With Tradition* (Columbia: University of Missouri Press, 1987), p. 87.

4. See Phillip Marcus, *Yeats and the Beginning of the Irish Renaissance* (Ithaca: Cornell University Press, 1970), pp. 105 & 125.

5. George Bornstein, *Transformations of Romanticism*, pp. 46-7. Harold Bloom has been stung into remarking that Yeats's response to Wordsworth in *AVB* 134 is not even interesting caricature (*Yeats* [New York: Oxford University Press, 1970), p. 251.

6. There has been valuable critical discussion about Yeats's relation to particular poems such as 'The Solitary Reaper,' the Immortality Ode and *The Excursion*. One indispensable study of Wordsworth's influence on Yeats is 'Revolutions French and Russian: Burke, Wordsworth and the Genesis of Yeats's "The Second Coming"' in Patrick J. Keane's *Yeats's Interactions With Tradition* (1987).

7. Patrick Keane, *Yeats's Interactions with Tradition*, p. 88.

8. *Yeats*, p. 8.

9. Patrick Keane, *Yeats's Interactions with Tradition*, p. 87.

10. The version of the poem used here is the one available to Yeats in *The Poetical Works of William Wordsworth*. 7 vols. Ed. Edward Dowden. London: G. Bell & Sons, 1892 (*YL* 2292), hereafter 'Dowden ed.'. For some of the other poems, see Wordsworth's *Poems in Two Volumes, and Other Poems, 1800-1807*. Ed. Jared Curtis, *The Cornell Wordsworth* (Ithaca and London:: Cornell University Press, 1983).

11. Dowden ed., II, 'Poems of the Imagination', xxxvi, pp. 174-5.

12. See William Wordsworth, *Selected Poems and Prefaces*. ed. Jack Stillinger (Boston: Houghton Mifflin, 1965). The eight year gap between the 'occasion' and the poem is not long for Wordsworth: there were other admonishments from relatives. In 1802 the love affair with Mary Hutchinson was facing the opposition of her family, who, according to Stephen Gill, considered the poet 'a man without a profession, no better than 'a Vagabond' (p. 206). Gill cites *The Letters of Mary Wordsworth 1800-1855*, ed. Mary E. Burton (Oxford, 1958), p. xxv, n. 13. See also Stephen Gill, *William Wordsworth: A Life* (Oxford: Clarendon Press, 1989), p. 80. Ernest de Selincourt refers to 'Dear child of Nature' as her 'brother's prophecy and dearest hope for Dorothy' (*Dorothy Wordsworth: A Biography* [Oxford: Clarendon Press, 1933], p. 323). Mark L. Reed suggests that the poem was composed early in 1802 (*Wordsworth: The Chronology of the Middle Years, 1800-1815* [Cambridge, Mass: Harvard University Press, 1975], p. 141). Wordsworth's own note makes it clear that they were companion poems, composed at Grasmere. 'Composed at the same time and on the same view as 'I met Louisa in the shade': indeed they were designed to make one piece' (*The Poetical Works* ed. Ernest de Selincourt and Helen Darbishire [Oxford, 1940-9], II, p. 471).

13. The quotation is from *The Early Letters of William and Dorothy Wordsworth* I, *The Early Years 1787-1805* 2nd. ed., ed. Chester L. Shaver (Oxford: Clarendon, 1967), pp. 113-14.

14. See Hazard Adams, *The Book of Yeats's Poems* (Tallahassee: Florida State University Press, 1990), p. 112.

15. For an illuminating analysis of this poem within the context of class and gender, see Michael Baron's *Language and Relationship in Wordsworth's Writing* (London & New York: Longman, 1995), pp. 174-6.

16. See W. B. Yeats, The Wild Swans at Coole; *Manuscript Materials*, ed. Stephen Parrish (Ithaca and London: Cornell University Press, 1994), p. 87. Hereafter, Parrish, *Manuscript Materials*.

17. Chariots of fire are common to the ancient mythologies of east and west, of Hinduism as well as Judaism and Christianity.

18. Yeats's original version was 'Beaujolet,' emended to 'Beauvarlet', referring to Jacques Firmin Beauvarlet (1731-97), who was, like Blake, an engraver, and who is best known today for fine reproductions in the style of other artists on the usual Christian and classical subjects. 'His first manner was bold and free, and his plates in that style are preferred by some to the more finished and highly-wrought prints that he afterward produced, although it must be confessed that the latter are executed with great neatness and delicacy' (Bryan's *Dictionary of Painters and Engravers* [enl. ed., N.Y.: Kennikat Press, 1964, ed. George C. William], I, p. 103). He was a 'celebrated engraver' of fashionable works including, for example, 'Cupid chained by the Graces' after Boucher, and 'Cupid holding his Bow' after C. van Loo (*ibid.*). He was a maker of *reproductions*, although a good one who often departed from his originals, a member of the l'Academie Royale (E. Benezit, *Dictionnaire critique et documentaire des peintres, sculpteurs,*

Dessinateurs et Graveurs [New ed. Librairie Grund, 1966], I), p. 498.

19. According to Yeats and Ellis, the 'term is taken from *Ezekiel* xxviii. 14, and is used by Blake in a perfectly correct sense, cherubs being always powers of bodily creation. He praises or denounces this Covering Cherub according to whether he considers it as a means whereby things, too far above us to be seen as they are, can be made visible in symbol and representative form, or as a satanic hindrance keeping our eager wills away from the freedom and truth of the Divine world. It has both aspects for every man' (*WWB1* 288). Yeats here seems to associate cherubs with sexual creativity. It has been argued that the Covering Cherub is always negative in Blake. But whether forces for good or evil, Blake's Cherubim, like Ezekiel's, are not to be taken lightly.

20. Our contemporary equivalent may be a work like Barry Lopez's marvellous *Arctic Dreams: Imagination and Desire in a Northern Landscape* (1986, New York: Bantam, 1987).

21. From *Letters Written During A Short Residence In Sweden, Norway, and Denmark*, in *British Literature 1780-1830*, ed Anne K. Mellor and Richard E. Matlak (New York: Harcourt Brace, 1996), p. 421.

22. Barry Lopez, *Arctic Dreams: Imagination and Desire in a Northern Landscape*, p. 17.

23. 'The Song of Wandering Aengus' resembles Wordsworth's 'Her Eyes are Wild', a poem marked in Yeats's copy of the Dowden edition (*YL* 305).

24. Parrish, *Manuscript Materials* pp. 8-9.

25. *Ibid., pp. 2-3.*

26. *Ibid.* pp. 10-11.

27. For a valuable analysis of the relation of speech and writing in Yeats and Wordsworth see Michael Baron's 'Yeats, Wordsworth and the Communal Sense' in *YA5* 62-82.

28. There is a peninsula on the southern end of Baffin Island, named by Elizabeth I, *Meta Incognita* (Lopez 363).

Seeing 'Last Things': Reading Yeats through the Eyes of Seamus Heaney

Colleen McKenna

IN 1978, SEAMUS HEANEY in a public lecture entitled 'Yeats as an Example?' argued that Yeats, through his perseverance, invention, and artistic commitment, is 'indeed, the ideal example for a poet approaching middle age'. Twelve years later, in the Oxford lecture 'Joy or Night: Last Things in the Poetry of W. B. Yeats and Philip Larkin', Yeats is cast as the ideal example for a poet approaching later middle age: one who might be beginning to contemplate his own (if still distant) last things, or at least conducting some mid-career literary stock-taking.[1] From the publication in 1980 of *Preoccupations* (which takes its title and epigraph from Yeats's *Explorations*) to the recent Nobel Prize acceptance speech *Crediting Poetry* (1995), Yeats might be thought to have ghosted Heaney's prose: he is frequently invoked and often implictly addressed, hovering in the writing like an admixture of Bloom's precursor poet and Bakhtin's superaddressee. However, although a persistent presence—especially in Heaney's essays, Yeats is also an unfixed one: Heaney, a seemingly committed literary revisionist, has, over the last two and a half decades, *constructed* different versions of Yeats—which, unsurprisingly, largely echo his own literary predilections.[2] The most recognizable Yeatsian departure is Heaney's embrace of a

221

secular transcendence as expounded in his 1983 lecture 'Among Schoolchildren' and subscribed to increasingly in the later poetry, especialy that of *Seeing Things* and *The Spirit Level*.[3] Nevertheless, a trawl through Heaney's *verse* in search of the ghost of Yeats, is, with a few exceptions, more likely to yield faint imprints—lingering much like those made by Heaney senior on the beach at Sandymount Strand—rather than overt allusions or imitations.[4] But, with a dialogic approach in which the poetry is necessarily read against the prose and vice versa, a fuller picture of Yeatsian influence emerges.

Furthermore, Heaney is a reader who takes a highly intertextual approach to literature, constructing in prose and verse what Wayne K. Chapman has termed the 'adaptive complex', a model of literary influence which depends upon the formation of clusters of two or more writers, often from different poetic traditions, who are arranged into mediatorial relationships. In particular, Heaney uses the dyad, a specialised binary example of the adaptive complex, and in Heaney's writing, Yeats is frequently paired in such a structure with other writers, as he is in 'Joy or Night' with Philip Larkin.[5] In order to praise Yeats's visionary verse in this lecture, Heaney constructs an opposition between Yeats and Larkin, and in so doing, he is forced to revise his general appraisal of the poets (notably Larkin) and his previous readings of the particular poems.

Finally, 'Joy or Night' consolidates much of Heaney's recent work on Yeats and serves as an implicit gloss for some of his own later poems, particularly those from the 'Squarings' section of *Seeing Things*. Given the self-reflexiveness of his *oeuvre*, it is both appropriate and illuminating to read several of these poems by the light of this lecture.

The (Changing) Case Against Philip Larkin

Like Yeats, Philip Larkin has been the object of Heaney's critical gaze on numerous occasions, and if he never attains Yeats's stature in Heaney's eyes, his measured voice, ear for vernacular, reigned-in world view, and curious combination of resignation and non-specific vision hold much appeal for Heaney and mark him out as an original force in twentieth century poetry. Heaney's *version* of Larkin, however, is highly unstable, and in essays leading up to and including 'Joy or Night' Larkin is transformed from tacit symbolist to bleak materialist. As with Yeats and others, Heaney has manipulated and revised 'Larkin' to suit his own aesthetic programme to such an extent that the poetic analyses reveal as much about Heaney as they do his subject.[6] In the earlier 'The Main of Light', (first published in 1982 in Anthony Thwaite's *Larkin at Sixty*, and later collected in *The Government of The Tongue*, 1988), Heaney paints Larkin as a reluctant but capable symbolist with an eye for vision and *likens* (rather than opposes) him to Yeats:[7]

> That sweetness flows into the poetry most reliably as a stream of light. In fact, *there is something Yeatsian* in the way that Larkin, in *High Windows*, places his sun poem immediately opposite and in answer to his moon poem . . . In 'Sad Steps', the wary intelligence is tempted by a moment of lunar glamour. The renaissance moon of Sir Philip Sidney's sonnet sails close, and the invitation to yield to the 'enormous yes' that love should evoke is potent, even for a man who has just taken a piss . . . . Light, so powerfully associated with joyous affirmation . . . is refracted even more unexpectedly at the end of 'High Windows' when one kind of brightness, the brightness of belief in liberation and amelioration, falls from the air which immediately fills with a different, infinitely neutral splendour . . . All these moments spring from the deepest strata of Larkin's poetic self, and *they are connected with another kind of mood that pervades his work and which could be called Elysian . . . these are visions of 'the spiritual, Platonic old England', the light in them honeyed by attachment to a dream world that will not be denied because it is at the foundation of the poet's sensibility.*[8]

Heaney could hardly be more exuberant and celebratory of the vision in Larkin's work in this fulsome appraisal: he seems to think Larkin as 'riddled with light' as either Yeats or Dante—the two supreme luminaries in Heaney's literary pantheon. He closes the piece by suggesting that 'Larkin also had it in him to write his own version of the *Paradiso*' (*GOT* 22). Or did he? In the more recent lecture 'Joy or Night', Heaney's interpretation of Larkin is formed on the basis of a retrospective reading of the *oeuvre*. Whereas, in the 1982 essay, Heaney had read Larkin by the bright but ephemeral rays of vision in poems like 'Solar', 'Sad Steps', 'Whitsun Weddings', in the 1990 lecture, he overlays the bleakness of the late 'Aubade' onto the Larkin corpus, and argues that his poetry is grounded in a comfortless, Hardy-esque world:

> . . . it is surely a God-curst sun that creates the glassy brilliance at the end of his poem 'High Windows'. Certainly it is the opposite of

whatever illuminates the scene where Yeats's protagonist 'cried and trembled and rocked to and fro.' . . . It [Yeats's vision] is, on the contrary, an image of superabundant life, whereas Larkin's sunstruck distances give access to an infinity as void and neuter as those 'blinding windscreens' which flash randomly and pointlessly in 'The Whitsun Weddings' (*JN* 152).

. . . he insists on taking full account of the negative evidence and this finally demoralizes the affirmative impulse (*JN* 153).

. . . his vision got arrested into a fixed stare at the inexorability of his own physical extinction. Human wisdom, therefore seemed to him a matter of operating within the mortal limits, and of quelling any false hope of transcending or outfacing the inevitable (*JN* 147).

Throughout, one is struck by the heavily oppositional language of 'Joy or Night', in which the contrast is drawn too crudely, but more surprising is the cheerless gloss offered here by Heaney in light of his previous assessments of Larkin.

With this reading, the earlier evaluation has been largely reversed: one would hardly imagine Heaney still to be naming Larkin the potential author of a latter-day *Paradiso*, as he had above. The comparison of these Larkin critiques also demonstrates the way in which readings are relativized: in the second essay, Heaney explicitly creates a binary opposition in which this recent version of Larkin, which displaces the 'Elysian' Larkin of 'The Main of Light', has to play 'night' to Yeats's 'light'. The contrast is starker still, because Heaney revises Yeats in the opposite direction: he sets up 'Joy or Night' as though Yeats's 'The Man and the Echo' is, to recall Julia Kristeva paraphrasing Bakhtin, an absorption of and a reply to another text, in this case Larkin's 'Aubade'.[9] Earlier Heaney assessments of 'The Man and the Echo' in *The Place of Writing* (1989) lingered on the doubt and palpable suffering of the piece. In 'W. B. Yeats and Thoor Ballylee', he writes of the 'tower dweller' who 'is helpless against the unaccommodated cry of suffering nature. The man's composure is certainly assailed by the mocking echo of his own doubting mind, but it is finally most vulnerable to the yelp of pain in a hurt creature . . .'.[10] In the essay, 'Variations on a Theme from Ellmann', collected in the same volume, Heaney writes, 'These are the last-ditch words of the man, instructed in hopelessness by the echo's portentous 'Lie down and die,''Into the night.'(*POW* 57)

Both these readings of 'The Man and the Echo' make a point of registering the achievement of the artistic event itself, but the piece is still largely interpreted as an exclamation of despair. However, in the later 'Joy or Night', which is organised around the contrary impulses of mortal limits and transcendence, Heaney, while still alert to the doubting mind, changes the *emphasis* of his appraisal and hails the poem as a ratification of the human spirit:

> Where Larkin's 'Aubade' ended in entrapment, 'The Man and the Echo' has preserved a freedom, and manages to pronounce a final *Yes*. And the *Yes* is valuable because we can say of it what Karl Barth said of the enormous *Yes* at the centre of Mozart's music, that it has weight and significance because it overpowers and contains a *No*. Yeats's poetry, in other words, gives credence to the idea that courage is *some* good; it shows how the wilful and unabashed activity of poetry itself is a manifestation of 'joy' and a redressal . . .'
> (*JN* 163)

This sanguine reading of the poem (particularly the confidence with which Heaney proclaims the final lines a resounding 'yes') under-scores the fact that 'Aubade' represents the definitive 'no' and caps Heaney's passionate promotion of the transformative powers of the Yeats vision, even in his bleakest hour. He also implicitly designates Yeats the quintessential poet-seer: 'The poet who would be most the poet has to attempt an act of writing that outstrips the conditions even as it observes them' (*JN* 159).

Heaney leaves us in no doubt that for him Yeats is 'the poet who would be most the poet', and yet, is not this praise given with touch of self-recognition? Heaney's project in *Seeing Things* (the very title of which suggests well-honed powers of observation and perhaps transformation) is nothing if not an outstripping of observed condi-tions. One Bloomian explanation would be that in this lecture (and elsewhere), Heaney insists upon re/misreading Yeats in a bid to remake him in the mould of his own (Heaney's) most recent image. Much like the speaker in 'The Skylight'[11] who removes the roof from his snug but claustrophobic bedroom to reveal 'extravagant sky', Heaney has undergone a well-documented transition from embracing the ground 'Antaeus-like' in his poetry to revelling in potent spaces, strange illuminations and things unearthed and ephemeral—qualities he associates with Yeats's work. For example, in 'Joy or Night' he commends 'The Cold Heaven' for the 'marvel-

lous sense of both physical visitation and intellectual apprehension
in the phrase 'riddled with light'' (*JN* 149), a phrase very like 'shifting brilliancies' with which his own poem 'i' (also the plight of the
new ghost in the winter cold) opens. In fact, this piece, which,
according to its author, 'imagines the soul being called away on its
journey after death to undergo a particular judgement'[12] is similar in
theme and vision to 'The Cold Heaven' and can also be read as an
absorption of and reply to the final question of Yeats's quickening
ghost.[13] 'i' concludes,

> And after the commanded journey, what? . . .
> Just old truth dawning: there is no next-time-round.
> Unroofed scope. Knowledge-freshening wind. (*ST* 55)

While the poem rejects an orthodox representation of rebirth and
afterlife, it is alert to something vague and potential: 'unroofed
scope'. And 'unroofed scope' is a fitting epithet for the 48-poem
sequence ('Squarings') to which 'i' is the entrance. Particular preoccupations here are the crediting of the spirit, the place of the
imagination, and a fascination with oppositional impulses whose
struggle is perpetually renewed, like the reconciling of the
'diaphanous' with the 'massive' in 'x'; indeed, all poems in the
sequence contribute in some way to the overarching contest: the
celebration of the material world vs. the transcendence of it. Yeats's
presence is unmistakable.[14]

Determining whether Heaney is recasting Yeats in his own image
through rereadings such as the one offered above in 'Joy or Night'
or whether he has shaped his own poetic progress with a Yeatsian
aesthetic in mind is rather less important than the realisation that he
has demonstrably revised his approach to Yeats and that this revision coincides with his own poetic agenda. After all, when asked in
an interview in 1979 'How do you face up to Yeats?' Heaney
replied, 'I don't face up to him; I turn my back and run!'.[15] After following a literary path approximating Harold Bloom's agonistic
learning curve—which included the swerve away from and the later
cautious embrace of Yeats—Heaney's recent prose discourse with
his precursor (in *The Field Day Anthology*, 1991, *The Place of Writing*,
1989, *The Redress of Poetry*, 1995, and *Crediting Poetry* 1995) is conducted with almost unreserved approval and greater self-awareness;
and, as I will show below, his dialogue with Yeats is increasingly
played out in verse.

In fact, we can see in the relationship between 'Joy or Night' and Heaney's poetry, similarities to the Yeatsian correlation between prose and poetry. 'Joy or Night' casts light on Heaney's reading of Larkin and Yeats, the most prominent 20th century writers who figure in *Seeing Things*; their individual significance and their dialectical relationship made clearer by the lecture, which in true Yeats fashion, buttresses and decodes the poetic volume. Larkin, 'a nine-to-five man who had seen poetry' (and whose shade opens part one of the collection with 'The Journey Back') is indicative of the more rational, anchoring poetry we encounter in the first half. But, as the turn in the closing sonnet of section one, 'Fosterling', predicts: 'So long for air to brighten, | Time to be dazzled . . .', the Yeatsian spirit obtains in part two.

The Poem and the Echo

Heaney constructs his own model of dialogic discourse when he describes in *Crediting Poetry*, (his unofficial defence of poetry) his alertness to other voices—actual and imagined—and the poetic necessity of straining towards them. He opens the lecture with a recollection of the child-poet as a receiver and interpreter of sounds (some intelligible, some garbled) and closes with an image of the adult labouring to glimpse the speech-acts themselves and acknowledging the revisionist impulses which perpetuate this process:

> But the thing uttered by the speaker I strain towards is still not quite the story of what is going on; it is more reflexive than that, because as a poet I am in fact straining towards a strain . . . . As if the ripple at its widest desired to be verified by a reformation of itself, to be drawn in and drawn out through its point of origin.[16]

So the poet-receiver, ear and pen poised, labours to go beyond the poem itself and detect the strain informing the original utterance which can then be reformed in a new context. In the following section, I want to consider poem 'x' of 'Squarings' (*ST* 64), in which traces of 'The Man and the Echo' are seemingly rearticulated, as a product of such an act of assimilation.

'The Man and the Echo' is one of the most frequently discussed poems in Heaney's recent criticism and in 'x' a faint but recognizable reverberation is audible in terms of place, imagery, and the doubting imagination. Like Yeats's Man, ('In a cleft that's christened Alt | Under broken stone I halt | At the bottom of a pit' [*VP* 632]), Heaney's subject is poised against a cliff-face and grapples with the antithetical qualities of solidity and sheerness; the massive and the diaphanous. An attempted reconciling of the body and the soul seems only a trope away. Indeed, although 'x' (unlike 'The Man and the Echo') is a highly impressionistic piece and not explicitly a meditation on the journey of the soul, one can, given the poem's context and explanatory comments by Heaney, interpret the 'cargoed brightness' as an oblique reference to the spirit. 'Lightenings', the 12-poem sequence in which 'x' appears was composed following the deaths of Heaney's parents, and the opening piece ('i') specifically imagines the journey of the soul after death.[17] The concluding poem of 'Lightenings' ('xii') repeats and consolidates the brightness/spirit metaphor:

> And lightening? One meaning . . .
> A phenomenal instant when the spirit flares
> With pure exhilaration before death— (*ST* 66)

The anxiety, personal culpability, and fear of the unknowable—all underpinned by the insidious echo—are undoubtedly stronger in 'The Man and the Echo', but a general sense of uncertainty, possibly artistic self-doubt, is still communicated in 'x' when the subject is compelled to ask:

> '. . . could you reconcile
> What was diaphanous there with what was massive?
>
> Were you equal to or were you opposite
> To build-ups so promiscuous and weightless?' (*ST* 64)

Although these questions are met with no formal echo in the poem, the repetition of phrases and words ('on the quarry face', 'on the quarry floor', face, 'ultimate', 'up' and 'quarry') in such a short poem effect the sense of an echo. Yeats's poem is a metaphorical facing of the music; Heaney, lest the piece has been too subtle, urges in the final line: 'Shield your eyes, look up and face the music. (l. 12)' However, in the latter the music is decidedly not the cry of a stricken rabbit and the poem resides, even if only provisionally, with the 'cargoed brilliance' and the 'diaphanous'.

However, while alert to Yeatsian sounds and themes, Heaney is neither *repeating* nor *copying* Yeats's poem.[18] 'x' is clearly his own work: he stamps it (in an almost exaggerated manner) with his own idiom: 'rock-hob', 'ultimate fathomableness', 'stony up-againstness'; his own halted metre, here lurching under the weight of such bulky diction; his own form (the 12-line poem); and a strong sense of context (placed in the midst of a 48-piece series and paired with another piece).[19] He is adapting Yeats while simultaneously staking out his own literary claim; he converses with his precursor while asserting his own poetic identity in a manner akin to Chapman's description of Yeats's process of composition.[20]

Furthermore, 'x' (which ultimately looks into the light rather than the night) at times resembles more closely the account Heaney gives of 'The Man and the Echo' than 'The Man and the Echo' itself. The following commentary from 'Joy or Night' could easily accompany Heaney's 'x', a meditation at the 'quarry face' of mystery, where momentarily human limitation and the creative impulse are held in a single thought:

'The Man and the Echo' [is] a poem where human consciousness is up against the cliff-face of mystery, confronted with the limitations of human existence itself. Here the consciousness of the poet is in full possession of both its creative impulse and its limiting knowledge. . . Yet in the poem the spirit's impulse still remains creative and obeys the human compulsion to do that 'great work' of spiritual intellect. (*JN* 160)

Indeed, it is Heaney's poem—as the speaker looks up and faces the brilliance—rather than Yeats's, that more closely concludes with the final *Yes* that Heaney so desires to see in 'The Man and Echo'. The two pieces are at the very least part of the same ripple.

'x' is both a poem spoken unmistakably in the Heaney voice and an interpretive act—grown out of an intersection with Yeats's 'The Man and the Echo'—and in this and other responses to the poem, Heaney acts as both reader and writer of Yeats, the boundaries between analysis and poetic creation being blurred, perhaps approaching Bloom's notion of verse-criticism.[21] Indeed, the literary terrain comprising modern Irish poetry is overrun with staked claims, so much so that poems are often necessarily responding to and determined by other pieces. Heaney, here writing in an essay on modern Irish poetry and drama, is clearly attuned to the artistic resonance resulting from this nexus of intertextual relationships:

> This perception—that any writing is to some extent an unwriting not only of previous writings but even of itself—is one that has been greatly elaborated into systems of reading. . . Indeed my theme from Ellmann concerns this doubleness of the fully empowered imagination, its compulsion to unwind the winding path, to encompass within its lift-off an acknowledgement of the gravity that pulls it down.[22]

Where does Spirit Live?

A piece which more self-consciously engages in poetic unwinding, or even deconstruction, is poem 'xxii' of *Seeing Things*, another literary conversation in the ongoing Yeats-Heaney dialogue and one which is also illuminated by the lecture 'Joy or Night'. Heaney's convicting charge against Larkin in this lecture is that he lacks faith in the immaterial world and thus denies 'spirit'. Heaney then takes his inquiry into spiritualism further, differentiating between the beliefs manifest in the verse of Yeats (here represented by 'The Cold Heaven') and Hopkins: Hopkins's construction of the spirit stands upon a theological, God-fearing, foundation whereas Yeats's notion of spirit is not bounded by orthodox religion:

> . . . the difference is that, in Hopkins, the terror has its given co-ordinates; the Deity, doubted though He may be, does provide a certain theological longitude and latitude for what is unknown and unknowable. In 'The Wreck of the Deutschland' and 'The Terrible Sonnets', *Hopkins's intensity is the intensity of dialogue, of blame and beseeching: a 'thou' is being addressed, a comforter is being called upon* . . . In Yeats, on the other hand, this personal God has disappeared and *yet Yeats's poem still conveys a strong impression of direct encounter*. The spirit still suffers from a sense of answerability, of responsibility, to a something out there. . . (*JN* 148-9, emphasis added).

Edna Longley writes that 'most Irish writers, Protestant and Catholics, even today are only a generation away from religious orthodoxy. "Morally naked and spiritually hungry", they are likely to be closer . . . to Thomas Hardy than to Philip Larkin'.[23] In some ways, it would be a supreme irony if Heaney were to satisfy a spiritual craving through Yeats, yet it would appear that Yeats, rather than Hardy (and certainly in preference to Larkin), has written into being a version of the transcendence of the material world close to that which Heaney seeks.[24] Furthermore, in the above quotation, Heaney places emphasis upon the notion of 'direct encounter' in both poets' relationships with a spiritual Other and he writes of these encounters using a vocabulary which suggests dialogic interaction: 'dialogue', 'addressed', 'called upon', 'answerability'.[25] In 'Joy or Night', Heaney considers Yeats's spiritual project (primarily *A Vision* and related writings) and his communications with 'ghostly instructors'; he then juxtaposes this with a conversation of another kind: Dorothy Wellesley's questioning of Yeats shortly before his death about the soul's existence in the afterlife. The perplexing and perplexed poem 'xxii' takes this topic as its theme. Here, in the midst of the series 'Squarings', Heaney's own poetic treatise on things spirtual, the ghost of W.B. and his construction of the spirit are 'assailed for reassurance'. Unlike an earlier address to a then unnamed Yeats, 'The Master' (*Station Island*), Heaney no longer needs the Sweeney mask or the cloak of circumspection to engage in dialogue with his precursor, here appealed to directly and with less deference.

'xxii' first appeared under the title 'Small Fantasia for W. B.'—and the piece is a fantasia in that it is a potpourri of Yeatsian images, poetic structures, and ideas woven into a loosely-bound composition.[26] Yeats is confronted both as past poet and as oracle, expected to respond to questions which are at once spiritual and aesthetic, philosophical and critical. Yet, the series of set questions contains some which are necessarily unanswerable and some whose answer is limited by anticipatory remarks; and in the course of the interrogation Heaney seems to be rhetorically demonstrating the lack of fixity and the plurality of the Yeats vision.

In both the article and the poem, Heaney calls attention to the complexity and contradiction of Yeats's representation of the ageing self. He writes in 'Joy or Night' of his alertness to both 'bodily decrepitude' and a supernatural liberation of the spirit and applauds his refusal 'to foreclose' on either possibility. Similarly, the poem combines the defiant, physical self with the 'melody and stamina of the resurgent spirit'[27] and the tension generated therein holds the piece together: the seabird is poised against the otherworldly soul in stanza one (with the 'made things, things unmade' and forming a neat internal counterpoise);[28] the physically and socially imposing marble bust is opposed to the windy light in the third stanza; and while not necessarily antithetical, the mystical 'dawn cold' (often the haunt of the newly dead in Yeats) is balanced in sound and position against the more tangible 'jackdaw's nest' in the second stanza.

When Heaney analyses in 'Joy or Night' Yeats's laughter in response to Wellesley's comment that he was 'hurrying us back to the arms of the Catholic Church', he suggests that this seemingly evasive gesture:

> established a *conversational space* where the question [about the soul's relationship to God] could move again. It was the social expression of that frame of mind which allowed the venturesomeness of a supernatural faith to co-exist with a rigorously sceptical attitude.[29]

Rather than a conversational space, I suggest that in 'xxii' Heaney is establishing a literary space in which his own well-documented respect for and celebration of the Yeatsian project can co-exist with a measure of cautionary scepticism. Furthermore, the intentional vagueness and the loose weave of this readerly piece, mean that Heaney can suggest a range of versions of late Yeats without offering a definitive reading. We see the imperious marble bust in line 7, weighted with Ascendancy hauteur, augmented by the verb 'commanding' and reinforced with the later 'assailed' (though this word is mitigated by 'reassurance' in the same line.)[30] By contrast, the 'dungy sticks' (l. 5) call to mind a coarser, earthier image of the Yeats shade; the cold, crying 'soul' (l. 3-4) implies a bewildered, vulnerable being. Yeats as poet and visionary is suggested by the references to 'perfected form' and the inhabited 'windy light' (l. 8-9) which signal one of the poem's more significant intertexts 'A Tower on the Apennines' (*E&I*) in which a great, aged poet, seemingly Yeats's self-projection, appears in a moment of reverie.[31] In the passage, the windy light illuminates a numinous site of the imagination and by finishing the third stanza with this allusion, Heaney concludes the direct questioning with a nod to the spiritual intellect. Although the final stanza, with its assailing of the 'held line'[32] can be read as an interrogation of what he has referred to elsewhere as Yeats's 'self-absolutism', this activity recalls Yeats's own poetic self-questioning, his own wariness of the cornucopia being 'undermined by the image of life as an empty shell', and by its very existence is ultimately a compliment to the Yeats project.[33]

Early in 'Joy or Night', Heaney asks whether Larkin's rejection of Yeats's romanticism has been 'too long and too readily approved of' (*JN* 147). Certainly for Heaney it has, and with some revision and extension of his previous appraisals, he pits the ageing Yeats against late Larkin and attempts to redress the critical balance. However, he arguably effects a more enduring defence of the Yeats vision by responding directly to the poet in verse and incorporating into his own work images, ideas, and places which are part of the same ripple, and which thereby 'circulate' with a 'new perspective' ('vii').

NOTES

1. 'Joy or Night: Last Things in the Poetry of W. B. Yeats and Philip Larkin' (dated 30 April 1990—roughly the same time that the poems for *Seeing Things* were being written and revised) was delivered at Oxford, and given again as the W. D. Thomas Memorial Lecture at the University College of Swansea in January 1993: this version has been published in pamphlet form by the College under the same title. A further revised version is included in *The Redress of Poetry: Oxford Lectures*, Seamus Heaney, (London: Faber and Faber, 1995), pp. 146-163). Subsequent references to the London edition will be included in the text and referred to as *JN*.

2. I use the term here as defined by Harold Bloom: 'As the origins of the word indicate, it is a re-aiming or a looking-over-again, leading to a re-esteeming or a re-estimating. We can venture the formula: the revisionist strives to *see* again, so as to *esteem* and *estimate* differently, so as then to aim 'correctively.' Harold Bloom, *A Map of Misreading* (New York: Oxford University Press, 1980) p. 4.

3. The move towards a Yeatsian aesthetic is adumbrated in a 1966 interview: 'Most of the poems in *Death of a Naturalist* have a very sturdy basis of anecdote or story or incident—which I don't apologize for because that was the way it came then, but I would like to get more suggestiveness, more of what Yeats might have called symbolism into the verse . . . . But I'll never like to kick away the real, factual, physical world from me. I think I depend on it more than a lot of other poets; I mean I don't think I could be what I think as John Crowe Ransom calls a platonic poet, a poet who works in the realm of ideas; I'm more akin to what he would call a physical poet—someone who depends upon the natural world for his wisdom' ('Seamus Heaney Talks to Peter Orr' 7 September 1966, British Council Tape 1185 [National Sound Archive, 1288R]).

4. See 'The Strand' in *The Spirit Level*, Seamus Heaney, (London: Faber and Faber, 1996), p. 62.

5. Chapman writes, 'The measure of his [Yeats's] indebtedness depends on his use of individual authors—a fact warranting an extension of the theory of the adaptive complex to reflect his generally binary habit of thinking about and remembering the work of other poets.' *Yeats and English Renaissance Literature*, (London: Macmillan, 1991) pp. 66-7. The dyadic construction in 'Joy or Night'

is a critical variation on the dyad as Chapman defines it. In his essay, Heaney is not strictly speaking about the joint influence of Larkin and Yeats upon his *own* writing (Chapman's concern), yet such a concern can be read as a subtext.

6. Recently, Edna Longley has suggested that Heaney retrospectively imposes an image on Patrick Kavanagh, which actually reflects Heaney's own poetic interests: 'Yet this may be . . . too determined by Heaney's own artistic agenda. Now he exaggerates Kavanagh's airiness, as formerly his weightiness'. See her *The Living Stream: Literature and Revisionism in Ireland*, (Newcastle upon Tyne: Bloodaxe, 1994) p. 212.

7. In fact, since the publication of this piece, Heaney has been regarded as one of the foremost proponents of a symbolist reading of Larkin's verse. Stephen Regan finds that the 'most impressive appraisal of Larkin's symbolist potential is undoubtedly Seamus Heaney's fine essay, "The Main of Light". . .'. See Stephen Regan, *The Critics Debate: Philip Larkin* (London: Macmillan, 1992), p. 52.

8. *The Government of the Tongue: The 1986 T. S. Eliot Memorial Lectures and Other Critical Writings* (London and Boston: Faber and Faber, 1988), pp. 16-17, 21 (emphasis added). Subsequent references will be included in the text and referred to as *GOT*.

9. Julia Kristeva, 'Word, Dialogue and Novel' in *The Kristeva Reader*, ed. Toril Moi (Oxford: Basil Blackwell, 1986) p. 39.

10. Seamus Heaney, *The Place of Writing* (Atlanta: Scholars Press, 1989) p. 33. Subsequent references will be made in the text and referred to as *POW*. Heaney continues, 'Behind the large firm gestures of Yeats's last poems, where the humanist effort is racked upon a wheel that is a paradigm of hollowness, we can already make out the shuffling, unappeasable decrepitude of Beckett's heroes going on refusing to go on' (*POW* 34).

11. Seamus Heaney, *Seeing Things* (London: Faber and Faber, 1991) p. 37. All subsequent quotations will be included in the text and referred to as *ST*.

12. Seamus Heaney, *Stepping Stones* (London: Penguin Audiobooks, 1995). See n. 17 for a full version of the quotation.

13. . . . Ah! When the ghost begins to quicken,
Confusion of the death-bed over, is it sent
Out naked on the roads, as the books say, and stricken
By the injustice of the skies for punishment? (*VP* 316).

14. Heaney has written elsewhere that Yeats's imagination could not 'repose for too long in the consolations of the material world' (*POW* 26), and for Heaney, this dialectical movement between the physical and the metaphysical is one of the supreme Yeatsian poetic achievements.

15. Robert Druce, 'A Raindrop on a Thorn: An Interview with Seamus Heaney' *Dutch Quarterly Review* (9: 1979) 25-6. Note the similarity to Yeats's comment to Lady Gregory that he was able to write 'with a new confidence[,] having gotten Milton off my back' (3 Jan., 1913, quoted in A. Norman Jeffares, *Yeats Man & Poet* (London: Routledge and Kegan Paul, 1949, 1962) p. 167.

16. Seamus Heaney, *Crediting Poetry* (County Meath: The Gallery Press, 1996) p. 28. Heaney has also expressed this concept in verse:
. . . a ripple that would travel eighty years
Outward from there, to be the same ripple
Inside him at its last circumference. ('Squarings', vi, *ST* 60)

17. 'x' is part of a series of 12 poems called 'Lightenings' and Heaney has said of these that '[t]hey could be said to form a sort of constellation around the image of an unroofed space and I am sure that that image had to do with the fact that the poems were written soon after both my parents had died. *The first one, for example, imagines the soul being called away on its journey after death to undergo a particular judgement and the place where this otherworldly encounter happens is an unroofed wallstead and the soul appears at the door in the figure of a shivering beggar*. . . (emphasis added) Heaney, *Stepping Stones*.

18. Bloom, Kristeva and other theorists of intertextuality might use the term 'imitation' to describe the relationship between these two poems, but Chapman argues effectively for the use of 'adaptation' in such a case: 'For reasons now obvious, the word *adaptation* might be preferred to *imitation* whenever the concept is employed as understood in England in the sixteenth and early seventeenth centuries. Yeats was of two minds about *imitation*, as are most modern readers. As we do, he sometimes associated it with copying. However, he just as often argued for its use, in the older, radical sense of what the word meant, which always involved the transformation and synthesis of one's materials'. See Wayne K. Chapman, *Yeats and English Renaissance Literature*, p. 10.

19. The companion poem ('xi') posssibly alludes to Yeats's well-known 'bundle of accident and incoherence that . . . has been re-born as an idea, something intended, complete' (*E&I* 509):

   To turn light outside in and curb the space
   Where accident got tricked to accuracy' (*ST* 65).

20. Wayne K. Chapman writes, 'The generally complicated nature of the adaptive complex—by which writers distort and *modify the stuff of originals into new originals*—is confirmed by a particularly characteristic adaptive habit: the erstwhile student and editor of Spenser must first 'own' what he will permit himself to expropriate . . . Yeats's characteristic approach to his craft involved an intuitive dependence on his own faculties while those channels were open to the advice of his predecessors' (emphasis added). See *Yeats and English Renaissance Literature* p. 218.

21. Poem 'x', when read alongside 'The Man and Echo' would seem to satisfy Bloom's definition of verse-criticism: 'These relationships depend upon a critical act, a misreading or misprision, that one poet performs upon another, and that does not differ in kind from the necesary critical acts performed by every strong reader upon every text he encounters. The influence-relation governs reading as it governs writing, and reading is therefore a miswriting just as writing is a misreading. As literary history lengthens, all poetry necessarily becomes verse-criticism, just as all criticism becomes prose-poetry'. (Harold Bloom, *A Map of Misreading*, p. 3.)

22. *POW* 56. Edna Longley has written widely on intertextuality in Irish writing. Here she is in *The Living Stream*: '. . . I found that I was tracing a textual web, and that the term 'intertextuality', applied to Northern Irish poetry in a special living sense: not as a theoretical dead letter, but as a creative dynamic working upon mechanisms of tradition and cultural definitions alike' (p. 51).

23. Edna Longley, 'Louis MacNeice: "The Walls are Flowing"' in *Across a Roaring Hill: The Protestant Imagination in Modern Ireland* eds. Gerald Dawe and Edna Longley (Belfast; The Blackstaff Press, 1985), p. 119.

24.   Heaney emphasizes this aspect of Yeats in his essay on the poet in *The Field Day Anthology*: 'Nobody doubts his fundamental importance as the creator of a cultural idea in and for Ireland, but that is only the beginning of his greatness. His extreme exploration of the possibilities of reconciling the human impulse to transcendence and subversion with the antithetical project of continuity and consolidation is universally and inexhaustibly relevant.' Seamus Heaney, 'William Butler Yeats' in *The Field Day Anthology of Irish Writing* ed. Seamus Deane, (Derry: Field Day Publications, 1991) II, p. 789. In an earlier essay, Heaney wrote approvingly of Yeats's 'Among Schoolchildren': 'Its final stanza is a guarantee of our human capacity to outstrip the routine world. . . And what it suggests is the necessity of an idea of transcendence, an impatience with the limitations of systems, a yearning to be completely fulfilled at all levels of our being...' (Heaney, *Among Schoolchildren* published by the John Malone Memorial Committee, Belfast, 1983, pp. 15-16.)

25.   Throughout *Seeing Things*, Heaney incorporates other poetic voices and constructs imagined dialogues between poets and even has poets quoting other poets. By putting words spoken by other poets in italics, he draws attention to the *activity* and achievement of quoting the words of another, while simultaneously emphasizing the double-voiced discourse of these pieces. The opening poem, in which Heaney has Larkin's shade quote from the opening of the *Inferno* puts the whole concept of dialogue at the forefront of the volume and identifies the process as one of its chief preoccupations.

26.   'Small Fantasia for W. B.' appeared in the *TLS*, 27 January, 1989 and the final stanza read,
>   What was learned from the midwife and the hangman?
>   What's the use of a held note or held line
>   That cannot be assailed for reassurance?

The allusion is to 'Swedenborg, Mediums, and the Desolate Places': 'I was comparing one form of belief with another, and, like Paracelsus who claimed to have his knowledge from mid-wife and hangman, I was discovering a philosophy' (*LE* 48). In *Seeing Things*, Heaney obviously eliminates the title to fit with format of the 'Squarings' sequence and therefore removes Yeats's name. However, he then revises the final stanza and reinstates Yeats's name in the last line, thus guaranteeing the poet's *named* presence (*ST* 78).

27.   Heaney, *The Field Day Anthology of Irish Writing*, II, p. 788.

28.   Heaney is perhaps also invoking Derek Mahon's 'Courtyards in Delft': '. . . Perfection of the thing and the thing made'. See Derek Mahon, *Selected Poems*, (Harmondsworth: Penguin, 1993) p. 120.

29.   *JN* 151, emphasis added. Heaney comments similarly *The Government of the Tongue*; his ideas about artistic space sharing common ground with Barthes's theories of textuality: 'Instead, in the rift between what is going to happen and whatever we would wish to happen, poetry holds attention for a space...Poetry is more a threshold than a path, one constantly approached and constantly departed from . . .' (p. 108.)

30.   The 'marble bust commanding the parterre'(l. 7), almost certainly refers to Lady Gregory's bust of Maecenas which Heaney considers both a symbol for the aristocratic and enlightened approach to and patronage of art which Yeats and Gregory embraced *and*, more pejoratively, a representation of cultural

hegemony:

> Society was indeed to prove very rude to the system of values and manners which sustained Coole Park in its prime, but more of that in a moment. Just now I want to come in close-up on one feature of the Coole Garden. This is a neo-classical bust, a white cropped head of carved marble, drawn from Italy by wagon and boat in the ninteenth century, to be planted in the rough Atlantic weather of Co Galway. This bust represents the Roman aristocrat, Maecenas. Friend of the Emperor Augustus and patron of the arts, Maecenas stands in the European mind for the possibility of a benevolent link between power and art, between imperium and imagination, and as such, he was the proper guardian spirit within a good landlord's garden . . . Maecenas in Coole Park. . . . it remains as an enduring emblem of the covenant which architects must surely still observe, a covenant with classical achievements, with powerful patrons, with images of order, with projects of salutary beauty and force. (Heaney, 'From Maecenas to MacAlpine' edited text of lecture given to the RIAI Annual Conference in Dunadry, Co Down, 1986) p. 69.

31.   'The other day I was walking towards Urbino . . . I was alone amid a visionary, fantastic, impossible scenery. . . I saw suddenly in the mind's eye an old man, erect and a little gaunt, standing in the door of the tower, while about him broke a *windy light*. He was the poet who had at last, because he had done so much for the word's sake, come to share in the dignity of the saint. He had hidden nothing of himself, but he had taken care of "that dignity . . . *the perfection of form* . . . this lofty and severe quality . . . this virtue." . . . He has in his ears well-instructed voices . . .' (*E&I* 291, emphasis added).

The description seems almost to prefigure Heaney's conceptual place of writing as defined in *The Place of Writing* and *The Redress of Poetry*. A reference to the 'windy light' also appears in 'The Grey Rock' and references to perfected form can be found throughout Yeats's work:

> 'Why are they faithless when their might
> Is from the holy shades that rove
> The grey rock and the windy light?' (*VP* 275)

32.   Heaney would seem to be simultaneously be alluding to MacNeice's set question in 'Western Landscape', a poem probing the permanence of place:

> But what
> Is the hold upon, the affinity with
> Ourselves of such a light and line . . .

Louis MacNeice, *Collected Poems*, (London: Faber and Faber, 1979) p. 525. 'Western Landscape' twice alludes directly to Yeats, thereby increasing the complexity of the intertexuality of the Heaney piece.

33.   Richard Ellmann, *Four Dubliners* (London: Hamish Hamilton, 1987), p. 48. The phrase is quoted frequently by Heaney.

'MASTERING WHAT IS MOST ABSTRACT': A FORUM ON *A VISION*

Yeats and the Thirteenth Æon

Ron Heisler

THE RICHNESS OF YEATS AS A POETIC THINKER (which is far from being the same as the issue of his status as a mere common or garden thinker) is unquestionable. But it is a richness that fascinates as much by those aspects that remain resolutely opaque as by those territories of his mind which seem obligingly—or deceptively—transparent. Hitherto the chief eye-sore amid the ruinous landscape of Yeats's obscurantist tendencies has generally been reckoned to be the concept of the 'thirteenth cycle' (alternatively called 'sphere','gyre', 'cone' or 'vortex') which features so prominently in *A Vision*. The way in which this concept has flummoxed authority after authority has been a constant joy to Yeatsian critics huddled in the safety of the side-lines, who, without being capable of providing any adequate answers themselves, were able to appreciate the bafflement of great reputations.

Graham Hough, in his highly intelligent *The Mystery Religion of W. B. Yeats*, dryly catalogues supposed meanings for the *Thirteenth Cone*: 'a locality, a historical period, an undifferentiated slice of time, a state of affairs or a supernatural force'.[1] This usually acute commentator appears impatient to bury the corpse of the thirteenth whatever-it-is, whilst dispensing with a proper *post-mortem*. Richard Ellmann mystifies our understanding of the *Thirteenth Cone* with the caution, 'Here too reality inheres, and nothing can be known of it'. He assures us that the 'source of the Thirteenth Cycle, as well as of the other twelve, was a reminiscence in either his [Yeats's] mind or his wife's, of Christ and the Twelve Apostles'.[2]

And what does George Mills Harper have to say, for whose edition of *Yeats's* Vision *Papers* we will be eternally grateful, despite Colin McDowell's largely valid strictures (*YA11* 157-70)? The editor slips in his thoughts in a single paragraph in the second volume:

> The Thirteenth Cone . . . remains an enigma in *A Vision*, seeming to represent an escape from the cycles of reincarnation, 'deliverance from birth and death' (*AV B* 240). Graham Hough describes it as 'Yeats's joker' (p. 117) and notes that superimposed on the machinery of the twelve cycles which nothing can alter or turn aside we find in the end a volition and a choice,and that the last word on human destiny is theirs (p. 118). See also *AV B* 193 ('ultimate reality'), 202 and 210 ('Within it live all souls that have been set free') and *MYV* II 105. A14[3] above supports Ellmann's suggestion 'that the Thirteenth Sphere or Cycle is Yeats's equivalent for God' (Hough, p. 117). (*YVP 2* 543 n. 36).

Alas, the editor has given the reader short measure here, apparently lacking a developed opinion of his own and relying on shards of speculation by other writers. But at least he has recognized that the concept has something to do with God!

Harold Bloom's contribution to the debate is more substantial, the product of a mind that has read widely in many areas of literature and which is prepared to follow its instincts gutsily. But Bloomian judgements, which lesser mortals query at their peril—who dare contradict his presumption that Wallace Stevens will be remembered when W. H. Auden is long forgot?—sometimes take on a complexion that some might mistake as idiosyncratic; and Bloom, I must report, is awfully keen to yoke Yeats into William Blake's stream of influence at any cost. Blithely, Bloom tells us that the *Thirteenth Cone* is 'a happily Urizenic name for God' and that

> In Blake's Milton one finds the fullest and likeliest source for Yeats's twenty-eight Phases, in the twenty-eight Churches that mark off the divisions of fallen human history.[4]

But Bloom, it must be allowed, retrieves his position somewhat by sensing the Gnostic pull that runs through *A Vision*: 'perhaps no other major poet is so much of a Gnostic in his mature vision' as Yeats. Bloom also notes that 'In *Anima Mundi*, Yeats takes on the curse of poetic influence as a Gnostic adept would . . . '. Elsewhere he isolates 'a Gnostic reaching after some place on a scale-of-being that is other than human, that distinguishes Yeats's subjectivity not only from Blake's or Shelley's, but from any of the major Romantic quests for truth . . .'. For Bloom, the 'Gnostic poet [Yeats] enters the shadows in order to gain knowledge that will hasten the Judgement.' The critic writes with insight of how Yeats 'found himself prophesying a hidden divinity' of the kind that 'Martin Buber grimly calls the "composite god" of the historicists and Gnostics, the god of process, a dehumanizing divinity'.[5]

To be so close to, and yet fall so short of, the truth! Bloom's downfall lies in his shirking a more exhaustive exploration of Gnostic thought itself[6]—the price to be paid for the rather hubristic assumption that '[o]nly a few rudiments are necessary for understanding the Thirteenth Cone . . . the immediate meaning of the Thirteenth Cone, for Books II and III, is man's freedom, or all of freedom that Yeats desires, anyway'.[7] What does Yeats himself tell us about the thirteenth whatever-it-is in *A Vision*? He is much taken with achieving the 'free' Spirit, which 'if it died amidst some primitive community', might 'be called by the *Thirteenth Cone* to the care of the newly dead . . . (*AVB* 233). And then there is 'the *Purification*'—the precondition for the freeing of the Spirit—which 'may seek the assistance of those living men into whose "unconsciousness" or incarnate *Daimon*, some affinity of aim, or the command of the *Thirteenth Cone*, permits it to enter . . .'. 'An unconscious mind', the poet reminds us elsewhere, can be inhabited by 'messengers of the *Thirteenth Cone*' (*Ibid.* 234, 237). And a 'bond' can exist 'between an incarnate *Daimon* and a *Spirit* of the *Thirteenth Cone*. This bond . . . will pass through the same stages as if it were between man and some ordinary discarnate spirit . . . . *Victimage* for a *Spirit* of the *Thirteenth Cone* results from the prevention or refusal of experience itself,' which may arise from pride or asceticism.

> . . . it may have any cause, but the *Spirit* of the *Thirteenth Cone* is starved. Such Spirit may itself create the events that incited the man to refuse experience, St. Simon may be driven to his pillar (*AVB* 239).

Yeats's fascination with dreams and visions is well-known, and it is unsurprising that he should explain how the *Spirit*, under the influence of '*Teaching Spirits—Spirits* of the *Thirteenth Cone*—may not merely dream through the consequences of its acts but amend them, bringing this or that to the attention of the living.' These *Teaching Spirits* have

> representatives who may be chosen from any state, and are those who substitute for *Husk* and *Passionate Body* supersensual emotion and

imagery . . . the *Spirit* itself being capable of knowledge only . . . Our actions, lived in life, or remembered in death, are the food and drink of the *Spirits* of the *Thirteenth Cone*, that which gives them separation and solidity (*A V B* 228-30).

Yeats now invokes the concept of the *Phantasmagoria*, 'which exists to exhaust . . . emotion, and is the work of *Teaching Spirits*', which complete not merely physical and moral life, but also imagination (*A V B* 230).

Yeats talks of spiritual norms set by 'traditional attitudes' (the rough equivalent of 'roles', or social 'types')', which he exemplifies as 'lover, sage, hero, scorner of life', and which, he adds, may, 'if permitted by the *Thirteenth Cone*, so act upon the events of our lives as to compel us to attend to that perfection which, though it seems theirs [i.e., the traditional attitudes'] is the work of our own *Daimon*.' With the assistance of the *Thirteenth Cone*, the *Spirit* 'can so shape circumstances as to make possible the rebirth of a unique nature' (*A V B* 234, 235).

'Cruelty and ignorance . . . constitute evil as my instructors see it, and are that which makes possible the conscious union . . . of the *Daimon* of the Living and a *Spirit* of the *Thirteenth Cone*, which is the deliverance from birth and death' (*A V B* 240). Yeats then proceeds to throw further light on our ultimate quarry. The '*Thirteenth Cone* is a sphere because sufficient to itself; but as seen by man it is a cone. It becomes even conscious of itself as so seen . . .'. The most crucial moment for the *Thirteenth Cone* is at the coming of Christ, which is characterized by 'antithetical influx' and a 'particular antithetical dispensation', which reaches its 'complete systematization at that moment when . . . the Great Year comes to its intellectual climax' (*A V B* 240). At this point, it 'must reverse our era and resume past eras in itself; what else it must be no man can say, for always at the critical moment the *Thirteenth Cone*, the sphere, the unique intervenes.

> Somewhere in sands of the desert
> A shape with lion body and the head of a man
> A gaze blank and pitiless as the sun,
> Is moving its slow thighs, while all about it
> Reel shadows of the indignant desert birds. (*A V B* 263)

It is a tired, dejected Yeats who sums up his efforts in *A Vision* in the coda entitled 'The End of the Cycle', as if his great *credo* ultimately dissatisfied him—had not found that ideal completion of form and content which was ever his ambition. 'I have already said all that can be said,' he laments, as if his *Daimon* had somehow failed him—or rather, his *Daimon* bonded with a *Spirit* of the *Thirteenth Cone*. Surely it was a rueful man—one denied the great secret by some frustrating element—who penned such succeeding sentences as these:

> The particulars are the work of the *Thirteenth Cone* or cycle which is in every man and called by every man his freedom. Doubtless, for it can do all things and knows all things, it knows what it will do with its own freedom but it has kept the secret' (*A V B* 302).

What light do Yeats's prolific manuscripts cast on the *Thirteenth Cone*? Yeats spoke of 'some fifty copy-books of automatic script, and of a much smaller number of books recording what had come in sleep'. Writing in 1975, George Mills Harper stated he could only find 36 notebooks or envelopes with questions and answers. We will no doubt eventually see in print Yeats's 'large notebook which contains many diagrams, sketches of gyres, Phases of the Moon, etc.'—the poet's first attempt at organizing his materials as the automatic writing experiment approached its end.[8] The automatic writing sessions—the *Vision* Papers—already take up three bulky printed volumes (*YVP 1-3*), and more are promised.

In those published, George Yeats plays a crucial equal role, but the evidence is dispiritingly thin as regards the *Thirteenth Cone*. Over three years, from November 1917 onwards, we encounter a disparate sequence of allusions to the *Cone*, but these leave very little mark on the eventual text of *A Vision*. For a while, Yeats played with the notion of there being a Fourteenth Cone, a *cul-de-sac* he finally abandoned. At one stage, in the early phase of the automatic writings, Yeats puts the intriguing question: 'Does then the fool reincarnate[?]', receiving the reply: 'In the final incomplete perfection only into 13th Cycle'.[9] Here, some aspect of the lost tarot card system, which Yeats had been concocting two decades before, seems to have emerged.[10] It was but a brief flurry, and is not followed up in subsequent sessions. Even more intriguingly, we stumble on an exchange which hints at ritual—either actual and realized, or merely contemplated in Yeats's mind, we cannot say. Some collective acceptance is broached, triggering the question: 'Is this acceptance initiation[?]' The reply cryptically runs: 'Cycle 13/final initiation yes' (*YVP2* 27). We also find a throwback to Yeats's theosophical days—or to those incessant conversations he had had in the late 1880s and 1890s with his dear friend, Æ. Yeats begins questioning whether the Avatar is a '13th cycle soul incarnated between Libra-Scorpio'. Frostily, George's instructors retort,

'I am tired of saying the avatar will be multiple . . . (*YVP2* 173). But nothing else is recorded to this effect. We learn, too, of 'perfected men' existing in the *Thirteenth Cone*, who, unlike Daimons, were in 'contact with many' men (*YVP3* 392). The plunge of the Yeatses into absolute Gnosticism arises with the issue of the Frustrators, for we learn that the

> 13th Cone Frustrators are *Evil* that is to say the opposite principle to the 13th Cone Spirits that assist us. Absolute evil as distinguished from absolute good . . . . Yet both sort are from God for in 13th Cone He divides into two. Human souls on reaching 13th Cone are first absolutely good & then absolute evil (*YVP3* 102).

And so to my thesis: the closest parallels to Yeats's *Thirteenth Cone* scheme are to be found in the Gnostic systems which so enthralled theosophists in the years around 1890 and maintained a distinct purchase on Theosophical thinking thereafter. Gnostic interest in Britain had been on the up and up in the 19th century, having lagged somewhat behind developments on the Continent. A key work in this Gnostic revival was *The Gnostic Heresies of the First and Second Centuries* by Henry Longueville Mansel, Dean of St. Paul's, which saw print in 1875, being based on lectures given at Oxford in 1868. An odd cove was Mansel, who owned a magical *grimoire*, was an arch-Tory and almost certainly wandered in the illuminated circle of Bulwer Lytton. His discussion of possible Gnostic traces—of the appearances of the word 'æon'—in the New Testament probably gave many a Victorian lay person a first inkling that an esoteric tradition lay concealed within the then primly conceived world of the early Disciples. Against Mansel's scholarly fastidiousness, we should set the enthusiasm of C. W. King, whose *The Gnostics and their Remains* was esteemed enough after its first edition of 1864 to justify a much revised second edition in 1887. We can guess that it was this book that inspired G. R. S. Mead—a fervent Blavatskian—to engage in his great life-work, first, the translation of the Gnostic classic attributed to Valentinus, the *Pistis Sophia*, and, second, the dissemination of the Gnostic creed. King had apparently made a complete English translation of the *Pistis Sophia* before relinquishing this world, but when in 1895 Mead proposed to the literary executors that he edit the manuscript for publication, they killed the project stone dead.[11] But Mead's own incomplete translation had seen its way into several issues of *Lucifer*, the magazine of the Theosophical Society, between April 1890 and April 1891. Now it happens that Yeats's membership of the London Theosophical Society overlapped with this Gnostic dawn in *Lucifer*. He seems to have joined in December 1888 and last appeared at a meeting in August 1890, though he continued to lecture to branches of the Society after his enforced resignation. A member of the Esoteric Section—which met but infrequently (it must be said)—Yeats clearly was quite familiar with Mead at that stage, who was Blavatsky's private secretary and later General Secretary of the English Section of the Theosophical Society. In a journal entry for 20th December 1889, the poet caustically saw Mead 'whose intellect is that of a good sized whelk' as 'a little over-righteous as usual' (*Mem* 282). Later on, Yeats's attitude mellowed, and he found qualities in Mead he had not appreciated earlier on. The 'friendly, intelligent *man*' (*Au* 182, emphasis added) whom, as secretary, Madame Blavatsky dispatched to serve Yeats with his expulsion notice, was, in my view, almost certainly Mead and not Annie Besant, and for the obvious reason.[12] Geoffrey Watkins, of the great occult bookshop, recollected occasions when Yeats and Mead, meeting by chance in the shop, would 'talk at length on Plotinus, the Gnostics, and Indian philosophy' a custom happily maintained by others right down to this present day. Yeats often visited the weekly meetings of Mead's breakaway group, the Quest Society, originally held in Kensington Town Hall, but later transferred to a studio in Clareville Grove in South Kensington. Mead's periodical, *The Quest*, also reprinted 'The Mountain Tomb' in April 1913.[13] Yeats's catalogue of his library, written out in the 1920s, shows his keen interest in Mead's work: there are fifteen books listed by the Gnostic proselytizer (*YA4* 286). Strangely, there is no copy of the translation of *Pistis Sophia* listed (though Yeats might have read in *Lucifer* Mead's translation of this work, undoubtedly of the profoundest import for his subsequent intellectual evolution).

The psycho-drama of the *Pistis Sophia* is centred on the battle for salvation: 'knowledge is salvation of the inner man' for the Valentinians, wrote Irenaeus. Pistis Sophia's[14] sufferings arose from her exclusion from her natural habitat, the thirteenth æon. Jesus comes to rescue Sophia, taking away a third of the power of those excluding her, but anticipating that her enemies would 'raise a loan from those who know the mysteries of the magic of the thirteenth æon'.[15] Situated in the thirteenth æon was a foe, the 'third triple-power', who had been disobedient, desiring to rule over the whole æon. The great triple-powered 'emanated from himself a great lion-faced power',[16] which, despite the differences, nevertheless reminds us that when Yeats invokes the *Thirteenth Cone*, 'the sphere, the unique' intervening, 'A shape with lion body and the head of a man' manifests itself.[17] The great triple-powered was to be transmuted in Yeats's eventual system into the Frustrators. Jesus, in Valentinus's system, was obliged, at the commandment of the First Mystery, His Father, to go down into the chaos, where he 'directed [his] attack against that lion-faced power, which was shining exceedingly, and took from it all its light; I prevented all the emanations of Arrogant from entering from that hour into their region, which is the thirteenth æon'.[18] Jesus, too, had been insistent that 'all the emanations of the thirteenth material æon shall fear the mystery of thy [Sophia's] light, and thus cause the others to put on the glory of their light'.[19] Jesus's role in the *Pistis Sophia* had one other important resonance for Yeats, for chs. 12 and 13 deal with Christ's entry into the spheres. In the 1921 edition, Mead conveniently sets out a cosmological scheme 'underlying' the *Pistis Sophia*, the third world of which (there are two higher light-worlds, with the Ineffable and his Limbs beyond even those) offers a distinct, if imperfect, parallel for that of *A Vision*:

III The Lower Light or Æon-world, or The Mixture of Light and Matter

  i. The Region of the Left.
    1. The Thirteenth Æon.
    2. The Twelve Æons.
    3. The Fate.
    4. The Sphere.
    5. The Rulers of the Ways of the (Lower) Midst.
    6. The Firmament.

  ii. The World (Kosmos), especially Mankind.[20]

Mead, whose completed translation of the classic saw first publication in 1896, with a second revised edition in 1921, seems embarrassed by the *Lucifer* extracts and the curious commentaries he and Madame Blavatsky provided. He assembled eventually a thorough bibliography of the publishing history of the *Pistis Sophia* in European languages, but as for those extracts, he merely mentions that they were issued in a 'Magazine'. A modest man, indeed! The commentary—alas, the contributions of Mead and Madame Blavatsky are not individually signed and some could be a joint effort—contains one big fresh idea: an attempt at the geometrization of the Valentinian system. This surely left its indelible mark on Yeats and was the origin of those geometric illustrations with which *A Vision* abounds. The double cones or vortexes were independently derived, clearly, but the Mead-Blavatsky 'Chart of the Plerôma according to Valentinus'[21] looks suspiciously like an early inspiration for Yeats's general system—the seed planted in his subconscious.

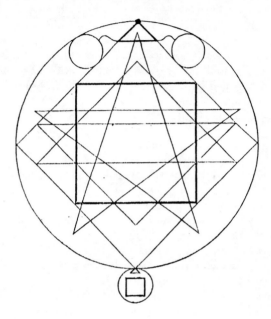

Part of the *Lucifer* commentary is worth reproducing

> Our author was right in comparing the Valentinian system with those of
> Pythagoras and Plato and in declaring that it had a mathematical basis.
> The *Gnosis* at all times and in all countries has been based on *natural
> laws*, and the different branches of mathematical science are simply the
> methods of expressing these laws. To vindicate these sublime systems of
> antiquity, and to *prove* that they were based on something more than
> 'superstitious imagination', some figures will now be given, and some
> hints to their explanation attempted. It must, however, be remembered
> that as such figures are infinite, and that the permutations and combina-
> tions of their properties, correspondences and qualities are equally
> infinite, no more than the roughest possible outline can be given in a
> short paper. . . . It is hoped that by these figures students will be given
> the clearest possible proof that, as Plato said, 'The Deity geometrizes'.[22]

The Gnostic interest among theosophists was more than a mere fad.
George Russell explained that 'a compositor's difficulty' with 'Æon'

(with which word Russell had signed an article) had 'suggested the pen-name now familiar to many who could not tell the poet's real name'.[23] 'ÆON'had been whispered to him in a vision, although it was some years before he properly discovered the Gnostics.[24] The former Chartist radical, Gerald Massey, who became a polymathic amateur historian of early Christianity, took as one of his principal themes the Gnostic trans-mission belt between Egyptian religion and the gospel of St. Luke, a thesis he was propounding in a lecture of 1887.[25] Under her Golden Dawn motto of S.S.D.D., Florence Farr published her *Egyptian Magic* in 1896, quoting a long passage from the Gnostic Papyrus (Bodleian) relat-ing to remission of sins, in which Jesus explains that 'the Light of the Purifying Æon [Thirteenth] will purify the twelfth Æon'.[26]

Nevertheless, there are great difficulties in charting how Gnostic notions may have indirectly entered Yeats's field of vision for the simple reason that we have no history of Gnosticism in British intellectual life to fall back on. Only very recently has it suggested that William Blake's complex organization of male and female figures in the major extended poems reflect Gnostic syzygies.[27] The modern history of the *Pistis Sophia* is intimately bound up with the London of Blake's time, for Dr Askew, who bought the unique manuscript on his travels in Italy and Greece, sold it to the British Museum in 1785, where C. G. Woide, the leading Coptic scholar of his day, was stationed as librarian. Woide, in fact, had been taking a keen interest in the text for some time. The appeal of Blake's poetry for Yeats during the years 1889-1892 was at its height as he worked with E. J. Ellis on their edition of the *Works*, during that seminal phase when Yeats's engagement with the Theosophical Society came crashing to the ground and when G. R. S. Mead was publishing the first English translation of the *Pistis Sophia*. The confluence of influences, and Yeats's reaction to them, provide a foundation, I would suggest, for his early crisis of intellectual identity. He would have been acutely self-conscious of his lack of a developed *weltanschauung*. Being Yeats, the self-willed man *par excellence*, he could not borrow someone else's ready-made system of thought, lock, stock and barrel. But to evolve his own system there was the question of acquiring a suitable vocabulary of con-cepts. Like Autolycus, he never walked away from a situation—from an intellectual crisis—without pocketing some unconsidered trifle. The Thirteenth Æon was of this order of acquisition. But part of Yeats's *per-sona* was the quality of evasion, and thus, in the naming of parts, the Thirteenth salvational realm could be called cycle, sphere, gyre, cone, or vortex—anything, in fact, but 'Æon'.

NOTES

1. Graham Hough, *The Mystery Religion of W. B. Yeats* (Brighton: Harvester Press, 1984), p. 113. I am very grateful to Roger Nyle Parisious for several conversations on numerous, unacknowledged points in this article, especially those involving the tarot.

2. Richard Ellmann, *The Identity of Yeats* (London: Macmillan, 1954; rptd. Faber and Faber, 1964) p. 159. Ellmann withholds the basis for this remarkably specific statement from his readers. It is likely that the source of the remark is a conversation with Mrs Yeats (of which Ellmann had many, from 1946 onwards), but if so, it is not recorded here.

3. Answer 14 (*YVP2* 26) replies to Question 14 'If all accept does it never incarnate again' and reads 'After the 13 incarnation if in all it accepts it becomes equal with God & is free to choose'. Some light is provides, a comment somewhat dto d by Answer 15 (to the question 'Is this acceptance initiation'?), 'Cycle 13 final initiation yes'. The exchange seems to prefigure Yeats's assertion that the *'Thirteenth Cone* or cycle . . . is in every man and called by every man his freedom' (*AVB* 302).

4. Harold Bloom, *Yeats* (New York: Oxford University Press, 1972) pp. 274, 206.

5. *Ibid.* pp. 185, 219, 220.

6. A critique of Bloom's ahistorical assumptions about Yeats's grasp of Gnosticism in his later books is provided in Warwick Gould's review essay on *The Anxiety of Influence, A Map of Misreading, Kabbalah and Criticism, Poetry and Repression,* 'A Misreading of Harold Bloom', *English,* XXVI:124, (Spring, 1977), pp. 240-254.

7. Harold Bloom, *Yeats,* p. 274.

8. George Mills Harper, 'Yeats's Occult Papers' in *Yeats and the Occult* ed. George Mills Harper (Toronto: Macmillan of Canada, 1975) p. 6. I have not consulted those plentiful volumes and scraps still unpublished.

9. *YVP2* 154. The Fourteenth Æon is occasionally mentioned by Gnostic writers and stands for the boundary enclosing the other æons.

10. On Yeats's 1898-9 notes for the Celtic Mystical Order involving the four talismans (Sword, Stone, Spear and Cauldron) which, said Yeats, 'related themselves in my mind with the suits of the Tarot', see *Mem* 125 and Richard Ellmann, *The Identity of Yeats* p. 29.

11. R. A. Gilbert advises in a private communication that the executors' reason was that as the translation was 'far from complete its publication would do no credit to his memory. Some of it had already appeared in *The Gnostics and their Remains'* (16 Jan., 1997). G. R. S. Mead's translation was *Pistis Sophia: A Gnostic Gospel (with Extracts from the Books of the Saviour appended) originally translated from Greek into Coptic and now for the first time Englished from Schwartze's Latin Version of the only know Coptic MS. and checked by Amélineau's French Version with an Intoduction by G. R. S. Mead B.A. M.R.A.S.* (London, New York, Benares, Madras: The Theosophical Publishing Society, 1896) There was a 'new and completely revised edition' published by John. M. Watkins in 1921 and reprinted in 1947. The texts differ significantly, and in what follows are distinguished as '1896' and '1921'.

12. cf., George Mills Harper, *Yeats's Golden Dawn* p. 8.
13. See *Wade*, p. 111 and Geoffrey M. Watkins, 'Yeats and Mr. Watkins' Bookshop', in George Mills Harper (ed.) *Yeats and the Occult*, pp. 308-9.
14. 'Pistis Sophia' means 'knowledge-wisdom'.
15. *Pistis Sophia* (1921), p. 23.
16. *Pistis Sophia* (1896), p. 45; (1921), p. 35; cf. *Daniel* 7:4.
17. See *A V B* 263. I fully recognise that the iconography of Yeats's manticore is a complex and much-discussed affair: for a list of appropriate articles see *J* DD 574-608, and see also *NC* 204-5.
18. *Pistis Sophia* (1896), p. 139. The 1921 edition reads '. . . approached the lion-faced power . . . and took its whole light in it and held fast all the emanations of Self-willed [the great triple-powered], so that from now on they went not into their region, that is the thirteenth æon' (p. 117).
19. *Pistis Sophia* (1896), p.p. 63-4 cf 1921, p. 52.
20. An Underworld including Chaos and Outer Darkness subsists beneath this region. See *Pistis Sophia* (1921), p. l-li.
21. This was the first of a series of eighteen interdependent figures, densely annotated and discussed by Mead, who found 'triumphantly shown forth' in them 'the great Hermetic axiom, "As above, so below"' (itself of crucial importance to Yeats, *vide VP* 556) Mead found it 'hardly necessary to point out the wonderful concordance of this system with that of *The Secret Doctrine*' (*Lucifer* vi [March-August 1890], 237-8).
22. *Lucifer* VI (March-August 1890) 237, 238. There are two further unnumbered pages of geometric diagrams between these pages. Further explanation of these are given on pp. 237-239. I am grateful to R. A. Gilbert for identifying the 'Magazine' as *Lucifer*, and for suggesting that whilst the technical footnotes and commentary on Gnosticism are the work of Mead, the occult commentary (probably including this quoted passage) is the work of Madame Blavatsky.
23. John Eglinton, *A Memoir of AE* (London: Macmillan: 1937), pp. 27. Though the name began as the diphthong or ligature 'Æ', 'AE' and later 'A. E.' became more common as his self-signatures.
24. Kathleen Raine, *Yeats the Initiate: Essays on Certain Themes in the Work of W. B. Yeats* (Mountrath: The Dolmen Press, 1986), p. 65.
25. Gerald Massey, *Gnostic and Historic Christianity. A Lecture* (1887). Articles by Massey turn up in *The Theosophist* III:3 (27) Dec. 1881. See also David Shaw, *Gerald Massey: Chartist, Poet, Radical and Freethinker* (London: Buckland Publications Ltd., 1995). Roger Nyle Parisious tells me that he once examined a copy of Massey's *Ancient Egypt the Light of the World: a Work of Reclamation and Restitution in Twelve Books* (1907), heavily annotated, possibly by Æ among others. Yeats and Æ founded the Dublin Hermetic Society, Æ also joining the Esoteric Section of the London Theosophical Society—but after Yeats had left.
26. S.S.D.D., *Egyptian Magic*, No 8 in W. Wynn Westcott's *Collectanea Hermetica* (London: Theosophical Publishing Co., 1896), reprinted with an introduction by Timothy d'Arch Smith (Wellingborough: Aquarian, 1982), p. 80
27. Stuart Curran 'Blake and the Gnostic Hyle: A Double Negative' in Nelson Hilton (ed.), *Essential Articles for the Study of William Blake, 1970-1984* (Hamden, Conn.: Archon Books, 1986), pp 15-37. See also Peter J. Sorensen *William Blake's Recreation of Gnostic Myth: Resolving the Apparent Incongruities* (Lewiston, New York; Salzburg: The Edwin Mellen Press, 1995).

'That Which is Unique in Man': The Lightning Flash in Yeats's Later Thought

T. Jeremiah Healey III

THE LIGHTNING FLASH in Yeats's thought receives extensive treatment in his later works, beginning with his interpretation of a personal experience and gradually evolving into a comprehensive view of the relationship of human identity to artistic pursuit. Yet it is a notion which has never been fully understood, for while it is a major tenet of Yeats's thought, it is not a part of his 'public philosophy'.[1] It is, therefore, hardly surprising that so many critics have passed over the matter, or been confused by its significance. To help resolve the existing uncertainty, this paper will propose a new understanding of the lightning flash, defining it as a form of communication, descending from *Daimon* to poet, which bestows a detailed knowledge of self and makes possible the craft of poetry.

The definition proposed here can be defended in two ways: by examining the lightning flash as presented by Yeats, and then by inspecting the one significant attempt to understand it, that of Professor George Mills Harper. The poet's conception can only be understood if the lightning flash is viewed as a single, essential notion, one which underwent continual development, but never altered its fundamental meaning. To ensure such an understanding, we must analyze the three major stages of development in turn, drawing from *Per Amica Silentia Lunae*, *Autobiographies*, and the writings known as the *Vision* Papers. What will emerge is both a key component to Yeats's understanding of poetry and an illustration of the freedom and self-actualization present in what many have labelled a deterministic philosophy.

I

Yeats's usage of the lightning flash image, though clearly influenced by those before him, was primarily rooted in personal experience. The first stage of its development was the result of inspiration that came to Yeats after a dream experienced at Tulira Castle, home of his friend Edward Martyn, in which he 'saw between sleeping and waking, as in a kinematograph, a galloping centaur, and a moment later a naked woman of incredible beauty, standing upon a pedestal and shooting an arrow at a star' (*Au* 372). In consultation with W. Wynn Westcott, 'a London coroner . . . learned in the Cabbala, whom I had known once' (*Au* 374), it was revealed that

> 'the centaur is the elemental spirit and the woman the divine spirit of the path Samekh, and the golden heart is the central point upon the cabbalistic Tree of Life and corresponds to the Sephiroth Tiphareth.' . . . He reminded me that the cabbalistic tree has a green serpent winding through it which represents the winding path of nature or instinct, and that the path Samekh is part of the long straight line that goes up through the centre of the tree, and that it was interpreted as the path of 'deliberate effort'. . . but he could not throw light on the other symbols except that the shot arrow must symbolise effort, nor did I get any further light (*Au* 375).

This twofold symbolism creates a dichotomous conception of how fulfillment might be achieved. The first method is the 'natural' method, represented by the green serpent or the 'winding path of nature'. This is the way by which persons normally develop, a literal back and forth movement, slowly proceeding upwards, a form of development in keeping with the doctrine of progression by contraries Yeats inherited from Jacob Boehme and Wiliam Blake. The other path is very different. It seems to be the path of a select few only, a group composed of those who have chosen to make 'deliberate effort'. This is a rather ambiguous phrase, so it is not surprising to find that it is interpreted by Westcott as being those 'who could attain to wisdom by the study of magic, for that was "deliberate effort"' (*Au* 375). Such an explanation would hold an obvious attraction for both Westcott and Yeats, themselves deeply involved in magical studies, as it would confirm the worth of their task. But it is certainly not the only way to understand the distinction posited by the vision, so it is not surprising to find that this notion undergoes significant development later on. However, it is not until the writing of *PASL* that Yeats would indicate the changes that had occurred in his thought in the intervening thirty years.

II

Per Amica Silentia Lunae marks a key shift in Yeats's thought by recording significant changes in his interpretation of the dream.

> Many years ago I saw, between sleeping and waking, a woman of incredible beauty shooting an arrow into the sky, and from the moment when I made my first guess at her meaning I have thought much of the difference between the winding movement of Nature and the straight line, which is called in Balzac's *Séraphita* the 'Mark of Man', but is better described as the mark of saint or sage. I think that we who are poets and artists, not being permitted to shoot beyond the tangible, must go from desire to weariness and so to desire again, and live but for the moment when vision comes to our weariness like terrible lightning, in the humility of brutes. . . . We seek reality with the slow toil of our weakness and are smitten from the boundless and the unforeseen. Only when we are saint or sage, and renounce experience itself, can we, in imagery of the Christian Cabbala, leave the sudden lightning and the path of the serpent and become the bowman who aims his arrow at the centre of the sun (*Myth* 340).

This marks an interesting shift in emphasis, in three ways. The first is the redefinition of the categories, such that the path of the arrow has now been identified with 'saint or sage'. This path is now predicated not upon the prerequisite of magical study, but rather upon an action of renunciation. The second change is Yeats's grouping together of the natural path and the 'sudden lightning', which suggests some expansion of the presentation in *Autobiographies*. And the third is that Yeats has quietly shifted his own identification. Following his conversation with Westcott, it would seem that Yeats, by virtue of his magical studies, believed himself to be following the path of the arrow. In *Per Amica Silentia Lunae*, however, he quite clearly considers himself a poet, and assigns poets to the path of nature. This re-identification is first shown by the explicit differentiation he makes between the poets of the first path and the saints and sages of the second. The separation is again confirmed by the clear placement of the poet's role within the world of experience, 'the tangible'—precisely what the sage must reject. 'For a hero loves the world till it breaks him, and the poet till it has broken faith; but while the world was yet debonair, the saint has turned away, and because he renounced experience itself, he will wear his mask as he finds it' (*Myth* 337).

Yet, despite having reimaged the role of the poet, Yeats leaves it to us to puzzle out its ambiguous relation to the newly introduced category of the hero. The hero and the poet must certainly be related, however, both because of the association of the two in the quote above, and because he indicates elsewhere that there are only two paths available.[2] Both the hero and the poet, then, must exist somehow upon the path of nature. From other comments in *Per Amica Silentia Lunae*, it would seem that the poet, though 'a man like all other men', is differentiated from the hero by his goal. He writes, 'It is not permitted to a man who takes up pen or chisel, to seek originality, for *passion* is his only business . . .' (*Myth* 339, emphasis added). It is this quest for passion which limits poets to the world of reality, focusing their attentions on precisely what the saint must renounce. Because poets will not renounce experience, they can only proceed along the serpent's path. But there is still room for something else. As Yeats writes, 'we seek reality with the slow toil of our weakness and are smitten from the boundless and the unforeseen' (*Myth* 340). This 'smit[ing]' is the key. In contrast to the hero, whose life of action leaves little room for transcendence, the poet can hope for some sort of ill-defined other contact. It would therefore seem that though the hero is a paradigm of the natural path, the poet, though similar in the main, occasionally wanders off it. It is this ability to depart from the path of nature which explains the statement cited above: 'I think that we who are poets and artists, not being permitted to shoot beyond the tangible, must go from desire to weariness and so to desire again, and live but for the moment when vision comes to our weariness like terrible lightning, in the humility of brutes' (*Myth* 340). It is this vision which makes the artist.

Yeats has given the poet the paradoxical burden of seeking visions through knowledge of earthly passion. This is certainly an unusual combination, and its effects are unclear. While he intimates an impressive quality to these visions, Yeats is hesitant to indicate their contents. But some sense is given in a cryptic passage near the end of *Per Amica Silentia Lunae*:

The Daimon,[3] by using his mediatorial shades, brings man again and again to the place of choice, heightening temptation that the choice may be as final as possible, imposing his own lucidity upon events, leading his victim to whatever among works not impossible is the most difficult. He suffers with man as some firm-souled man suffers with the woman he but loves the better because she is extravagant and fickle. His descending power is neither the winding nor the straight line but zigzag, illuminating the passive and active properties, the tree's two sorts of fruit: it is the sudden lightning, for all his acts of power are instantaneous. We perceive in a pulsation of the artery, and after slowly decline. (*Myth* 361)

This 'sudden lightning' must be identified with the vision that 'comes like terrible lightning' to the poet. The implication is that this, the Daimon's 'descending power',[4] is, in fact, the communication of the knowledge of 'the passive and active properties,' a phrase which seems to have its basis in the Yeats's doctrine of the self and anti-self, or mask.[5] The 'creation' spoken of in the diary must be the 'choice' the Daimon brings about, the adoption and 'touch[ing] with gold the cheek' (*Myth* 339) of the mask of the poet. While this is rather vague, we must acknowledge one crucial element, namely, Yeats's constant emphasis that the choice is clearly the provenance of the individual. The Daimon may 'heighten choice', and 'impose . . . lucidity', but it cannot control the outcome. The process is clearly one of self-determination, not of determinism. Poets are left to shape themselves.

III

It is in the obscurity of the Vision Papers that the lightning flash becomes a completed notion, tying together both the concerns of the individual and Yeats's greater cosmology—or, as *Per Amica Silentia Lunae* would have it, 'Anima Hominis' and 'Anima Mundi'. This final stage of development comes with Yeats's articulation of the phasal system, which represents the individual stages through which all persons must pass. The key is the fact that the individual performs the cycle not merely once within the course of a lifetime, but also in a series of twelve wheels, ie., at least 336 lives.[6] While the individual is only concerned with, and aware of, the events of its present existence, his or her identity must therefore be far greater than that. The person can be truly known only if the selves and anti-selves of all the lives lived can be seen at once. While this degree of knowledge is beyond human capability, it is not beyond that creatures who is 'the ultimate self of [a] man' (*A V B* 83), and whose memories determine the outlines of our lives, i.e., the *Daimon*. The *Daimon* may communicate portions of the totality of identity which only it can see, if it so chooses. It follows, then, that the lightning flash diagrams in the text of the *Vision* Papers are simply a schematic view of this understanding of a person's experience, illustrating in a visual format the decisive points of an individual's history, as seen from the Daimon's perspective. Yet even the diagrams do not give the whole story, as they are quite explicitly incomplete.[7] Clearly, then, no person's identity is merely an enumeration of their successive masks. The reason is simple: because the life of every person differs, the lightning flash must be unique for every individual.[8] Despite Yeats's repeated attempts at formulaization, it is not possible to derive the self-knowledge of the lightning flash from one's horoscope, nor can communicated knowledge be used to anticipate the future. The lightning flash is a record, not a cause. It is unnecessary to provide a synopsis of the hard-learned lessons of the Vision sessions. Having finally accepted the dimensions of the notion presented to him, Yeats summarizes his knowledge of the lightning flash in an entry in one of his notebooks, which, as is so often the case with the *Vision* materials, represents a significant expansion of the materials provided to him by the 'instructors'.

> The Lightening Flash because of its irregular and incalculable movement expresses that which is unique, that which cannot recur just as wheel & cone expres all that is seasonable. . . .Taken as expressing not merely the nature of successive forms of emotional experience in external life, but as the nature of the emotional life it self at every moment of its existence they are that which is unique in man. His entire emotional past as always present. The Lightening Flash is therefore the man in emotional relation to his past, made present; & in intellectual relation to his future conceived as present. It is because of this that he is an individual & not merely a type of his phase. at every moment he chooses his entire past & his entire future, though he is not conscious of his choice till on the threshold of the Beatific Vision. (*YVP3* 115)

This passage seems to confirm precisely the notions we have seen developing. There can be little doubt that we are now dealing with a notion much larger than obscure rituals of the Golden Dawn. The lightning flash is even more significant than a mere guide to identity, as Yeats seems to understand it in the early dialogues of the *Vision* Papers. Rather, in its most developed form, the lightning flash is a record of human experience and self-actualization, one which may, in part, be given to the poet by the *Daimon*. This has two results. First, it gives the poet knowledge of him- or herself. This is possible because of the poet's acceptance of the passionate reality of the life which the saint rejects, which is necessary because of poetry's roots in the individual's history.[9] The second is that it serves as a representation of the person as a self-determining individual, a counterweight to the formulaic mechanism of the phasal system. It is an idea which unifies personal and universal experience, the concrete and the abstract. It is an idea, therefore, which serves as the perfect basis for poetic inspiration.

IV

Although the lightning flash as understood here is clearly key to Yeats's thought, it is unfortunately absent from the text of *A Vision*. This is not surprising. Yeats himself complained that 'I have not dealt with the whole of my subject, perhaps not even with what is most important, writing nothing about the Beatific Vision, little of sexual love' (*AV A*, xii).[10] Clearly sexual love is related to the lightning flash, since for Yeats, 'it may be [that] 'sexual love,' which is 'founded upon spiritual hate,' is an image of the warfare of man and Daimon . . .' (*Myth* 336). And the Beatific Vision may be linked to the flash even more closely, as is implied by his previously quoted comment, in a passage on the lightning flash, that 'at every moment [the individual] chooses his entire past & his entire future, though he is not conscious of his choice till on the threshold of the Beatific Vision' (*YVP3* 115). Quite simply, the lightning flash belongs to an category of Yeats's philosophy which he never published. Yet the reconstruction of the lightning flash presented here ties in closely to what we do know of Yeats's philosophy. Clearly some sort of aid must be necessary for a poet who was convinced that all poetry is rooted in one's own identity, while simultaneously admitting that he knew very little of himself. The lightning flash, and possibly the Beatific Vision, are quite at home in Yeats's own conception of poetic vision, which is rooted not in the transcendental sacrifice of the saint or sage, but in the expression of the depths of one's own soul. Yeats himself said it best, in a meditation upon the human condition. 'When I remember that Shelley calls our minds "mirrors of the fire for which all thirst," I cannot but ask the question all have asked, "What or who has cracked the mirror?" I begin to study the only self that I know, myself, and to wind the thread upon the pern again' (*Myth* 364). And from that thread, poetry is woven.

V

George Mills Harper treats the lightning flash (to some degree), in both his *The Making of Yeats's 'A Vision'* and *Yeats's Vision Papers*. In his view

> [t]he LF is patterned on the Flaming Sword of the GD rituals. The descending path of the LF follows a zig-zag pattern, the points of which are marked by phasal numbers representing characters in the play and are marked by phasal numbers representing characters in [*The Only Jealousy of Emer*] and in Yeats's life . . . (*YVP1* 521).

This is a fascinating proposition, one which, in light of Harper's knowledge of the Golden Dawn, requires the most serious consideration. Unfortunately, this assertion is never given detailed discussion in his works.[11] This is unfortunate, for while the flash is certainly a useful interpretative tool in the context which he mentions, such an approach seems rather reductionistic for a notion to which Yeats gives such serious treatment. This disregard is especially puzzling because Harper is clearly familiar with some of Yeats's most explicit presentations of his views. In fact, Harper directly transcribes some of the most important and revealing lightning flash texts directly into *The Making of Yeats's 'A Vision'*, when he briefly discusses Yeats's attempt to relate the lightning flash to other, rather more prominent material. 'As the term suggest, [the lightning flash] represents an instantaneous revelation. Yeats attempted for several months to relate it to the Initiatory and Critical Moments'. While this seems an excellent beginning for a consideration of the lightning flash, Harper's final statement on the matter is terse and unfortunate: 'Since the Flash was not one of the Moments, it was difficult to connect' (*MYV2* 232-3).

For Harper to derive such a conclusion hardly seems fair. It is his lack of interest in the subject, coupled with his single-minded conviction in the lightning flash as a tool for interpreting *The Only Jealousy of Emer* and Yeats's own, admittedly complicated, romantic history, which gives the reader the uncomfortable impression that the depth of the poet's consideration is being given short shrift. More importantly, the unchallenged assumption that the lightning flash is derived from some previous source ignores the startling originality of Yeats's notion, and fails to recognize its larger application to his thought. It is only in the light of the poet's history that the lightning flash can be understood. Given Yeats's use of the lightning flash as a tool for self-understanding, this seems only appropriate.

NOTES

1. Yeats would sometimes distinguish between his 'public philosophy', the published ideas contained primarily in *A Vision*, and his 'private philosophy', which 'is the material dealing with individual mind which came to me with that on which the mainly historical Vision is based. I have not published because I only half understand it' (*L* 916).

2. Yeats wrote, 'in so far as a man is like all other men, the inflow finds him upon the winding path, and in so far as he is a saint or a sage, upon the straight path' (*Myth* 361).

3. Always italicized in Yeats's later usages, the *Daimon* plays an extraordinarily complex role, well beyond the scope of this paper. It is particularly complicated when considering the time period of *Per Amica Silentia Lunae*, as so much of scholarly opinion is coloured by the statements of *A Vision*. This investigation will make no assumptions about the nature of the *Daimon*, other than to recognize the importance of memory in the *Daimon*, and to adopt the vague definition of *A Vision*: 'the *Daimon* [is the] ultimate self of [a] man' (*A V B* 83).

4. The idea of descent reinforces the contrast of the poet and saint. Unlike the saint, whose action of renunciation allows the seeking of wisdom, the active choice of shooting arrows upward, the poet must await the whim of the *Daimon*, who communicates downward to the poet without warning.

5. The mask is an idea most simply explained by Yeats in a excerpt from one of his diaries: 'I think that all happiness depends on the energy to assume the mask of some other life, on a re-birth as something not one's self, something created in a moment and perpetually renewed . . .' (*Myth* 334). The distinction between 'passive and active properties' in this context is particularly appropriate for Yeats, who states that the contrast between his own self and anti-self is characterized by a move from 'reaction' to 'action only' (*Myth* 325).

6. Colin McDowell alerted me to the number (28 x 12).

7. This fact is demonstrated in the script of 1 May 1919:

    1. Do all lightening flashes in subjective nature end in 15?
    1. No Your do not end in fifteen

    2. They did in diagram
    2. There are further points (*YVP2* 273).

8. The instructors' insistence on autonomy may be seen, e.g., in the script of 6 May 1919:

    6. How many angles in lightening flash?
    6. varying

    7. what causes the character in each lightening flash?
    7. The uniqueness of every ego

    8. Is lightening flash the most complete expression of that uniqueness.
    8. Yes

> 9. Does flash of one incarnation develop from that of incarnation
>   before?
> 9. Yes
>
> 10. Can that development be reduced to law?
> 10. I said *unique* (*YVP2* 281)

There is little ambiguity here.

9.   'We make out of the quarrel with others, rhetoric, but of the quarrel with our-
      selves, poetry' (*Myth* 331).

10.   This remains little changed in *A Vision*: as Colin McDowell comments, 'If Yeats
      treats these important matters in the second edition it is not in an obvious man-
      ner'. See Colin McDowell, 'To 'Beat Upon the Wall': Reading *A Vision*' (*YA4*
      220).

11.   While other references are made, they consist of nearly identical programmatic
      statements, such as, 'the Lightning Flash represents an adaption of the Flaming
      Sword, a Golden Dawn Symbol, to the personal themes of the A[utomatic]
      S[cript]' (*MYV1* 85).

SHORTER NOTES

J. B. Yeats's Marginalia in
The Wanderings of Oisin and Other Poems

Michael J. Sidnell

I

THE PUBLICATION IN 1889 of *The Wanderings of Oisin and Other Poems* enhanced W.B. Yeats's growing reputation and, as a sign of the twenty-four-year-old poet's productivity and promise, gratified his father.[1] But the son's achievement was galling, also, since it came at a time when the father's career had stalled. At fifty-one, John Butler Yeats's achievement as a painter was modest and he was descending into chronic financial dependency on his family and friends. JBY's biographer observes that as 'Willy was rising to prominence . . . John Butler Yeats came as close to emotional breakdown as it was possible to do without going over the edge.'[2] JBY always remembered this as a time of 'incessant humiliation'.[3] His son's new book had the effect of further marginalising him and it was in its margins that he asserted himself.

One of JBY's problems—the fundamental one according to WBY's assessment many years later—was an 'infirmity of will which has prevented him from finishing his pictures and ruined his career.'

He even hates the sign of will in others. It used to cause quarrels between me and him, for the qualities which I thought necessary to success in art or life seemed to him 'egotism' or 'selfishness' or 'brutality'. I had to

265

escape this family drifting, innocent and helpless, and the need for that
drew me to dominating men like Henley and Morris.[4]

For the son's view of the father, in this respect, Tennyson's 'Will' is an
apposite text and, as it happens, one well known to JBY. The second
stanza of 'Will' goes:

> But ill for him who, bettering not with time,
> Corrupts the strength of heaven-descended Will,
> And ever weaker grows through acted crime,
> Or seeming-genial venial fault,
> Recurring and suggesting still!
> He seems as one whose footsteps hault,
> Toiling in immeasurable sand,
> And o'er a weary sultry land,
> Far beneath a blazing vault,
> Sown in a wrinkle of the monstrous hill,
> The city sparkles like a grain of salt.[5]

As noted below, WBY's 'wrinkled moon' triggered in JBY a recollection
of Tennyson's poem of which, significantly, he carried at least the final
lines in memory.

Despite the opposition and opposite career trajectories of father and
son, they remained uncommonly communicative on aesthetic and
philosophical matters, and JBY's views were sometimes conveyed with a
marked zeal. At the very beginning of his 'unpublished autobiography'
WBY recounts, with some relish, how 'a quarrel over Ruskin came to
such a height that in putting me out of the room he broke the glass in a
picture with the back of my head.'[6]

Always a sharp critic of his son's thought and work, JBY could also be
an approving one, but on the occasion of the appearance of that first collection of poems the intensity of his scrutiny was especially keen. This is
attested by a most notable recent acquisition by the Thomas Fisher Rare
Book Library at the University of Toronto, a copy of WBY's *The
Wanderings of Oisin and Other Poems* with marginalia by JBY. This
unique document is a moving testimony of the painter's responses to his
son's poetry, and of the critical burden the poet bore. JBY's notes, corrections and observations come from an animated reading and are not
above mockery and sarcasm. They include four marginal sketches, two of
them proffered as visual critiques of WBY's words.

JBY's most eloquent, though mute, observation is in relation to lines
that refer to the 'hanging mansion' of 'the golden-crested wren.' 'Hang-

ing' is twice underlined by JBY and his sketch at the foot of the page is conclusive—a wren's tiny 'mansion' rests securely in the crotch of a branch, as nature sensibly ordains (Plate 8). A poet with WBY's pretensions to intimacy with the Irish countryside, its plants and creatures, should doubtless have been better informed about the nesting habits of the king of all birds.[7] And how could one of the horse-riding gentry write that a 'careful pastern pressed the sod'? JBY's reproof of WBY's anatomy-defying euphony is spelt out. (His words are represented here by bold type and all underlines are his):

But no horse "presses the <u>sod</u>" with his "<u>pastern</u>" but with his <u>hoof</u>.

JBY's delicate sketch of the lower part of a horse's leg (Plate 6) exhibits his superior precision of observation but he does not, by any means, condone pictorialism—quite the contrary:

O, let us have done with 'the <u>painted</u> birds.' [pictaeque volucres] Nature does <u>not</u> 'paint,'—nor 'gild' either,—nor even 'silver.'

The resort to Virgil (*Aeneid* IV, 525) is a low blow. JBY (like his father and his grandfather) had the advantage of a Trinity College education but lacked the means (and desire) to send WBY there. And WBY's attempts at Latin (as at French and Irish) were ineffectual. Indeed, in his youth, even his English syntax was defective, perhaps because his father's tuition was so impatiently energetic.

(grammar?) (or syntax) is at issue for JBY in 'How Ferencz Renyi Kept Silent,' especially in the following interrogation of the captive Renyi:

> Hiding the rebels worm in yonder wood
> Or yonder mountains. Where?

In three margins JBY does his best to unravel WBY's meaning:

? Hiding the <u>rebel worms</u> in yonder wood ? Hiding the <u>rebels</u> (<u>Worm</u>!) in yonder wood ? Hiding the rebels, worm (verb, imperat: 'do thou worm'—i.e. 'hide like a worm') in yonder wood.'

and again:

Hiding the rebels (who), worm (who do worm'. worm' being a verb, 3rd person pl. pres.) in yonder wood.

and again:

"The rebels,—hiding,—(do) worm' in yonder wood."

Eventually, he divines a typographical mischief with **rebel swarm?**, which was nearly what had appeared in the earlier printing and was doubtless very close to what WBY intended. WBY also intended a political statement, comparing Hungarian and Irish subjugation and offering 'Libations from the Hungary of the West'. JBY pointed out the prepositional solecism in a Buck Mulliganish mock:

(**Libations to the thirsty wld be more appropriate**).

In the event, WBY chose not to reprint this poem, which JBY thought **Good (but rather spoilt)**.

How JBY came to suspect ineptitude rather than a printer's error with that 'rebels' swarm' may be gauged from his difficulties with the following passage from 'Jealousy', in which the stars are apostrophised. The text is printed in italic: underlined roman shows JBY's underlining of it:

Sing, turning in your cars,
Sing, till *ye raise your hands and sigh, and o'er* your car heads peer
With all your whirling hair, *and* drop *through space* an *azure tear.*

One of JBY's marginal comments on this passage goes:

**which heads? whose whirling hair? will the heads (how many?) drop
an azure tear between them?   And why should they (the stars at
night) Sing till the hands drop an azure tear when they stop singing?**

But he thought better of this, and of another comment of a similar tenor, erasing them both.[8]

Though JBY was early convinced that WBY was a true poet, he was often irritated by his son's metrical practices, which arose from WBY's habit of 'composing in a loud voice manipulating of course the quantities to his taste'.[9] On several occasions (**Metre**) in the book's margin indicates JBY's dissatisfaction on this score and, more precisely, his accents over certain syllables flush out the author's manipulations of the 'quantities', or stresses. So JBY offers to correct and criticise the following lines, deleting the words in brackets, underlining a weak line, adding a word and the notations in the margin and exposing what he takes to be WBY's bad metres:

The doves whose <u>growing forms</u> he'd watched. Not these
           old
<u>He numbers. He a brown^ farm house sees,</u>
(metre?)

Where shadow of cherry, and [s̸h̸a̸d̸o̸w̸] of apple trees,   **(?-)**
    /   / /   /   /   /
Enclose a quiet place [of beds] box-bordered, bees, **(Alexandrine)**

In a simpler example, JBY's accent on a final syllable, his line under it
and his marginal note economically expose the manipulations of the
accent:
               /
Thy name, thy kin, and thy <u>country</u> **countree**

In this instance, WBY appears to have been attentive, since the next pub-
lished version would read, 'But where are your noble kith and kin, | And
into what country do you ride?' (Later still he changed 'into' to 'from',
which would have pleased JBY even better.)

Since so much of the contents of this first collection was never
reprinted, it is unsurprising that few of the objects of JBY's criticisms
survived. But it is also likely that, since they were living in the same
house at the time, WBY actually saw and considered the marginalia
addressed to him; and this is consistent with the evidence of this volume.
It was JBY, apparently, who alerted WBY to the important fact that the
name of the faery bride with whom Oisin rides off is pronounced as one
syllable only:

    **but is not "Niam" (Niambh) pronounced Neev'? as one syllable? Not
    'Nee-am'?**

WBY adopted 'Neave' in the next version and 'Niamh' later (though
there was editorial slippage in various printings). But a criticism that he
partly and properly ignored was JBY's tetchy response to the line, 'Her
hair was of a <u>citron</u> tincture'. JBY might have enlarged his vocabulary
(and perhaps his palette) instead of demanding in the margin:

    (citron <u>fruit</u> ? or what? yellow? or brown? what colour is "citron?").

It was the indefinite 'tincture', not the colour, that was excised. The line
became, 'A citron colour gloomed in her hair'.

JBY's marginalia are spread throughout the volume but some poems are particularly favoured with his comments. One such is 'How Ferencz Renyi Kept Silent', which has been mentioned. Another, also about a man who goes mad, is 'King Goll', which excited JBY's superciliousness:

> Has he caught the fever again, poor man. Was he a sort of Celtic Nebuchardnezzar (or <u>was</u> he a Celt?).

JBY had the wit to cancel this query with a wavy line meant to make it illegible. Elsewhere he is more troublesome, though he may not mean to be:

> If King Goll was a legendary character there ought to be here an explanatory note. "3ʳᵈ Cent." explains nothing, & is an absolutely useless addition—((absolutely useless to the general reader—ut mihi—at least).

And one point, he demands,

> What is it happened? What is the story of King Goll? (Had he anything to do with King Cole?).

The poem had been written in 1884 and first published in 1887, in *The Leisure Hour*, as 'King Goll, An Irish Legend', along with WBY's long explanatory note.[10] JBY must have recalled this printing, since the poem was illustrated by his drawing of mad King Goll done in 1885 with WBY as his model.[11] It was one of JBY's rare successes in getting an illustration accepted for publication.[12] As to the explanatory note, by 1889 WBY would have learned that he had carelessly misread his chief and precisely-identified source, conflating Gall, an adolescent prince of Ulster, with Goll Mac Morna, a mature Connacht chieftain.[13] But WBY stuck with his mythological hybrid and for later printings adopted a strategic vagueness about the source. As to JBY, he thought well enough of his King Goll illustration to turn it, in 1900, into a painting. And John Quinn, New York lawyer and patron of the arts, thought well enough of the painting to offer to buy it.[14] The work had already been sold but Quinn's offer was the first contact between JBY and the man who would become his lifelong patron. So Goll (or Gall), in whose place of refuge 'all the madmen of Ireland would gather were they free' (*VP* 796), was a rather critical link between father and son both before and after JBY offered his marginal edifications.

In addition to the interrogations, comments and sketches, JBY also jotted down snatches of verse. With these, his intentions are not entirely clear but it appears that WBY's verse has in each case reminded him of others' lines, and he may be alerting WBY to an inadvertent echo or poetic cliché. On page 2 of the book, the image-association of dew and eyes apparently links WBY with Sir Walter Scott and Robert Montgomery in JBY's mind, though WBY does not use the 'eyes' | 'lies' rhyme that links the couplets attributed to Scott and Montgomery. JBY's inscription on page 53, 'Life of the mountains on the moon', which is the verbal counterpart to his sketch of a moonscape may be a quotation, though I have not been able to place it. This inscription and the sketch appear on the same page as his quotation from Tennyson's 'Will', which is more revealing of JBY's preoccupations than of any resemblance between WBY's lines and Tennyson's; though 'wrinkled' clearly echoes 'wrinkle' in JBY's mind, and his note on page 54 criticizes WBY's double application of the adjective. With the King Goll quatrain on page 77 (which he may have made up) JBY is putting on an antic disposition to a rather deflating effect, it seems, as with his shrewd, if not very helpful mention of Old King Cole.

Mosada: A Dramatic Poem (1886), WBY's first published book, was an off-print from a periodical.[15] JBY paid for the binding of it and also insisted on adorning it with his frontispiece portrait of his son, rather than with a representation of some scene from the play, which WBY thought more seemly. WBY's second book, *The Wanderings of Oisin and Other Poems,* was published by Charles Kegan Paul under a muddled subscription arrangement that caused its author annoyance and embarrassment. Five hundred copies were printed, of which three hundred were bound and issued in January 1889. Fifty more copies were bound in the following month and six months later another fifty. The sheets remaining (fewer than a hundred copies) were transferred, in 1892, to T. Fisher Unwin and published by him in May of that year as *The Wanderings of Oisin Dramatic Sketches Ballads & Lyrics,* in the uniform binding of his Cameo Series, with a cancel title and a frontispiece representing Oisin, Niam and Saint Patrick, specially done by Edwin J. Ellis.

Remarkably, the De Lury Collection in the University of Toronto's Thomas Fisher Library held (before the recent addition) two of the 1889 copies (in their slightly different, original bindings) and a copy of the rarer 1892 issue. The volume under discussion (which happens to be in yet another variant of the 1889 binding) was purchased from the collection of the late Robert O'Driscoll, who had acquired it from the late Mícheál O h-Aodha, the broadcaster, Abbey Theatre Director and book collector, probably in the early 1970s. Not only is it richly annotated by JBY but it may be the only extant copy of a book by Yeats with marginalia by his father.

II: Description and Transcription

This is a copy of *Wade* 2. The cloth binding is the same colour (dark blue) as the variant reported in *Wade* (not the lighter blue of another *Wade* 2 copy in the Fisher Library), though it does not have the spaced 'T H E' and it does have publisher's monogram stamped blind on the back cover.

There is no bookplate or indication of ownership. All inscriptions and sketches are in pencil, unless otherwise noted. JBY's erasures and deletions of his inscriptions and his cancellations of them (done with wavy lines intended to produce illegibility) are noted below. Where possible, erased or deleted material is transcribed; otherwise a dash replaces an unidentified letter.

Page references are to *Wade* 2. Lines in which JBY's underlines or other markings appear are reproduced and are located by reference to page and line number in the *Variorum Edition of the Poems*, thus: *VP* 720:8. (In *VP*, rather confusedly, the same line occasionally appears under different numbers in the main text and the collation, as at *VP* 83: 17/19.) Transcriptions are made page by page except in those cases in which the two-page opening has been treated as a single unit by JBY.

The inscriptions on pages 134-35 are different from the rest in that they are in brown crayon, and in other ways. They may possibly be in another hand. Otherwise, the underlines and strike-outs, the square and round brackets, braces and carets below represent JBY's own markings. JBY's inscriptions are in **bold type**. The locations of inscriptions and sketches are indicated as follows: L = left margin; R = right margin; T = top margin; B = bottom margin. Slashes in the transcriptions indicate line ends in the marginalia. Curly brackets { } enclose editorial comments.

Page 2: *The Wanderings of Oisin.*

VP 2:7w   Whose <u>careful</u> pastern <u>pressed the sod</u>

L   {Sketch of the lower part of a horse's leg and hoof.}

R   **But no| horse| "presses the| <u>sod</u>"| with his| "<u>pastern</u>"| but|
             with his| <u>hoof</u>.**

VP 2:7z
> shoes
> For gold his <u>hooves</u> and silk his rein

B¹⁶

> "The dew that on the Violet lies
> Mocks the dark lustre of thine eyes"
> (Scott.

> And the bright dew-bead on the Bramble lies
> Like liquid rapture upon Beauty's Eyes"
> (R. Montgomery.

> {The word 'rapture' is written over another word, possibly 'rap-
> tre'.}

Page 3: *The Wanderings of Oisin.*

VP 3:24
R
> Her hair was of a <u>citron</u> tincture
> <(citron <u>fruit</u> ?| or what?| yellow? or| brown?| what|
> colour is| "citron"?)

VP 4:28
> For <u>brooch</u> 'twas bound with a bright sea-shell

VP 5:40
R
> "We think on Oscar's <u>pencilled</u> urn
> ? {Questioning "pencilled".}

Page 4: *The Wanderings of Oisin.*

VP 5:44

R
> /
> Thy name, thy kin, and thy countr<u>y</u>
> {JBY underlines the 'y' of 'country' and places an accent above
> it}
> countree

VP 5:49
L

R
> Is <u>Niam</u>, daughter of the King
> but is not| "Niam"| (Niambh)| pronounced| Neev'? as| one
> syllable?| Not Nee-am'?
> Thierna nan Oge

VP 6:54
> Clear fluted then that <u>goblin</u> rare—

VP 7:65-6	And glorious as <u>Asian</u> birds <u>At evening</u> in their rainless lands.
L&B	**why at| evening?| There are no| Birds I fancy| in any <u>rain- less</u>| parts of Asia.| Çertainly| no very| beautiful| ones.**

Niamha
  (Neeva)

Page 5: *The Wanderings of Oisin.*

VP 7:75	Young Niam, and thou shalt be <u>callen</u>
VP 8:82	Where the voice of <u>change</u> is the voice of a tune

Page 9: *The Wanderings of Oisin.*

*VP*14:191 R	Of bitterns and fish-eating <u>stoats,</u> **otters?**

Page 14: *The Wanderings of Oisin.*

VP 22:330	Across your wandering <u>ruby</u> cars

Page 15: *The Wanderings of Oisin.*

*VP*22:338	The <u>ever-winding</u> wakeful sea

Page 16: *The Wanderings of Oisin.*

VP 23:355	Of bitterns and <u>fish-eating stoats</u>!

Page 18: *The Wanderings of Oisin.*

VP 26:396 L[17]	And as they sang, the <u>painted</u> birds
	O, let us have| done with "the| <u>painted</u> birds."| [pictaeque volucres]| [Nature does <u>not</u>| "paint," — nor| "gild" either, — nor even| "silver."]
VP 27:416	A storm of birds in the <u>Asian</u> trees

Page 26: *The Wanderings of Oisin.*

re
VP 35:89   "Ay, and huge. Wheń ye have led

Page 35: *The Wanderings of Oisin.*

VP 47:9   Were we days long or hours long in riding, when rolled in a
                 <u>grisly</u> peace,

VP 48:16   Dripping and doubling landward, as though they would hasten
                 away
                 Like an army of old men longing for rest from the moan of the
                 seas
L   , {JBY probaby intends to insert the comma after "away".}

Page 37: *The Wanderings of Oisin.*

VP49:35   And, shaking the plumes of the grasses and the leaves of the
                 <u>mural</u> glen

Page 40: *The Wanderings of Oisin.*

VP 52:76   <u>Square</u> leaves of the ivy moved over us, binding us down to our
                 rest.

Page 41: *The Wanderings of Oisin.*

VP 53:89-90   Came Blanid, Mac Nessa, Cuchulin; came Fergus who feastward
                 <u>sad slunk,</u>
                 Cook Barach, the traitor; and warward, <u>the spittle on his beard</u>
                 <u>never dry,</u>

Page 44: *The Wanderings of Oisin.*

VP 55:120   But to be 'mid the <u>shooting of flies</u> and the flowering of rushes
                 and flags."

VP 55:123-4   As she murmured, "Oh, wandering Oisin, the strength of the
                  <u>bell-branch</u> is naught,
                  For moveth alive in thy fingers the <u>fluttering</u> sadness of earth.

Page 46: *The Wanderings of Oisin.*

VP 57:142-4   Grey sands on the green of the grasses and over the dripping
                  trees,
                  Dripping and doubling landward, as though they would hasten
                  away,
                  Like an army of old men longing for rest from the moan of the
                  seas.
L   {A vertical line marks the above passage, probably signalling
                  approval.}

VP 57:150   Snatching the bird <u>in secret</u>, nor knew I, embosomed apart,

VP 57:152   For Remembrance, <u>lifting her leanness</u>, keened in the gates of
                  my heart.

Page 47: *The Wanderings of Oisin.*

T   **What is a Grass-barnacle?**
                  Barnacle-goose?

VP 57:156   From the great <u>grass-barnacle</u> calling, and later the shore-weeds
                  brown.
                         /   /
VP 58:157   If I were as I once was, the gold hooves crushing the sands and
                  the shells
                  {JBY's accents over 'were' and 'once' imply, probably, a metrical
                  criticism}

Page 48: *The Wanderings of Oisin.*

VP 58:167   Awaiting in patience the <u>straw-death</u>, crosiered one, caught in
                  thy net—

Page 52: *The Wanderings of Oisin.*

1

*VP*63:222   For lonely to move 'mong the soft eyes of b^est ones a sad thing
were—
{JBY changes 'best' to 'blest'.}

Page 53: 'Time and the Witch Vivien'.

T   {JBY's sketch of a moonscape of volcanic mounds and craters
fills most of the space above the title and into the top margin,
about a quarter of the page (Plate 7)}

*VP*720:8   Hide where he will, in wave, or <u>wrinkled</u> <u>moon</u>,

R   ?   {Questioning the underlined phrase.}

B[18]

**"Sown in a wrinkle of the monstrous hill
   The city sparkles like a grain of salt . . . "**

Life of the mountains on the moon?

Page 54: 'Time and the Witch Vivien'.

VP 720:16   The <u>wrinkled</u> squanderer of human wealth

VP 720:18-20   *Time.*   Lady, I nor <u>rest</u> nor sit.
Vivien. Well then, to business; what is in your bag?
*Time (putting the bag and hour-glass on the table
      and* <u>*resting*</u> *on his scythe).*
{The underlines and an oblique line linking 'rest' and 'rest-
ing' draw attention to the contradiction.}

B   **Time and the Moon are both wrinkled.**

Page 59: 'The Stolen Child'.

VP 88:31   <u>That scarce could bathe a star,</u>

Page 62: 'Ephemera'.

VP 80:14   Fell <u>like faint meteors in the gloom</u>, and once

Page 63: 'Ephemera'.

VP 81:24c   The little waves <u>that walked in evening whiteness</u>,

Page 64-5: 'An Indian Song'.

VP 77:3   The <u>pea-hens dance</u>, in <u>crimson</u> feather
L   ?   {Questioning the underlined phrase above.}

R   (What pea-hens| are crimson?)| (Do pea-hens| dance?| even
               in| India?)

VP 77:5d-e   And Love is kindly and <u>deceitless</u>,
               And all is over save the murmur and the <u>sweetness</u>.

VP 78:17   That moans and sighs <u>a hundred days</u>;
L   ? {Questioning the underlined phrase above.}

B   "deceitless"
               "sweetness"}
               [deceitness]

Page 68: 'Kanva on Himself'.

VP 723:3   Wandering of yore in forests <u>rumorous</u>,
               Beneath the <u>flaming eyeballs</u> of the night,

                              innumerous
VP 724:6   Of <u>Rajas</u> and Mahrajas beyond number?

VP 724:8   Hast thou not known a <u>Raja</u>'s dreamless slumber?

Page 70: 'Jealousy'.

VP 72:18   *Sigh, oh ye little stars! oh, sigh and shake your <u>blue</u> apparel!*
               {Underlined roman shows JBY's underlining of printed italic}

VP 72:26   *Vijaya.*   The hour when Kama* with a <u>sumptuous</u> <u>smile</u>,
R   ?   {Questions the underlined phrase. The asterisk is in the
printed text to provide a footnote key.}

Page 71: 'Jealousy'.

VP 73:43   <u>The van of wandering quiet</u>; *ere ye be too calm and old,*
Sing, turning in your <u>cars</u>,
Sing, <u>till</u> *ye raise your hands and sigh, and o'er* <u>your</u> <u>car—heads</u>
<u>peer</u>
<u>With all your whirling hair</u>, *and* <u>drop</u> *through space* <u>an</u> *azure tear.*
Anashuya. What know the <u>pilots</u> of the stars of tears?

L   **car-heads, the heads of the cars?**
R   **(sky-pilots)** {referring to the underlined 'pilots'}

{The underlined roman represents JBY's underlining of italic,
and the hyphen in 'car-heads' has been added by JBY. The
underlinings, though fully represented above, have been partly
erased. Long inscriptions in the left and right margins have been
erased leaving only the short inscriptions transcribed above. Of
the two long inscriptions that on the right, unlike that on the
left, is written over an erasure. An attempt to reconstruct the
erased inscriptions follows. Some readings are conjectural.
Illegible letters are represented by dashes.}

L   **which heads?| whose| whirling hair?| <u>will</u> the | heads (how|
many?)| drop|
an azure| tear| between| them| And <u>why</u>|
should they (the stars at night)| Sing <u>till</u> the hands drop|
an azure tear when | they stop singing?**

R   **Do several| heads peer| (with all| (whose| -----| hair| the
stars| whirling| hair or| the heads?| or| are the| stars|
the heads?)| but do several heads peer| each car?|
The heads are the heads from|
pilots of the cars apparently ("sky- pilots").**

Page 72: 'Jealousy'.

VP 74:63   The daughter of the <u>grey old wood-cutter</u>,

VP 74:73   Of <u>aweless</u> birds, and round their <u>stirless</u> feet

VP 75:75   Who never heard the <u>unforgiving</u> hound.

Page 73: 'Jealousy'.

VP 75:90   May never-<u>restless fay with fidget finger</u>
                {JBY erroneously inserts the hyphen.}

R   **Is this Indian?**   {Questions the underlined phrase. }

Page 74: 'Song of the Last Arcadian'.

VP 65:4   Grey Truth is now her <u>painted</u> toy;
R   ? {Questions 'painted'.}

VP 65:12   Word be-mockers? —<u>By the rood</u>,

VP 65:16   In <u>the verse of Attic story</u>

Page 75: 'Song of the Last Arcadian'.

VP 66:39   Rewording in melodious <u>guile</u>

Page 76: 'Song of the Last Arcadian'.

VP 67:46b   And <u>birdly</u> iteration is

Page 77: 'King Goll'.

T   **Old King Goll**
                Erst ---- jer toll
                Oui, tout folle,
                Poor old King Goll.
                        {The second word of the second line is indecipherable}

VP 81	KING GOLL (Third Century.)
R	? {Against the title}
R	? {Against the parenthesis}

R If King Goll was| a legendary| character there| ought to be| here an| explanatory| note.| "3rd Cent."| explains| nothing, &| is an absolutely| useless| addition—(—| (absolutely| useless to the| general| reader—ut| mihi—at least)[19]

VP 81:2	Wolf-breeding mountains, galleried Eman,
L	What sort| of galleries?

VP 82:5	Chaired in a cushioned otter-skin,
L	Emania

Page 78: 'King Goll'.

VP 83:17/19 From rolling vale and rivery glen,

L What is it| happened?| What is the story| of King Goll?| (Had he anything| to do with| King Cole?) {JBY inscribes the above alongside the stanza beginning "But slowly as I shouting slew" (*VP* 83:25)}

VP 84:33	And crumpled in my hands the staff
L	crumbled?

VP 84:34-5 Of my long spear, with scream and laugh
And song that down the valleys rolled.

VP 84:38	Where summer gluts the golden bees,
R	(?) {Questioning the underlined phrase.}

VP 84:39	Or in autumnal solitudes Arise the leopard-coloured trees;
L	{A vertical line marking these lines apparently signals JBY's approval.}
B	(good)| (only what should an| Irish King of the 3rd Centy| know of the colour of| leopards?)

Page 79: 'King Goll'.

VP 84:42   The cormorants <u>shiver</u> on ther rocks
R   **<u>Cormorants</u>| don't| shiver; — | shiver my timbers| if they do.)**

VP 85:54   A tramping of tremendous feet/,
            {JBY substitutes the comma for a full stop.}

VP 85:62   With eyes of sadness <u>rose</u> to <u>hear</u>,
            (From pools and rotting leaves,) <u>me</u> sing
            {JBY inserts the brackets and links the new parenthesis with 'rose' to indicate the syntactical relation. He also deletes the comma after 'leaves'.}

Page 80: 'King Goll'.

VP 86:65   My singing sang me <u>fever-free</u>;
R   **Oh, it was a fever| was it?**
            {JBY cancels this inscription so as to make it scarcely legible.}

VP 86:69   (<u>For my remembering hour is done</u>)—
            {JBY adds the brackets}
R   **Has he| caught the| fever| again,| poor man.| Was he a sort of| Celtic Nebuchardnezzar| (or <u>was</u> he a Celt?)**
            {JBY's cancellation atttempts to make this inscription illegible}

Page 81: 'The Meditation of the Old Fisherman'.

R   **metre** {Conjectural. JBY cancels this inscription so as to make it illegible. An allusion to the strongly anapaestic metre?}
L   **X** {Against the title.}

VP 91:10   Is heard on the water, as they were, the proud and <u>apart</u>,

Page 82: 'The Ballad of Moll Magee'.

L   **X good** {against the title}

Page 85: 'The Phantom Ship'.

R   √ **good**   {against the title}

VP 718:6   Ah! <u>it dwelt within the twilight as a work within the nut.</u>

Page 86: 'The Phantom Ship'.

?

VP 718:12   See the darkness slow <u>disgorging</u> a vessel blind with <u>squall</u>

Page 87: 'The Phantom Ship'.

VP 719:25   Stands each grey and silent phantom on the same <u>regardless</u>
spot—

L   ? {Questions 'regardless'.}

VP 719:30   Then <u>the stars grow out of heaven</u> with their countenances fair.

?

VP 719:32-34   Prayed those <u>forgotten</u> fishers, till in the eastern skies
Came olive fires of morning and <u>on the darkness fed,</u>

-

By the slow^heaving ocean—<u>mumbling mother of the dead.</u>
{JBY interpolates the question mark and the hyphen.}

Page 91: *Mosada*.

R   **Good**   {Against the title.}

Page 94: *Mosada*.

/

VP 693:64   <u>And spiders are my friends; I'm theirs, and they are</u>
R   **metre** {Cancelled. The accent over 'they' may be a substitute
for this marginal note.}

Page 99: *Mosada*.

VP 698:51   Who giveth to the golden-crested wren
                Her hanging mansion. Give to me, I pray,
L?   {Cancelled. Probably in favour of the sketch below.}

B   {Sketch of a wren's nest, showing the bird's tiny 'mansion' rest-
                ing in a crotch between branches, rather than 'hanging'.}

Page 100: *Mosada*.

VP 699:4   That rustles in the reeds with patient pushes,

Page 101: *Mosada*.

VP 700:40   The burghers of the night fade one by one.
B²⁰
                There is no appropriateness to the person or the occasion|
                in this "burghers-of-the-night" applied to the stars.|
                It is only a most unnecessary variant of|
                "sentries of the night" (which would of course|
                be equally inappropriate here), 'Burghers' don't fade.

Page 103: *Mosada*.

VP 702:75   Dear heart, there is a secret way that leads

VP 702:77   Where lies a shallop in the yellow reeds.

Page 106: 'How Ferencz Renyi Kept Silent'.

L   **X Good (but rather spoilt)** {Against the title.}

VP 709:5   Libations, from the Hungary of the West.
R   **(Libations to| the thirsty| wld be| more| appropriate)**

VP 709:8   The Austrian Haynau he, in many lands

VP 709:11   Schoolmaster he, a dreamer, fiddler, first

In every dance, by children sought.   "Accurst⁄!
{JBY changes comma to exclamation mark.}

Page 107: 'How Ferencz Renyi Kept Silent'.

T   ? Hiding the <u>rebel worms</u> in yonder wood|
                    ? Hiding the <u>rebels</u> (<u>Worm</u>!) in yonder wood|
                    ? Hiding the rebels, worm (verb, imperat: "do thou|
                    worm" -- i.e. "hide like a worm")|
                       in yonder wood."
                    ?
VP 709:14   <u>Hiding the rebels 'worm' in yonder wood</u>
                    {JBY adds the quotation and question marks.}
L   (grammar?)
R   rebel swarm?
R   Hiding the rebels (who),| worm ('who do worm'.|
                    'worm' being a verb,| 3ʳᵈ person pl. pres.)| in yonder wood.|

R   "The rebels, -- | hiding, -- (do)| 'worm' in| yonder| wood."

VP 710:19   Flashing and flickering with e̶v̶e̶r̶-undulant wing,
                    {JBY deletes 'ever' and inserts the final comma.}
L   (metre?)   {The question applies to the above line.}

VP 710:21-4 The doves whose <u>growing forms</u> he'd watched. Not these
                                                        old
                    <u>He numbers. He a brown^farm house sees,</u>
                    Where shadow of cherry, and [s̶h̶a̶d̶o̶w̶] of apple trees,
                             /   /   /   /   /
                    Enclose a quiet place [of beds] box-bordered, bees,
                    {At the left, JBY joins the above 4 lines with a brace. He inter-
                    polates 'old', the bracketing and deletion of 'shadow', the brack-
                    eting of 'of beds' and the accents, as indicated above. He also
                    adds the following comments below.}
R   (metre?)   {Against line 22}
R   (?-)   {Against line 23}
R   (Alexandrine) {Against line 24}

VP 710:29   With berries. <u>Placid</u> as <u>a homeward bee</u>,
R   (<u>Are</u> homeward bees| placid?)

VP 710:30   Glad, simple—nay, he sought not mystery
R   (Why should he?)

VP 710:33   Why those who do good often be not good/;
                    {JBY changes the final comma to a semi-colon.}

VP 711:35   Clogged in a marsh where the slow marsh-clay clings,—
                    {JBY adds the hyphen and the final dash.}

VP 711:36   Abolished by a mire of little things,—
                    {JBY adds the dash.}

               Page 108: 'How Ferencz Renyi Kept Silent'.

T   **Support his lameness upon death? How?**
               What is the meaning of a man turning death into a crutch?
VP 711:35   Were here, he would turn death into a crutch;
R   ?

VP 711:39   But this one--this one.
                         Now his head drops low,
L   ? {Questioning the first half-line.}

VP 711:40   Drops on his bosom, sombre, moist and slow.
R   ? What is| moist| & slow?| The Head| drops slow(ly)|
               I suppose.| The Bosom| (or head?) is| sombre—|
               or the head| drops| sombre(ly)?| The Head|
               (or the| bosom?)| is moist? or the| head| drops| moist(ly)?

VP 711:54   The soldier thus/; and Haynau— 'Peasant/ ! speak
               {JBY changes the first comma to a semi-colon and the second
               one to an exclamation mark}

               Page 109: 'How Ferencz Renyi Kept Silent'.

VP 713:82   Like small brown moths, a tremble.
L   (!?)

VP 713:83   Where worm the rebels, or my bullets lay
R   ("worm" plainly| is a verb,| after all)

Page 110-11: 'How Ferencz Renyi Kept Silent'.

VP 713:82	Assassin, my assassin! thou who let'st me die,
L	**(metre?)** {Against the above, unchanged line.}

VP 714:109	With quiet shade its ever-dewy-plot.
	{JBY adds the first hyphen and deletes the second.}

B	**Assasin! Mine! O thou who let'st me die,**

VP 715:112	Creeping along the heavens' <u>purple cup</u>,

VP 715:117	Haynau, thine hour has come, <u>thy followers far</u>
	<u>Beside the willow</u>.
R	**(What a fool!)**

VP 715:119	Yon <u>bauble of the heavens</u>, he lifts his hands,

Page 123: 'The Fairy Pedant'.

VP 708:21	O shining ones, lightly with <u>song pass</u>,

VP 708:23	My mother drew forth from the <u>long grass</u>

VP 708:26	<u>Of</u> birds even, longings for aery

Page 124: 'The Fairy Pedant'.

VP 708:26	Come away while the moon's in the <u>woodland</u>,
	Though the youngest of all in our <u>good band</u>,

Page 125: 'She Who Dwelt Among the Scycamores'.

VP 715:2	Saw on the wood's edge gleam an ash-grey <u>feather</u>/;
	{Here and below, JBY's line under 'feather' is continued obliquely upward. He may be drawing attention to the rhyme.}

*VP*715:6-7	Followed a ring-dove's ash-grey gleam of <u>feather</u>/.
	Noon wrapt the trees in veils of violet <u>weather</u>,

Page 127: 'A Legend'.

R   X   {against the title}

Page 128: 'A Legend'.

VP 725:26-8   A cock came by upon his toes;
              An old horse looked across a fence,
              And rubbed along the rail his nose
L   {A vertical line marking this passage may signal JBY's approval
              of it.}

Page 133: 'To An Isle in the Water'.

VP 89:5-6   She carries in the dishes,
              And lays them in a row
L   ? {Quesions the above lines.}

VP 89:13-14   And shy as a rabbit
              Helpful and shy.

Page 134-5: 'Quatrains and Aphorisms'.

              {Uniquely, these pages are marked in brown crayon}
Page 135

VP 734:1   The child who chases lizards in the grass
R   >   {Against the above line}

VP 734:11   Not even 'I long to see thy longing over,'
R   >   {Against the above line}

VP 734:13   The ghosts went by with their lips apart

Page 135

T&R[21]   {The partly-erased, very faint outline of a woman's face in which
              the lips and hair are the prominent features.}

VP 735:17-18   This heard I where, amid the apples trees,
                  Wild indolence and music have no date,
L   >   {Placed between these lines, though it may refer to the first
                  of them.}

VP   735:21 "Around, the twitter of the lips of dust,
               {The inverted commas are deleted and the final comma added,
               both in ink.}
L   >   {An uncertainly formed mark placed after the above line.}

VP   735:21 In the deep alcove's dimness smiles and hides"
               {The inverted commas are deleted in ink.}

B   {The inscription in the bottom margin appears to be an additional (parodic?) quatrain. It has been vigorously erased. Readings are conjectural. Illegible letters are represented by dashes.}

> --- heard I where --- ---- critic ----- |
--- ---- --- ----- ---- --- judge |
--- --gh-- upon ----- ---d --- of your |
To -- --- ---- or good --- budge

Page 156: *The Island of Statues.*

{A small pencil mark, possibly accidental, after the last line of WBY's printed text.}

NOTES

1.   Richard Landon, Director of the Rare Books and Special Collections at the University of Toronto was most helpful from the very beginning of the preparation of this article; Gayle Garlock is editor of *Halcyon: The Newsletter of the Friends of the Thomas Fisher Rare Book Library*, in which (No.18, November 1996) a shorter version appeared; for *The Halcyon* Maureen Morin produced digital images which she has kindly allowed *YA* to reproduce; D. I. Alexander, Paul Beidler, Gretchen Beidler, Dino Felluga, Jerome McGann and Jane Millgate helped me with the scouting of quotations, and George Rigg recognised Virgil; John O'Neill of the Art Gallery of Ontario and Emrys Evans of the Thomas Fisher Library helped with the decipherment of JBY's erasures; and the staff of the Thomas Fisher Library have been unfailing not only in their courtesy but their keen interest—I thank all of them most cordially.

2. William M. Murphy, *Prodigal Father: the Life of John Butler Yeats* (Ithaca: Cornell University Press, 1978), p. 161.

3. *Ibid.*, JBY to John Quinn, April 1919.

4. WBY to John Quinn, 30 November 1921, quoted in B. L. Reid, *The Man from New York and his Friends* (New York: Oxford University Press, 1968), pp. 493-94.

5. *The Poems of Tennyson in three volumes*, edited Christopher Ricks, (London: Longman, 1987), II, p. 493.

6. 'One night a quarrel over Ruskin came to such a height that in putting me out of the room he broke the glass in a picture with the back of my head' (*Mem* 19).

7. In 'Stories of Michael Robartes and his Friends', WBY's late, fantastic story about an ornithologist who would teach cuckoos how to build nests, might be found an *amende* for this youthful aberration (*A V B* 46-49).

8. They are partially legible but it required the Art Gallery of Ontario's x-ray equipment and close scrutiny by three of us—John O'Neill, Emrys Evans and me—to completely decipher them.

9. JBY to Edward Dowden, 7 January 1884. See J. B. Yeats, *Letters to his Son W.B. Yeats and Others: 1869-1922,* ed. Joseph Hone (London: Faber & Faber, 1944), p. 53.

10. The poem was reprinted in *Poems and Ballads of Young Ireland* (1888, 1890, 1903) and *A Celtic Christmas* (1898) (*Wade* 279-80, 330).

11. See *YA4* pl 16, *L* 705 and *Prodigal Father*, p. 573. The illustration also accompanied the poem when it was reprinted in *A Celtic Christmas* in December 1898. See *Wade* 330.

12. Rather curiously, WBY writes, on 1 August 1889 to Laurence Housman that 'Two or three of the shorter poems, by the way, were written to illustrations of my fathers which were printed with them in one or two magazines' (*CLI* 177n). The only poem to which this seems to apply at all is 'King Goll', but it was not 'written to' JBY's illustration.

13. See Frank Kinahan, 'A Source Note on "The Madness of King Goll"', *YA* 4, 189-194.

14. *Prodigal Father*, pp. 234-5.

15. For the details of publication I am indebted to John S. Kelly, 'Books and Numberless Dreams: Yeats's Relations with his Early Publishers', in *Yeats, Sligo and Ireland*, ed. A. Norman Jeffares (Gerrards Cross: Colin Smythe, 1980), pp. 232-253.

16. (a)   'The dew . . .' appears in 'The Lord of the Isles', canto 1, st. 3 by Sir Walter Scott (1771-1832). Edith, the Maid of Lorn, on her wedding day, is being urged by minstrels to wake and so allow her beauty to match Nature's, which, at the moment, is ahead of hers. See *The Poetical Works of Sir Walter Scott*, edited J. Logie Robertson (London: Oxford University Press, 1908), p.413.
(b)   'And the bright dew-bead . . . ' appears in Part One of 'The Omnipresence of The Deity' by Robert Montgomery (1807-55). At this point in the poem, Montgomery is describing a transition from storm to calm weather. See Robert Montgomery, *The Omnipresence of The Deity: A Poem*, 13th edition, revised and enlarged (London: Simpkin and Marshall, 1834), p. 48.

17. The phrase, meaning 'ornate birds', is from the *Aeneid* IV, 525.

18. Lines 19-20 of 'Will' by Alfred, Lord Tennyson. See n. 5 above.

19.   As WBY may not have known, 'ut mihi' is short for 'ut mihi videtur', meaning 'as it seems to me.'
20.   JBY may possibly have in mind the angels who 'watch as winged sentries all the night' in 'An Orphan's Family Christmas' by Gerald Massey (1828-18??), or perhaps the (human) 'sentry of the Night' in 'The Tower of Babel' by Alfred Austin (1835-1913).
21.   The face of Niam in the frontispiece done by Edwin Ellis for *The Wanderings of Oisin: Dramatic Sketches Ballads & Lyrics* 1892 (*Wade* 3) is curiously reminiscent of the sketch on this page.

Variant Covers of *The Secret Rose*

Virginia Hyde

BECAUSE *THE SECRET ROSE* (1897) has one of the most famous bindings in a decade of spectacular bindings—dark-blue stamped in gold with an ornate tree design—it is surprising to see variant cloths of red and brown, but both exist. A newly-discovered copy bound in brilliant magenta red in the Holland Library of Washington State University,[1] possesses a cover that does not fit the standard description of *Wade* 21, and joins two other copies of the book with non-standard covers listed in App. 5 of *The Secret Rose, Stories by W. B. Yeats: A Variorum Edition* (1992), p. 276 n. 20. These are another magenta copy in the D. W. Weldon Library, the University of Western Ontario,[2] and a brown copy (with a slight rust cast) in the Harry Ransom Humanities Research Center, the University of Texas at Austin.[3] All three of the variant copies are bound in ribbed cloth.[4] All bear the date 1897. The publisher's name on the spines, 'Lawrence and Bullen', shows that all were created before the dissolution of this publishing firm in late 1900, which resulted in subsequently bound copies bearing the name 'A. H. Bullen' (see *Wade* pp. 41-42).

Like the standard, published copies, all three variants bear the distinctive cover design depicting a cabbalistic (and biblical) tree of life, created by the Irish artist, Althea Gyles, whom Yeats knew in London.[5] This design is familiar to some readers who have never seen the original cover because several Yeats studies have reproduced it.[6] While Gyles was not a member of the Hermetic Order of the Golden Dawn (as Yeats was), she was clearly aware of some of its symbolism. The tree, with its roots entwined in the skeleton of a dead knight and its crown displaying three roses (echoing the central rose that represents a 'rosy cross' at the tree's 'heart'), is composed of Celtic interlace that culminates in an image of kissing lovers. The standard copy possesses continuous decoration, completed by the back design of the alchemical rose, a rose-cross contained in a diamond-like configuration of pointed spears and a circle, thus a 'squared circle'. But the WSU and Western Ontario variants, while they have the standard decorated spines, lack the back design, as do all the copies for the American market,[7] suggesting that all may have been printed very early, possibly before the lower-board design was available.

Washington State processed its book in 1974 while Western Ontario received its copy after the 1933 death of the donor Rufus Hathaway, a well-known Toronto book collector and author of articles on rare books. The Texas copy, part of the extensive Yeats collection (perhaps the largest ever) assembled by the bibliographer William Matson Roth, came to the HRHRC in 1949-50. The Roth copy's binding, aside from its colour, is otherwise standard; internally, however, it is the most unusual of the three books, lacking all seven of the illustrations by John Butler Yeats, despite the fact that the title page, like those of other copies, calls attention to the illustrations: *THE SECRET ROSE | BY W. B. YEATS, WITH | ILLUSTRATIONS BY J. B. | YEATS*. Lacking these plates, the book has none of the slightly dual effect created in standard copies between the highly symbolic art of the cover and the relatively more realistic work of J. B. Yeats, modulated though it is to accommodate its myth-like subjects. But it is hardly likely that the book was contemplated without the inside plates, which in standard copies were tipped in after binding and were possibly unavailable when this sample was bound. When the book was acquired by the HRHRC, it was listed as an early 'trade book'; but neither Wade nor Roth, in his *A Catalogue of English and American First Editions of William Butler Yeats*,[8] lists a trade copy with a brown binding. More significantly, the title page's reference to the J. B. Yeats illustrations would surely have been removed if the book had been intended for sale without them.

All three variants are evidently the publishers' trial copies, not reflecting Yeats's own colour choices. While there is no extant record of his colour preference before publication, he later found the dark-blue binding of *The Secret Rose* a model. A year and a half after its publication, when he disliked a 'proof' for the cover of *The Wind Among the Reeds*

(1899), he wrote to publisher Elkin Mathews, 'The colour should be the same dark blue as my "Secret Rose"'; moreover, he later wrote to Mathews to say how pleased he was with the blue cover that was eventually used on the published *The Wind Among the Reeds*.[9] Even in 1927, when expressing a preference for the cover of *The Stories of Red Hanrahan and the Secret Rose* (with illustrations by Norah McGuinness), the Yeatses chose 'the darkest blue—a fine colour in itself' (*VSR* 284). Since 'Rosa Alchemica' refers to 'Dante in the dull red of his anger' (*VSR* 127), Yeats, in London at the relevant time, might well have 'seen red' when inspecting the trial bindings of *The Secret Rose*. Though there is no surviving evidence, he was in London at the time and in close contact with Bullen and it would be unusual if he had not looked at trial bindings. Yet his covers were often far more diverse in appearance than readers imagine,[10] and Allen Wade even confessed despair at 'ever keeping track of the variant bindings of W. B. Yeats's earlier books' (*Wade* 58).

Notes

1. Hereafter WSU. I gratefully acknowledge the assistance of John Guido and Leila Luedeking at the E. O. Holland Library of Washington State University; John Lutman and John Martin at the D. B. Weldon Library of the University of Western Ontario; Cathy Henderson and Barbara LaBorde at the Harry Ransom Humanities Research Center of the University of Texas at Austin; and Thomas Taylor, dealer in rare books, Austin, Texas.

2. See Steven Winnett and Beth Miller, 'Addenda to *Wade*. Item 21: *The Secret Rose*', *The Canadian Association for Irish Studies Newsletter* 5 (November 1974).

3. All three are designated by the Library of Congress numbering system as follows: WSU: PR 5904 .S3 1897 HOL; Western Ontario: PR 5904 .S3 1897 DBW SPE; Texas: PR 5904 .S3 1897 HRC. The WSU copy bears the book plate of one Paul Steinbrecher. In the inside cover of the Western Ontario copy is a handwritten note, evidently by Hathaway, about the book's red colour (which he believed was characteristic of an entire issue). The Texas copy contains pencilled notes, possibly by Victor Reynolds (whose name is also pencilled in with the date 'April 26, 1901') or by a bookseller, stating that the book is rare because of its brown colour and lack of plates. An additional pencilled note in another hand, probably a bookseller's, refers specifically to the 'Publisher's Trial Binding'. The Roth purchase included items belonging to Olivia Shakespear (see Warwick Gould, 'Books by W. B. Yeats in Olivia Shakespear's Library', *YA9* 295-308), and one WSU holding, a 1973 purchase from the bookseller Thomas Taylor, was traced to her family (see Wayne K. Chapman, 'The Annotated *Responsibilities*: Errors in the *Variorum Edition* and a New Reading of the Genesis of Two Poems', *YA6* 129-30); but these copies of *The Secret Rose* are apparently not connected with her. I am indebted to Thomas Taylor of Austin, Texas, for information in a letter to me of 1993.

4. Ribbed cloth was used for the first issue (blue) of the first state bindings, and is found on Yeats's presentation copies, eg., those to George Pollexfen and Olivia Shakespear. See *VSR* 263 and *YA9* 299. Subsequently, a finer, smooth blue cloth was used.

5. See Yeats's 1898 essay on Gyles's art, 'A Symbolic Artist and the Coming of Symbolic Art' (*UP2* 132-137), his 1900 note on her for an anthology (*P&I* 118), and a prose sketch of her (unnamed) in *Au* 411-412. See also the account of her in *CL2* 680-83, and Ian Fletcher, 'Poet and Designer, W. B. Yeats and Althea Gyles' in Robert O'Driscoll and Lorna Reynolds (eds.), *Yeats Studies: an International Journal* 1 (Bealtaine 1971), 42-79.

6. Besides *VSR*, pl. 1, see Fletcher, *loc. cit.,* p. 59; Richard Ellmann, *The Identity of Yeats* (London: Macmillan, 1954; Faber and Faber, 1965), p. 65 (redrawn by Mary Gelb); *The World of W. B. Yeats: Essays in Perspective,* ed. Robin Skelton and Ann Saddlemyer (Dublin: Dolmen, 1965), pl. 3 & pp. 152-7; Richard J. Finneran, *The Prose Fiction of W. B. Yeats: The Search for 'Those Simple Forms'* (Dublin: Dolmen Press, 1973), pl. 1, showing a copy of the 2nd issue, with 'A. H. Bullen' on the spine; A. Norman Jeffares, *W. B. Yeats: A New Biography* (London: Hutchinson, 1988), p. 90; and Wayne K. Chapman, *W. B. Yeats and English Renaissance Literature* (London: Macmillan, 1991), pl. 7. See also descriptions by Jacqueline Genet, 'Villiers de L'Isle Adam and W. B. Yeats', in *Yeats the European,* ed. A. Norman Jeffares (Savage, Maryland: Barnes and Noble, 1989), pp. 63-64; Steven Putzel, *Reconstructing Yeats:* The Secret Rose *and* The Wind Among the Reeds (Dublin: Gill and Macmillan; Totowa, N. J.: Barnes and Noble, 1986), pp. 22-25; William H. O'Donnell, *A Guide to the Prose Fiction of W. B. Yeats* (Ann Arbor: UMI Research Press, 1983), pp. 90-91.

7. The standard copies for the American market (with Dodd, Mead & Co. named on the spine) were bound (probably in London) in ribbed blue cloth and had cancel titles.

8. New Haven: 1939.

9. See *CL2*, 279-80, 402, cf. James G. Nelson, *Elkin Mathews: Publisher to Yeats, Joyce, Pound* (Madison: University of Wisconsin Press, 1989), 78.

10. *The Tables of the Law. | The Adoration of the Magi.*, privately printed by Bullen in 1897 after he had excluded these two stories from *The Secret Rose,* was printed in an edition of 110 copies, bound in red buckram, while *Stories of Red Hanrahan and the Secret Rose* (1927), despite Yeats's preference for gold on blue, was also issued more cheaply in red cloth, with the design and lettering in blue. This issue has the undeserved reputation of being rare.

W. B. Yeats and *The Oxford Magazine*

Declan D. Kiely

THE OXFORD MAGAZINE was established in 1883 and enjoyed an impressively long and distinguished run as a University journal until its demise in the summer of 1973.[1] Its principal interest for students of Yeats lies in the fact that during his lifetime thirteen reviews of his work were published there, only two of which have been previously recorded.[2] The *Magazine* also published reviews of plays by Yeats, Synge, Lady Gregory, and other Irish playwrights, which were performed by the Abbey company during visits to Oxford, as well as providing a record of some of Yeats's activities during his periods of residence in Oxford, including details of his Presidency of the Oxford Branch of the English Association for the year 1921-1922.

The first issue of *The Oxford Magazine* appeared on 24 January 1883, and it was published weekly during term thereafter. It was founded upon somewhat vague literary intentions following the example set by *The Cambridge Review* (which preceded it in 1879), and in response to what were perceived to be the widening interests of the University at this time. The founders were Richard Lodge, a young History don at Brasenose, and Thomas Herbert Warren of Magdalen. Lodge was its first editor and in its earliest days editing and writing were unpaid activities. The initial success of the *Magazine* was due to the way in which it quickly established an audience among undergraduates and dons. It was later 'widely read outside the University'.[3] Another factor in its success must be attributed to the brilliance and determination of some of the other founding figures, which included D. S. MacColl, J. W. Mackail, Percy Matheson, Oliver Elton, Michael Sadler, and Anthony Hope Hawkins.[4]

As Arthur Quiller-Couch, another of its early contributors and later Assistant Editor, noted in his letter published in the Diamond Jubilee issue of the *Magazine*, 'the careers of bright university journals are notoriously brief'.[5] Despite its longevity and apparent robustness, *The Oxford Magazine* cannot be said to have flourished consistently. There were times when it teetered on the brink of being a lost cause, particularly in the period following the First World War when circulation fell and production costs increased.[6] The *Magazine*'s prestige and visibility were also eclipsed, to a certain extent, by the advent of *The Oxford Outlook* and *The Oxford Review* in the 1920s. It operated as a limited company from 1898 until 1921. T. H. Warren, President of Magdalen, had been elected Chairman of Directors.[7] A watchful eye was kept on the fortunes of the whole enterprise and it was the enduring interest and care of its first editors which provided the *Magazine* with the necessary continuity and stability required in its vulnerable early years. At no point in its history could it have been considered an undergraduate production. It secured a circulation among the dons because from the outset the book reviews were contributed 'by persons of authority'.[8] For instance, Warren had enlisted J. A. Symonds, and among other notable early reviewers were W. P. Ker, Arthur Sidgwick and Walter Pater.[9] In 1948 it was observed that 'it may not be commonly known that the Editors of the paper during the time it was published at the [University] Press were all Dons, and it was printed to air their views. The only undergraduate contributors were the writers of College Notes, the sporting articles, and an occasional poem.'[10] The reviews of Yeats's work are of more interest since they reflect not the undergraduate reception but the more sophisticated and learned response of members[11] of the Oxford academic community, albeit a response perhaps initiated by some discreet log-rolling.

The first attention paid to Yeats's work occurred only in passing within a review of the third issue of the *Dublin University Review* which included Act I, scene 1 of 'The Island of Statues'. Yeats is not referred to by name and his 'Arcadian Faery Tale in heroic verse, of which only one scene is given, does not strike us as yet as very happy: Colin and Thernot speak in the metre of Gay; but their euphuism is as the euphuism of the Victorian minor poets, and that needs no further comment'.[12] Nevertheless, any kind of notice was a tribute, and one in which his father's Oxford friends, such as Oliver Elton and York Powell,[13] might have begun to exert some influence.

The evidence is apparent in the anonymous *Oxford Magazine* notice of *The Celtic Twilight*, which is probably the work of York Powell.

It is not an easy thing to write of Ireland, and yet absolutely and altogether avoid politics. Mr. Yeats, however, has done this thing, for which reason his book is a pure joy, and loyalists and nationalists alike may join in its praise. Mr. Yeats knows his people in all their moods, and has the native power of changing from grave to gay as he will. Indeed he would have us believe that he too has seen what the grosser Saxon eye may never see, and tells his tale with a belief that might convert even a scientific professor. Whether he is writing of brides or babes carried off to 'the bloodless land of Faery; happy enough, but doomed to melt out at the last judgement like bright vapour, for the soul cannot live without sorrow'; or of Paddy Flynn, whom the gift of a large bottle of whisky 'filled with a great enthusiasm,' so that 'he lived upon it for some days and then died,' Mr. Yeats is always delightful. Fain would we say more of his people, real and unreal, of 'the woman of the log and Clooth-na-bare,' of whom it is written that 'the great winds came and took them up unto themselves,' and of 'Zozimus,' eponymous hero of short-lived comic papers, whose pictures we have ourselves beheld on the Dublin quays; but it may not be. One story we must quote, and then leave our readers to seek further for themselves. A prisoner was defending himself on the ground 'not unknown in Ireland, that some heads are so thin you cannot be responsible for them. Having turned with a look of passionate contempt towards the solicitor who was prosecuting, and cried, "that little fellow's skull if ye were to hit it would go like and egg-shell," he beamed upon the judge, and said in a wheedling voice, "but a man might wallop away at your lordship's for a fortnight."'[14]

The last quotation is from 'The Thick Skull of the Fortunate' (*Myth* 95-6), Yeats's tale about the hammer-resistant skull of the Icelandic bard Egil Skalla-Grimsson (d. c. 990 AD) who was so menacing and irritable that he became subject of an Icelandic saga.[15] In a letter of 21 April 1899 Powell compared Yeats to Egil, who had evidently become something of a shared allusion. Claiming that *The Wind Among the Reeds* would 'assuredly live', Powell averred that Yeats had 'the gift of immortality in your hands, as far as immortality goes in this world. Your songs will live as long as this English speech endures. Like Egil you may have your quarrel with the Lord of Hosts . . . but . . . you may say he has given you a great gift of song—lyric song: and like Egil you will feel that he had few greater gifts to bestow upon those he loved best' (*CL2* 400-01n.).

The Land of Heart's Desire 'as we might have expected a work of this kind coming from Mr. Yeats would be' is characterised as 'a pleasant fairy fancy', though some perplexity is expressed over 'the exact significance of the massive-waisted female, and of the black and white marks, which adorn the cover', a comment on Beardsley's design—the only *Oxford Magazine* comment on the cover design of a Yeats book.

The enthusiastic reviewer of *The Secret Rose* was only too ready to pad out his review with extended quotations before concluding abruptly and with cryptic self-satisfaction that 'some such things may need interpreters, but they have a voice for those who know'.[16] The reviewer of *Poems* found the content 'too vague and unordered for the permanent pleasure of any class of readers' but discovered that there is 'in this highly visionary poetry . . . a real cry of the human spirit'.[17] Yeats's large claim for *Cuchulain of Muirthemne* is doubted by the confused reviewer while 'it appears to us that scholars will not care for an eclectic edition of these legends, and that the ordinary reader, in this country, will not care for the book as a story'.[18]

Yeats had lectured in Oxford in May 1902 at the St. John's College Essay Society and subsequently reported to Lady Gregory that 'a number of persons of mature years, whom I afterwards discovered to be Dons, asked me a number of commonplace questions' *CL3* 185).[19] Shortly after this Yeats wrote a letter to the *Times Literary Supplement* taking issue with John Churton Collins (Professor of English at Birmingham from 1904) over a reading of Blake and put on the record his 'opinion that many a cultivated woman without learning is more right about these matters than all the professors'.[20] Yeats's antipathy was, therefore, well-established by the time he wrote the unflattering lines on 'The Scholars' (*VP* 337) who 'cough in ink' and 'wear the carpet with their shoes'; the repeated 'All' in line 7 and at the beginning of lines 8-10 registers a far more emphatic dismissal of dons. It is unlikely that Yeats's opinion would have been reversed if he had read some of the reviews of his work which appeared over a period of fifty-five years in *The Oxford Magazine*.

Many of the reviews until 1919 had been short and filled out with quotations rather than analysis, and there was an interval of well over a decade before Yeats's work was noticed again, this time with increased bafflement. The review of *Per Amica Silentia Lunae* begins: "The higher flights of Mr. Yeats's "perfervid genius" are baffling to the unitiated [sic]' and concludes by admitting that 'the average reader will get lost, but he will be left with a haunting feeling that it is his own fault and not Mr. Yeats's.' The work is appreciated for possessing 'some profound observations, passages of great literary beauty, and much quiet humour'. The reviewer of *The Wild Swans at Coole* is, like Middleton Murry, disappointed with the volume: 'Mr. Yeats's philosophy is vague and is wearing rather thin; and the diction is rougher than it used to be.'[21] He looks forward to the volume of new plays promised in the Preface and 'shall welcome it the more heartily, in the hope that through this congenial medium the poet we seem to be in danger of losing may reveal himself once more.' *The Cutting of an Agate* is altogether more pleasing: 'Mr. Yeats's prose . . . gives no hint of falling off'. The essay on Spenser is picked out for special praise while observing that 'these random papers are bound together by a unity of beauty and principle with those which take Ireland as their defined subject; while Mr. Synge's work and personality pervade the whole so perceptibly that they form a fitting memorial'.

Nearly a decade later *The Oxford Magazine* returned its attention to Yeats who, 'now that Mr. Hardy is dead . . . is probably the greatest living writer of English poetry'. This high praise comes with a reservation, however, because it can 'hardly be maintained that *The Tower* is on the same level as *The Countess Cathleen* or that splendid volume *The Wild Swans at Coole*'. This reviewer is perceptive in his comments about the unity of the volume: 'There are here about twenty lyric poems, all formally independent, but bound together very closely by their theme—the ordering of life for old-age'. The later verse of Yeats is appreciated as being 'far finer than his earlier, both in depth and seriousness.' The drawback to this is 'that obscurity has come with depth, and what is worse—symbolism'. This criticism is offset by a recognition of a perfected style which is 'all lucidity and directness, often almost brutal directness'. At this time Macmillan began to advertise Yeats's books in the pages of the *Magazine*. These were usually placed for two to three weeks and often included brief extracts from reviews which had appeared in other publications. *The Tower*, *The Winding Stair*, *Collected Poems* (1933), *Wheels and Butterflies*, *Collected Plays* (1934), *A Full Moon in March*, *Dramatis Personae*, *The Oxford Book of Modern Verse* and *Last Poems and Plays* were all advertised prior to or immediately following their publication.[22]

The short review of *Dramatis Personae*, subsumed in a review of several other books, is rather incompetent. Yeats's account of 'the difficulties encountered [by the Irish National Theatre Movement] seem incomprehensible and unnecessary to the English mind' but there is 'a generous sketch of Lady Grigour' [sic]. Stuart Hampshire's review of *The Oxford Book of Modern Verse* does not differ in its estimate of Yeats's editing from those of most other reviews of the book at the time.[23] The final review divided its attention between *Last Poems and Plays* and *Scattering*

Branches but concentrates on the latter. It concludes favourably that 'some of the pieces here, like 'The Wild Old Wicked Man' and the 'Fierce Horsemen' ['Three Songs to the One Burden'], are as fine as anything he ever wrote'.

The reviews of plays performed by the Irish National Theatre Society (always referred to as 'The Irish Players' in the *Magazine*) show a much more informed awareness of the objectives of the literary theatre movement than of Yeats's poetry. The Abbey players were always extremely welcome in Oxford, providing some relief from 'the usual diet of musical dullnesses or laughless and lifeless comedies and farces supplied by most English theatres.'[24] According to the reviews published in *The Oxford Magazine* almost every visit of the Company was a great success.[25] Plays by Lady Gregory, Synge, Boyle and St. John Ervine were always more popular with audiences than Yeats's, but his nevertheless did not fail to impress and were invariably appreciated for their 'poetic grandeur' which left audiences 'breathless and enthralled.'

The Oxford Magazine records that Yeats served as successor to John Masefield as President of the Oxford Branch of the English Association during the 1921-22 academic year after he had 'allowed himself to be nominated for the office'.[26] Yeats addressed the Association as its President on 2 December 1921 in the Hall of Oriel College but there is no report of proceedings in the subsequent issue.[27] Yeats chaired the two meetings which followed in the Hilary and Summer terms, arranging a lecture by Laurence Binyon on 'Tradition and Re-actions in Modern Poetry' which took place on 17 February 1922, and a lecture by Professor Ernest de Selincourt on 'Thomas Fuller'.[28] During this period Yeats also made a memorable contribution to the Oxford Union debate on the motion 'That this House would welcome complete Self Government in Ireland, and condemns reprisals'. After several speakers the *Magazine* records that

> Mr. W.B. Yeats, who was very well received by the House, immediately gave expression to his feelings on the Irish question. He gave an oration rather than a debating speech, holding the attention of the House by the manner in which he passionately extolled Sinn Fein justice, denounced the Prussianism of the 'Black and Tans,' and appealed to the England of Gladstone and Disraeli. We have never heard so full a speech delivered in seven minutes.[29]

On 1 June 1933, the *Oxford Magazine* noted that Yeats was due to appear on the following Monday evening of 5 June in the Taylor Institute, where he would 'read his poems and discuss his writings before a meeting of the English Club', but did not subsequently report the event. The *Oxford Mail*, however, printed a photograph of Yeats with some members of the group which had organised the event on its front page (Plate 9). The report noted that 'in spite of the hot weather a large crowd filled the theatre of the Taylorian Institute'. They were treated to what seems to have been a fairly general lecture in which Yeats talked about his influences and the evolution of his style. He remarked upon the influence of Shelley on his early work and his 'desire for simplicity and a desire to introduce the scenes of my own country' into his poetry. Yeats read "The Lake Isle of Innisfree", and commented wryly that he would not give the name of the small island to which the poem referred 'since tourists had already identified it to their own satisfaction'. There was little that needed explaining in this poem 'except that the words "purple glow" refer to the reflection of the heather in the water'. The article reported that Yeats also 'dealt with the influence of religion upon his poems, and how he once made a shrine at which he might make offerings.'[30] After this he told how 'he was influenced by realism', and 'read a number of poems to illustrate the different types of influence'.[31]

Derek Patmore recalls Yeats's visit to Oxford for the purpose of delivering this lecture in *Private History: an Autobiography* (1960). His account contains an amusing anecdote about Yeats's preparations for the lecture. Excusing himself from the cocktail party, which Richard Rumbold had arranged for him, on the grounds that 'I always like to be quiet before I lecture', Yeats withdrew to his rooms in one of the towers of Christ Church. When Patmore and Rumbold returned to collect Yeats some time later in order to take him to the Taylorian Institute, they 'found him sitting in a darkened room apparently lost in thoughts of his own. He had dressed and was wearing a somewhat old-fashioned tail-coat, but Richard and I were horrified to see that his dressing left much to be desired. He had put on his clothes oblivious of buttons and other tiresome details which make English evening clothes such an unnecessary nuisance, and all his trouser buttons were undone. But neither of us dared comment upon this fact, and hoped that Yeats would see what was wrong and arrange himself before we reached the Taylorian.'

During the journey by taxi Yeats 'seemed more animated. Like an actor about to give a performance, his eyes were bright and he was filled with a secret force.' As they approached the Taylorian 'Yeats suddenly looked down at his trousers and hastily buttoned them up. Richard and I secretly heaved a sigh of relief. When we arrived . . . he looked just right—the slightly old-fashioned suit and the flowing bow tie giving the right poetical touch.'

Patmore remembered that 'a roar of applause greeted Yeats as he stepped on to the platform, and he bowed graciously like a king accepting his due.' The audience listened to Yeats reading his poems in hushed silence and after the recital was over they realized that 'never again should we hear a modern poet read his own poems with such eloquence and expressiveness.'

An obituary notice which appeared in the first issue of the *Magazine* after Yeats's death fondly recalled this lecture of the summer term of 1933, remembering how Yeats had

> rewarded his listeners with reminiscence, gesture, reading in abundance. The years had begun to tell on him, but he still retained the romantic aspect which had been part of the London scene forty years earlier. He set out by rebuking the public for expecting him to recite the lyrical triumphs of his youth, and went on to offer some of his less familiar poems; but at last (and close observers thought they detected a touch of despondency) he obliged with 'Innisfree' and 'The Sally [*sic*] Gardens'. And very good they were.

The obituarist felt it was unnecessary to 'record his career or estimate his genius as a poet', but chose to 'lament him as a figure well known in Oxford,' remembering that while resident in Oxford 'Yeats was delightfully benevolent' towards students of that generation, 'even to the extent of encouraging or at least not discouraging them, in bringing their poetical productions to his notice.'[32] Recent broadcasts had 'suggested that he might still return to discuss the subject [of poetry] with "his Oxonians"—to quote his hero, Dean Swift—but that hope has vanished'.[33]

NEWLY DISCOVERED REVIEWS OF WORKS BY W. B. YEATS

1. ANON.: *Oxford Magazine*, 3:10 (29 Apr 1885), 192 (notices Part of *The Island of Statues* in *Dublin University Review*).

2. ANON.: *Oxford Magazine*, 12:17 (25 Apr 1894), 280 (reviews *The Celtic Twilight*).

3. ANON.: *Oxford Magazine*, 12:23 (6 June 1894), 380 (reviews *The Land of Heart's Desire*).

4. ANON.: *Oxford Magazine*, 16:5 (17 Nov 1897), 96 (reviews *The Secret Rose*).

5. ANON.: *Oxford Magazine*, 20:9 (22 Jan 1902), 155-6 (reviews *Poems*, 3rd edition, revised).

6. ANON.: *Oxford Magazine*, 22:13 (Feb 1904), 232-3 (reviews *Samhain*).

7. ANON.: *Oxford Magazine*, 36:2 (24 May 1918), 286 (reviews *Per Amica Silentia Lunae*).

8. ANON.: *Oxford Magazine*, 38:3 (31 Oct 1919), 52-3 (reviews *The Wild Swans at Coole* and *The Cutting of an Agate*).

9. J. R. H.: *Oxford Magazine*, 46:21 (31 May 1928), 582 (reviews *The Tower*).

10. F. G. M. F.: *Oxford Magazine*, 'Books for Actors and Playgoers,' *Oxford Magazine*, 54:24 (18 June 1936), 716 (reviews *Dramatis Personae*).

11. A. D. W.: *Oxford Magazine*, 59:2 (24 Oct 1940), 30-31 (reviews *Last Poems and Plays* and *Scattering Branches*, ed. Stephen Gwynn).

REVIEWS OF PERFORMANCES BY THE IRISH NATIONAL THEATRE SOCIETY:

1. 'The Irish Plays', *Oxford Magazine*, 24:7 (29 Nov 1905), 113 (reviews *On Baile's Strand*, *In the Shadow of the Glen*, *Spreading the News*, *The Well of the Saints*, *Kathleen Ni Houlihan*).

2. 'The Theatre', *Oxford Magazine*, 25:22 (5 June 1907), 390-391 (reviews *The Gaol Gate*, *Hyacinth Halvey*, *The Rising of the Moon*, *The Shadowy Waters*).

3. 'The Theatre', *Oxford Magazine*, 25:23 (12 June 1907), 407-8 (reviews *The Playboy of the Western World*).

4. 'The Theatre', *Oxford Magazine*, 27:24 (17 June 1909), 380 (reviews *Dervorgilla*, *The Playboy of the Western World*).

5. 'The Theatre', *Oxford Magazine*, 29:21 (1 June 1911), 362-3 (reviews *Riders to the Sea*, *Birthright*, *The Workhouse Ward*).

6. 'The Theatre', *Oxford Magazine*, 31:21 (22 May 1913), 356 (reviews *Riders to the Sea*, *The Playboy of the Western World*).

7. 'The Irish Plays', *Oxford Magazine*, 32:21 (28 May 1914), 358-9 (reviews *The Kings's Threshold*, *Damer's Gold*, *Spreading the News*).

8. 'The Theatre', *Oxford Magazine*, 40:11 (9 Feb 1922), 207 (reviews *Kathleen Ni Houlihan*, *Riders to the Sea*, *The Building Fund*).

9. C. Mac. D.: 'The Irish Players,' *Oxford Magazine*, 40:19 (18 May 1922), 363 (*The Witness to the Will*, *In the Shadow of the Glen*, *The Eloquent Dempsey*).

NOTES

1. Its full title was *The Oxford Magazine: A Weekly Newspaper and Review*. It was not new in 1883; there had been a journal of the same name from 1768-1776 and the name had also been briefly revived in 1845. The current *Oxford Magazine*, founded in 1985, is 'essentially new and distinct' according to the editor, Professor T. J. Reed. (Letter to D. Kiely, 27 Aug, 1996.)

2. Eleven of these reviews are listed here for the first time. The others are 'E. F.'s review of *Wheels and Butterflies* and *Collected Plays* (1934) in 53:17 (2 May 1935), 536-7 and S[tuart] N. H[ampshire]'s review of *The Oxford Book of Modern Verse* in the issue for 4 Feb 1937, (p. 343): see *J* items G666 and G1215.

3. W. T. S. Stallybrass (editor 1914-1919), '"The Magazine" During the Last War', *Oxford Magazine* 61:9 (21 January 1943), 137-8.

4. Dugald Sutherland MacColl, Keeper of the Tate Gallery 1906-1911 (later a Trustee), was the painter, critic and controversialist whom Yeats suggested to Lady Gregory as the most suitable candidate to write a biography of Sir Hugh Lane and whose style, in Yeats's opinion, 'fitted him to deal firmly with Sir Hugh Lane's Dublin enemies'. Yeats seems to have maintained his respect for MacColl despite their protracted antagonism over the Lane Pictures (*L* 616-623, and *UP2* 425). The biography was abandoned during the controversy over the codicil to Lane's will.
    J. W. Mackail (later OM) became Professor of Poetry at Oxford from 1906-1911. Percy Matheson succeeded Lodge as editor of the *Magazine* from 1884-5. John Butler Yeats described Oliver Elton as 'the most loyal and ardent friend of your work I know' in a letter to WBY of 1899 (*JBYL* 60). Anthony Hope Hawkins (pseud. 'Anthony Hope'), author of *The Prisoner of Zenda*, began by writing reports of football matches for the *Magazine* as an undergraduate.

5. Sir Arthur Quiller-Couch in *The Oxford Magazine* 61:9 (21 January 1943), 136. Part of this letter was reprinted in the *Illustrated London News*, 202 (20 February 1943), 216.

6. This is reflected in the *Magazine*'s changes of publisher at various critical moments in its history. *The Oxford Magazine* was first published by James Thornton. In 1884 it was transferred to the University Press where it remained until 1921. It was then adopted by *The Oxford Chronicle*, who undertook to publish it at their own risk, until the goodwill was disposed of to the Oxonian Press at the end of the University year in 1926 and in whose hands it remained until 1960.

7. The other directors were Lodge, Matheson, Charles Cannan, A. D. Godley, J. Wells, and C. E. Brownrigg.

8. D. S. MacColl, 'Early Days of the Oxford Magazine', *The Oxford Magazine* 51:9 (19 January 1933), 294-6.

9. Pater wrote two reviews for *The Oxford Magazine*: 'Love in Idleness' 1:7 (7 March 1883), 144-5 (unsigned), and 'The English School of Painting', 3:6 (25 February 1885), 113, signed 'W. H. P.'.

10. Letter from E. L. Gass to Mr. Batey, 20 March 1948, PKT 191 Oxford University Press Archives. Gass had been responsible for the publication of the *Magazine* when it was published by the University Press. I am grateful to Mr. Peter Foden for his assistance at the archives of the Oxford University Press.

11. Aubrey de Selincourt (editor 1925-1929) refers to the reputation that the *Magazine* enjoyed as 'a weighty and respectable organ of Oxford opinion' in his article '"The Magazine" Ten Years After the Last War', *The Oxford Magazine*, 61:9 (21 January 1943), 139.

12. *The Oxford Magazine*, 3:10 (29 April, 1885), 192.

13. Regius Professor of Modern History from 1894 and a don at Christ Church, Powell facilitated Yeats's second visit to Oxford, in August 1889, when he copied out the *Hypnerotomachia Polipholi* of Fra Colonna. See *CL1* 65, 177-181.

14. *The Oxford Magazine* 12:17 (25 Apr 1894), 280.

15. According to legend, his skull was dug up in Iceland 150 years after his death and was so thick that it could withstand the hardest blow from an axe: he is now thought to have suffered from Paget's Disease.

16. *The Oxford Magazine*, 16:5 (17 November, 1897) 96.

17. *The Oxford Magazine*, 20:9 (22 January, 1902) 155-6.

18. *Oxford Magazine* 21:4 (24 November 1902), 71.

19. *The Oxford Magazine* noted this lecture in its 'Calendar of Events' but carried no report of the proceedings of what was, according to other accounts, a successful evening.

20. *CL3* 191. Yeats had taken a more youthful view of Churton Collins when transcribing Aesop in the Bodleian in 1888: 'a most cheerful mild pink and white little man full of the freshest unreasonablest enthusiasms'. But then on that occsion the whole of Oxford had seemed 'so beautiful . . . like an Opera' (*CL1* 92-3).

21. J. Middleton Murry's 'Mr. Yeats's Swan Song' had appeared in *The Athenaeum* on 4 April 1919, (rpt. in *CH* 216-20).

22. Two of Macmillan's advertisements quote from reviews not recorded in *J*: one, of *The Tower*, 'Mr. Yeats's New Poems'appeared in *The Scotsman*, 20 Feb 1928 (2) and the other, a review of *Dramatis Personae 1896-1902* by Robert Lynd, appeared in the *News Chronicle*, 22 May 1936 as 'Mr. Yeats and George Moore' (4).

23. See above n. 2. Another review of *The Oxford Book of Modern Verse* in *New Verse* 23 (Christmas 1936), 21, unrecorded in *J*, is attributed to Geoffrey Grigson by B. C. Bloomfield. See *An Author Index to Selected British 'Little Magazines', 1930-1939* (London: Mansell Information/Publishing Ltd., 1976), pp. 56 and 152. I am grateful to Mr. Daniel Adamski for bringing this item to my attention.

24. Francis N. B. Palmer, "The Irish Players", *The Oxford Fortnightly Review* 3:31 (24 February 1922), 360-363, at 363.

25. The reviewer of Synge's *Playboy of the Western World*, with fine understatement, commented that 'this play, when first produced at Dublin in January, created such uneasiness in the auditorium that it became impossible to proceed'. It subsequently claimed that the performance in Oxford on 5 June 'was, therefore, the first actual exhibition of the whole play'. See 'The Theatre', *The Oxford Magazine*, 25:23 (12 June 1907), 407-8.

26. 'The English Association', *The Oxford Magazine* 39:23 (9 June 1921), 378.

27. See however, 'Plays and Politics: Mr. W. B. Yeats at Oriel College', *Oxford Chronicle*, 9 Dec. 1921, 3.

28. The summer meeting of 5 May was reported by a correspondent for *The Oxford Magazine*, 40:18 (11 May 1922), 338, who wrote that the 'lecture on Friday broke completely new ground, and brought to a successful close the third year of the Association's activities in Oxford'.

29. 'The Union', *The Oxford Magazine* 39:14 (25 February 1921), 225. L. A. G. Strong recollected that Yeats's speech at the Union debate 'brought that most formidable of audiences cheering to its feet with a torrent of oratory' (*I&R* 148). A. Norman Jeffares gives a fuller account of this speech before the Oxford Union on 17 February in his *W. B. Yeats: A New Biography* (London: Hutchinson, 1988), 206.

30. For a photograph of the shrine in Yeats's rooms in 1904, see *YA5* frontispiece and *CL3* pl. 10. See also *CL3* 303&n.

31. 'Mr. W. B. Yeats Recalls His Poet's Shrine: Readings and Reminiscences for the Oxford University English Club', *Oxford Mail*, 6 June 1933, 1, 6.

32. As L. A. G. Strong recalled (*I&R* 142).

33. 'W. B. Yeats', *The Oxford Magazine*, 57:11 (2 February 1939), 327-8. The obituary records that 'At a much later date the University signified its awareness of his literary achievement with the degree of D. Litt.'. The conferment of an honorary doctorate on 26 May 1931 had not been previously reported in *The Oxford Magazine*.

McGowan's Code: Deciphering John Masefield and Jack B. Yeats

Philip W. Errington

LADY GREGORY REPORTS that W. B. Yeats once told John Masefield 'You'll be a popular poet—you'll be riding in your carriage and pass me in the gutter'.[1] In later life, however, Masefield was sought out by those who wanted to discuss not his own work, but that of Yeats.[2] It is not this later period of Masefield's life I wish to discuss, however (nor indeed his connections with W. B. Yeats) but the friendship between Masefield and Jack B. Yeats that proved particularly productive for Masefield in a more relaxed and flippant vein. In contrast to Masefield's connections to WBY, the friendship with Jack Yeats was the friendship of escapism and the desperately juvenile which enabled a release upon which both men thrived. The collaborative productions between Jack Yeats and Masefield, in addition to a substantial correspondence and holidays spent together suggest that the two were particularly close.

Masefield's early books carry revealing dedications,[3] and in choosing to dedicate *On The Spanish Main*[4] to Jack B. Yeats, Masefield publically acknowledges a *shared* specialist interest. (Similarly, 'The Tarry Buccaneer' in *Salt Water Ballads* was originally dedicated to Jack Yeats[5]). Yeats's spirited illustrations to Masefield's piratical verses in *A Broad Sheet* suggest that both men enjoyed stories of the high seas, buccaneers, smuggling and piracy. Piracy, at least for Masefield, encapsulated the romance, spirit and daring of the sea and was, in itself, escapism. The young Masefield, although destined for a career at sea, had found himself a poor sailor. He yearned for the beauty of marine life and its sense of history, not the banal existence of most seamen. The autobiographical *New Chum* presents obvious evidence that Masefield was not attuned to the sailor's life:

> I took careful observations of the movements of the clouds; those were interesting to me; the ships were beautiful; their building and rigging were wonderful to me. It was, however, quite clear to me, that something was very much amiss somewhere; there was too much grab, too much snatch, and I knew very well, that I did not want to belong to it. I wanted to be clear of the type of man who gave iron walls and a shelf, and a little daily offal, in exchange for a life's work.[6]

Tales of buccaneers and pirates removed, for Masefield, the immediacy of harsh naval life and replaced it with the rose-tinted material of which tales were told. With Jack Yeats the character of Theodore the pirate cabin-boy was born: a thieving mischievous rogue in love with the beautiful Constanza.[7] Theodore and his exploits worked their way into Masefield's correspondence to Yeats, in prose, verse and, occasionally, excerpts of drama. Such was Masefield's sense of fun that self-parody is included. Contrast, for example, the opening stanza of 'Captain Stratton's Fancy':

> Oh some are fond of red wine, and some are fond of white,
> And some are all for dancing by the pale moonlight,
> But rum alone's the tipple, and the heart's delight
> Of the old bold mate of Henry Morgan.[8]

with the following manuscript verse in a letter to Yeats:

> Oh some are fond of cow's milk and some are fond of gore
> And some are fond of sailoring & some are fond of shore
> But I am fond of writing of the pyrat Theodore
> The cabin-boy to beautiful Constanza.[9]

A volume of Theodore verse was, at some stage, contemplated by Masefield but this was abandoned. Perhaps it was felt that the verse might have only limited appeal: it was simply the result of instant creativity in a flippant style. Yet Masefield's children's stories have survived into today's book market in contrast to his adult fiction perhaps because he refused to take himself seriously,[10] and such liberated freshness and vigour is also to be found in Masefield's Theodore compositions.

If piracy enabled Masefield and Jack Yeats to recapture a boyhood sense of adventure, then two examples are good evidence of this boyish escapism: the manufacture and sailing of toy boats, and the use of a secret code within correspondence. In 1909 Yeats published *A Little Fleet* in which he detailed the manufacture and adventures of toy boats. Within the text, explaining why a stretch of the Gara River was called 'Pirate's Leap', Yeats writes that it was:

> called that because a poet who had been a pirate, I expect, was thinking about a poem when he ought to have been shoving the vessel off the rocks, and so he fell in.[11]

The reference is almost undoubtedly to Masefield and it is known that Masefield bought miniature brass canon with the cheque he received for publication of 'Hall Sands' in *The Speaker*. Additionally, in his introduction Yeats states he is 'indebted to the Fleet Poet for the verses through the book'. This has often been identified as Masefield and a listing of this verse now appears for the first time:

[Untitled lines on the 'Monte']

'And now by Gara rushes,' (pp.[9-10]).

[Untitled lines introducing the 'Moby Dick']

'She sailed down Gara Valley,' (p.[11]).

[Untitled lines on the 'Moby Dick']

'She came to flying anchor', (p. [14]).

[Untitled lines on the 'Theodore']

'And let no landsman doubt it,' (p. [18]).

Yeats was not alone in writing of exploits with toy boats: both Jim and Hugh sail boats in *Jim Davis* whilst Kay Harker and the Jones children navigate a model ship in *The Box Of Delights*. Sharing a passion for toy ships and the romance of skull-duggery, it is not surprising that the two men devised and corresponded with a secret code. It seems likely that it was Yeats who devised the symbols (in an undated letter around 1904, Masefield thanks him for 'the perfect alphabet'[12]) and it is employed in the same light vein of the correspondence. There are, however, a few examples known to me of Masefield specifically using the code for private and confidential comments. One passes judgement on a recent play by Bernard Shaw whilst another refers to 'the human hairpin' (who remains unidentified). Breaking the code was comparatively easy, for a simple system of pictures substituted for letters is employed whilst standard spacing between words is retained (with occasional punctuation). The crucial clue, however, was Masefield's use of the word 'bloody'. Bloody was first published by Masefield in *Salt-Water Ballads* and glossed as an 'intensive derived from the substantive "blood"'. . .',[13] but when *The Everlasting Mercy* was first published in *The English Review* in October 1911, the decision was taken to replace the offensive word with blank spaces. The sensation was, nevertheless, unavoidable with Masefield accused of debasing poetic diction.[14] For code breaking purposes the word is particularly useful since it contains a repeated vowel and, in combination with 'Hell', a consonant in the first word is repeated twice in the second. The first excerpt of code to be broken thus spelt 'By Bloody Hell This Song Goes Well' (see Plate 10). To complete the task it is also possible to find reasons for the symbols chosen: Breeches for 'B', Sea for 'S', Hills for 'H', pieces of Eight for 'E' and, of course, Theodore hiding behind a rum cask for 'T'. Although I have so far failed to locate any letters from Yeats to Masefield using the code,[15] Yeats certainly used it, even in print. His map 'A View Of Pirate Island'[16] includes 'Here Theos Treasure Was Buried' in code whilst *A Broadside* No.7 (Fourth Year) for December 1911 includes Yeats's illustration 'The Pirate Sentry' which shows code as graffiti on a wall reading 'Constanza Pity Me'. As is to be expected, however, Yeats's drawings are far clearer and more assured—although this may merely show the differences between private correspondence and published work.

With such verses entitled 'Theodore To His Grandson' (signed 'Wolfe T. MacGowan') in *A Broadside*, I have long had suspicions about the pseudonym. Hilary Pyle in her biography of Jack B. Yeats states that 'the evidence among [Jack B.] Yeats's papers and the crude quality of the verse tends to indicate [Jack B.] Yeats as the author'.[17] In a helpful letter Dr Pyle has given details of sources and also remarks 'it was widely accepted in Dublin that the Wolfe Tone and Robert Emmet pseudonyms were adopted by Jack B. Yeats'. One source to which Dr Pyle refers finds Liam Miller noting, with reference to *A Broadside*:

> Jack B. Yeats contributed several verses, some anonymously and some signed with his pseudonyms 'R. E. MacGowan' and 'Wolfe Tone Mac-Gowan'.[18]

Evidence, however, suggests the traditional view of the pseudonym requires revision. A letter from Elizabeth C. Yeats to an unknown correspondent dated 31 June 1924 provides a listing of Masefield's verse. E. C. Yeats writes:

> I enclose a list of any verses written by John Masefield in 'The Broadside' [*sic*]. I think these are all—& I am not quite certain of one called 'Captain Kidd'—my brother Jack B. Yeats . . . compiled the Broadsheets—so he will of course know where he got each ballad—but I fancy he would not like to tell you which was Masefield's without Mr Masefield's permission—I don't think the thing of any great importance so I do not mind giving you what information I have . . .[19]

There then follows a listing. On the authority of this listing and after referring to copies of *A Broadside* I have prepared the following list of dates, titles, first lines and signatures for all poems contributed by Masefield:

No. 1 (First Year) Jun, 1908

'Campeachy Picture'

'The sloop's sails glow in the sun; the far sky burns,'
[signed, 'John Masefield']

No. 4 (First Year) Sep, 1908

[untitled]

'Bring wine, and oil, and barley cakes,'
[signed, 'Wolfe T. MacGowan']

'A pleasant new comfortable ballad upon the death of Mr. Israel Hands, executed for piracy.'

'My name is Mr. Israel Hands'
[signed, 'Wolfe T. MacGowan']

No. 8 (First Year) Jan, 1909

'Theodore To His Grandson'
'O gamfer : you are lined and old,'
[signed, 'Wolfe T. MacGowan']

No. 1 (Third Year) June, 1910

'A Young Man's Fancy'

'All the sheets are clacking, all the blocks are whining,'
[signed, 'R. E. McGowan'[20]]

No. 1 (Fourth Year) June, 1911

'Captain Kidd'
'"My name is Captain Kidd["]',
[unsigned]

No. 4 (Fourth Year) Sept, 1911

[untitled]
'O Irlanda, Irlanda,'
[signed, 'Wolf [*sic*] T. MacGowan]

No. 12 (Fourth Year) May, 1912

'Die We Must'

'Die we must and go to dust'
[signed, 'Wolfe T. MacGowan']

No. 3 (Sixth Year) Aug, 1913

'The Gara River'

Oh give me back my ships again
[signed, 'Wolfe T. MacGowan']

What is significant is that E. C. Yeats attributes all *Broadside* verses with the MacGowan name to Masefield. (There are, additionally, several unsigned shanties not mentioned by E. C. Yeats which, although not original work, were presumably provided by Masefield). Regarding the

authenticity of the Captain Kidd poem, it is of interest to note that
Masefield writes the following untitled poem to Yeats in a letter dated
August 15, 1906:

> O have you seen my Broad Sheet with the wood Cut on the Top
> It is the finest Broad Sheet in the ballad Monger's Shop
> It is the finest Broad Sheet that ever I did see
> It has a wood Cut done by you and a ballad by Me.
>
> You may tell a proud Broad Sheet in the Shop where it lies
> There's a picture of a Schooner with her Spars in the Skies
> She's a red bold Banner flying and she logs a steady Ten
> It is lucky that her Story is not known among Men.
>
> For O the poor housemaid she would let the Guards go
> There is never a red guardsman would ever have a show
> If she saw a red guardsman she would say to him Aroint
> (And this is how a poet can wander from the Point)
>
> And underneath the picture, where the salt waves shake,
> There is the bulliest ballad a man did ever make
> It is the bulliest ballad that poet ever did
> It is all of Admiral Morgan and of Captain Kidd
>
> It's an old sad ballad of sad and sorry times
> There's the noise of the waves breaking in the slow fall of the rhymes
> For poets say, as pirates said, (the witty saying sticks)
> 'Let Judges win by honours, and we'll win by tricks'.[21]

The date does not exactly correspond and Masefield mistakenly uses the
name of the earlier, and by then terminated publication; however, this
verse is additional evidence if not absolute proof. The verse in *A Broadside* is crude but this is no reason to deny it is Masefield's: his hasty verses
are often rough and the style is that of the private Theodore verse.
Indeed, the untitled verse beginning 'O Irlanda, Irlanda' is present in an
undated letter (approximately April 1909) to Jack B. Yeats[22] which confirms E. C. Yeats's reliability. After Masefield's numerous contributions
to *A Broad Sheet* it would seem curious to record that he only contributed one verse to the first issue of *A Broadside* (the signed
'Campeachy Picture') and with Masefield often content to remain
unacknowledged (as previously noted with *A Little Fleet*), the listing
above confirms a view of Masefield that emerges from the correspond-

ence—light, flippant verse was to be enjoyed as just that whilst a pseudonym was merely part of the type of fun that evaded true meaning and gave rise to secret code.

The friendship of John Masefield and Jack B. Yeats thus gave rise to a productive collaboration: *A Little Fleet*, an edition of Reynolds's *The Fancy*, Yeats's frontispiece to Masefield's *A Mainsail Haul*, and the collaboration even includes a sketch by Yeats to accompany Masefield's article on whippet racing in *The Manchester Guardian* for 19 August 1905. One collaborative study of London life, *The Jolly Londoners* failed to appear but it is amusing to note one of Masefield's earliest suggested titles for the book was *The New Corinthians*—the name of a boat in the Gara fleet. A letter from early 1903 even reveals Masefield's intention to dedicate his autobiography to Jack. B. Yeats,[23] but this volume never appeared. Masefield and Yeats eventually drifted apart; nevertheless Yeats's influence remained with Masefield: whilst writing his narrative poem *King Cole* (a poem inhabiting the Yeatsian world of circuses), Masefield wrote to Elkin Mathews regarding the process used for printing illustrations in *A Broad Sheet*.[24] When the poem first appeared it was accompanied by numerous black and white illustrations Yeatsian in spirit but, admittedly, not so assured or skilled. The illustrator was Masefield's daughter (christened 'Isabel Judith Yeats Masefield').[25] The childishness of John Masefield and Jack B. Yeats was manifested afresh in her drawings.

NOTES

1. Daniel J. Murphy (ed.), *Lady Gregory's Journals Volume One* (Gerrards Cross: Colin Smythe, 1987), p. 385. I am grateful to the Society of Authors as literary representative of the Estate of John Masefield, to the Bodleian Library, and the Houghton Library, Harvard University for permission to reproduce Plate 10.

2. The example of Daniel Hoffman's visit in 1961 is cited by Alison Lurie in 'Opening the Box of Delights', *The New York Review of Books*, 21 December 1995, 48-53.

3. Masefield's future wife is included in the dedicatees of *Salt-Water Ballads*, the dedication of *The Tragedy Of Nan and other plays* reveals Masefield's self-confessed debt to WBY's guidance whilst Masefield's edition of *Dampier's Voyages* is courteously dedicated to Lady Gregory.

4. Sub-titled *Some English Forays On The Isthmus of Darien With a Description of the Buccaneers And A Short Account of Old-Time Ships and Sailors* (London: Methuen, 1906).

5. The 1902 Grant Richards edition of Masefield's first book is significantly different to the 1913 Elkin Mathews reissue. The deletion of all dedications is merely one example of change.

6.   John Masefield, *New Chum* (London: William Heinemann Ltd., 1944), p. 186.
7.   Yeats's illustration, 'The Pirates Ashore' in *A Broadside* No. 2 (Third Year) for July 1910 amusingly shows Constanza as an old crone in charge of rum with a large cigar protruding from her mouth. This is not, however, her usual appearance.
8.   'Captain Stratton's Fancy', *Ballads* (London: Elkin Mathews, 1903), p. 20-22.
9.   John Masefield, undated letter to Jack B. Yeats (Bodleian MS. Eng. poet. d. 194, f. 16).
10. A view presented by Professor Alison Lurie in her lecture 'The Children's Books of John Masefield' (Trinity College, Cambridge, Clark Lecture, 1995).
11. Jack B. Yeats, *A Little Fleet* (London: Elkin Mathews, 1909), p. [6].
12. John Masefield, undated letter to Jack B. Yeats (Bodleian MS. Eng. poet. d. 194, f. 28).
13. John Masefield, 'Glossary', *Salt-Water Ballads* (London: Grant Richards, 1902), p.109.
14. Muriel Spark reports that Lord Alfred Douglas claimed the poem was 'nine-tenths sheer filth' and that Masefield exceeded the 'wicked licentiousness' of Marlowe. See Muriel Spark, *John Masefield* (London: Hutchinson, 1991), pp. 4-5.
15. Seven letters (mostly from 1905-1906) held by the Harry Ransom Humanities Research Center, University of Texas are described as 'illustrated', and these illustrations may constitute code.
16. First printed in Ernest Marriott, *Jack B. Yeats: being a true and impartial view of his pictorial and dramatic art* (London: Elkin Mathews, 1911) and also reproduced in T. G. Rosenthal, *The Art of Jack B. Yeats* (London: André Deutsch, 1993), p. 3.
17. Hilary Pyle, *Jack B. Yeats* (London: André Deutsch, 1989), p. 96.
18. Liam Miller, *The Dun Emer Press, Later The Cuala Press* (Dublin: Dolmen Press, 1973, p. 120. 'A View of Pirate Island' includes 'McGowan's Garden' and 'McGowan's House'.
19. Elizabeth C. Yeats, letter to unknown correspondent, 31 June 1924 (Houghton Collection, University of Harvard, Autograph file).
20. Conceivably 'R[obert] E[mmett] McGowan?
21. John Masefield, letter to Jack B. Yeats, August 15, 1906 (Harvard, bMS Eng 849 [*44M-301F]).
22. John Masefield, undated [approximately April 1909] letter to Jack B. Yeats (Harvard, bMS.Eng.849 [*44M-301F]).
23. John Masefield, undated [early 1903] letter to Jack B. Yeats (Bodleian MS.Eng.poet. d. 194, f.2).
24. John Masefield, letter to Elkin Mathews, 15 September 1920 (*British Publishers' Archives—Elkin Mathews* [Bishop's Stortford: Chadwyck Healey Ltd., 1973], ff. 1038-39).
25. Judith Masefield has herself mentioned that one of the toys her father built for her was a soap box with 'a mast with sails that furled, and correct rigging'. See her 'Introduction' to Corliss Lamont, *Remembering John Masefield*, (London: Kaye and Ward, 1972), p. 10.

Crosby Gaige and W. B. Yeats's *The Winding Stair* (1929)

Colin Smythe

IN THE AMERICAN PUBLISHING WORLD, the years before the Wall Street crash of 29 October 1929 produced a number of small publishers whose aim was the production of books of the highest quality not only in design but in content. Among the most interesting are those that were connected with and distributed by Random House, including the Bowling Green Press, the Fountain Press and that of Crosby Gaige.

Random House was the creation of Bennett A. Cerf, Elmer Adler and Donald S. Klopfer, and it published its first book in January 1928, a splendid edition of Voltaire's *Candide*. It also acted as the American distributor for the books of the Nonesuch and Golden Cockerell Presses from England, and distributed other American publishers of limited editions, including Centaur, Fleuron, and Rimington & Hooper, so it was connected with some of the most impressive publishers of the period. But, according to John Tebbel, none 'could match the Crosby Gaige list for quality and sheer beauty'.[1]

The three American houses were all based in New York and run by a small group of people, all friends of Cerf: Crosby Gaige, James R. Wells, Elbridge Adams and William Edwin Rudge. Wells had founded the Bowling Green Press and ran it until 1 May 1929 when it was taken over by Rudge (who must already have possessed a printing house, as many if not all of Gaige's books were, according to their colophons, 'printed at the printing house of William Edwin Rudge'). Wells then joined with Adams to form the Fountain Press.

Crosby Gaige was probably the most colourful of this group: born Roscoe Conkling Gaige, he amused himself by adopting the name Crosby and an entire Revolutionary War ancestry. His career had been in the theatre, first joining the theatrical agent Elisabeth Marbury, and then becoming a partner with Edgar and Arch Selwyn, producing Broadway hits including Bayard Veiller's *Within the Law* (1912), which played for 541 performances, and Jesse Lynch Williams' *Why Marry?* (1917, 120 performances), and after severing his connections with the Selwyns, on his own, producing such successes as George S. Kaufman's *The Butter and Egg Man*, and Channing Pollock's *The Enemy* (both 1925) on which he had made a fortune.[2] When Cerf was starting Random House, his list was enhanced by his friendship with Gaige, who had one of the best private libraries of the time, and also handset and printed fine editions on a press he kept in a huge barn at his home. At Cerf's suggestion, he had started his publishing house in 1927, asking leading writers to provide him with original works that could be produced in limited editions, usually signed by their authors whom he paid handsomely. Before the Crash in 1929 which wiped out his $5m. fortune[3] he had produced twenty-two titles, whose authors in order of publication, included Liam O'Flaherty (two books), Siegfried Sassoon, A.E. (George William Russell), Richard Aldington, James Joyce, Humbert Wolfe, Joseph Conrad, Walter de la Mare, Carl Sandburg, Virginia Woolf, Lytton Strachey, Thomas Hardy, James Stephens, George Moore and, lastly, W. B. Yeats.

Although Yeats's *The Winding Stair* was the last title to be produced by Gaige—the publication programme was taken over by the Fountain Press, distribution continuing through Random House—it was by no means the end of Mr Gaige. Such was the esteem that he was held in by his friends that, following his financial ruin, those who were more fortunate than he (such as Raoul Fleischmann, owner of *The New Yorker*, kept him in the manner to which he was accustomed for the rest of his life, and he even produced some further hits, such as Samson Raphaelson's *Accent on Youth* (1934, 229 performances). While he seemed perpetually short of cash, he never went without the best food and wines, as among other things he had been a founder of the International Wine and Food Society—based in London, with André Simon as its first President—and his contacts with restaurateurs and hoteliers such as Claudius Philippe of the Waldorf Hotel in New York, continued.

In February 1946, John Tebbel, the future historian of American publishing, was an associate editor with E. P. Dutton when he met Gaige for the purpose of ghosting his memoirs *Footlights and Highlights*.⁴ In the summer of that year Tebbel and his wife moved up to Gaige's home at Watch Hill Farm, living in an apartment over the three-car garage. He resigned from Dutton at the end of the year, and remained at the farm, acting as ghostwriter, companion, and friend, until Gaige's death in March 1949. He well remembers the excellent meals, the many famous guests, and the theatrical productions and printing activities that took place in the estate's massive barn. Gaige continued to produce books, assisted by friends such as Cerf whom he finally drove away through his insistence on varying every single copy of everything he produced—for example by the use of various coloured papers—so that general biblio-graphical descriptions of any particular title are an impossibility. In these he was assisted by James Hendrickson, a designer and typographer, who had worked for Knopf and had a weekend apartment in Gaige's vast barn. A biography of Crosby Gaige is needed, and I very much hope that John Tebbel will at least put his memories of those years down on paper.

But to return to W. B. Yeats's *The Winding Stair*: James R. Wells had visited Yeats in September 1927 asking him for 16 pages—about 150 lines—of poetry (to be written in two months) suitable for publication as a signed limited edition, and offering Yeats £300.00⁵ for six months' use.

Evidently Wells, who represented Gaige, had given Yeats the erroneous impression that he himself was the company's President, as on 16 September 1927 Yeats wrote to Sir Frederick Macmillan from 82 Mer-rion Square:

> The other day an American came here and asked me for 16 pages to be privately printed in America, and I am hard at work (having asked for two months to write them in) and it may be only the Poet's delusion but I think I am writing better than I ever did. He wants the Poems for twelve months so they would be free next Autumn, dating from Sept 15 last (his name is—James R. Wells, and he is President of the Crosbie Gage Publishers and he will try to get you to handle the book in England)⁶

A fortnight later, on 2 October, Yeats was writing to Olivia Shakespear:

> My dear Olivia: I owe you a letter but I have been writing verse. Two or three weeks ago an American with a private press offered me £300 for six months' use of sixteen or so pages of verse. I had about half the amount. I agreed and undertook to write a hundred and fifty lines in two months. I have already written 50 or 60 lines, and he has already paid £150. I am giving him 'The Woman Young and Old' a poem called 'Blood and the Moon' (a Tower poem) which was written weeks ago, and I am writing a

new tower poem 'Sword and Tower',[7] which is a choice of rebirth rather than deliverance from birth. I make my Japanese sword and its silk covering my symbol of life . . . (*L* 728-9).

Composition did not go smoothly, however, and George Yeats wrote to Lady Gregory, as recorded in her diary entry of 13 October: 'today G.Y. writes that Willie is ill "First he was writing poems against time for an American publisher who offered him a large sum for sixteen pages of verse not previously published, and then he got 'flu and has a slight congestion of left lung. He is <u>not</u> <u>at</u> <u>all</u> seriously ill, but is rather weak and has to be kept very quiet".'[8] And on 29 November, in another letter to Olivia Shakespear

> . . . I want to finish that book for the American before some doctor gets at me—and I am going to allow myself when I am in the mood to write a little in the afternoon. How strange is the subconscious gaity that leaps up before danger or difficulty. I have not had a moment's depression—that gaity is outside one's control, a something given by nature—yet I did hate leaving the last word to George Moore (*L* 733).

In an effort to improve his health the couple visited Mentone and on 16 January 1928, Lady Gregory received a letter from Yeats, after indicating that they would return for a second opinion on the general state of his health via Switzerland,

> It was like 'God cared for the ravens', one of my family mottoes, the way that American private Press enabled me to make an utterly unforeseen £400 as if in preparation for all this expense.[9]

Yeats completed the collection in early March,[10] and on the 13th Mrs Yeats sent Wells the complete script of the poems, and Yeats inscribed the pages to Gaige (as requested), 'To Mr Gaige [who] is about to put these poems into such a beautiful book W. B. Yeats'.[11]

On 15 June, Lady Gregory (who was staying at 82 Merrion Square) recorded that 'W. B. Y. is correcting his poems for the little expensive American book'.[12] The book was designed by Frederic Warde. Warde had started with Princeton University Press and then freelanced, first in London, chiefly for Cambridge University Press and the Julian Press in 1925, at the Officina Bodoni in Switzerland (1926), in Paris (Pleiade and Pegasus, 1926-27), Berlin and for the Department of Art and Archaeology of Princeton University Press, and others (1927-28), and in New York for Gaige and the Bowling Green Press (1928-). He then joined the printing firm of William Ellis Rudge, who had already printed a number of the books that he designed. On his death his ashes were buried under a foot-path in the formal garden at Watch Hill, with the inscription (using a typeface that he designed) on a flat stone in the path, 'Here lie the ashes of Frederic Warde, in a garden of his own designing'.

The description of the published volume is as follows: THE | WIND-ING STAIR | BY | W. B. YEATS | NEW YORK | THE FOUNTAIN PRESS | MCMXXIX | [The last five lines are enclosed in a design incorporating a fountain.] 22.4 x 15.2; pp. xii, 28: comprising pp. [i-vi] blank; half-title bearing author's signature, verso blank, pp. [vii-viii]; title, verso with copyright notice and printing information, pp. [ix-x]; con-tents, verso blank, pp. [xi-xii]; fly-title, verso blank, pp. [1-2]; text, pp. 3-[26]; colophon, verso blank, pp. [27-28]. Issued in dark blue cloth, pattern stamped in gold on front and back covers; title stamped in gold with two small red leather labels lettered in gold "YEATS" pasted on at head and "FOUNTAIN PRESS" at foot of spine; purple end-papers flecked with gold and lined white; top edges gilt, others untrimmed. The colophon reads:

"OF THIS EDITION OF THE WINDING STAIR, SIX HUN| DRED AND FORTY-TWO COPIES WERE PRINTED ON KAL| MAR PAPER IN THE PRINTING HOUSE OF WILLIAM EDWIN | RUDGE. SIX HUNDRED NUMBERED COPIES, SIGNED BY | THE AUTHOR, WILL BE FOR SALE. DISTRIBUTED IN | AMERICA BY RANDOM HOUSE, AND IN GREAT BRITAIN | BY GRANT RICHARDS AND HUMPHREY TOULMIN, AT THE | CAYME PRESS LIMITED. DESIGNED BY FREDERIC WARDE. | THIS IS COPY NUMBER   ".

The copies are numbered in red ink.

Contents

In Memory of Eva Gore Booth and Con Markiewicz
Death
A Dialogue of Self and Soul
Blood and the Moon
    First appeared in *The Exile*, Spring 1928.
Oil and Blood
A Woman Young and Old
    I   *Father and Child*
    II *Before the World was Made*

   III   A First Confession
   IV   Her Triumph
    V   Consolation
   VI   The Choice
  VII   Parting
 VIII   Her Vision in the Wood
   IX   A Last Confession
    X   Meeting
   XI   From "The Antigone"
Notes.   *Dated Rapallo, March, 1928.*

The final version of the title page of Gaige's planned edition reads: 'THE |
WINDING STAIR | BY | W. B. YEATS | [publisher's device] |NEW YORK
CROSBY GAIGE MCMXXIX'. It would appear that Gaige's original intention for *The Winding Stair* was to have an edition of 700 copies, later
reduced to 642 copies printed on white handmade paper plus twelve
copies on green paper. The Harry Ransom Humanities Research Center
in Austin, Texas possesses an early mock-up of this edition on which
there are some pencilled notes that indicate that it was sent to England
(to Yeats or Macmillan?) on 8 May 1928 and returned on 22 November
that year. Then a further note: 'New Half Title for poets signature send
Dec. 18. [1928]'.

In 1966 Mr David A. Randall of the Lilly Library informed Russell
Alspach that the Library owned a set of sheets with the Gaige imprint,
and sent him a photocopy of the title and colophon pages, the latter reading

'OF THIS EDITION OF *THE WINDING STAIR* | SEVEN HUN-
DRED COPIES ON HANDMADE PAPER AND | TWELVE
COPIES ON GREEN PAPER HAVE BEEN PRINTED | AT THE
PRINTING HOUSE OF WILLIAM EDWIN RUDGE | NEW YORK
| SIX HUNDRED AND FIFTY COPIES WILL BE SOLD AND | DIS-
TRIBUTED BY RANDOM HOUSE | TYPOGRAPHY BY
FREDERIC WARDE | [signature of W. B. Yeats]'.

The Lilly Library now has no record of these sheets. Mr Randall had
been dealing with Crosby Gaige's collection when he was with Scribners,
but his letter does not indicate that the set of proofs was anywhere else
but in the Lilly Library which, however, does have an advance copy of
the Gaige 'edition'. It had evidently been bound up as a display sample
for it lacks a printed half-title on the last leaf of the first gathering, but

having a notation in pencil 'half title | The Winding Stair | [vertical pointing arrow] W B Yeats | author to sign here' in its place. The colophon page is as follows:

'SIX HUNDRED AND FORTY-TWO COPIES PRINTED BY | WILLIAM EDWIN RUDGE. EACH COPY SIGNED BY THE | POET. | SIX HUNDRED COPIES WILL BE FOR SALE. THREE | HUNDRED COPIES ARE RESERVED FOR ENGLAND. | DISTRIBUTED IN AMERICA BY RANDOM HOUSE. | NO. | TYPOGRAPHY BY FREDERIC WARDE'

over which have been written the words 'sales copy'. The binding is identical to that of the Fountain Press edition except that the casing lacks the red leather labels (which were added to the Fountain Press copies in order to cover up 'GAIGE' at the foot and—for the symmetry of the design—'YEATS' at the head of the spine).

A set of proofs, identical to the 'Randall' set, signed by Yeats, was stated to have been acquired in 1970 by the Library of the Russell Sage College, Troy, N.Y., but its present whereabouts is unknown. Stephen Goode, the Director of Libraries at that time, wrote: 'We have recently acquired advance proof sheets of the Crosby-Gaige edition of the *Winding Stair'* which admits no doubt. It would be pleasant to think that this was the same set that was earlier in the possession of David Randall, for both these sets of sheets have had a curious life, popping in and out of existence like sub-atomic particles.

The Humanities Research Center in Austin not only owns the original typescript of this work inscribed to Gaige as mentioned above, but also Gaige's copy of his own edition, bound in brown goatskin. Both the half-title and colophon (which is the same as the 'Randall' and Russell Sage College sets) are signed by Yeats. Its page size is 22.8 x 15.5 cm, and there is a gathering of four blank leaves at the front of the book and another at the back, one leaf of each being used as the pastedown endpaper (an arrangement trade book-binders in Britain refer to as 'self-ends').

The Lilly Library also owns a copy of the Fountain Press edition printed on green paper, with endpapers of the same green paper instead of the first and last gatherings of four leaves (therefore lacking the half-title leaf), bound in black cloth, and t.e.g. The spine blocking and leather labels are the same as on the standard edition. In the HRHRC collection is an unnumbered copy printed on green paper in which Wells has written below the colophon where the number would be, 'One of four printed on green paper. J. R. W.' (copy no. A9Y348929W). In the Yale University exhibition held in 1939 which contained many books from his own collection, William M. Roth exhibited a copy of the Fountain Press edition, printed in green paper, bound in black cloth, and numbered 72 (item 214). Unfortunately I do not know where this copy is now, but I suspect that the number was inserted by an unauthorised hand.

According to Will Ransom's *Private Presses and their Books*,[13] 'early in 1929' Gaige's publications (including *The Winding Stair*, which was supposed to have been already published in an edition of 550 copies at $15.00) were taken over by the Fountain Press which was owned by his friends James R. Wells and Elbridge Adams. Wells had founded the Bowling Green Press, running it until 1 May 1929, when it was taken over by William Ellis Rudge. Wells and Adams then formed the Fountain Press. According to John Tebbel's *History of Book Publishing in the United States*,[14] however, Gaige continued to publish books until he lost his fortune in the stockmarket crash at the end of October 1929, *The Winding Stair* being the last production before the Fountain Press took over his list.

Both authors agree that *The Winding Stair* was the last book published by Gaige, but in their books both fail to take into account why the imprint was changed—or how—after publication. Alan Wade states the book was published on 1 October, Tebbel that it was the last production before the Crash, which occurred on 28 October. If the book had been in print for a month, there would be many copies extant with the Gaige imprint, and there would have been no need to change it. Ransom—although writing at the time—states that the book had been published before Gaige's firm was taken over by the Fountain Press, which had only been formed after 1 May after Rudge had acquired the Bowling Green Press. Unfortunately, none of the colophons mention dates or publishers. The extant evidence makes it obvious that *The Winding Stair* had not been bound at the time the Fountain Press bought Gaige and its bookstocks, although the casings with the Gaige imprint had already been made: the title, verso and colophon pages of the published volumes are not cancels. Wells and Adams, as the Fountain Press, were able to print new sheets, both for the standard as well as for the green paper copies, decide whether to print 700 or 642 copies, and have the casings modified to incorporate the name of the new publisher. Ransom was wrong when he states that the book had been published—though the sheets may well have been printed—by the time Wells and Adams formed the Fountain Press. Ransom's book also states that the Fountain Press had in preparation an edition of *Oedipus at Colonus*, 500 copies of which were to be printed in Kelmscott type signed by Yeats, printed by R. & R. Clark, Edinburgh, and selling at $15.00, but this edition never got beyond the proof stage, as Macmillan insisted on buying up the edition to ensure the best market for the proposed *de luxe* edition that was to be published after the depression, and Yeats had to return 'a quite substantial sum of money'. As Yeats wrote on 20 February 1932 to James Starkey, when recounting this experience, 'I cannot start on any more such adventures if for no other reason that they are too racking for the nerves'.[15]

The question arises as to how much we should rely on Ransom's book. At first glance, as it is contemporary to the events being described, we might feel the answer to be 'a very great deal', but although published in 1929 it would appear that parts of it were completed earlier and not updated, or were based on inaccurate information, and I suspect that parts were written about future events as if they had taken place. On p. 173 Ransom states that 'early in 1929 the Gaige program was taken over by the Fountain Press, and in the next chapter, ten pages later, that

> One other private press in the making stimulates a sort of breathless anticipation. Crosby Gaige and Frederic Ward are assembling equipment 'somewhere up the Hudson,' part of which is being specially manufactured for their purpose. Of mechanism, however, there is to be no more than an irreducible minimum, as 'nothing but the human hand' is to produce their results. Knowing the past record of both these men, it is no surprise that there will be uncommon, even unique types and that reprints are to have no place in the program, which is to consist of unpublished material of R. L. Stevenson, Rudyard Kipling, Rupert Brooke, Lafcadio Hearn, and others not so well known.

This would appear to be a new project, using material mainly from dead authors, and would account for Tebbel's assertion that Gaige was continuing to produce books right up to the Crash. It could also be taken—or mistaken—for a description of the original idea for Gaige's first list since, apart from the authors named, it describes the nature of that list, which contains books printed in Caslon, Granjon, Scotch, Cochin, and Brimmer types (with two titles, one being *The Winding Stair*, for which the type face is not specified). According to p. 173, Gaige had 'not only arranged for the best bookmaking but also exercised unusual discrimination in selecting literary content, most of the issues being first editions of important and significant material.'

Ransom's bibliography (p. 289) notes that the twenty-second and final title on the Gaige list is *The Winding Stair*, describing the edition as being of 550 copies (a figure given nowhere else), signed, and selling at $15.00. It is followed by the words: *'This completes the Gaige list, continuation of which is taken over by the Fountain Press early in 1929.'* If *The Winding Stair* was published before the transfer, then why did it appear with a Fountain Press imprint? The answer should be that the information Ransom was using had been overtaken by events. At this point the date of transfer is irrelevant, more important is what was in production at the time of transfer, and it is obvious that Yeats's book had not been completed by that time, so that new title and colophon sheets could be printed and incorporated into the final volume, with suitably modified casings, and only copies with a Fountain Press imprint were sold to the trade: the Gaige edition was never published, and Ransom is therefore incorrect on this point.

The Winding Stair must have been one of the first, if not the first to be published with a Fountain Press imprint. Or should have been. The three titles listed in the bibliography (p. 283) as having already been published by it were printed by the Spiral, Harbor and Grabhorn Presses respectively, and the first six announced were mostly to be printed by the Merrymount Press, Pynson Printers, R. & R. Clark, and Earl Wideman. The seventh and final entry, that for James Stephen's *The Symbol Song*, does not name the proposed printer, while the sixth is Yeats's aborted *Oedipus at Colonus*, mentioned above. No more titles were to be printed by Rudge.

That Ransom is wrong about *The Winding Stair* can only mean that there were gaps in his knowledge of the New York publishing scene, and that therefore his text should not be treated as gospel, in spite of its contemporaneity. Had the transfer of Gaige's titles taken place as smoothly and when he stated, then *The Winding Stair* would certainly have been published under the Gaige imprint. The fact that the Fountain Press published it with their imprint, and that it was only entered for copyright at the Library of Congress in October 1930, a year after the generally accepted publication date, indicates that the situation was much more complicated than at first sight. Unfortunately I have not yet found any copies with a dated inscription that might help date its appearance on the market nor, in spite of John Kelly's help, anything in Yeats's correspondence. The only firm date in the USA has been that of the Library of Congress registration.

The first three editions of Wade state that *The Winding Stair* was published on 1 October 1929, and while the Library of Congress copy is stamped Oct -4 1930, with the entering clerk's pencilled initials BEW and the date 10/7/30 (i.e. 7 October 1930), US copyright law required that copies of books published in the US only had to be deposited within twenty-eight years of first publication: a year's delay between publication and deposit could merely mean that someone forgot to send copies to the Library until a year later: a late delivery therefore need carry no implication regarding delayed publication. While the *Times Literary Supplement* only reviewed *The Winding Stair* in November 1930, which would have supported a delayed publication date, AE reviewed it in *The Irish Homestead* on 1 February 1930, so publication very likely was in October 1929 as stated by Wade. But this does not answer the question as to why Ransom got his facts wrong—if he did. In a 1983 letter to me, John Tebbel wrote:

> Herewith is what little I can tell you. That little is based on speculation, because I have searched my records, including Crosby's autobiography, 'Footlights and Highlights,' which I ghostwrote for him, and find no mention of the Yeats volume. My memory tells me that it was indeed called 'The Winding Stair,' and that it bore the Fountain Press imprint. The exasperating confusion arises from Crosby's extremely casual kind of publishing. Little of the printing he and Freddie Warde and Jim Hendrickson did at Watch Hill was commercial; it was mostly a form of self-expression, as he himself said. Yet some of the imprints he used—Fountain Press was among them—were picked up and used again by Random House when it re-published these volumes commercially. An edition on green paper with a Fountain Press imprint would almost certainly have been printed at Watch Hill, since this was a favorite whimsical gesture of Crosby's, to print editions in off colors, or even interspersed different colors—whatever happened to be in the shop. It maddened Bennett Cerf and crazed later bibliographers. Cerf would <u>never</u> have done an edition on green paper. My guess is that WINDING STAIR was published at Watch Hill in one edition in 1929, just before the October Great Crash completely wiped out Crosby's fortune, all five million dollars of it, and was then republished next year by Random House in a non-green edition but employing the Fountain Press imprint. I feel certain that this is the case, but unfortunately I can't document it for you. Freddie would know, but he's dead, and so would Jim, but I haven't the remotest where he would be found, or even if he's still alive.

Tebbel's speculative scenario—'se non è vero, è ben trovato'—probably does come very close to the truth, but unless we are exceptionally fortunate, I doubt that we shall ever know the exact chronology of events—or even all the most important facts concerning the publication of *The Winding Stair*. In the meantime I can only be extremely grateful that John Tebbel was able to provide me with so much information, without which this essay would have been very much the poorer. If we are more fortunate than I fear, and there is anyone who can answer any of the questions posed here, please would they write to me at P.O. Box 6, Gerrards Cross, Buckinghamshire SL9 8XA, UK: I would hate to hand over the text of the next edition of *Wade* to Oxford University Press only to find out the facts too late to include them.

NOTES

1. *The History of American Book Publishing,* (New York: R. R. Bowker, 1929), pp. 173, 289.
2. Gerald Bordman, *The Oxford Companion to American Theatre,* (Oxford, 1984).
3. At the time of the Crash, five million dollars would have had the purchasing power of over fifty million now. (Inflation in the US has been much less than in Britain.)
4. New York: E. P. Dutton, 1948.
5. According to the Cost of Living index in *Whitaker's Almanac* (1995), this sum would have an equivalent buying power now of over £8,500—£2 a line then, nearly £60.00 a line now.
6. *BL Add MS* 55003 f. 101.
7. Finally called 'A Dialogue of Self and Soul'.
8. *Lady Gregory's Journals: Volume Two, Books Thirty to Forty-Four, 21 February 1925—9 May 1932* ed. Daniel J. Murphy, with an afterword by Colin Smythe (Gerrards Cross: Colin Smythe, 1987), p. 207.
9. *Lady Gregory's Journals etc.,* p. 229.
10. As David R. Clark has pointed out, the date of 'Her Triumph' was misread by Ellmann and Mrs Yeats, both of whom understood 'Nov. 29' to mean November 1929. Clark himself argues that the year of composition was 1926. For further discussion on this point by Clark, see his *Yeats at Songs and Choruses,* (Gerrards Cross: Colin Smythe Ltd; Amherst, MA.: University of Massachusetts Press, 1983), pp. 249-50.
11. The Winding Stair (1929) *Manuscript Materials,* by W. B. Yeats, edited by David R. Clark (Ithaca and London: Cornell University Press, 1995), pp. xxvi-xxvii.
12. *Lady Gregory's Journals etc.,* p. 276.
13. (New York: R. R. Bowker, 1929), pp. 173, 289.
14. Vol III (New York and London: R. R. Bowker, 1978), p. 168.
15. *L* 792. I am indebted to Professor David R. Clark, Mr John Tebbel, Mr David Warrington, William R. Cagle and the staff of the Lilly Library, Bloomington, Indiana, for the information they have given me over this problem.

REVIEWS

Questing for an Appropriate Style of Dance

Sylvia C. Ellis, *The Plays of W. B. Yeats: Yeats and the Dancer* (Basingstoke & London: Macmillan Press, 1995) xiii + 370 pp.

Richard Allen Cave

THE RESEARCH AND SCHOLARSHIP that, on the author's admission, over fifteen years have gone to the making of this volume are nothing short of prodigious. The result is of value not only to the Yeatsian scholar but also to researchers in the fields of dance, theatre and cultural history. Sylvia Ellis's inspiration was Frank Kermode's pioneering study, *Romantic Image* of 1957; but she has pursued in considerable depth what he often chose merely to gesture at in attempting to define the significance of dance and dancer within Yeats's work. Her overall focus is different in that she is seeking to determine the intellectual and cultural milieu, the *zeitgeist*, within which Yeats came inexorably to create his dance plays. The study falls into four lengthy chapters; the first three each approach Yeats's work from different perspectives (the plethora of literary and theatrical depictions of Salome; the growing interest in Britain after the 1850s in all manifestations of Japanese culture and their underlying aesthetic principles; and the range of genres of theatre dance available to Yeats and his circle of friends after 1890); the final chapter brings all this material together as the basis for an interpretation of Yeats's many plays for dancers, which here include *The Land of Heart's Desire*, *The Cat and the Moon*, *The Resurrection*, *The King of the Great Clock Tower*, *A Full Moon in March* and *The Death of Cuchulain*.

Starting with a detailed comparison of the two biblical accounts of Salome's dance and coveted reward, Dr. Ellis studies the complex history of this archetype and the possible reasons for its fascination for poets, novelists, playwrights, painters, opera composers as well as choreographers after Heine published the seminal *Atta Troll* in 1841. Remarkably the choreographers and dancers (Maud Allan and Karsavina) join the catalogue rather late, as if their attention were drawn to the subject by the preoccupation of other kinds of artists whose medium of expression was not the dance but who were enticed by the challenge of defining movement through words, oils or music. What impresses here is the sensitivity with which the changing cultural contexts are established through a critique of each work by Mallarmé, Heywood, Banville, Regnault, Flaubert, Massenet with Milliet and Gremont, Lorrain, Huysmans and Moreau, Laforgue, Wilde, Sudermann and Yeats (only Strauss and his librettist, Lachman, receive but glancing mention in relation to Wilde). This allows Dr. Ellis to make some subtle discriminations between the versions, especially in terms of the kind of dance being evoked, the differing relationships between Salome and her mother, Herodias, and the particular psychology being communicated through the representations of the princess. Yeats was always keen to point out that his versions of a tale involving a dance and a beheading owed little to Wilde's *Salome* and this meticulous contextualising gives Dr. Ellis a secure base on which to build a defence of *A Full Moon in March* as decidedly different from Wilde's tragedy and the prevailing tradition in deriving 'from something more than an easy misogyny' (best, perhaps, defined by Arthur Symons's depiction of the *femme fatale* as 'the eternal enemy') since Yeats's 'fascination with the dancer stems more from a preoccupation with meaning' (p. 79). Yeats on this showing clearly rethought the significance of the elements making up the tale, making three major psychological changes which had far-reaching moral and emotional consequences: his Swineherd dies as a profound expression of his ardour for the Queen and so he is not killed like Jokanaan for rejecting the woman who yearns for him; secondly his Queen 'is dangerous in knowing herself and of what cruel deed she is capable', whereas Wilde's Salome is 'dangerous in her lack of self-knowledge'; lastly while Yeats's Queen discovers the limitations of secular power through the death of the Swineherd and learns through her body a new kind of authority and awareness, Salome is on the point of discovering the reality of the power invested in her sexuality at the moment when Herod orders her killing. From this standpoint Wilde's interpretation seems obvious to the point of cliche, where Yeats is voyaging into highly original territory to explore the sexual dynamic between the genders and, since his focus is on power and its manifestations, the politics of sexuality.

The question that lies behind the second chapter is why Yeats came to the Noh so late (there is no mention of this form of Japanese dance drama in his writings before 1913). What Dr. Ellis demonstrates in this essay is the sheer extent of information that was steadily accumulating about Japanese art for the English and Irish intellectual long before the momentous occasion of Pound's introduction of Yeats to the Noh with his editing of the Fenellosa papers. From the late 1890s *The Times* regularly ran features on aspects of Japanese culture, including in 1906 an extensive article by a Mrs. Hugh Fraser on a visit to a Noh performance; Sada Yacco was one of several performers to act in London in Kabuki where she was seen by Yeats's friend, the artist Charles Ricketts, who—to judge by his diary entries—responded to her artistry with great insight; in 1910 Marie Stopes published an account of her visit to Japan which included an extensive and informed description of a Noh performance; several art journals to which Yeats contributed such as *The Dome* contained essays about and illustrations of ukiyo-e; he studied Japanese art in detail on at least one occasion in the British Museum when, after the founding of the Abbey, he was trying to determine a style of design for staging open-air scenes in plays that would relieve him of the need to deploy conventional scene-painting; and Ricketts, who was continually consulted by Yeats as a mentor in matters to do with stage design, began after 1906 seriously to put theorising into practice while working as a designer for the London stage on productions where his work showed a developing Japanese influence, to such a degree that he was actually invited to design for a Japanese company. While all this clearly excited a measure of interest from Yeats, none of it stimulated an imaginative engagement. The fact perplexes Dr. Ellis.

What is apparent from this is that Yeats turned *creatively* to Japanese art only when in quest of a solution to a specific problem he was facing at a particular time (the question of deploying principles of stylisation for outdoor settings). And this is characteristic of the way influences tended to come to prominence for Yeats: namely, in answer to a felt need or a crisis of confidence about the development of an aspect of his work. His reading and cultural awareness were keenly attuned, especially to forms of innovation, so that he generally had a potential influence at the ready when a need became manifest. This was, surely, the nature of his hesitant progress towards an engagement with the Noh? For one thing the Noh was noticeably the least written about of the cultural forms being presented to excite Western interest at the time and for good reason: as

Marie Stopes comments in her account of seeing a performance of a typical cycle of such plays, 'all are so highly specialised and conventionalised that it is hard even for most Japanese to understand them'. The Noh troupes catered for a very limited *cognoscenti* as spectators in Japan ('fit audience though few', which was part of the attraction for Yeats once he discovered Noh) to the extent that they were one of the last exemplars of a performance-tradition to be deployed as a cultural export. When Pound and Yeats met Michio Ito in 1915 (he was then working at the Coliseum as a dancer, having recently completed his studies with Dalcroze) and invited him to demonstrate the style and principles informing the danced sections in Noh, Ito was at first, to their evident surprise, disparaging about a form of theatre he deemed old-fashioned (visits as a child had bored him). Ironically Yeats's enthusiasm seems to have awakened Ito to the potential of the form.

From the standpoint of Yeat's career as dramatist, it is clear that until 1913 he was not *ready* in creative terms to respond to that potential in Noh. In the crucial period defined by Dr. Ellis between 1906 and 1910 Yeats was preoccupied with establishing the Abbey as a repertory theatre with a substantial repertoire, with facing the consequences (within the theatre as well as in his private life) of the death of Synge, and his chief enthusiasm was for Craig's system of screens and how they might become a permanent feature of his and the company's stagecraft. Elements within his own plays over this period (song, dance, the deployment of a chorus, the increase in dramatic effect occasioned by the use of masks, the extremely stylised settings consequent upon using Craig's screens) anticipate features that constitute the conventions of Noh; but Yeats had not yet seen how these features might all be united within one coherent and organic structure. That is the insight that Noh brought him, but only at a point in time when the collapse of his plans for staging Sophocles' *Oedipus* and the difficulties of reconciling the narrative with the complexities of the symbolic scheme he had designed for *The Player Queen* had brought his creativity as playwright to a state of impasse. The time was suddenly right and Yeats's engagement was immediate and profound. What Dr. Ellis does not comment on here is the remarkable accuracy of his insight into the physical demands of Noh on the actor. She quotes (p. 131) from *Certain Noble Plays of Japan*:

> There are few swaying movements of arms or body such as make the beauty of our dancing. They move from the hips, keeping constantly the upper part of their body still, and seem to associate with every gesture or pose some definite thought. They cross the stage with a sliding move-

ment, and one gets the impression not of undulation but of continuous straight lines.

Where did this level of perceptive observation into the weighting, carriage, elevation and directional flow of the actor-dancer's body come from? Was it the product of an intense imaginative engagement with Ito's efforts at imitation? Did Ito, the trained dancer, bring his awareness to focus on how his body was being deployed, where the sites of tension and softness were distributed, and then describe these perceptions to answer Yeats's incisive questioning? Was Yeats, the trained artist, bringing his knowledge of the human figure from 'life' classes to interpret the physical significance of what he observed? Or was Yeats, intent now on devising his own dance plays, growing sensitive to the power of the body as a medium of expression in movement and looking for forms of dance where the meaning of the body's expressive potential would not be confined within what he considered the predictable codes of classical ballet and other currently popular genres of theatre dance? There is no firm answer to such speculation, of course; indeed, all these possibilities could in some measure have some bearing on the case. It is the accuracy of observation and the confidence with which it is articulated which impress, and the degree to which Yeats's imagination is alive to the *speaking* body. Ironically, the dance in Noh is as tightly codified as in classical ballet. And it was here that Yeats was to make his biggest departure from the practice of Noh in performance: his ideal dancer and preferred interpreter of his plays for dancers when he found her in Ninette de Valois was most admired by him for her improvisatory skills in the contemporary genre of *free* dancing.

The range of dance styles available to Yeats in the theatre between 1890 and 1930 against which he came to define his ideal are the subject of the third chapter. Two of his friends were ardent connoisseurs of the dance: Symons regularly reviewed performances for the *Sketch*, the *Star*, and the *St James's Gazette* and visited Paris in pursuit of this interest; Ricketts became a positive fan of Diaghilev's company after their second London appearance in 1911 (two years later he was to take Yeats to a performance that included Nijinsky dancing in *Le Dieu Bleu*). What Dr. Ellis demonstrates is why Loie Fuller and de Valois were at different stages of his life such important influences on Yeats's thinking about the nature of the dance. To do this she examines the contemporary responses to classical ballet (Lanner, Genee, Pavlova, Karsavina), to the *cancan* and *chahut* dancers who fascinated Symons (Avril, La Goulue, Nini Patte-en-l'Air), the numerous imitators of Fuller's skirt-dancing, the *Ballets Russes*, and the initiator of the modernist school, Isadora Duncan, with her belief in the extemporised and the *free*. Dr. Ellis speculates on the routes by which Yeats might have become aware of current opinion about these performers and, where possible, records Yeats's own impressions; as his theatregoing visits to dance performances were limited, the visits he did make were clearly deliberate and the impact that they made crucial. He was quick to discriminate himself from the prevailing taste: music hall and, especially, *cancan* dancing he dismissed for its obtrusive sexuality; where many, including Beerbohm, found Fuller's 'art of manipulating layers of gauze' doll-like, mechanical, lacking in 'personal importance', Yeats considered her style impressive for precisely those qualities of impersonality and stylised abstraction; ballet in its severely classical manifestations was to him overly artificial, its modes of stylisation lacked 'abundance of life'; Duncan had that abundance but lacked the discipline and control that created the dignity of both the ballet dancer and Loie Fuller. There is a valuable observation quoted by Dr. Ellis (p. 193) from Karsavina's autobiography, *Theatre Street* (1930), made after she had watched Duncan perform in Paris: 'It was possible for us with our training to have danced as she did, but she, with her very limited vocabulary, could not have emulated us'. What Yeats required for his dance plays was a disciplined dancer with the confidence to improvise from a range of styles at her command; Ninette de Valois, when he first met her in 1927, was classically trained, had danced with Diaghilev's company, and was alert to the post-War development in Germany of abstract expressionism, which she was exploring in choreography for herself and her school of dancers. She fulfilled Yeats's ambitions for the dance more securely than even Michio Ito could; and she possessed one further skill invaluable to Yeats's aesthetic of performance in that she had considerable experience of dancing with masks (a more difficult matter for the dancer than for the modern actor) as a consequence of assisting her cousin, Terence Gray, at his theatre in Cambridge as movement instructor on his productions of Greek tragedy, Expressionist drama and Yeats's *On Baile's Strand* and *The Player Queen*.

This issue of the masks is an important one. The hawk-costume designed by Dulac for Ito in the first performances of *At the Hawk's Well* was more in the nature of a hood that half-covered the face; it was made of the same stiffened, but nonetheless malleable, material as the dress and wings. As such it was different in kind from the proper masks worn by Henry Ainley and Allan Wade playing Cuchulain and the Old Man, which covered the whole head to create a fixed physionomy. It was this kind of mask which de Valois had experimented with in Cambridge at the Festival Theatre in 1926 and which Hildo Krop had designed for

Albert van Dalsum's production of *The Only Jealousy of Emer* in Amsterdam in 1922 (revived 1926)—designs which so impressed Yeats that he had had them copied for the Abbey production with de Valois of *Fighting the Waves* in 1929 and which, subsequently, he had incorporated within a woodcut to illustrate the title-page of *Wheels and Butterflies*. This style is closer to what is thought to be the Greek model than to the Japanese Noh mask, which is a tied-on facial covering of carved wood, or the half-mask deployed in *commedia dell'arte*, which is the style generally preferred by the modern actor because it creates fewer problems of resonance when speaking.

Yeats's letters show that he had some trouble with Ainley during rehearsals for *At the Hawk's Well*, which he rather loftily dismisses with gibes about the vanity of professional actors. But in 1916 few English or Irish actors had ever worked with masks and they do require care in the handling: actors can be profoundly disconcerted by having their heads covered and an alien face imposed on what many consider their most expressive feature as a performer. Yeats may have wanted to invest his actors with a complete impersonality by deploying such masks, but the resulting loss of self can expose the actor to all manner of insecurities; that Ainley proved 'difficult' is hardly surprising under the circumstances; clearly Yeats was over-impatient, anxious to get the stylised effects he wanted quickly, when time was what was required steadily to re-build the actor's lowered confidence. Perhaps the experience of working with Ainley made him doubt for a time the style of mask he had chosen as proper for his dance plays (certainly his comments on seeing Krop's designs imply a renewed conviction that his first thoughts on the matter were the right ones).

It may have been this uncertainty that impelled Yeats to the New Oxford Music Hall in the spring of 1921. By a remarkable piece of extended scholarship Dr. Ellis has pursued a chance reference to this visit in a letter of 17 May to Olivia Shakespear which records how Yeats 'spent 19/- to see a woman dance in masks' to discover that the woman in question was an American, Grace Christie and that the masks were from the New York workshop of a Polish artist, W. J. Benda (best known as an illustrator of magazines). The show in which Grace Christie appeared was *The League of Nations* mounted by Cochran and it had run at the New Oxford for some months, during which time it was widely reviewed, but noticeably in greatest detail in the *Irish Times* of 24 January 1921. The masks which were the occasion for a series of dances comprised 'a beautiful Oriental girl', a 'flapper' with pouting lips and rouged features, a fantastic face embellished with peacock feathers and a grotesque 'devil', which is in a highly decorated style suggestive of

Indonesian shadow-puppets; all covered the whole head and, to judge by the photographs Dr. Ellis includes in her study from *Theatre Magazine*, *The Dancing Times*, *The Play Pictorial* and the *Sketch*, completely transformed Christie's appearance, since each dictated a different kind of body-line and range of movement. The performer's identity is wholly subsumed within that of the mask. The photographs reveal an exact representation of what on the one hand Yeats believed acting ideally should entail and on the other the principles of stylisation informing his prescriptions for the staging of all his plays for dancers.

Where one has to take issue with this otherwise admirable study is with regard to the interpretation of Yeats's plays, not only in the final chapter but throughout the volume. Given the sensitivity Dr. Ellis shows elsewhere to the dance scene contemporary with Yeats's exploration of his new dramatic form, one is the more surprised by the infelicity with which she handles the episodes of dance in the plays and the relation of dance to the surrounding action. During the fifteen years the author confesses that she has been working on her study, the nature of the performed text has been subjected to numerous theoretical deconstructions which have defined it at its best as being an open-ended entity. Dr. Ellis starts her discussion of the plays by examining where Yeats stands in relation to two schools of thought about the nature of dance in performance: the one arguing that dance is a kind of language and therefore capable of direct interpretation; the other asserting that movement in being 'self-begotten and self-referring' is more than metaphorical. The latter view, which Yeats came in time to espouse, clearly makes for a performed text which is open-ended and Dr. Ellis, in seeking ultimately to place Yeats within an on-going tradition of performance, quotes views about the work of Jan Fabre which stress how movement work is inevitably multivalent, shaping different significances for different spectators. It is surprising, therefore, in the body of her analysis of the dance plays to find her offering *categorical* interpretations of the sequences of movement. She sees Emer's dance with the severed heads in *The Death of Cuchulain* as expressing triumph on two counts: in having 'finally ousted all her rivals...and...reinstated herself as the woman to take priority in his death'; and in celebrating 'the destruction of the man who betrayed and humiliated as well as loved her' (pp. 68-9). This is to ignore Yeats's carefully enigmatic stage direction ('*She moves as if in adoration or triumph*') which leaves interpretation by the spectator *open* to a range of responses. Even then I doubt whether Dr. Ellis's view would come readily to one's mind during a performance, since it completely ignores the context of the dance. The whole play till now has been about the laying to rest of old enmities and hatreds: Emer has *herself* after all sent Eithne proffering love to Cuchulain in the opening scene in an attempt to prevent him going out to what Emer knows will be a fatal battle (hardly the gesture of a woman harbouring malice and vindictiveness); when Cuchulain senses trickery afoot in Eithne's confusion, he refuses to blame her in any way for what may happen; the scene with Aoife and Cuchulain shows the one-time antagonists rising above all the bitterness that has created antipathy between them; faced with death in the third episode Cuchulain does not curse the Blind Man but calmly accepts his fate. Cuchulain in dying has a transcendent perception of his soul as embodied in the form of a bird. At the conclusion of Emer's dance, the actress is required to pause, her whole body reaching upwards in a posture suggestive of attentive listening; she and the audience hear briefly a few faint bird calls as the scene ends; this suggests so intense a sympathy with Cuchulain that she shares his moment of vision. Sympathy is about loss of self in concern for another, whereas jealousy is wholly self-centred. Would a triumphantly vindictive Emer be capable of such a degree of insight as the scenario requires? The meaning of 'triumph' in Yeats's directions lies beyond the cheap melodramatics of Dr. Ellis's interpretation.

Of the Soldiers' dance in *Calvary*, Dr. Ellis observes: 'Their steps are calm and stately because no further action is possible' (p. 140). But this is to ignore the implications of Yeats's direction which describes them as joining hands to '*wheel* about the cross'. Yeats used words with precision; and 'wheel' here must surely evoke images of controlled (wheeling is a continuous motion within a distinct circle) but mindless energy. What is there within the context of the dance to suggest the stately, since the consequence of it all is not to cheer Christ (as the Soldiers intend) but to bring him to his last great cry of despair at his cosmic loneliness. At a later point in her argument Dr. Ellis remarks that 'cynicism and a sense of the absurd are the very components which constitute their [the Soldiers'] nature' (p. 293). If this is so, then is a 'calm and stately' dance likely to express that nature best in terms of movement? Yeats is meticulous in not dictating a precise style for the dance, but he as meticulously shapes a dramatic context for it, which helps to define the emotional tenor that the choreographer should seek to achieve.

Dr. Ellis is not always sensitive to Yeats's use of words. Referring to his letter to his father about the rehearsals for *At the Hawk's Well*, she quotes his remark that 'the abstract is incompatible with life' (p. 195) and goes on to comment that 'stillness, the stasis of death, is what the poet demanded of his actors'. Within the context Yeats is referring to actors and his dislike of fussy, realistic acting with its preoccupation with business that draws attention to the performer and away from the dramatic action. Stillness was a hallmark of the Abbey style as instilled in the company from the first by the teaching of Frank and Willie Fay; it was what most excited critics like A. B. Walkley when the company first toured to England; it was what specifically marked out the Irish players as *different* from their English contemporaries; and Yeats took pride in that difference. But 'stillness' in a theatrical context does not mean 'the stasis of death', but rather a refining away of unnecessary movement so that what remains becomes profoundly significant by sheer contrast. Within a play where the dramatic climax is to be created through dance, there is good reason to observe restraint in terms of other kinds of stage movement. Yeats was, after all, dealing with two English actors who had not had the benefit of the Fays' training and he was bent on eradicating mannerisms that were alien to his attempt to realise a performing style akin to the clarity of the Noh; and stillness in the Noh occurs generally where the emotional and psychological tension is mounting. Stillness in a good actor or dancer is always exciting theatrically, because it is replete with the potential for movement.

How one judges rhythm is a highly personal matter and this affords another instance with poetic drama of why the form is so open in its possibilities of interpretation. But again one has to respond to the total dramatic context, which with Yeats is not likely to be simple. How accurate is it, therefore, within the context of Fand's dancing about the prostrate Ghost of Cuchulain and their ensuing scene together in *The Only Jealousy of Emer*, to describe their rhymed speech as 'mechanical' and 'jangling' and her movements as 'staccato and frenzied because she is desperate for a consort' (pp. 289-90)? This is to ignore the sonorities of the vowels within the verse-lines of their dialogue which, it could be argued, impose an eerie, hushed expectancy on this moment of spectral seduction. If Fand is to be sensed as the worthy opponent of Emer and a being whose power is so great that it can only be overthrown by what to Emer is the ultimate sacrifice, then the actress would surely be advised to eschew a vocal delivery of the verse that treated rhythm and rhyme as 'jangling'? Yeats asks in his stage direction that Fand's mask and dress should make her appear like an idol fashioned out of some precious metal; though he further prescribes that the 'metallic suggestion' should include the appearance of her hair, he does not add that it should also affect the timbre of her voice. One might also argue that it is somewhat simplistic to describe the rhythms of the closing lyric of *At the Hawk's Well* as 'harsh and intransigent' (p. 283) or those in which the Musicians evoke the coming of dawn in *The Dreaming of the Bones* as 'rollicking and boisterous' (p. 287). The dramatic contexts for these songs suggest a troubled return to the normal world (a longing for settled content in the first instance and for the coming of the light in the second), in which relief is desperately sought from the awesome events with which the stage action has been engaged and which still permeate the Musicians' awareness. All too often Dr. Ellis goes for the obvious, when a subtler suggestiveness is present in the text.

There are any number of related judgements which are open to debate [that Yeats invests *The Dreaming of the Bones* 'with the current and specific rather than the universal' (p. 136); that Yeats 'choreographed his dances' (p. 266); that the Peacock was a conventional proscenium theatre; or that a '*reckless* modern energy sound the final note' of *The Death of Cuchulain*] but there is one that cannot go unchallenged since it totally misinterprets Yeats's ambitions for these plays in performance. Dr. Ellis quotes the description of the setting for *The King of The Great Clock Tower*, noting that the inner curtain 'should represent "perhaps a stencilled pattern of dancers"' and comments that 'such hesitation and seeming self-doubt are typically found in Yeats's stage-directions'. She glosses this with the qualification that Yeats was 'always experimenting but was also ever open to new suggestions and ideas' (p. 310). The last remarks are true and consequently could well be applied to the stage direction to draw a very different inference from it than what is implied by 'hesitation and seeming self-doubt'. Yeats was a consummate man of the theatre and he had become so as a consequence of being open to advice, influence, observation and, most crucially, through the openness that is an essential aspect of collaboration. Successful collaboration demands total respect between the partners involved in the enterprise. It is wholly apparent from Dr. Ellis's research that Yeats over the years in which he observed dance came to a decided idea about the style he required, even if he lacked the requisite choreographic skills to teach that style to a performer himself. His practice as dramatist shows him creating contexts within which a dancer-choreographer is free to display her or his own artistry. This is not self-doubt or hesitation; this is a recognition that, for the complex uniting of skills, insight and creativity that are necessary in collaborative ventures to occur, there must be freedom and room for each of the collaborators to expand in imagination within an agreed scheme. Yeats knew perfectly well what he was doing and he was doing it out of complete respect for Ninette de Valois in the particular instance of *The King of The Great Clock Tower* as an artist equal in standing within her own chosen aesthetic discipline. It is clear from her writing about the experience of dancing in this play, which Yeats wrote for her expressly, that at each performance de Valois improvised around a prepared sequence of movements and that her inspiration came each evening (during the long period at the start of the play where the Queen must remain totally still and silent) from letting the suggestive power of Yeats's language and rhythms take complete possession of her awareness. She trusted him to inspire her and he constructed around her a context of meanings within which an audience might appreciate her virtuosity and the strange potency of dance.[1] Ninette de Valois has described the style of her dancing and movement as 'abstract expressionism'; it is apparent from photographs of the production that this was the style also deployed in Albert van Dalsum's production of *The Only Jealousy of Emer* in Amsterdam. Despite the fullness of Dr. Ellis's explorations in earlier styles of theatre dance that may have influenced Yeats, she chooses to leave this particular field deriving throughout the post-war years from Germany and the work of Wigman and Laban wholly untouched. As de Valois was Yeats's ideal dancer and abtract expressionism her preferred style in performing his plays, then this is a huge omission, given the scope of Dr. Ellis's debate. It mars what appears otherwise as an exhaustive study of the influences from contemporary theatre dance that went to the shaping of Yeats's plays for dancers.

NOTE

1. The collaborations between Yeats and Ninette de Valois are the subject of one chapter in my forthcoming book, *Border Crossings: Studies in the Relation of Dance and Drama*. Many of the ideas expressed in this review-article draw on research undertaken while preparing this volume of essays.

Lady Gregory's Diaries 1892-1902, edited and introduced by James Pethica (Colin Smythe: Gerrards Cross; New York: Oxford University Press, 1996) pp. xxxviii + 346.

Adrian Frazier

Any book so well done as this book is a pleasure to have. Colin Smythe has produced a volume in style and format comparable to the Oxford University Press edition of Yeats's *Collected Letters:* wrapped and covered in dark blue, with paper of a good weight, fine printing in conservative fonts, a trustworthy biographical appendix, and binding that looks as though it will last—which is only right, as the book will be useful for many years to come.

That is owing to the editorial work of James Pethica, who with this *debut* looks to be a scholar who will continue to make truly significant contributions for years to come. The research that went into making the scrawl of these notebook diaries into a fascinating history of late Victorian English and Irish societies is . . . what are the proper terms of praise? Staggering, humbling, delightful? There are, for instance, notes identifying and often giving the private history of forty-nine members of Lady Gregory's Persse family, much of it, to judge from the acknowledgements, gathered from interviews with five living members of the family. These notes as a group make up a great lost story of the decline of a landlord family in the West of Ireland: the grandfather who changed his will after being committed to a lunatic asylum; the father who then illegally suppressed a deed to steal an estate from his brother, and later set up a sawmill at Roxborough taking, in face of his children's horror, all the best trees of the wood, so that Dudley Persse, Lady Gregory's brother and the heir, enlisted in the British Army, only to be seriously wounded in the Crimean War. We are also introduced to Lady Gregory's proselytizing mother, whose local curate preached that the great mortality among the local peasants came from the priests' putting of poison into extreme unction, so that the demon papists could get the death dues; the brother William, Master of the Roxborough home, delusional from alcholism, who, to the relief of his family, died at age 56; and to Lady Gregory's sister Adelaide, who divorced her parson husband, Rev. James Lane—he kept a mistress—leaving the future of their son, Hugh Lane, for Lady Gregory to arrange. Considering this family and its past, it is no wonder that Lady Gregory chose to identify herself with the traditions of Coole, which, after the death of Sir William Gregory in 1892, were hers to redefine.

The Balzacian saga of the Persse family is, however, only an episode pointillistically charted through the 1,400 footnotes of this edition. Lady Gregory's diaries, once amplified by Pethica's scholarship, throw light on many more prominent figures. Sir William Gregory, in twelve years of marriage to Lady Gregory, had introduced her to several of the best circles of British society: Irish landlords, such as Lord Morris; art collectors, such as the Director of the National Gallery, Sir Frederic Burton; and Foreign Service officers (Sir William was once Governor of Ceylon), such as Sir Austen Henry Layard; and London literary people, among them Henry James, Marc-André Raffalovich, and Sir Alfred Comyns Lyall. Readers can imagine the value of a dated diary, even in the early years before Lady Gregory had given herself to the Irish literary movement, of someone with such access to notables, who knows what is genuinely quotable, and who is herself possessed of a remarkably piquant, even acerbic style of observation.

During her early years of widowhood, Lady Gregory was bent on keeping up a profile in London, so her young son Robert would, upon coming of age, have prominent friends to help make his way in life an easy one. Consequently, she got about London society with a purpose and earned herself a reputation as an excellent dinner guest, studying for the part by keeping abreast of current reading, so that she could discover trends in their emergence. By regular dining-out, she knew gossip others did not know, but where she came by the wonderful tact with which she deployed it is harder to say.

Lady Gregory's diary is not an accidentally important book; it seems that she sought from the first to make it one (or the basis of one). Her first major project after her husband's death was the properly widow-like one of completing his autobiography; next she assembled the life and correspondence of his grandfather and namesake, Under-Secretary for Ireland 1813-31. Her work on these volumes seems to have strengthened her idea of what the value to posterity could be of a wise daily record. The silent blessings of scholars will now fall upon her, for not simply recording what minor Royalty she's met, or what woman was on the arm of Sir —— at the opera. Not all chroniclers are so astute. T. P. Gill, for instance, through his career as Nationalist MP, *Daily Express* editor, and Secretary of the Department of Agricultural and Technical Instruction, kept a diary for decades, and recorded, alas, almost nothing but his cab fares. Lady Gregory taxied around London from house to house, often four or five an afternoon, in search of good material, but she recorded conversation not receipts. Just take her record of her nightly chats in Queen Anne's Mansions with Paul Harvey, an orphan in whom both she and Henry James took a parental interest (Lady Gregory emerges here as a very Jamesian woman, one who was an artist in the material of other's marriage prospects, but neither Isabel Archer nor Madame Merle, a little too knowing for the first, and too decent for the second). During the Boer War, Harvey was a private secretary in the Foreign Office, and when the weight of Imperial affairs was too much for him, he disburdened himself to the aunt/mother figure of Lady Gregory. Her notes on these late-night confessions throw many shafts of light on dark events from the Jameson Raid to Mafeking night.

Pethica here as elsewhere is an expert in decryption, who can tell us with each of the figures that turn up in the record, no matter how little their lives finally amounted to, when they were born and died, who their relations were, what books they wrote or offices they held, if any, how they came to be in relation to Lady Gregory, and, when possible, if there is further corroboration of the event, for instance in another unpublished diary, such as those by Lady Layard or Horace Plunkett. This is work very well done, not just information from the *DNB*, but original work.

Pethica's introductory essay will lend force to the movement to establish Lady Gregory as a major literary figure in her own right (a movement well underway with Mary Lou Koufeldt's biography and Lucy McDiarmid and Maureen Waters' recent Penguin edition of Lady Gregory's selected writings). Without puffery on the one hand or condescension on the other, he traces her character from the age of 39 and to 50, when she moved from being the Unionist author of the unsigned anti-Home Rule pamphlet, 'A Phantom's Pilgrimage' to the advanced Nationalist 'Felons of Our Land,' from the social circles of elderly friends of her late husband to the network of the major figures of the Irish cultural revival, then centered in her own home of Coole Park, from someone who makes herself invisible as an author by anonymous publication and quiet editiorial work to someone who redrafts her diaries into published memoirs that magnify her role, from the editions and minor short-stories to 'the threshold of lasting literary prominence', at the end of her 'apprenticeship in the politics of self-representation'.

This apprenticeship is mostly in relation to her chosen master, W. B. Yeats. Pethica confirms George Moore's account in *Hail and Farewell!* that Lady Gregory saw her need in Yeats at once. Before the famous meeting at Coole in early August, 1896, she had already read Yeats's poems, proselytized for *The Celtic Twilight*, made her own solitary trip to Aran years earlier, and, immediately prior to her hastening to Tillyra when the poet showed up there, she had gathered folklore to give to him. As Pethica says, 'the scent of careful planning hangs over Lady Gregory's part in the meeting' (xxxvi).

She cemented her relation to the thrilling young poet once she got back to London. In February of 1897, she invited him to a rapid sequence of dinners, before the first of which she typed out the folklore she had in the interim gathered. Then, using her confident skills as a hostess in selecting guests for small dinner-parties, and managing the conversation, she brought him together with her wide circle of acquaintance, which now included the MPs, Barry O'Brien (Nationalist) and Horace Plunkett (Unionist, but patriotic). After this sequence of dinners in February and March, by April she had Yeats signed up to stay the summer at Coole. It was the beginning of a major change in life for both of them.

It is extraordinary, by the way, just how many dinners Yeats ate at Lady Gregory's apartments in Queen Anne's Mansions in London. He not only lived at Coole for months every summer and sometimes into the autumn, but once she returned to London, usually right after Christmas, he was there to meet her on the day of her arrival, and thereafter showed up almost daily (sometimes he was, to her bitter regret, off chasing Maud Gonne) around dinnertime, or at least teatime. It looks like the man would have starved without her, and he was not ashamed to let her know it. By the winter of 1899, she had also taken up other members of the Yeats family. She found buyers for Jack Yeats's pictures during his February 1899 Exhibition, and bought heavily herself. A month after helping Jack with his exhibition, in March, 1899, she has arranged and 'assist[ed] at W. Peel's portrait' by John Butler Yeats. How did this 'assistance' work? When Lady Gregory tried to entertain the sitter through uncommonly protracted sittings, she happened to say that Robert's headmaster at Harrow gave a sermon saying that the two ideals for a boy are the British Empire and the Church of Christ. JBY cried '& both shams!' It was all she could do to get Peel to come back after lunch for yet another sitting.

Through this period of involvement with Yeats and his family, Lady Gregory progresses, as Pethica shows, from folklore gatherer (yes, and WBY really did wait in the cart while she went to the cottage doors!), to private secretary, to prose collaborator, to sage counsellor, to contributor of sentences (e.g., to 'Diarmuid and Grania'), to author of all-but-all of *Cathleen ni Houlihan*, to work on her own. At the halfway point of this transformation in her role, there is a heartbreaking reflection recorded in a notebook completed in March 1900: 'I dreamed that I had been writing some article & that W.B.Y. said, "It's not your business to write—Your business is to make an atmosphere"'. But if the poet of her dreams failed to see early on that his hostess wanted herself to be a great author, the real WBY ultimately did so. The diaries end with scattered reflections in 1909, after she has written many plays and established herself as bread-winner of the Abbey Theatre. One of the last of these reflections is that her friendship with Yeats continues, and 'I owe to him what I have done of late years—he gave me belief in myself'. That is certainly the best of gifts, and all honor to the giver. One can see that she gave him at least as much in return—not only the many dinners, the summers at Coole, and the dialogues for plays, but a constancy of purpose through her counsel, and a whole new sense of life: the dignity of a landed aristocrat of long (if half-imagined) traditions, with a sincere love of Irish folk, a deep feeling of duty to help others with less wealth and education, and a resigned but not embittered acceptance of the end of landlordism with the coming of national independence. (Yeats was a slow learner of this last lesson.)

One of the painful and beautiful stories that emerges from the diaries is that of Lady Gregory as mother. Widowed in 1892, she reconceives of her role as no longer wife, but mother of the one son that remains to her: she will for his sake clear Coole of debt, for his sake keep up a London profile, manage his entrance into Harrow, and then Oxford, and preserve good relations with the tenants, even if it means liberal reductions in rent. She imagines a future for him as head of the class at Harrow, with a First at New College, and then a career in the Foreign Office. But Robert, while mostly a dutiful boy and gentle, is rather idle at Harrow, and after a good start drops by the end to the bottom of his class. Once at Oxford, reports come back to her that he does not work much, has no settled interest, except maybe art, and he finally graduates late (in 1903) with a third-class degree. His favourite activities are playing cricket and shooting birds (often with Douglas Hyde, whose letters to Lady Gregory keep a running tab of the hundreds of birds he has bagged). What is more, when the Boer War heats up, Robert begins to part company with his mother on political matters: he is full of imperialist excitement, and not just about South Africa. By this time, Lady Gregory is well on her way to advanced nationalism, and emotionally she is completely com-mitted to Yeats. She is afraid that by nationalism she will lose her son; and he is afraid that by nationalism he will lose himself. In July 1900, she records a touching dream that Robert has: he fears that if he goes sketch-ing with AE and Yeats and looks at faeries, he will lose his eyesight and won't be able to play cricket. For some, de-Anglicization could be a nightmare. In 1902, when Robert turns 21, and should become the Master at Coole Park, Yeats is well established in his stead (as com-fortably in possession as a stepfather), and Robert has to make off for Paris and London, where he studies art. The mother who lived for her son, her largest horizon the family, has become the author involved in a national cultural movement with a great poet.

One could not have figured out Lady Gregory's relationship to Yeats, or to much else, by the version of these diaries Lady Gregory published as *Seventy Years*. A detailed comparison of Pethica's edition of the *Diaries* will show many another scholar besides myself how it was that their chronology of the Irish Literary Revival became irreconciliably confused. In 1897-98, she mislaid one of her notebooks, and took up another; then found the original, and continued in it, in the process contorting the chronology of the beginnings of the Irish Literary Theatre. Furthermore, in *Seventy Years*, she leaves out all but the occasional month and day, and sometimes gives those incorrectly. Thus, part of the great value of the diary, its chronology, was not only lost, but in place of it we put our trust in a false chronology.

In writing *Seventy Years*, Lady Gregory went in for a thoroughgoing bowdlerization. She left out the best parts from the point of view of the biographer and the literary historian: barbs of truth aimed at friends, signs of intimate feelings for her 'charming lovable companion' W. B. Yeats, favourable remarks about her subsequent enemy George Moore, acid detestation of Maud Gonne, general chilliness toward the wives of all the male artists she patronizes (AE, Hyde, Jack Yeats, etc.), and anything else not consonant, as Pethica points out, with her 'conciliating self-image.' Along with *Our Irish Theatre*, *Seventy Years* makes her seem from the start like a central figure in the Irish Literary Theatre, when the *Diaries* show that (until the Summer of 1902) she was simply an enthusiast, gatherer of guarantees, and bearish protector of WBY's interests.

On 24 January 1900, for instance, when Edward Martyn came to her asking for her support in an effort to supplant George Moore's *The Bending of the Bough* (then in rehearsal for a February 20 opening) with his own already rejected *The Tale of a Town*, saying he only needed a 'majority of the committee' of the Irish Literary Theatre, she says she does not believe herself to be on that committee: it is only WBY, Moore and Martyn. However, at this stage, she is beginning to take a role in delilberations that would suggest to others that she is a director, at least virtually through her influence on Yeats. After *The Bending of the Bough* turns out to be a tremendous success (to the nearly equal disappointment of Lady Gregory and Martyn), she determines along with Yeats that such successes must not be repeated, even at the price of disappointing the audiences, because 'we must try & keep politics out of plays in the future.' Since Yeats had been, along with AE and T. P. Gill, one of those chiefly responsible for putting the politics into *The Bending of the Bough*, and Yeats only weeks earlier had been ecstatically proud over doing so, it may be that Lady Gregory here was beginning to play a chief role in setting the course of the Irish Literary Theatre, by emboldening Yeats to force out of the theatre Ibsenesque satirical treatments of the Irish middle and upper classes, and to include only strictly literary (if in another sense no less political) heroic and folk theatre. But the matter remains unclear. For all the value of the diary, when Lady Gregory says that Yeats agreed with her that so-and-so was the case, it is not easy to tell whether she said something very firmly, and WBY nodded, and said, 'Of course, Lady Gregory'; or whether he soliloquized on the carpet, and she was satisfied to find him saying something she had beforehand already believed. The transmission of opinions between two people so intimately dependent on one another, bound together by multiple forms of candor, and multiple forms of discretion too, is a highly mysterious process.

My own chief interest in first reading these diaries was in the appearances of George Moore, of whom I am writing a biography. He turns up on 64 different pages, at teas, dinners, theatres, galleries, story conferences, at Tillyra and Coole in Galway, at the Shelbourne in Dublin, in Lady Gregory's apartment or his own in London, as literary lion to adorn the guest-list of a dinner party, then as close friend of her new friend W. B. Yeats, as acquaintance of her friends Edward Martyn and William Geary, as the suddenly vigorous stage-manager of the first season of the Irish Literary Theatre, then as the more and more dominant presence in Yeats's life, taking *The Tale of a Town* from Martyn, getting involved (to her horror) in rewriting *The Shadowy Waters*, then shockingly seizing upon the Irish language as his to promote (which had been her particular field of expertise and management), and more and more becoming somebody she wanted to get out of Yeats's life. In the beginning of this sequence, she is rather distantly impressed by him as the author of *Esther Waters*, a novel which consolidated her myth of herself as mother living through hardship for the sake of her son. Later she is constrained to record that he is often an 'amiable', 'agreeable' person at many a dinner party. By the end, she cannot keep herself from speaking of him as 'an absurd creature' (p. 289). In the course of the *Diarmuid and Grania* collaboration, on 2 October, 1900, she joins with Yeats at the Coole dinner-table in twitting and teasing GM for his choice of words ('soldier' for Finn); then she firmly pushes Yeats to stick by a no-concessions policy on stylistic revisions, not even to talk with GM about compromises on 19 November. When at Arthur Symons's urging, Yeats does go on 20 November, the two get on amicably and have no subsequent difficulties over their collaboration. While it was normally Lady Gregory's role to play the conciliator, and in *Seventy Years* this is always her role, in the Yeats/Moore friendship she seems to have been consistently the instigator of trouble, by feeding Yeats's pride and hurting Moore's, with the intention of protecting Yeats's central position and her central relationship to him.

On the whole, these diaries offer the first day-by-day contemporary record to set beside Moore's narrative in *Hail and Farewell!*. One would expect that they would lead one to correct what has always been said (first by its victims) to be a book more novel than history, more libel than truth, more vanity than wisdom. A comparison of Lady Gregory's contemporary record with GM's narrative based on his memory, however, leads one to be impressed the accuracy of Moore's memory. The diary provides the dates and footnotes to Moore's narrative, but it does not substantially undercut its truth. Generally, Moore outraged people by telling unseasonable truths, not by lieing.

Without the fine editorial work done on this volume, without indeed the fine literary intelligence expressed in the diaries themselves, I would have a far poorer picture of one period in the life of George Moore. I am therefore grateful to James Pethica and Colin Smythe for doing a first-class job with this book. There will be many another scholar who will feel similiar gratitude. Those that are interested in Henry James, Sir Henry Layard, Sir Frederic Burton, John Gray, Edward Martyn, Horace Plunkett, George Russell, Douglas Hyde, and, most importantly, Lady Gregory herself, will find this to be henceforth an essential book.

William M. Murphy, *Family Secrets: William Butler Yeats and His Relatives* (Syracuse: Syracuse University Press, 1995) pp. xxvii + 534.

Gifford Lewis, *The Yeats Sisters and the Cuala* (Dublin: Irish Academic Press: Dublin, 1994) pp. xiv + 199. Joan Hardwick, *The Yeats Sisters: A Biography of Susan and Elizabeth Yeats* (London: Pandora, 1996) pp. viii + 263.

James Pethica

WRITING OF THE PRESSMARK used by Dun Emer and then the Cuala Press between 1907 and 1926, Elizabeth (Lollie) Yeats, the long-time manager of those presses, commented in 1932 to a Scottish bibliophile that its design, the figure of 'The Lady Emer Standing by a Tree', hadn't had 'any meaning—except that our press was started as a woman's press. She is a very limp figure is she not? Much as Cuala makes me feel'. The comment serves as a telling reminder of the way that gender was a crucial factor both in the inception of Dun Emer and Cuala, and, more significantly and corrosively, in the personal lives of Lollie and her sister Lily (Susan) Yeats. While their creative abilities were always likely to have been affected, positively as well as negatively, by growing up under the influence of the forceful personality of their father, and by having to work in the ever-widening shadow of fame cast from the 1890s on by WBY, it is clear that their sex and the gender politics of the Ireland of their time were factors which shaped the course of their lives at least as significantly as their particular family heritage. These books by William M. Murphy, Gifford Lewis and Joan Hardwick constitute a welcome surge of new attention to the hitherto largely overlooked sisters, but they signal quite sharply that the matter of gender remains a contentiously unresolved factor in critical assessment of their work.

William Murphy's *Family Secrets* complements his many writings about the Yeats family—most notably his biography of John Butler Yeats, *Prodigal Father* (1978)—and reflects many years of research on the mass of surviving family papers. His notes alone here comprise nearly 90 pages of precise documentation of manuscript sources from a dozen major public and private repositories and numerous other locations. The volume opens with chapters on the Yeats and Pollexfen lineages and on

'Home Life amongst the Yeatses' up to around 1900, and concludes with a chapter on Jack B. Yeats and another on John Butler Yeats's epistolary 'affair' with Rosa Butt—this latter being perhaps the only family 'secret' promised by the title not to have been addressed to some degree by other critics. At its heart, though, are four chapters which focus on Lollie and Lily Yeats, the formation and collapse of Dun Emer, and the fortunes of the Cuala Industries. Much here is new and valuable, particularly Murphy's detailing of the formative parts played by Evelyn Gleeson and Augustine Henry in the inception of the Dun Emer co-operative. As he demonstrates, the 'Yeats sisters were not founders of Dun Emer except in the most tangential way', joining the enterprise only following an approach made by Henry in 1902, and from the first misunderstanding Gleeson's primary executive role in the new business. Murphy's charting of the stages of the gradual break-up of Dun Emer, the formation of Cuala in 1908 after the Yeats sisters' split with Gleeson, and then the strains which beset Cuala in the years which followed, draws extensively on the financial and legal records of the two organizations, and makes copious use of the sisters's unpublished correspondence. His account adds substantively to the previous record of the practical dealings of the Cuala Press, of the personal tensions between Lollie and Lily, and also of WBY's part as both series editor for the Cuala volumes and as lender of last resort in keeping the operation afloat in the 1930s.

Regrettably, though, Murphy's treatment of the sisters is conditioned throughout by his obvious privileging of, or perhaps simply internalization of, JBY's view of events—a view centred on a crude genetic theory of the difference between the 'Pollexfen' temperament and the 'Yeats' temperament—and by a basic antipathy towards his subjects. For JBY, Lollie was all Pollexfen—moody, withdrawn, 'primitive'—while the conciliating Lily embodied the essential qualities of the personable Yeatses. Murphy follows this schema loyally, detailing reams of damning evidence against Lollie, to draw a portrait of her as loose cannon—psychologically crippled, socially dysfunctional and a constant irritant to her family—while Lily becomes the preyed-upon victim, who deserved much better. Murphy takes little or no account of the way Lollie, in particular, served as the dominant breadwinner for the Yeats family in the 1890s, earning as much as £300 a year—an extraordinary sum for a single woman at that time—through her teaching and successful publications, money she willingly spent to fill the financial void left by the impractical JBY and a slow-earning WBY who had been warned away by his father from the dangerous world of regular work. At least some engagement with the fact that Lollie thereby compromised her chances for marriage or other forms of self-fulfillment, serverd as an essential figure in sub-sidizing her brother's success, and might have had good reason to be bit-ter later in life, should have featured here. Instead, what we are presented with is a simplistic good girl | bad girl dyad, in which the compliant Lily, earning her money through appropriate 'woman's work' as an embroiderer, becomes a figure for admirable self-sacrifice, whereas the transgressive Lollie, an assertive and ambitious professional who entered the mainly male domain of printing and later even had the temerity to baulk at her celebrated brother's imperious insistence that things be done his way, becomes a dangerous, unbalanced virago. Murphy entitles his fourth chapter simply 'W. B. Yeats and the Weird Sisters', and it is clear that he finds Joyce's mocking epithet basically appropriate to describe the pair. His preface tells us that he is 'under no illusion that [their] story would be of interest to the world if they were not sisters of a great poet' and his narrative thus takes no interest in their unusual achievement in running a women-only business, in the remarkable accomplishment of Cuala as a Press, or the way they epitomised the kind of marginalization suffered by intelligent women in their time. Alternately referred to as 'ladies' and 'girls' (the latter even when in their fifties and older), they are judged here as much for their skills in 'social graces' and their willingness to comply with the wishes of the Yeats males, as for their creative capa-cities.

Murphy indeed exposes a clear antipathy in this volume to assertive women of any kind: Evelyn Gleeson and Annie Horniman are overbear-ing and 'patronizing', while Maud Gonne is 'extreme and irrational' in her politics and 'almost insanely' committed to violence. The 'homely' Katharine Tynan, giving 'encouragement' to the young WBY, is by implication more womanly and correct than these hysterical and emo-tional old maids. Meanwhile, WBY's 'arrogance and righteousness' and JBY's 'overpowering personality' are markers of genius rather than signs of intolerance, narcissism or emotional dysfunction, and we are expected, like Auden, simply to forgive them 'for writing well'. Murphy's imagina-tive identification with JBY and his view of events is clear in his final chapter charting the racy correspondence with Rosa Butt, which treats the letters as an 'utterly fascinating' testament to the elder Yeats's pas-sionate intensity. Most readers, however, will surely be inclined to find JBY's fixation on his one moment of of limited physical intimacy with Butt, and his efforts to rekindle it by post, merely pathetic. In 1906, when she came to Dublin specifically to see him—and, one must assume, find out whether his epistolary fervour might lead to lovemaking or mar-riage—he proceeeded as far as amorous groping but no further. From the thoroughly safe distance of New York he would posture for the next decade and more as a fire-eater and *enfant terrible*, thrilling at the thought of painting her 'pink nipples' and imagining heroic passion at their next encounter, but his accomplished discourse in the letters only thinly veils an infantile self-absorption and, typically, his complete lack of practicality. Murphy construes Butt's apparent refusal to rise to the bait of postal titillation as a sign of her quintessental Victorian repression and prudishness, but a commonsense recognition of JBY's masturbatory immaturity seems as likely as explanation.

Family Secrets is an attractively produced book, richly illustrated and packed with hitherto unpublished source materials. As a treatment of the inner workings of the Yeats family, however, it is of limited value, not least since Murphy deliberately shies from serious interpretative engagement with the materials he uncovers, and indeed seems to be in shocked withdrawal over the critical developments of the past few decades. 'Psychoanalytic probing', we are told, 'is a dangerous business' from which 'Marxists, Freudians, Deconstructionists, New Historicists, and assorted other 'ists' and 'ians' do not shrink, but one which the person of ordinary common sense approaches with caution'. Theory of any sort is suspect here—with Feminism symptomatically being unnamable in the list of demons—while instead the 'open mind' and a 'simple humanist' position are repeatedly extolled. The result is that we indeed get plenty of 'facts' and 'simple biography', but very little reflective literary criticism. Major work within the field is basically evaded or assimilated lazily—a footnote tells us that John Purser's 1991 book on Jack Yeats appeared 'too late' for substantial use in this work, published in 1995—and crude personal preferences are brandished as 'common sense' (Yeats's involvement with the occult, for instance, generate epithets ranging from 'bizarre' and 'ludicrous' to 'mumbo jumbo' and 'eccentric'). The volume presents a remorselessly male-centred system of values, and ends up essentially simply reaffirming the central narratives offered in WBY's and JBY's own writings

Gifford Lewis's *The Yeats Sisters and The Cuala*, by contrast, positions itself candidly and vigorously in the opposing court. The dust-jacket immediately signals the recuperative work the volume attempts by highlighting the way the sisters funded their 'self-absorbed and improvident father' and by noting that WBY's opinion of them was 'rather blinkered and patronizing'. The opening chapter fleshes out the first of these charges effectively, crisply accusing JBY of having psychologically 'maimed' his wife, cramped his daughters' prospects and evaded the responsibilities of being a husband and father, all the while blaming those 'primitive' Pollexfen genes and rarely himself. Despite the limits on them, Lewis argues, Lollie and Lily succeed anyway. Reconceived in her scheme as essentially late century 'new women', they resisted convention in crucial ways, actively resisting marriage (rather than simply lacking opportunities), and seeking out financial independence as best they could. While far from feminist triumphs—Lewis is throughout judiciously measured in her claims—the sisters were significant achievers despite all the forces working against them, with the Cuala Press volumes in particular constituting in her view a quite remarkable achievement in the otherwise 'male' sphere of printing. The archival material she deploys in support of these readings is almost always arresting, particularly an 1863 letter in which JBY figures himself as an ineffectual wife-figure and Susan Pollexfen Yeats as the dominant force: 'I know that in your reserve, quiet strength and common sense you are more a man than a woman[,] only I hope you won't henpeck me . . . what a milksop I'll be thought and what a tyrant you'll be thought'. Such semi-erotic fantasies on JBY's part nicely undercut the simple and essentialist male-female binaries which inform Murphy's work, and hint at the potential impact of his impracticality and 'effete' passivity on his four talented children. Lollie, in short, did 'become' the man of the house in the 1890s, though the dominance she earned in the practical and professional realm earned her few lasting credits with her father or brother.

Lewis, who has written extensively on Somerville and Ross, is shrewdly attentive to the particular concerns of women artists and entrepreneurs in this book. Evelyn Gleeson's suffragist views, for instance, are stressed as a factor in the establishment of Dun Emer, while figures such as Susan Mitchell and Lady Gregory are enlisted as examples of contemporaries ambitious, like the Yeats sisters, to find a creative out-lets for themselves. Her treatment of the strains and personal tensions both between the sisters, and between Lollie and WBY, is likewise judicious and does much to undercut Murphy's 'genetic' reading in which Lollie was simply the 'problem' sister. Lewis notes, for instance, that it was Lollie who was the regular guest of notables on her weekends, while Lily tended to stay home, and that it was Lily who interfered in Lollie's relationship with Louis Purser, whereas Murphy depicts Lolllie in later life as little more than a pathological liar and always socially incompetent, and Lily simply as the 'good sister'. Lewis acknowledges Lollie's abrasiveness, noting that WBY and Lollie were 'very alike in their unpleasant qualities of self-absorption and self-righteousness', but she argues that these qualities stemmed in both from the same perfec-tionism and drive, and that Lollie was routinely criticized simply because her ambition and directness were 'unexpected then in a woman'. Lewis's narrative, unlike Murphy's, also emphasizes the moments of collaboraative concord and joint-achievement which punctuated the many strains in the sibling relationships, stressing the way that WBY and Lollie 'painstakingly' worked together to achieve the most satisfactory layout in the early Dun Emer texts and noting the way their 'two handwritings converse with each other' on the proofs of *In the Seven Woods*.

The Yeats Sisters is almost always insightful, and particularly valuable in its focus on Lollie and Lily's accomplishment as designers. Lewis, trained as a typographer and letterer, and formerly a designer at Irish University Press herself, treats the reader to a concise account of the development of Irish script, engaging commentary on Lollie Yeats's accomplishments with and publications on brushwork, and concise overviews of matters such as the history of Irish printing. Her admiration for the Cuala Industries work and for the sisters' design-work is manifest, and the volume includes a rich selection of illustrations and photographs of Cuala embroideries, lettering, bookplates and other works. In its effort to cover a very broad terrain rather quickly—it after all treats family history and biography, Cuala as a business, Cuala as an artistic enterprise, and much more in a very limited space—the volume does move rather too quickly across fertile areas, being content to offer provocative comments and speculations and then move on, and its use of archival materials is somewhat limited. One would wish, in short, that this book were much expanded. A more severe shortcoming is the lack of scholarly notes identifying sources, particularly given the many choices vignettes Lewis culls from the archives. Written with pace and energy, the volume overall certainly succeeds in its stated task of urging 'separate notice' for the Yeats sisters and their accomplishments, and will surely spur further attention to and documentation of the now widely-dispersed production of the Cuala workshop.

Joan Hardwick's *The Yeats Sisters: A Biography of Susan and Elizabeth Yeats* offers a populist feminist portrait of the sisters, which professedly sets out to 'rescue Lily and Lolly from the shadows of their male relatives'. Hardwick, who acknowledges in her Introduction that '[t]wo years ago I had never heard of Susan and Elizabeth Yeats' paints heroes and villains here with a rather broad brush, and her narrative, which lacks the more subtle revaluative readings of gender in Lewis's book, proceeds with reductive confidence across the masses of material she has assimilated in her two years. There is a modicum of use of new sources here, but most of the text simply decants wine from older barrels and pours it into a rather flat new narrative of oppression.

Hazard Adams, *The Book of Yeats's Vision: Romantic Modernism and Antithetical Tradition* (Ann Arbor: The University of Michigan Press, 1995) pp. xiv, 178.

Colin McDowell

THE SUBJECT MATTER AND ODD STRUCTURE of *A Vision (B)* have combined to cause problems for those wishing to classify its genre and hence understand what it is trying to accomplish. Is it a philosophical or a literary work? Is it unified enough for it to be classified either way? *The Book of Yeats's Vision* details an approach to *A Vision* which was first adumbrated by the author some forty years ago in *Blake and Yeats: The Contrary Vision*, and repeated by him several times since. Adams argues 'that Yeats fictionalized and satirized his own persona in *A Vision*, that the comic in Yeats should not be underestimated, that the work ought to be treated as a literary text, and that the frame of *A Vision* is important' (p. 166). The book is full of novel and intriguing insights, and Adams's case is argued with sensitivity, passion, intelligence and good humour. Such an approach is well worth taking, and I have not read anything else on *A Vision* with so much pleasure for quite some time. Still, whether it is altogether convincing is another thing entirely.

In my view, *A Vision* is primarily a discursive work and the non-expository parts are ultimately dispensable: the so-called 'frame' is hardly deserving of the title, and certainly doesn't manage to pull all of the fragments together, whereas the expository parts in themselves are pulled together by Book II, 'The Completed Symbol'. You can decide to view a water buffalo from the perpective of the ticks in its ear, and ticks are certainly interesting creatures, perhaps even amusing, but the water buffalo is quite able to survive without them. I say this to warn the reader of my bias.

What I wish to suggest in this review is that Adams's approach leads him to make palpable errors in emphasis and interpretation. This by no means disqualifies his viewpoint. What Adams has to say will have to be digested by the Yeats community as a whole. Given the difficulty of *A Vision*, I don't think this will happen for some time yet; but if Adams's work encourages people to try reading the book for themselves, it will have served a noble purpose.

Exposition of a system demands completeness and consistency; fiction may be satisfied with neither, as Sterne has demonstrated. Adams's principal argument for his contention that *A Vision* is a literary work is summarized in the statement that 'When Yeats simplifies or delays, he tends to obfuscate' (p. 96). If this were true, it would seriously qualify one's trust in Yeats as propounder of a system, unless of course Adams is correct in believing that such a situation has been projected as part of a comic persona. Instead of taking Yeats's statements at face value, as incidental or *ad hoc* expressions of his awareness of how odd the tale of the Instructors must appear to outsiders or as signs of the author's sympathy for the reader faced with the difficulty of mastering a complex geometry, Adams asks us to believe that they have been deliberately planted to cast doubt on Yeats's motivation and to draw the reader further into the trap. The book is, for him, narrative and not exposition, and 'Yeats' assumes the status of unreliable narrator or Kennerian arranger. 'Exposition' exists merely to dramatize the theory that 'consciousness is conflict', and consistency exists only in similitude, or at a minimal level, so that the reader does not give up in disgust. For Adams, the difficulties and apparent *non-sequiturs* become part of a ploy to increase the reader's frustration and heighten tension. Consciousness is brought thereby to an exquisite pitch of intensity, and if the text does not quite generate a frisson recognizable as aesthetic emotion, at least one feels as though one is undergoing an experience.

At least two things may be said against this view. First, it is a double-take, the convenience of which verges on the venal. If you cannot make sense of a piece of exposition, you can always save face by claiming that it was not intended to make sense. In other words, there is no way the claim can be falsified. The theory works better if there is open warfare between individual passages of exposition, and its proponents are happier to find that confusion and ambiguity abound: hence the number of times that Adams delights in finding that chaos 'threatens' the system (pp. 67, 102, 107). In short, it discourages the reader from attempting to understand. Secondly, it is simply not true that Yeats obfuscates. It may be taken as an axiom that whenever Yeats says that something is more convenient or simpler, and it does not appear to be so, this is because the reader has not followed his instructions or has made one or more fundamental errors in interpretation; and that whenever he delays, but says that he will return to a topic later in *A Vision*, he inevitably returns to it. Here, at least, we leave the realm of opinion for one where logical argument can be brought to bear.

I do not deny that Yeats's Part I, 'The Principal Symbol', of Book I, 'The Great Wheel', is hard going; but when Yeats suggests that it is 'more

YEATS ANNUAL 13   359

convenient' (*AV B* 80) to move from diagrams of gyres to a diagram of a wheel, it seems to me that this is a simple statement of fact. Yeats is drawing diagrams to explain a reciprocal waxing and waning of pairs: as one pair expands, the other contracts. He could have explained his concepts with pictures of pistons and cylinders just as easily, although he would have had to draw twenty-eight of them, and would not have been able easily to indicate relationships. The abrupt way in which Adams turns the discussion from gyres to wheel is indicative of either a lack of understanding on his part or a desire to make Yeats seem more arbitrary than he is. 'The two gyres are also a wheel', he writes (p. 74), and the reader is entitled to ask, 'Why?' It is true that Yeats sometimes uses 'gyre' and 'wheel' interchangeably, but in any diagram consisting of a single line which joins its beginning and end, designated points on the line can be plotted on a wheel. For example, the four corners of a square can be represented as points on a wheel, but you don't go on to say things like 'The square is also a wheel' unless you explain what it is you are doing. It seems as though Adams is looking for a syntagmatic relationship between gyre and wheel, whereas the correct relationship is a paradigmatic one. This suspicion is confirmed when he later claims that 'The wheel is what Blake called "the bound or outward circumference of Energy"', where Energy is identified by Adams as the activity of the two interlocking whirling gyres (pp. 68-9). It must be stressed that Yeats does not attempt seriously to relate his gyres to his wheel in this fashion, although he flirts with the idea when he discusses Empedocles (*AV B* 67-8). He merely wants to show us a representation of proportionality and direction, and the relationship between the two symbols is purely abstract.

This is not the only place where Adams seems to want to do things with the geometry that it was not designed to do. When Yeats tells us that, 'Taken in relation to the wheel, the diamond and the hourglass [of the Principles] are two pulsations, one expanding, one contracting. I can see them like jelly-fish in clear water' (*AV B* 200), he is offering a throwaway simile whose picturesque quality may or may not add sparkle to the text and assist the reader. But there is no warrant for Adams's interpretation:

> This suggests still another movement. As the two cones [of the hourglass] whirl opposite to each other they turn inside out, while the diamond, whirling in the clockwise direction, does the same (p. 103).

Adams is here importing a piece of mystification from Owen Aherne's Introduction to the 1925 edition (*AV A* xxiii; cf. 175), but it is never explained how it is meant to arise out of Yeats's figure.

It is disappointing that Adams tends to get the wrong end of the stick when discussing the geometry, given that his introduction of the term 'mathesis' (p. 23) is a genuine contribution to debate, pointing up a distinction Yeats was working towards but never formulated, and that Adams, unlike most readers of *A Vision*, adopts the excellent strategy of drawing diagrams which Yeats did not supply. Unfortunately, some of the diagrams he gives are not precise, and the more complex ones are downright misleading, so that my advice to those who wish to use his diagrams is that they should do so only with extreme care. To begin with, the template used for the twenty-eight phase wheel depicts each phase by a point on the circumference, rather than as a segment with extension, and the points are erratically spaced. This results in the lop-sided diagram on p. 75, and contributes, one suspects, to the appalling diagram on p. 104, where the lines to show the extent of the zodiacal signs are all over the place.

It could perhaps be said these complaints about the template relate to the merely cosmetic aspects of Adams's book, although it is important to be able to grasp Yeats's symmetries at a glance; but let us examine the latter diagram more closely. Adams first discusses it when expounding the division of the Great Wheel into sets of three phases, excluding phases 1, 8, 15 and 22. His comment on this division is that 'It is not until a later book of *A Vision* that we learn the instructors are speaking here in terms of a solar wheel of twelve months rather than a lunar one of twenty-eight phases' (p. 82). In fact, Yeats is talking simply of dividing the lunar wheel in a different way, and Adams is wrong to think that the solar wheel should be brought in here. He thinks this, of course, because he has taken to heart Yeats's statement that 'This wheel [of twenty-eight phases] is every completed movement of thought or life, twenty-eight incarnations, a single incarnation, a single judgement or act of thought' (*AVB* 81). The statement becomes Adams's licence to apply what he calls the principle of radical synecdoche wherever and whenever he sees fit: each wheel becomes every other wheel. But before you can conflate, you need to distinguish; in other words, you must know thoroughly what it is you wish to conflate. What is above may be what is below, and what is below may be what is above, but it's still nice to know which way is up. Yeats introduces the hermetic principle in order to simplify, not to complicate, and what he says of the Great Year of the ancient Greeks applies to his own wheels: 'it is always the simpler, more symbolic form, with its conflict of light and dark, heat and cold, that concerns me most' (*AVB* 246). Yeats is interested in circularity, and in the points which disrupt the circularity, moments of highs and lows, of crisis and reversal, and every wheel may be said to have these. Yeats often uses shorthand by discussing them in terms of Phases 1 and 15, or 8 and 22, Aries and Libra, Cancer and Capricorn, and could have referred just as easily to half-way and three-quarter points, but he does not expect us to confuse matters by filling in the intervening points in every case.

Thus, in Adams's diagram of the solar and lunar wheels, Yeats's instructions have not been used as they are intended, merely to position the solar wheel in relation to the lunar wheel; Adams assumes that the solar wheel must also be divided into twenty-eight phases, and adds various features from different parts of the system. He has in fact fallen for the temptation of trying to construct a multi-purpose diagram, a single figure which can be used a reference point for all (or most) discussions of the book's geometry. This makes it simpler for him to claim that Yeats is being complicated for complication's sake. In his diagram, Adams identifies the quarters where individual Faculties and Principles dominate; specifies the directions 'Toward Nature' and 'Toward God' (but gets them wrong, both for a lunar wheel, where 'Phase 1 to Phase 15 is towards Nature' and 'Phase 15 to Phase 1 is towards God' [*AVB* 104], and for a solar, where 'Toward God' should go towards the quarter where Celestial Body dominates, and 'Toward Nature' should go towards the quarter where Passionate Body dominates); and adds 'Pagan Era (Antithetical)' and 'Christian Era (Primary)' to identify halves of the wheels (although it may appear to casual inspection that the directional arrows are also meant to apply to the Eras). He also writes 'Sun' against solar North and 'Moon' against solar South. In other words, his so-called solar wheel is almost identical to a lunar wheel, with the lunar wheel's phases, Eras, directions and full Sun and full Moon.

But what of the superimposition itself? Adams takes the basic principle for constructing his diagram from *A Vision* where Yeats writes:

> If, however, we were to consider both wheels or cones [i.e. of *Faculties* and *Principles*] as moving at the same speed and to place, for purposes of comparison, the *Principles* in a double cone, drawn and numbered like that of the *Faculties*, and superimpose it upon that of the *Faculties*, a line drawn between Phase 1 and Phase 15 on the first would be at right angles to a line drawn between the same phases upon the other. Phase 22 in the cone of the *Principles* would coincide with Phase 1 in the cone of the *Faculties*. 'Lunar South in [sic: is] Solar East'. In practice, however, we do not divide the wheel of the *Principles* into the days of the month [i.e. into 28], but into the months of the year [i.e. 12] (*AVB* 188).

Unfortunately, Adams interprets Yeats's sentence construction to imply a parallelism that does not exist, and equates Phase 22 in the cone of the

Principles with Lunar South, and Phase 1 in the cone of the *Faculties* with Solar East. Thus, his lunar wheel is like no lunar wheel that Yeats ever drew. For Yeats, lunar South is always Phase 15, and lunar North Phase 1. Adams reverses this. He also equates Aries with solar South, whereas for Yeats, Aries is always solar East. In fact, the diagram of lunar and solar wheels should be the same diagram that Adams attempts to supply on p. 124, with the substitution of zodiacal signs for the phases of the lunar wheel; but Adams also muddles up the positions of the solar signs in that diagram. Adams spoke more truly than he knew when he wrote, 'Our troubles began, after all, with the imposition [sic] of solar year on lunar month, and the difficulties have multiplied since that moment' (p. 103).

I sympathize with the reader who switched off during my last few paragraphs, but such discussions are a necessary part of coming to terms with *A Vision*. I also realize that there is no point in being smug about Adams's mistakes; anyone who has ever laboriously worked out how to construct Yeats's undrawn diagrams is likely sooner or later to come across a case where the diagram collapses as more information about the system emerges. Yet the reader must persist in drawing the diagrams, for an accurate representation of the geometry is surely necessary before it can be decided whether it explains anything. Life itself is complicated, and any explanation of it is going to be similarly complicated. The geometry has to get more complex as it incorporates more. Yeats simplifies as much as he can. But what is not needed is the addition of complications that were not intended by Yeats. And given that Adams has made such a mess of what is after all an elementary part of the geometry, how much credence should one give him when he claims that Yeats should never have attempted to superimpose a solar wheel on a lunar wheel, and that such superimpositions go nowhere?

Likewise, when Yeats promises, as he frequently does, that he will return to a topic 'presently', Adams prefers to find that the promised return as often as not does not occur. This too for him becomes part of the drama: these signposts to a supposedly non-existent destination are deliberate attempts to send the reader on a wild goose chase. Against this, readers who are sceptical about Adams's case, and even those who agree with it, may like to consider what it was like to organize a complex exposition in the days before word processing and the personal computer.

Let's look at the first of Adams's examples. On p. 72, he traces the phrase 'the interchange of the *tinctures*' from pp. 75, 89, and 105 of *A Vision (B)*, and concludes, 'elsewhere discussion of the interchange is promised for Book II, but never occurs'. It is a wise rule always to check on writers on *A Vision* who do not supply chapter and verse. Adams's unsupplied reference is to *A Vision (B)* 159. Yeats first of all says that something which *resembles* the interchange occurs at Phase 22 and is 'reflected' from 'the Wheel of the *Principles* I shall describe in Book II'. He does describe the Wheel of the *Principles* in Book II. Further down the page, he says he will discuss why a similar interchange, i.e. an interchange similar to the one which resembles the interchange of the *tinctures*, does not occur at Phase 8, promising that 'I will return to this omission in Book II'. To me, this is an obvious misprint for 'Book III', where the reason is duly given on p. 232, and Yeats has fulfilled his promise.

A further point needs to be made about returning to a topic. If you are looking for a phrase in a merely mechanical manner, and do not attempt to understand what is meant by it, you will often miss a reference. In the case of the interchange of the tinctures, you should also be looking out for phrases like 'old and new *antithetical* and *primary*', because the interchange changes old for new. There are thus more references than those to which Adams draws attention.

Adams does give one example where it seems that Yeats does not complete an exposition. After quoting a passage where Yeats explains that life is made vain by 'deceit', Adams writes:

> This comment is maddeningly followed by a remark that seems to offer a contrary situation, but explanation is withheld and never appears in the book: 'There are also Harmonies, but these which are connected with the whole figure can be best considered in relation to another part of the System' (94). It appears that there is something missing from *A Vision* as there was from the *Speculum* (p. 84).

It is perhaps only quibbling to note that Yeats does not specifically say he will return to this topic, merely mentioning that it does not belong to the present discussion. If we assume that Yeats has in fact promised to return to the subject, there are several options available to the reader who wants to find out more about 'Harmonies'. The first is look for the topic in a mechanical manner. This approach is certainly doomed to frustration, because I do not think Yeats uses the word 'Harmonies' or its cognates elsewhere in the book. Another is to assume that Yeats discusses the topic but uses a different terminology. Because the Harmonies are connected with the whole figure, perhaps the subject is touched on when Yeats discusses the Whole. By 'another part of the System', he must mean the Principles, as he has just been discussing the Faculties. It's unlikely, but within the realms of possibility, that he is referring *back* to p. 88, where Unity of Being is discussed as that state wherein 'Every emotion begins to be related to every other as musical notes are related'. Two or three other possible places emerge: one is in Book II, Section V, where Yeats lists 'certain interactions of *Faculties* and *Principles* which are not defined by diagrams' (*AV B* 195); another could well be where he discusses the Beatitude, in Book III, 'The Soul in Judgement'. But, within the confines of *A Vision B*, there is no way of telling if these guesses are correct. However, on occasion, Adams himself has not hesitated to refer to *Per Amica* or *A Vision A* to clarify his exposition, so why should one ignore the fact that Yeats's sentence above is taken over from *A Vision A* 25, with the substitution of 'the whole' for 'the centre of'? In *A Vision A*, Harmonies and harmonization are discussed on pp. 25, 139 and 172-3. In the section entitled 'The Cones of Sexual Love', 'Harmonization' is defined as 'the substitution of the sphere for the cone. . . . After harmonization the *Creative Mind* becomes Wisdom, *Body of Fate* Truth, *Will* Love, and *Mask* Beauty' (*AV A* 172-3). Doubtless, this explanation needs to be rewritten with the *Principles* in mind; but it is apparent Harmonization belongs to that part of *A Vision* which has to do with sexual intercourse and other ways in which it momentarily appears that the antinomies have been transcended. The subject is treated in the poem 'Chosen' and mentioned, in passing, in *A Vision B* (199-200).

Adams is free to believe that the non-appearance of this subject, or at least the non-appearance of a later use of the word 'harmony', in *A Vision B*, is part of a deliberate strategy of confusion; however, it seems simpler to put it down to an oversight or to Yeats's reluctance to reveal what is too personal. Whatever you decide, it cannot be maintained that the system itself reserves no place for the topic.

Finally, what of Adams's overall argument? *A Vision* is certainly a subtle exploration of the nature of belief, as Adams asserts. It can be this without at the same time being a work of literature, which is Adams's further corollary. In his Epilogue, Adams chronicles the reaction to *A Vision* of critics such as Blackmur, Frye and Bloom, who were ambivalent about the 'system' but who could not quite bring themselves to call it a fictive exploration. But how is his own assessment to be placed, as opposed to how he thinks it should be placed? If *A Vision* is an antithetical work, as he claims, does someone who attempts to explain it thereby perform a primary function, or does the work become primary to the critic's antithetical understanding? Is distortion of a text primary or antithetical? Insofar as it discounts difference, it must be primary; insofar as it seeks to disrupt and contradict, it must be antithetical. Systematization, one would think, is primary, which is why Adams plumps for drama over exposition.

As these suggestions indicate, there are limitations involved in using either of these characterizations, which is only to be expected, seeing that in all matters of thought *A Vision* demonstrates the importance of taking a perspectival and contextual approach. 'Stories', it should be noted, mocks the antithetical as much as the primary, although Adams does not take the hint, and Yeats nowhere describes *A Vision* and its system in terms of the tinctures. Instead, he talks about it as 'a system symbolizing the phenomenal world as irrational because a series of unresolved antinomies' (*AV B* 194). Apart from the fact that Yeats thinks the terms 'solar' and 'lunar' are more comprehensive than 'primary' and 'antithetical' (see, eg., *AV A* 139: Adams thinks they are synonyms), there is perhaps a good reason why *A Vision* itself cannot be thought of as antithetical. Considering that *A Vision* describes a context which is wider than the antithetical, the word 'antithetical' is not a good choice, unless you have antithetical$_1$ encompassed by antithetical$_2$ encompassed by antithetical$_3$ and so on in an infinite regress. Any introduction to set theory or the theory of logical types will explain why. The ecstasy arising from contemplation of the infinite is one of the compensations of *A Vision*, as Adams himself points out; but the problem remains. Adams alludes to it without quite addressing it in his most direct assessment of the status of *A Vision*:

> The Principles, being solar and encompassing the lunar Faculties, suggest that the whole 'system' is actually primary. But this is not quite the case, for two reasons. First, a next larger wheel would in turn be lunar, and so on in alternation. Second, the whole of the 'system' expresses antithetical commitment, not only to images but also to letting the primary have its place and say. The antithetical can open itself to contrariety with the primary, but the primary always tends to suppress or negate the antithetical (pp. 101-2).

Implicit in this passage is Adams's use of the Blakean terms 'negation' and 'contrary'. I have no wish to suggest that Adams does not understand the difference between a negation and a contrary, because of course he does, but the passage embodies some evident confusions and may mislead the reader. The first reason given here is simply not true in terms of *A Vision*, where a larger wheel is always solar as compared with a smaller wheel (*AV A* 149; *AV B* 268). Thus, what is antithetical from one point of view is primary from another, so that a next larger wheel, which is solar, changes what was previously a solar wheel into a lunar wheel. One person's antithetical becomes another's primary, as Yeats says when he explains that 'every Faculty is alternately shield and sword' (*AV B* 74). This is how Yeats interprets Blake's 'The Mental Traveller'. Similar considerations apply to the Kabbalistic Sephiroth, where one Sephira is feminine in relation to the Sephira above it, but masculine in relation to the Sephira below. Adams's statement implies, rather, a set nature for the antithetical, so that it becomes a reification rather than one half of a relation. The second reason given by Adams is almost, but not quite, equivalent to restating one's case as though the restatement itself constituted the proof. I leave it to others to decide whether the characterization of the antithetical here is consistent with the implied definition of the first reason. Part of the difficulty lies in Adams's interpretation of Yeats's reasons for introducing into *A Vision* the ideas of negation and contrary, although he almost gets it right on pp. 12-13. In his glossary, Adams defines them as forerunners of primary and antithetical respectively (pp. 169, 171). However, when Yeats talks about negations and contraries (*AV B* 72-3), he is not identifying them with his *tinctures*. Instead, he is saying that neither *tincture* can be understood without the other. They are thus contraries, and the primary is no more the negation of the antithetical than the antithetical is the negation of the primary.

Alasdair D. F. Macrae, *W. B. Yeats: A Literary Life* (Basingstoke & London: Macmillan Press , 1995), 204 pp.

Declan D. Kiely

THIS BOOK APPEARS TO BE AIMED at A-Level and undergraduate students reading Yeats for the first time. It is well constructed, telling the familiar story of Yeats's life in eight chronological chapters of approximately equal length. The account is spiced up with details from recent research, including some published in earlier *Yeats Annuals*, so that what you get is a more up to date version of the life than that provided by Ellmann or Jeffares. A 'literary life' implies a symbiotic treatment of 'the bundle of accident and incoherence that sits down to breakfast' and the author's 'intended, complete' work. The main emphasis of this book is on 'locating' Yeats, in placing his work within the wider context of his life and time. To this end Macrae has constructed each chapter so that the reader is given some impression of Yeats's literary activities and achievements, and of the important influences acting upon him at various stages of his developing life. The focus of the book moves back and forth between the life and the work, dwelling on the essential continuity of Yeats's themes and concerns. Drawing effectively on his teaching experience, Macrae anticipates the qualms, irritations and resentments which students sometimes have when reading Yeats. The writing style is always accessible and reassuring, the idiom adapted to accommodate the neophyte. Making no secret of the inherent difficulties posed by a study of Yeats, sentences characteristically begin: 'One of the problems for the reader . . .' or 'It is difficult, first of all, to understand fully what Yeats . . .'. Macrae elucidates and clarifies without evasion or oversimplification, and regularly lets Yeats's own contradictions stand, leaving the final judgment to the reader.

The first chapter, 'Family and Place', is excellent on some of the early influences upon Yeats, especially that of John Butler Yeats. Macrae alludes to but unfortunately does not fully develop Yeats's tendency to define himself *against* others. Throughout the book he excels at providing neat biographical sketches of Yeats's family, friends (and enemies), lovers, contemporaries, and collaborators. His account is refreshingly free from speculation and sticks to a straightforward presentation of the facts. The later related chapter, 'Friends and Loves' is absorbingly rich in anecdote, and the style is taut and compact. Like other parts of the book it adumbrates recent research, presenting Yeats in a fully rounded manner, as a man of flesh and blood.

The literary tradition of early Romanticism underlying Yeats's poetry is comprehensively set out in an extensive treatment of 'Yeats and the 1890s', a chapter which also comprehends Yeats's interest in folklore and his involvement with the Order of the Golden Dawn. Macrae traces Yeats's interest in symbols and symbolism back to Shelley and Blake, making clear that 'he did not discover it for the first time when he was reading the French poets'. He carefully delineates the difference between Yeats's use of symbols and that of the Symbolist poets. Importantly, he also insists upon the centrality and seriousness of Yeats's occult interests, refusing to understate or dismiss, and roundly castigates earlier critics for doing so: 'there is nothing superficial or glibly curious about Yeats's interest in the occult'.

The chapter dealing with 'Yeats and the Theatre', subtitled 'Baptism of the Gutter', locates Yeats and his involvement with the Abbey Theatre within wider movements of European theatre generally. Macrae is eager to destroy any lingering misconceptions about Lady Gregory, who it is suggested 'has often been presented as a frump, a dull literary groupie or a late Ascendancy manipulator'. He is angry at the way in which she has sometimes been ignored or marginalised in studies of Irish literature. Correspondingly the achievements of Lady Gregory, Synge, O'Casey and Shaw are well covered, but Yeats's own dramatic works are somewhat under-represented in favour of an exposition of his theories of the drama, and the chapter sells him short. This insufficiency is corrected in a later chapter on 'Masks and Development'.

On the whole the book makes some excellent and sound suggestions about how Yeats ought to be approached and understood without being prescriptive or pontifical. Macrae's respect and enthusiasm for his subject is evident and his exegesis consistently seeks to open up discussion. There are wide-ranging, apposite and lengthy quotations from Yeats's works and Macrae is content to withdraw to a discreet distance and let the great man speak for himself. All but one chapter concludes with Yeats's own words rather than Macrae's.

There are, however, a few things to take issue with. The book comes complete with a 'preliminary but substantial chronology of Yeats and contingent happenings' in which there are several errors and some surprising omissions. Placing contemporary events, such as the opening of London's first underground line (misdated) or the cinema release of

Chaplin's 'The Gold Rush', alongside a chronology of Yeats's life can be of only coincidental and therefore limited interest. The Introduction states that: 'the earlier struggle does not feature strongly in Yeats's projection of himself'. Yet one of the book's theses is that many of Yeats's achievements grew out of 'a disrupted childhood and fear or insecurity', and examples in the work where the earlier struggle impinges are often pointed out.

There is an irritating haphazardness about citations and references. Some quotations are endnoted while others are just located more generally within the text from which they are taken. Sometimes no source is given. My concern is that because of the lack of consistent referencing the student will find further reading is not adequately directed. Not surprisingly, given the limitations of space, the examples seem too often selective rather than exhaustive. There are also some odd inconsistencies between the Chronology and the main text. For example, two conflicting dates are given for Yeats's first meeting with Lady Gregory—both are incorrect. Additionally, the wrong date and title is given for Douglas Hyde's lecture 'The Necessity for De-Anglicizing Ireland' and this event is absent from the Chronology. Balzac's *Comédie Humaine* is said to have been read by Yeats in ninety-one volumes, a huge course of reading indeed! Perhaps the worst error is found on p. 149: 'Yeats was provoked by the philosopher's [Nietzsche's] call to go beyond good and evil now that God had been pronounced dead, but it may be significant that Yeats called the book of essays he published in 1903 *Essays on Good and Evil*, as if he had not quite jumped beyond'. Aside from the obvious mistitle this statement ignores the fact that Yeats acknowledged that he 'got the title of this book out of one of Blake's MSS works' in his inscription, dated March 8, 1904, in John Quinn's copy of the first American edition (*CL3* 313n).

The book shows recurrent signs of haste in other respects too: there are some outstanding mistakes in the quoted passages of poetry which range in severity from the occasional omission of punctuation or changes in a word to the complete omission of a whole line from, of all poems, 'He wishes for the Cloths of Heaven'! Yet despite these nagging errors this is a very competent introduction and can, with these reservations, be recommended to those new to Yeats studies.

Roselinde Supheert, *Yeats in Holland, The Reception of the Work of W. B. Yeats in the Netherlands before World War Two* (Amsterdam: Rodopi, 1995; Costerus, NS 104) viii + 319 pp. + 7 illustrations.

K. P. S. Jochum

YEATS IN HOLLAND is really two books in one. One of the two is a full description of a rather meagre subject, the history of academic English studies in the Netherlands. The first university to establish a permanent chair in Anglistics was Groningen in 1885; it took almost 30 years for the City University of Amsterdam to follow suit. The two largest universities, Leiden and Utrecht, waited until as late as 1950 and 1957, respectively. The curriculum was heavily biassed towards philology and historical linguistics; in literature few courses ventured beyond the early Romantics. By and large, Dutch academics of the first half of the 20th century found that contemporary English literature was not a fit subject for teaching. Roselinde Supheert argues that the reception of Yeats in the Netherlands will be better understood if the academic neglect of modern English literature is taken into account, but to this reviewer (at least) it is more than a little frustrating to read a lengthy disquisition on a non-event. Why does Supheert, to cite but one example, write two detailed pages on the Dutch scholar Clara Bille, who did *not* publish anything on modern literature, let alone Yeats (pp. 88-90)? This chapter might have benefited either from rigorous pruning or from the addition of some comparative remarks about the fate of other modern literatures (French, German) in early 20th-century Dutch academia.

The bulk of Supheert's dissertation is devoted to the early Dutch reception of Yeats's work which, I regret to say, was neither substantial nor exciting. Given the insignificance of English studies at Dutch universities, it comes as no surprise that Yeats and his contemporaries did not figure prominently in academic courses. It was only in 1925 that an Amsterdam lecturer, Gerard Anton Dudok, referred to him twice in a survey of 19th-century English prose. It appears that Dudok possessed a single Yeats book, the 1913 printing of *Plays for an Irish Theatre*, now in the Amsterdam University Library. Supheert notes that Amsterdam had the 'best academic Yeats collection of the 1910s' (p. 48), namely five titles. Groningen bought four volumes, which is remarkable since it did not care to acquire a single volume by Joyce, Eliot, Lawrence, and Virginia Woolf. There is virtually no academic writing on Yeats before 1933 when Rebecca Brugsma defended her thesis, *The Beginnings of the Irish Revival*, minutely reviewed by Supheert on four tedious pages, although she has to admit that it is only 'a patchwork history of Ireland and the Irish movement' (p. 91).

In those days, the best Yeats collection was that of the Royal Library. The library's director, W. G. Bijvanck, was responsible for these acquisitions, presumably because he was also one of the editors of *De Gids*, a journal interested in modern literature. This sad state of affairs was somewhat offset by substantial Yeats sections in several contemporary anthologies and literary histories. The best-known early pioneer was Willem van Doorn, whose anthology *Golden Hours with English Poets* (1910) included a generous selection. Van Doorn later wrote a number of articles and reviews on Yeats, notably in what is Holland's most significant contribution to Anglistics, the journal *English Studies* (founded in 1919). But van Doorn was not an influential figure; he never made it to a professorship.

The Yeats reception in the Netherlands also suffered from the paucity of translations. Supheert's first listing is a 1920 version of 'The Lover Tells of the Rose in His Heart' by A. Roland Holst (of whom more later); until 1939 there were only 25 translations of poems, published in various periodicals. Two plays were also translated but not a single prose piece.

All of this makes painful reading, especially when Supheert leisurely spreads her material over dozens of pages. Her book becomes somewhat more interesting, when she discusses three events connected with Yeats's life and work that elicited a substantial response, the award of the Nobel Prize for literature, his death, and the four Dutch productions of *The Only Jealousy of Emer* between 1922 and 1926. The response, presented in great detail and, helpfully, in translation, was almost exclusively restricted to the daily and weekly press and had virtually no impact on the academic world. The performances of *The Only Jealousy of Emer* were the work of Albert van Dalsum, an enterprising young actor who enlisted the help of the poet Hélène Swarth to translate the text, and of the sculptor Hildo Krop to construct the masks. The translation is lost, the masks survive in copies, and were photographed.

The masks in turn were much admired by Yeats and provided the inspiration for turning *The Only Jealousy of Emer* into its ballet version *Fighting the Waves*. The first performance of this work in 1929 was reviewed by P. N. van Eyck. Van Eyck was one of the three Dutch writers and modernist poets, who were instrumental in bringing Yeats to the attention of the reading public. The other two were J. C. Bloem, and, most importantly, Adriaan Roland Holst. They all collected Yeats's works, translated some of it, and wrote on him, but not very comprehensively. Roland Holst and van Eyck corresponded with Yeats; two of Yeats's letters are reprinted by Supheert.

The discussion of Yeats's importance for Roland Holst, van Eyck, Bloem and a few others is the subject of Supheert's longest and most valuable chapter. She makes extensive use of unpublished correspondence and notebooks, since these writers kept much of what they thought about Yeats to themselves. Supheert's approach is mostly biographical and bibliographical; she does not venture far into literary analysis or comparison. She does not discuss Yeats's influence on Roland Holst's work because others have been in the field before her. She writes only a few pages on the quality of Roland Holst's translations which, she cautiously suggests, is uneven. The single translation produced by van Eyck, that of 'Sailing to Byzantium,' is described as 'accurate' (p. 211) and at the same time criticized as being too simplistic.

On the whole Supheert's book is more relevant to the study of 20th-century Dutch writers; its contribution to Yeats studies, although valuable as an account of the dissemination of his works and reputation, is less substantial. This is only partly her fault; there is simply not enough material worthy of discussion and relevant to an understanding of Yeats's works, and its distribution is very limited. The reviews and notices that she has diligently unearthed from such periodicals as *De Groene Amsterdammer* and *De Maasbode* are often slight; moreover these publications are apparently nowhere on file except in some Dutch libraries. To fill her book, Supheert has to make a little go a very long way. Even so, she could have done better. Her reasons for restricting her investigations to the period before 1939 are unconvincing; she thinks that the later material is too bulky (which it isn't) and that 'the Dutch reception then loses its distinct character' (p. 2). She never spells out explicitly the nature and relevance of this character, and much of what she writes suggests that it simply did not exist, unless it is that of 'a romantic, typically Irish poet' (p. 244) which is too vague to be useful.

The 'image of the Yeats canon as it developed in the Netherlands' (p. 2) is, despite all her efforts, a very incomplete and lopsided one. After 1939, Dutch Yeats scholarship and translations of his work are more interesting than Supheert wants her readers to believe. Several of the studies assessing Yeats's influence on Roland Holst have at least the merit of placing the latter in a wider European context. These studies should have been cited; they are not. A scholar such as Maartje Draak has probably done more for an understanding of Irish culture than many of her insignificant predecessors whom Supheert treats with great but unnecessary circumstantiality; the same may be said of Jan van der Vegt and a number of others. Yet these writers are barely mentioned by Supheert and are not listed in her bibliography. Even some of the writers whom she does discuss are not documented correctly or properly. She refers to an article by P. N. van Eyck on Roland Holst and Yeats (p. 166), but does not give any details. I have been unable to locate it. The collection of poetry by Ko de Haan is listed in *Brinkman* as *Liefde and Leed* (not *Lief en Leed*); Jan Engelman's translation is in a book *Tuin van Eros* (not *De Tuin van Eros*). In her citations of contributions to newspapers, Supheert does not give page numbers, which necessitates cumbersome searches. And her statement that there are no studies of the reception of Yeats in Germany and France (p. 245) is plainly wrong; she has simply not bothered to get hold of the dissertations of Susanne Margarete Schaup ('William Butler Yeats in deutscher Sicht', Universität Salzburg, 1968), Joan Kellogg Renz ('Yeats and the Germans', University of Connecticut, 1979), and Margaret Stanley ('W. B. Yeats et la France', Université de Lille, 1977). These are duly listed in my bibliography and, though unpublished, easily obtainable.

Fashion and Cunning

Jonathan Allison (ed.) *Yeats's Political Identities; Selected Essays.* (Ann Arbor: University of Michigan Press, 1996.) 352pp.

Deborah Fleming. *'A Man Who Does not Exist': The Irish Peasant in the Work of W. B. Yeats and J. M. Synge* (Ann Arbor: University of Michigan Press, 1995.) 224pp.

W. J. Mc Cormack

'Only that historian will have the gift of fanning the spark of hope in the past, who is firmly convinced that even the dead will not be safe from the enemy if he wins. And this enemy has not ceased to be victorious.'—Walter Benjamin, in 'Theses on History' quoted by Seamus Deane in 'Muffling the Cry from a Hungry Past', *The Guardian* (17 June 1995) p. 29.

IN THESE NEW CONTRIBUTIONS to the gaiety of nationalists, the University of Michigan Press offers a collection of essays devoted to the ageing Yeats's politics and a specialist account of Yeats's relationship with his greatest disciple/rival. The monograph is a dogged achievement, uneasily shifting from inherited prejudice to instant political rightness. When readers pick up a copy of Jonathan Allison's anthology, however, they must stoop to pick up a page-long errata-slip which slips to the floor. This mild physical exercise provides a suitable warm-up for the task of reading *Yeats's Political Identities*, in the course of which more demanding acts of retrieval will be required.

With close on twenty essays (or extracts), an introduction and a usefully annotated bibliography, the book has brought together work published between 1965 and 1996 on the Irish poet's ideological orientation. Some players who regularly hold their place on the first team are present—Conor Cruise O'Brien, Elizabeth Cullingford, Seamus Deane—together with reservists. Among all of these there are, frankly, one or two who are past their prime. But we need not fear a very bruising encounter on the field; from an early moment in this collection, the editor indicates that the wise player takes a dive immediately behind the flying heels of the rightwinger. There is more taking up of positions than tackling.

That being the case, why should anyone devote more than flinging-away time to such a publication? For a positive answer to this question one needs to have regard to the larger political and/or cultural process which it obliquely addresses. This might be called the 'dangerous intersection' between postmodernist theory and Irish political activity, had not that useful metaphor been discredited in the hands of a prominent contributor to the anthology, Conor Cruise O'Brien. In search of metaphors to substitute for his cross-roads, one is made aware of the current professionalised hostility manifest towards all such tropes as evidence of a lamentable survival of humanistic credulity. The effort must be made, nevertheless, to argue against such silliness. The importance of articulating a reasoned case against the fashions of the North American academy is directly proportionate to persistent vitality among the killing clubs of Ulster. What follows might be read as a special application of Christopher Norris's *Truth and the Ethics of Criticism* (1994), though my immediate concerns are more practical than philosophical.

Three aspects of Allison's enterprise deserve scrutiny:—first, its representation of current opinion on the issue of Yeats's politics, especially in the United States; second, its account of the longer debate, reaching back to Yeats's last years in the 1930s; and finally, its position *vis-à-vis* the substantive issue of the poet's political behaviour and thought from (say) the death of Charles Stewart Parnell in 1891 to his own death in 1939. A fourth question, as to the likely origins of Yeats's politics in the mid-nineteenth century, could hardly have been accommodated in a book of the kind proposed—as this one was—by Maurice Harmon to Jonathan Allison. While its relevance should be noted, no attempt is made to deal with the issue of origins here and now. The omission is regrettable and certainly should be taken as no endorsement of the anthology's attitude towards history.

Much is revealed in the editor's choice of title, especially its insistence on the plural, *identities*. Among the contributors are Marjorie Howes, author of *Yeats's Nations*, Declan Kiberd, author of 'Inventing Irelands' in *Inventing Ireland*, and—less trivially—David Lloyd of *Anomalous States*. Indeed, Kiberd's contribution here is called 'Inventing Irelands', and is simultaneously published for the first time and saluted for having 'stirred the pot of revisionism' on its appearance more than a decade ago (p. 1). Roy Foster's 'Protestant Magic' is presented as possessing the same magical power over time; 'reprinted by permission from *Proceedings of the British Academy*, Vol 75 (1989)', it comes (courtesy of the editor and the University of Michigan Press) trailing footnotes which cite publications of 1991 and 1993. On the basis of this evidence—and there is more to follow—textual integrity matters little, basic chronology even less. Instead, we are serenaded from the hotel balconies of postmodernism. Politically, Yeats is everything and nothing; he is kitted out with identities for all seasons.

The indulgent, simulated idiocy of all this has much to do with the present state of the American educational industry. For example, Deborah Fleming would have us believe that the following passage from *The Aran Islands* proves Synge's discovery of a 'Celtic aristocracy' in 'the Irish peasantry':

> These strange men with receding foreheads, high cheek-bones, and ungovernable eyes seem to represent some old type found on these few acres at the extreme border of Europe, where it is only in wild jests and laughter that they can express their loneliness and desolation. (p. 62)

This might be taken as a venial repetition of something close to a Yeatsian gloss on an Edwardian text, were it not for Fleming's persistence in updating such nonsense. We are solemnly advised that 'In the early 1970s idealistic young English people emigrated to Ireland in order to find a more "spiritual," less materialistic, "natural," and "uncorrupt" life . . .' (p. 58). The quotation marks cannot be taken as indicating any reservation of the author's about the words so distinguished. They are scattered liberally over Fleming's work like Parmesan on pizza, with the result that we cannot tell her normative, quotative, and quizzical usages one from another: there are native Irishmen and 'native' Irishmen. The risks involved in these procedures are evident in an early attempted transposition of Edward Said's ideas to the Irish situation—'if we substitute "Great Britain" for "Europe" and "Ireland" for "Orient," we see how

Said's theory clarifies much about British attitudes towards its nearest colony' (p. 21). Perhaps only Walter Benjamin has been more travestied in being forcibly applied to the aforesaid situation than the author of *Orientalism*, notwithstanding his own intervention, *Nationalism, Colonialism and Literature: Yeats and Decolonization*.

The work collected by Jonathan Allison is less daffy but not less worrying. Given the strong links existing between the United States and Ireland, and the long *impasse* in Anglo-Irish relations and in Ulster, the intellectual stance (or pose) exemplified in these *Selected Essays* is frightening. Allison rightly points to the successful marketing in the United States of 'the *Crane Bag Book of Irish Studies* and of various Field Day publications, especially the three-volume *Field Day Anthology of Irish Writing*' (1991). What, as editor, he fails to concede is that his selection from the former is highly partisan, and serves to reinforce the 'national liberation struggle' view of Irish culture and of Irish affairs generally. From that Harp O'Marxist radicalism, however, Karl Marx is a notable refugee in hiding. Instead the cultural emblem of Irish nationalism supplies a forename, displacing what used to be known as politics.

The strategy is launched by an initial citation of 'the frenzied rhetorical pitch of the Marxist critic Sheila Ann Murphy', as—for example—in her remark that 'Bourgeois scholar despots are teaching William Butler Yeats's anti-people works all over the imperialist world in order to reinforce fascist ideology' (Allison, p. 8). What Allison conceals—or does not know—is that the source of this is a Maoist paper which circulated among some students in Trinity College Dublin in the early 1970s. Strategically within *Yeats's Selected Identities*, however, a bench-mark has been established through quotation of Sheila Ann Murphy which will late be used to characterise Terry Eagleton and myself as Marxist critics of Yeats—critics who are, of course and for that reason, excluded from the selection.

In the introduction which cites Murphy (a non-contributor, it need hardly be said), the final contributor, Ronald Bush, is trailered as finding against Eagleton and Mc Cormack that they 'continue to mistake one facet of that dialectic for the whole, overlooking the radical and pervasive scepticism which was always a component of the modernists' conflicted philosophical program' (pp. 22, 331). The dialectic in question was that (to quote Sandra F. Siegel's words) whereby 'Yeats advances an argument and then proceeds to devalue or repudiate the view he seemed to uphold. He thus asserts both his convictions and his doubts' (p. 331). We shall in due course encounter an instance of this dialectic and the pervasive scepticism it accommodated, though it may not be an instance comfortable to Yeats's admirers.

It is a low habit in reviewers to point out omissions but, with the political implications of Irish-American academia in mind, the habit must be indulged. Among those who contributed to the great debate launched by Cruise O'Brien's 1965 essay, 'Passion and Cunning', the following are excluded by Allison—David Bradshaw, Joseph Chadwick, Patrick Cosgrave, Denis Donoghue, David Fitzpatrick, Grattan Freyer, Joseph Hassett, Samuel Hynes, William Johnsen, John Kelly, Bernard Krimm, Michael North, Edward Said and Geoffrey Thurley (at least four of whom have published full-length books on the topic). None of the reviews of *In Excited Reverie* (the volume in which Cruise O'Brien's essay featured in 1965) is included, though a striking number of these concentrated on the political issue; the same restraint is extended to *Passion and Cunning and Other Essays* (1988). All in all, the anthology provides a distinctly 'skewed' narrative of the debate from 1965 to the present.

It is true that the anthology is not solely concerned with 'the fascist charge' against Yeats. Divided into four parts, it gives roughly equal space to that specific theme, then to 'Yeats and the Ascendancy', then 'Nationalism and Revolution', and (finally) to 'Some Responses'. There is strikingly little on Yeats and parliamentary politics, either of the Home Rule or Seanad Eireann varieties; indeed, only the judicious omission of an index inhibits me from declaring that there is nothing on Yeats and the politics of the 1880s and '90s. If, as Napoleon believed (and Yeats endorsed), to understand a man's mind one needs to study the world as it stood when he was twenty—Yeats reached that age in 1885—then the target is very widely missed in this collection.

Cruise O'Brien and Elizabeth Cullingford divide the honours in the first section, with no room for another opinion. The substantive debate on Yeats and fascism is thus cast as occurring between 1965 and 1981, no late-comers admitted. The second section—again, two items only—includes Marjorie Howes's 'Family Values: Gender, Sexuality, and Crisis in Yeats's Anglo-Irish Aristocracy', which genuinely appears for the first time. This innovation is welcome, but a studied avoidance of David Bradshaw's article on Yeats and eugenics (*YA 9* 189-215) undercuts any suggestion of radical feminism in the volume as a whole.

'Nationalism and Revolution' is the longest section, dominated by a team drawn from University College Dublin—Seamus Deane, Maurice Harmon, Richard Kearney, and Declan Kiberd. Of these Deane is undoubtedly the most able, intellectually and rhetorically. Harmon's 'Yeats, Austin Clarke and Seán O'Faolain' seems limply old-fashioned by contrast, until one realises that the recuperation of Civil War republicanism has its part to play in the casual comedy of postmodern discourses. To conclude, there are six 'Responses', several of which address in detail work excluded from the anthology. The fascist charge returns, but is represented mainly by ingenious plea-bargaining. The rest of the hearing has been struck from the record.

Before turning to consider what might be the meaning of this hide-and-seek, let us complete our three-aspect survey of the anthology, for the longer perspective remains to be examined. If it is acceptable that Yeats's political identities are likely to have included something 'constructed', 'fabricated', 'imposed' or 'produced' during his own lifetime, then the absence of any commentary from W. H. Auden or George Orwell is to be regretted. (This is not to restrict my regrets to the case of the English Left, such as it was: John Eglinton, Frank O'Connor, Sean O'Faolain and Walter Starkie might have been cited to good effect and without any kow-towing to a Popular Front mentality.) Not only does the decision to open the anthology with 'Passion and Cunning' confirm one's belief that the topic upon which the editor and his publishers seek to offer reassurance is indeed fascism, it fatally excludes the testimony of those who lived through the era of fascism.

Hence, of course, the imperviousness of virtually all the contributors to historical argument becomes evident, Roy Foster being the distinguished exception. Richard Kearney, for example, classifies James Clarence Mangan (1803-1849) among 'the great Fenian poets' (p. 177 n.1), though the Fenian Brotherhood was not founded until 1858. Historical implausibility is not limited to mere detail. Elizabeth Cullingford's *Yeats, Ireland and Fascism* (1981)—from which an excerpt is taken—proves, by concentrating on weak points in Cruise O'Brien's argument, that Yeats's interest in Mussolini was really only an extension of his admiration for Edmund Burke. The frailty of this as political analysis might be gauged from the fact that Yeats was far too honest to invoke such a convenient but fatuous explanation.

Postmodernism wholly disposes of the problem by denying in effect that anything like evidence exists. In a truly perverted way, it is the Althusserian dismissal of all methods of historical research, an anti-humanism recycled for use in the happy autumn fields of post-capitalism. There is nothing remarkable, according to this view, in Roy Foster's being set up as a man who cites books written years after the essay in which he cites them. And if Mangan died a Fenian poet, who is to quibble about the delay in laying down the conditions of that distinction? Paper never refused ink, my Granny always said. But the essays and extracts in *Yeats's Political Identities* reveal an anxiety to order the papers in a particular way, announce the verdict, and get on to other matters.

While this attitude is reprehensible, it is not wholly inexplicable. Frustrated ambition—in individuals and ethnic groups, for example, for whom words like justice or civil rights have lost their 'signified' in the latest seminar-room *coup*—is the counterpart of unfocused nostalgia. Fleming's point of departure is to assert that on behalf of Yeats and Synge (Fleming, p. 8). On a larger stage and willingly persuaded that neither historical research nor ethical reflection can advance the resolution of a grievance, the O'Marxists have additionally abandoned Karl's silly obsession with economics and with social structure. Contemporary poverty never features in their denunciations. In a parody of Weberian (or is it Veblenian?) sociology, they have reinvented the interest group and justified self-justification.

Few will dispute the contention that the issue of Yeats's political behaviour—including his utterances and his mute scepticism—is at once a political and a scholarly concern. Some will regret that it is both—the politicians keen to rid themselves of scholarly fussing, and the textual editors outraged by the consideration of anything other than ink. Ronald Bush's observation (Allison, p. 331) that Eagleton, Mc Cormack and other simpletons 'continue to mistake one facet of [Yeats'] dialectic for the whole, overlooking the radical and pervasive skepticism which was always a component of the modernists' conflicted philosophical program' is a brilliantly displaced diagnosis. For it is always only the pro-fascistic aspects of Yeats's thought which are explained away in this manner. His patriotism, his belief in fairies, his love of Maud Gonne, his attitudes to to censorship—these positions are rarely suspected of being pervaded by scepticism. Seen as 'one facet of that dialectic' each is entirely admirable, and admirably entire unto itself—whatever the evidence elsewhere might suggest—and there is apparently on these scores no need to invoke a second term in the dialectic. Indeed Sandra Siegel's formulation of this so-called dialectic—'Yeats advances an argument and then proceeds to devalue or repudiate the view he seemed to uphold. He thus asserts both his convictions and his doubts'—gives the game away, by insisting that the first term is certain (convictions) and the second merely speculative (doubts). So it seems that there never was a dialectic in Yeats's political thought as construed by Bush and Siegel, and the offensiveness of Eagleton, Mc Cormack & Co. remains just that—offensiveness. (And, of course, the spreading of news which can't be good for business. And perhaps truthfulness, if the word is tolerable on the hotel balconies.)

Evidence, it should be clear, is never available except in mediated form. Far from abandoning concern with accuracy in the face of this revelation, it behoves biographers, critics, editors, publishers, scholars, theorists and every other species of drudge to redouble their efforts to render fully accessible the sources upon which they draw, to articulate the processes where transmission and interpretation collude or collide, and to provide opportunities for the independent testing of hypotheses against as much diverse evidence as can be mustered. One of the aspects of Cruise O'Brien's essay which caused offence in 1965 was not just his charge of pro-fascism levelled against Yeats but his extensive citation of Yeats's private correspondence to back up his case. Wade's edition of the *Letters* is slowly being superseded by the vast multi-volume project of which John Kelly is General Editor. It would be a naive Harp O'Marxist who trusted that the greatly enlarged dossier will reduce the embarrassment quotient.

Yeats then remains unexploded, both in the sense that he has not been found out in his sustained and sympathetic interest in German fascism, and in the sense that he constitutes a danger. If he were found out, he would be become a far greater danger to his new Irish-American admirers than to Harvard liberals of the old school. But he constitutes a danger in a wider context. Even if his politics could, in some miraculous way, be entirely excavated and placed on view, it would not sit apart from all the other activities of his mind and body, nor would it remain unattached to the various 'societies' in which he lived, moved and had his being—European culture, the Protestant Irish middle class, American lecture circuits, the Abbey Theatre, the Order of the Golden Dawn, the Irish Free State, the Athenaeum, the Irish Republican Brotherhood, marriage to Georgie Hyde-Lees, Seanad Eireann, the Cheshire Cheese, to name but a few. Potentially at least, the examination of Yeats's politics promises to 'totalise' a body of literary texts previously regarded as coming from an era of peculiar fragmentation and generally acknowledged as voicing a strong sense of their own internal contradictoriness.

In the end, what is depressing about the movement represented by the strategies of *Yeats's Political Identities* is its opportunism. While in the Field Day perspective Irish nationalism remains an essentially unchallengeable presupposition of all negotiations, seasonal changes in ideological costume are borne with insouciance. This is not to say that Jonathan Allison is a crypto-nationalist nor that Seamus Deane is a sloppy editor, but it is to point out a larger intellectual climate in which 'anything goes' so long as it serves a need. Irish versions of post-colonial discourse have been obliging on the matter of US foreign policy, just as Harp O'Marxism has abandoned class politics and the poor. Textual accuracy scarcely matters as a third victim; after all scholarship takes too long. Yet it is through a politics of inaccurate scholarship that 'the enemy if he wins' will report success. But not to us, of course.

Publications Received

Note: A number of these titles will be reviewed in *YA 14.*

Keith Alldritt, *W. B. Yeats: The Man and the Milieu* (London: John Murray, 1997) pp. xviii + 388.

C. C. Barfoot, Theo D'haen and Tjebbe A. Westendorp (eds.) *The Literature of Politics, the Politics of Literature: Proceedings of the Leiden IASAIL Conference* Vols 1-5 (Amsterdam, Atlanta: Editions Rodopi, 1995). The separate vols are (i) Joep Leerssen, A. H. van der Weel and Bart Westerweel (eds.), *Forging in the Smithy: National Identity and Representation in Anglo-Irish Literary History*, 249 pp.; (ii) C. C. Barfoot and Rias van den Doel (eds.), *Ritual Remembering: History, Myth and Politics in Anglo-Irish Drama*, 204 pp.; (iii) Peter Liebregts and Peter van de Kamp (eds.), *Tumult of Images: Essays on W. B. Yeats and Politics*, 249 pp.; (iv) Theo D'haen and José Lanters (eds.), *Troubled Histories, Troubled Fictions: Twentieth-Century Anglo-Irish Prose*, 174 pp.; and (v) Tjebbe A. Westendorp and Jane Mallinson (eds.), *Politics and the Rhetoric of Poetry: Perspectives on Modern Anglo-Irish Poetry*, 205 pp.

Stephen Coote, *W. B. Yeats: A Life* (London: Hodder & Stoughton, 1997), pp. xii + 612.

Seamus Deane, *Strange Country: Modernity and Nationhood in Irish Writing since 1790* (Oxford: Clarendon, 1997), pp. x + 269.

Decadents, Symbolists, Anti-Decadents: Poetry of the 1890s: a facsimile reprints from Woodstock Books (Poole, U.K. and Washington, D.C.) chosen and introduced by R. K. R. Thornton and Ian Small.

John Davidson, *In a Music Hall* (1891) and *Ballads and Songs* (1894), (1993)
......................., *Fleet Street Eclogues* (1893, 1896, 1993)
Ernest Dowson, *Verses* (1896) and *Decorations* (1899), (1994)
Michael Field, *Sight and Song* (1892) and *Underneath the Bough* (1893), (1993)
W. E. Henley, *Poems* (1898, 1993)
A. E. Housman, *A Shropshire Lad* (1896, 1994)
Henry Newbolt, *The Island Race* (1898, 1995)
Arthur Symons, *Images of Good and Evil* (1899, 1996)
Oscar Wilde, *The Ballad of Reading Gaol* (1898, 1995)
..................., *Poems* (1892, 1995)
Theodrore Wratislaw, *Caprices* (1893), and *Orchids* (1896), (1993).

Deborah Fleming (ed.), *Learning the Trade: Essays on W. B. Yeats and Contemporary Poetry* (West Cornwall, CT: Locust Hill Press, 1993) pp. xxxi + 313.

R. F. Foster, *W. B. Yeats: A Life Vol I: The Apprentice Mage* (Oxford, New York: Oxford University Press, 1997), pp. xxxi + 640.

Toshi Furomoto, George Hughes, Chizuko Inoue, James McElwain, Peter McMillan and Tetsuro Sano (eds.), *International Aspects of Irish Literature* (Gerrards Cross: Colin Smythe, 1996). Irish Literary Studies Series 44, IASAIL-Japan Series 5. pp. xii + 450.

Hans Walter Gabler, George Bornstein and Gillian Borland Pierce (eds.), *Contemporary German Editorial Theory* (Ann Arbor: University of Michigan Press, 1996), pp. vi + 278.

Jacqueline Genet (ed.), *Rural Ireland, Real Ireland?* (Gerrards Cross: Colin Smythe, 1996). Irish Literary Studies Series 49, pp. 245.

.... and Wynne Hellegouarc'h (eds.) *Irish Writers and their Creative Process* (Gerrards Cross: Colin Smythe, 1996). Irish Literary Studies Series 48. pp. vii + 151.

Joscelyn Godwin, *Music and the Occult: French Musical Philosophies, 1750-190* (Rochester: University of Rochester Press, 1995), pp. x + 262.

William T. Gorski, *Yeats and Alchemy* (Albany, N.Y.: State University of New York Press, 1996). pp. xv + 223.

Hibernia: Literature and Nation in Victorian Ireland. A series of facsimile reprints from Woodstock Books (Poole, U.K., and Washington, D. C.), chosen and introduced by John Kelly.

William Carleton, *The Black Prophet* (1847, 1996), pp. xvii, 455.

James Fintan Lalor, *Collected Writings* (1918, 1997), pp. xxiv + 155.

James Clarence Mangan, *Poets and Poetry of Munster* (1885, 1997), pp. xxviii + 355.

John Mitchel, *Jail Journal* (1876, 1996), pp. xxiv + 320.

Gerald Griffin, *The Collegians* (1829, 1997), pp. xxii + 995 (4pp on 1)

A. Norman Jeffares, *W. B. Yeats: Man and Poet* (London: Kyle Cathie; Dublin: Gill and Macmillan, 1996) Third edition, corrected. pp. x + 338.

............................, *Images of Invention: Essays on Irish Writing* (Gerrards Cross: Colin Smythe Ltd., 1996). Irish Literary Studies Series 46, pp. x + 351.

Anthony J. Jordan, *Willy Yeats and the Gonne-MacBrides* (Dublin: Anthony J. Jordan, 1997), pp. 215.

Lorraine Janzen Kooistra, *The Artist as Critic: Bitextuality in* Fin-de-Siècle *Illustrated Books* (Aldershot: Scolar Press; Brookfield, Vermont: Ashgate, 1995), pp. xiv + 304.

Janis Londraville (ed.), *On Poetry, painting, and Politics: The Letters of May Morris and John Quinn* ((Selinsgrove: Susquehanna University Press; London: Associated University Presses, 1997), pp. 228.

W. J. Mc Cormack, *From Burke to Beckett: Ascendancy, Tradition and Betrayal in Literary History* (Cork: Cork University Press, 1994). Revised and enlarged edition of *Ascendancy and Tradition in Anglo-Irish Literary History from 1789-1939* (Oxford: Clarendon, 1985). pp. x + 470.

Mary Massoud (ed.), *Literary Inter-Relations: Ireland, Egypt, and the Far East*

(Gerrards Cross: Colin Smythe, 1996). Irish Literary Studies Series 47. pp. x + 428.

Patrick Parrinder and Warren Chernaik (eds.) *Textual Monopolies: Literary Copyright and the Public Domain* (London: Office for Humanities Communication; Centre for English Studies, School of Advanced Study, University of London, 1997), pp. x + 146. Contains Warwick Gould, 'Predators and Editors: Yeats in the pre- and post-copyright era' (pp. 69-82).

Marie Mulvey Roberts and Hugh Ormsby-Lennon (eds,), *Secret Texts: The Literature of Secret Societies* (NY: AMS Press, 1995) pp. xv + 349.

Michael J. Sidnell, *Yeats's Poetry and Poetics* (Basingstoke and London: 1996), pp. xvi + 192.

John Sloan, *John Davidson, First of the Moderns: A Literary Biography* (Oxford: Clarendon Press, xvi + 306 pp.

John Sloan (ed.), *Selected Poems and Prose of John Davidson* (Oxford: Clarendon Press, 1995), xxx + 206 pp.

TEXT: Transactions of the Society for Textual Scholarship Vols. 7 (1994) & 8 (1995).

Deirdre Toomey (ed.) *Yeats and Women* (London: Macmillan, 1997), pp. xx + 428. This is an enlarged edition of *YA 9*, adding some essays and presentations from other *Yeats Annuals*. The contributors are Elizabeth Butler Cullingford, Warwick Gould, John Harwood, Josephine Johnson, James Pethica, Deirdre Toomey and the volume includes an edited transcript of W. B. Yeats's 10 April, 1932 broadcast, 'Poems about Women'.

Ian Willison, Warwick Gould and Warren Chernaik (eds.), *Modernist Writers and the Marketplace* (Basingstoke: Macmillan, 1996), pp. xviii + 331. Contains Warwick Gould's '"Playing at Treason with Miss Maud Gonne": Yeats and his Publishers in 1900' (pp. 36-80).

YAACTS 12 (1994) pp. xiv, 281; *13 (1995)* pp. xvi, 377 [*sic*, both 1997].

Yeats Eliot Review 13, 1-2; 3-4 (Summer 1994, Fall 1995)

Yeats, W. B., *The Collected Letters of W. B. Yeats Vol II, 1896-1900* edited by Warwick Gould, John Kelly and Deirdre Toomey (Oxford: Clarendon Press, 1997), pp. lxxxi + 790.

.................., *Under the Moon: The Unpublished Early Poetry*, ed. George Bornstein (New York: Scribner, 1995).

.................., Last Poems: *Manuscript Materials by W. B. Yeats* edited by James Pethica (Ithaca and London: Cornell University Press, 1997), pp. lvi + 471.

.................., *Yeats's Poems*, ed. and annotated by A. Norman Jeffares, with an appendix by Warwick Gould (Basingstoke and London: Macmillan Press, 1996) 3rd edition, revised and corrected. pp. xxxi + 781.